NETWORK SECURITY HACKS™

Other computer security resources from O'Reilly

Related titles

Security Warrior

Network Security
Assessment

802.11 Security

Linux Security Cookbook

Practical Unix & Internet
Security

Secure Coding:
Principles and Practices

Hacks Series Home

hacks.oreilly.com is a community site for developers and power users of all stripes. Readers learn from each other as they share their favorite tips and tools for Mac OS X, Linux, Google, Windows XP, and more.

Security Books Resource Center

security.oreilly.com is a complete catalog of O'Reilly's books on security and related technologies, including sample chapters and code examples.

---

oreillynet.com is the essential portal for developers interested in open and emerging technologies, including new platforms, programming languages, and operating systems.

Conferences

O'Reilly & Associates brings diverse innovators together to nurture the ideas that spark revolutionary industries. We specialize in documenting the latest tools and systems, translating the innovator's knowledge into useful skills for those in the trenches. Visit *conferences.oreilly.com* for our upcoming events.

Safari Bookshelf (*safari.oreilly.com*) is the premier online reference library for programmers and IT professionals. Conduct searches across more than 1,000 books. Subscribers can zero in on answers to time-critical questions in a matter of seconds. Read the books on your Bookshelf from cover to cover or simply flip to the page you need. Try it today with a free trial.

NETWORK
SECURITY
HACKS™

Andrew Lockhart

O'REILLY®

Beijing · Cambridge · Farnham · Köln · Paris · Sebastopol · Taipei · Tokyo

Network Security Hacks™
by Andrew Lockhart

Copyright © 2004 O'Reilly Media, Inc. All rights reserved.
Printed in the United States of America.

Published by O'Reilly Media, Inc., 1005 Gravenstein Highway North,
Sebastopol, CA 95472.

O'Reilly Media, Inc. books may be purchased for educational, business, or sales promotional
use. Online editions are also available for most titles (*safari.oreilly.com*). For more
information, contact our corporate/institutional sales department: (800) 998-9938 or
corporate@oreilly.com.

Editor:	Rob Flickenger	**Production Editor:**	G. d'Entremont
Series Editor:	Rael Dornfest	**Cover Designer:**	Hanna Dyer
Executive Editor:	Dale Dougherty	**Interior Designer:**	Melanie Wang

Printing History:

April 2004:	First Edition.

RepKover™ This book uses RepKover™, a durable and flexible lay-flat binding.

ISBN: 0-596-00643-8
[C]   [8/04]

Contents

Credits

About the Author

Andrew Lockhart is originally from South Carolina but currently resides in northern Colorado, where he spends his time trying to learn the black art of auditing disassembled binaries and trying to keep from freezing to death. He holds a BS in computer science from Colorado State University and has done security consulting for small businesses in the area. When he's not writing, he currently works at a Fortune 100 company. In his free time, he works on Snort-Wireless (*http://snort-wireless.org*), a project intended to add wireless intrusion detection to the popular open source IDS Snort.

Contributors

The following people contributed their hacks, writing, and inspiration to this book:

- Oktay Altunergil is the founder of The Free Linux CD Project (*http://www.freelinuxcd.org*) and one of the maintainers of Turk-PHP.com (a Turkish PHP portal). He also works full-time as a Unix system administrator and PHP programmer.

- Michael D. (Mick) Bauer (*http://mick.wiremonkeys.org*) writes Linux Journal's "Paranoid Penguin" security column. By day, he works to keep strangers out of banks' computer networks.

- Schuyler Erle (*http://nocat.net*) is a Free Software developer and activist. His interests include collaborative cartography, wireless networking, software for social and political change, and the Semantic Web. Schuyler is the lead developer of NoCatAuth, the leading open source wireless captive portal.

- Bob Fleck (*http://www.securesoftware.com*) is Director of Security Services at Secure Software. He consults in the fields of secure development and wireless security, and is a coauthor of O'Reilly's *802.11 Security* book. The results of his more recent investigations into Bluetooth security can be found at *http://bluetooth.shmoo.com*.

- Rob Flickenger (*http://nocat.net*) is a writer and editor for O'Reilly's Hacks series. He currently spends his time hacking on various projects and promoting community wireless networking.

- Michael Lucas (*http://www.blackhelicopters.org/~mwlucas*) lives in a haunted house in Detroit, Michigan, with his wife Liz, assorted rodents, and a multitude of fish. He has been a pet wrangler, a librarian, and a security consultant, and now works as a network engineer and system administrator with the Great Lakes Technologies Group. He's the author of *Absolute BSD*, *Absolute OpenBSD*, and *Cisco Routers for the Desperate*, and is currently preparing a book about NetBSD.

- Matt Messier (*http://www.securesoftware.com*) is Director of Engineering at Secure Software and a security authority who has been programming for nearly two decades. In addition to coauthoring the O'Reilly books *Secure Programming Cookbook for C and C++* and *Network Security with OpenSSL*, Matt coauthored the Safe C String Library (SafeStr), XXL, RATS, and EGADS.

- Ivan Ristic (*http://www.modsecurity.org*) is a web security specialist and the author of mod_security, an open source intrusion detection and prevention engine for web applications. He is a member of the OASIS Web Application Security Technical Committee, where he works on the standard for web application protection.

- John Viega (*http://www.securesoftware.com/*) is Chief Technology Officer and Founder of Secure Software. He is also the coauthor of several books on software security, including *Secure Programming Cookbook for C and C++* (O'Reilly) and *Building Secure Software* (Addison-Wesley). John is responsible for numerous software security tools, and he is the original author of Mailman, the GNU mailing list manager.

Acknowledgments

I would first like to thank the illustrious DJ Jackalope (aka Karen) for all of her encouragement, support, and understanding throughout the writing of this book. Without her, it would have languished in the doldrums, and I don't think I could have done this book without her.

I'd also like to thank Nat Torkington for putting me in touch with Rob, my fearless (and patient) editor for this book, as well as my parents for having the faith to let me have time to tinker with computers and do silly things like read *Phrack* when I was a kid; if not for that, I might have ended up doing something completely different.

Preface

Nowhere is the term *hacker* more misconstrued than in the network security field. This is understandable because the very same tools that network security professionals use to probe the robustness of their own networks also can be used to launch attacks on any machine on the Internet. The difference between system administrators legitimately testing their own machines and a system cracker attempting to gain unauthorized access isn't so much a question of techniques or tools, but a matter of intent. After all, as with any powerful piece of technology, a security tool isn't inherently good or bad—this determination depends entirely on how it is used. The same hammer can be used to either build a wall or knock it down.

The difference between "white hat" and "black hat" hackers isn't the tools or techniques they use (or even the color of their hats), but their intent. The difference is subtle but important. White hat hackers find that building secure systems presents an interesting challenge, and their security can be truly tested only through a thorough knowledge of how to subvert such systems. Black hat hackers (more appropriately called *crackers*) pursue precisely the same knowledge, but without regard for the people who built the systems or the servers they attack. They use their knowledge to subvert these systems for their own personal gain, often to the detriment of the systems they infiltrate.

Of course, tales of daring international techno-robberies and black-clad, cigarette-smoking, laptop-wielding evil masterminds tend to sell better than simple tales of the engineer who built a strong network, and so the term *hacking* has a bad reputation in the popular press. They use it to refer to individuals who break into systems or who wreak havoc using computers as their weapon. Among people who solve problems, though, the term *hack* refers to a "quick-n-dirty" solution to a problem, or a clever way to get something done. And the term *hacker* is taken very much as a compliment, referring to someone as being *creative*, i.e., having the technical chops to get things done. The Hacks series is an attempt to reclaim this word, document the ways people are hacking (in a good way), and pass the hacker ethic of creative participation on to the uninitiated. Seeing how others approach systems and problems is often the quickest way to learn about a new technology. Only by openly discussing security flaws and implementations can we hope to build stronger systems.

Why Network Security Hacks?

Network Security Hacks is a grimoire of 100 powerful security techniques. This volume demonstrates effective methods for defending your servers and networks from a variety of devious and subtle attacks. Within this book are examples of how to detect the presence (and track every keystroke) of network intruders, methods for protecting your network and data using strong encryption, and even techniques for laying traps for would-be system crackers. Many important security tools are presented, as well as clever methods for using them to reveal real, useful information about what is happening on your network.

How This Book Is Organized

Although each hack is designed to stand on its own, this book makes extensive use of cross-referencing between hacks. If you find a reference to something you're interested in while reading a particular hack, feel free to skip around and follow it (much as you might while browsing the Web). The book itself is divided into several chapters, organized by subject:

Chapter 1, *Unix Host Security*

As the old saying goes, Unix was designed to share information, not to protect it. This old saw is no longer true with modern operating systems, where security is an integral component to any server. Many new programs and kernel features have been developed that provide a much higher degree of control over what Unix-like operating systems can do. Chapter 1 demonstrates advanced techniques for hardening your Linux, FreeBSD, or OpenBSD server.

Chapter 2, *Windows Host Security*

Microsoft Windows is used as a server platform in many organizations. As the Windows platform is a common target for various attacks, administering these systems can be challenging. This chapter covers many important steps that are often overlooked by Windows administrators, including tightening down permissions, auditing all system activity, and eliminating security holes that are present in the default Windows installation.

Chapter 3, *Network Security*

Regardless of the operating system used by your servers, if your network is connected to the Internet, it uses TCP/IP for communications. Networking protocols can be subverted in a number of powerful and surprising ways, leading to attacks that can range from simple denial of service to unauthorized access with full privileges. This chapter demonstrates some tools and techniques used to attack servers using the network itself, as well as methods for preventing these attacks.

Chapter 4, *Logging*

Network security administrators live and die by the quality of their logs. If too little information is tracked, intrusions can slip by unnoticed. If too much is logged, attacks can be lost in the deluge of irrelevant information. Chapter 4 shows you how to balance the need for information with the need for brevity by automatically collecting, processing, and protecting your system logs.

Chapter 5, *Monitoring and Trending*

As useful as system logs and network scans can be, they represent only a single data point of information, relevant only to the instant that the events were recorded. Without a history of activity on your network, you have no way to establish a baseline for what is "normal," nor any real way to determine if something fishy is going on. This chapter presents a number of tools and methods for watching your network and services over time, allowing you to recognize trends that will aid in future planning and enable you to tell at a glance when something just isn't right.

Chapter 6, *Secure Tunnels*

How is it possible to maintain secure communications over networks as untrustworthy as the Internet? The answer nearly always involves powerful encryption and authentication techniques. Chapter 6 shows you how to implement powerful VPN technologies, including IPSec, PPTP, and OpenVPN. You will also find techniques for protecting services, using SSL, SSH, and other strong encryption tools

Chapter 7, *Network Intrusion Detection*

How do you know when your network is under attack? While logs and historical statistics can show you if something is out of sorts, there are tools designed to notify you (or otherwise take action) immediately when common attacks are detected. This chapter centers on the tremendously popular NIDS tool Snort and presents many techniques and add-ons that unleash this powerful tool's full potential. Also presented are methods for setting up your own "honeypot" network to attract and confuse would-be system crackers.

Chapter 8, *Recovery and Response*

Even the most competent and careful network administrator will eventually have to deal with successful security incidents. This chapter contains suggestions on how to verify your system's integrity, preserve evidence for later analysis, and track down the human being at the other end of undesirable network traffic.

Conventions Used in This Book

The following typographical conventions are used in this book:

Italic

Indicates new terms, URLs, email addresses, filenames, file extensions, pathnames, directories, daemons, programs, and Unix utilities.

Constant width

Indicates commands, options, switches, variables, attributes, keys, functions, types, classes, namespaces, methods, modules, properties, parameters, values, objects, events, event handlers, XML tags, HTML tags, macros, the contents of files, or the output from commands.

Constant width bold

Shows commands or other text that should be typed literally by the user.

Constant width italic

Shows text that should be replaced with user-supplied values.

Color

The second color is used to indicate a cross-reference within the text.

The thermometer icons, found next to each hack, indicate the relative complexity of the hack:

    beginner   moderate   expert

Using Code Examples

This book is here to help you get your job done. In general, you may use the code in this book in your programs and documentation. You do not need to contact us for permission unless you're reproducing a significant portion of the code. For example, writing a program that uses several chunks of code from this book not require permission. Selling or distributing a CD-ROM of examples from O'Reilly books *does* require permission. Answering a question by citing this book and quoting example code does not require permission. Incorporating a significant amount of example code from this book into your product's documentation *does* require permission.

We appreciate, but do not require, attribution. An attribution usually includes the title, author, publisher, and ISBN. For example: "*Network Security Hacks* by Andrew Lockhart. Copyright 2004 O'Reilly Media, Inc., 0-596-00643-8."

If you suspect your use of code examples falls outside fair use or the permission given here, feel free to contact us at *permissions@oreilly.com*.

How to Contact Us

Please address comments and questions concerning this book to the publisher:

O'Reilly & Associates
1005 Gravenstein Highway North
Sebastopol, CA 95472
(800) 998-9938 (in the United States or Canada)
(707) 829-0515 (international or local)
(707) 829-0104 (fax)

We have a web page for this book, where we list errata, examples, and any additional information. You can access this page at:

http://www.oreilly.com/catalog/netsechacks

To comment or ask technical questions about this book, send email to:

bookquestions@oreilly.com

For more information about our books, conferences, Resource Centers, and the O'Reilly Network, see our web site at:

http://www.oreilly.com

Got a Hack?

To explore Hacks books online or to contribute a hack for future titles, visit:

http://hacks.oreilly.com

## CHAPTER ONE

Unix Host Security

Hacks 1–20

Networking is all about connecting computers together, so it follows that a computer network is no more secure than the machines that it connects. A single insecure host can make lots of trouble for your entire network, as it can act as a tool for reconnaissance or a strong base of attack if it is under the control of an adversary. Firewalls, intrusion detection, and other advanced security measures are useless if your servers offer easily compromised services. Before delving into the network part of network security, you should first make sure that the machines you are responsible for are as secure as possible.

This chapter offers many methods for reducing the risks involved in offering services on a Unix-based system. Even though each of these hacks can stand on its own, it is worth reading through this entire chapter. If you only implement one type of security measure, you run the risk of all your preparation being totally negated once an attacker figures out how to bypass it. Just as Fort Knox isn't protected by a regular door with an ordinary dead bolt, no single security feature can ultimately protect your servers. And the security measures you may need to take increase proportionally to the value of what you're protecting.

As the old saying goes, *security* isn't a noun, it's a verb. That is, security is an active process that must be constantly followed and renewed. Short of unplugging the machine, there is no single action you can take to secure your machine. With that in mind, consider these techniques as a starting point for building a secure server that meets your particular needs.

Secure Mount Points

#1   Use mount options to help prevent intruders from further escalating a compromise.

The primary way of interacting with a Unix machine is through its filesystem. Thus, when an intruder has gained access to a system, it is desirable to limit what he can do with the files available to him. One way to accomplish this is with the use of restrictive mount options.

A *mount option* is a flag that controls how the filesystem may be accessed. It is passed to the operating system kernel's code when the filesystem is brought online. Mount options can be used to prevent files from being interpreted as device nodes, to disallow binaries from being executed, and to disallow the SUID bit from taking affect (by using the nodev, noexec, and nosuid flags). Filesystems can also be mounted read-only with the ro option.

These options are specified from the command line by running mount with the -o flag. For example, if you have a separate partition for *tmp* that is on the third partition of your first IDE hard disk, you can mount with the nodev, noexec, and nosuid flags, which are enabled by running the following command:

```
# mount -o nodev,noexec,nosuid /dev/hda3 /tmp
```

An equivalent entry in your */etc/fstab* would look something like this:

```
/dev/hda3    /tmp    ext3    defaults,nodev,noexec,nosuid    1 2
```

By carefully considering your requirements and dividing up your storage into multiple filesystems, you can utilize these mount options to increase the work that an attacker will have to do in order to further compromise your system. A quick way to do this is to first categorize your directory tree into areas that need write access for the system to function and those that don't. You should consider using the read-only flag on any part of the filesystem where the contents do not change regularly. A good candidate for this might be */usr*, depending on how often updates are made to system software.

Obviously, many directories (such as */home*) will need to be mounted as read-write. However, it is unlikely that users on an average multiuser system will need to run SUID binaries or create device files within their home directories. Therefore, a separate filesystem, mounted with the nodev and nosuid options, could be created to house the users' home directories. In addition, if you've determined that your users will not need to execute programs stored in their home directories, you can use the noexec mount option as well. Similar situations also arise when looking at */tmp* and */var*, where it is highly unlikely that any process will legitimately need to execute SUID or non-SUID binaries or access device files. This helps prevent the possibility of an attacker leaving a Trojan horse in common directories, such as */tmp* or a user's home directory. The attacker may be able to install the program, but it cannot actually run, with or without the proper chmod bits.

Note that services running in a chroot( ) environment **[Hack #10]** may be broken if nodev is specified on the filesystem running under the chroot. This is because device nodes such as /dev/log and /dev/null must be available within the chroot( ) environment.

There are a number of ways that an attacker can still circumvent these mount restrictions. For example, the noexec option on Linux can be bypassed by using /lib/ld-linux.so to execute binaries residing on such filesystems. At first glance, you'd think that this can be remedied by making *ld-linux.so* nonexecutable, but this would render all dynamically linked binaries unexecutable. So, unless all of the programs you rely on are statically linked (they're probably not), then the noexec option is of little use in Linux. In addition, an attacker who has already gained root privileges will not be significantly hampered by filesystems mounted with special options, since these can often be remounted with the -o remount option. But by using mount flags, you can easily limit the possible attacks available to a hostile user before he gains root privileges.

Scan for SUID and SGID Programs

Quickly check for potential root-exploitable programs and backdoors.

One potential way for a user to escalate her privileges on a system is to exploit a vulnerability in an SUID or SGID program. SUID and SGID are legitimately used when programs need special permissions above and beyond those that are available to the user who is running them. One such program is passwd. Simultaneously allowing a user to change her password while not allowing any user to modify the system password file means that the passwd program must be run with root privileges. Thus the program has its SUID bit set, which causes it to be executed with the privileges of the program file's owner. Similarly, when the SGID bit is set, the program is executed with the privileges of the file's group owner.

Running ls -l on a binary that has its SUID bit set should look like this:

```
-r-s--x--x   1 root     root        16336 Feb 13  2003 /usr/bin/passwd
```

Notice that instead of an execute bit (x) for the owner bits, it has an s. This signifies an SUID file.

Unfortunately, a poorly written SUID or SGID binary can be used to quickly and easily escalate a user's privileges. Also, an attacker who has already gained root access may hide SUID binaries throughout your system in order to leave a backdoor for future access. This leads us to the need for scanning systems for SUID and SGID binaries. This is a simple process and can be done with the following command:

```
# find / \( -perm -4000 -o -perm -2000 \) -type f -exec ls -la {} \;
```

One important thing to consider is whether an SUID program is in fact a shell script rather than an executable, since it's trivial for someone to change an otherwise innocuous script into a backdoor. Most operating systems will ignore any SUID or SGID bits on a shell script, but if you want to find all SUID or SGID scripts on a system, change the argument to the -exec option in the last command and add a pipe so that the command reads:

```
# find / \( -perm -4000 -o -perm -2000 \) \
  -type f -exec file {} \; | grep -v ELF
```

Now every time an SUID or SGID file is encountered, the file command will run and determine what type of file is being examined. If it's an executable, grep will filter it out; otherwise, it will be printed to the screen with some information about what kind of file it is. Most operating systems use ELF-format executables, but if you're running an operating system that doesn't (older versions of Linux used a.out, and AIX uses XCOFF), you'll need to replace the ELF in the previous grep command with the binary format used by your operating system and architecture. If you're unsure of what to look for, run the file command on any binary executable, and it will report the string you're looking for.

For example, here's an example of running file on a binary in Mac OS X:

```
$ file /bin/sh
/bin/sh: Mach-O executable ppc
```

To go one step further, you could even queue the command to run once a day using cron and have it redirect the output to a file. For instance, this crontab entry would scan for files that have either the SUID or SGID bits set, compare the current list to the one from the day before, and then email the differences to the owner of the crontab (make sure this is all on one line):

```
0 4 * * * find / \( -perm -4000 -o -perm -2000 \) -type f \
  > /var/log/sidlog.new &&
  diff /var/log/sidlog.new /var/log/sidlog &&
  mv /var/log/sidlog.new /var/log/sidlog
```

This example will also leave a current list of SUID and SGID files in */var/log/ sidlog*.

HACK #3 Scan For World- and Group-Writable Directories

Quickly scan for directories with loose permissions.

World- and group-writable directories present a problem: if the users of a system have not set their umask properly, they will inadvertently create insecure files, completely unaware of the implications. With this in mind, it seems it would be good to scan for directories with loose permissions. Much like "Scan for SUID and SGID Programs" [Hack #2], this can be accomplished by running the find command:

```
# find / -type d \( -perm -g+w -o -perm -o+w \) -exec ls -lad {} \;
```

Any directories that are listed in the output should have the sticky bit set, which is denoted by a t in the directory's permission bits. A world-writable directory with the sticky bit set ensures that even though anyone may create files in the directory, they may not delete or modify another user's files. If you see a directory in the output that does not contain a sticky bit, consider whether it really needs to be world-writable or whether the use of groups or ACLs [Hack #4] will work better for your situation. If you really do need the directory to be world-writable, set the sticky bit on it using chmod +t.

To get a list of the directories that don't have their sticky bit set, run this:

```
# find / -type d \( -perm -g+w -o -perm -o+w \) \
  -not -perm -a+t -exec ls -lad {} \;
```

If you're using a system that creates a unique group for each user (e.g., you create a user *andrew*, which in turn creates a group *andrew* as the primary group), you may want to modify the commands to not scan for group-writable directories. (Otherwise, you will get a lot of output that really isn't pertinent.) To do this, run the command without the -perm -g+w portion.

HACK #4 Create Flexible Permissions Hierarchies with POSIX ACLs

When Unix mode-based permissions just aren't enough, use an ACL.

Most of the time, the traditional Unix file permission system fits the bill just fine. But in a highly collaborative environment with multiple people needing access to files, this scheme can become unwieldy. Access control lists, otherwise known as *ACLs* (pronounced to rhyme with "hackles"), are a feature that is relatively new to the Linux operating system, but has been available in FreeBSD and Solaris for some time. While ACLs do not inherently add "more security" to a system, they do reduce the complexity of managing permissions. ACLs provide new ways to apply file and directory permissions without resorting to the creation of unnecessary groups.

ACLs are stored as extended attributes within the filesystem metadata. As the name implies, they allow you to define lists that either grant or deny access to a given file based on the criteria you provide. However, ACLs do not abandon the traditional permission system completely. ACLs may be specified for both users and groups and are still separated into the realms of read, write, and execute access. In addition, a control list may be defined for any user or group that does not correspond to any of the user or group ACLs, much like the "other" mode bits of a file. Access control lists also have what is called an ACL mask, which acts as a permission mask for all ACLs that specifically mention a user and a group. This is similar to a umask, but not quite the same. For instance, if you set the ACL mask to r--, any ACLs that pertain to a specific user or group and are looser in permissions (e.g., rw-) will effectively become r--. Directories also may contain a default ACL, which specifies the initial ACLs of files and subdirectories created within them.

To modify or remove ACLs, use the setfacl command. To modify an ACL, the -m option is used, followed by an ACL specification and a filename or list of filenames. You can delete an ACL by using the -x option and specifying an ACL or list of ACLs.

There are three general forms of an ACL: one for users, another for groups, and one for others. Let's look at them here:

```
# User ACL
u:[user]:<mode>
# Group ACL
g:[group]:<mode>
# Other ACL
o:<mode>
```

Notice that in the user and group ACLs, the actual user and group names that the ACL applies to are optional. If these are omitted, it means that the ACL will apply to the base ACL, which is derived from the file's mode bits. Thus, if you modify these, the mode bits will be modified and vice versa.

See for yourself by creating a file and then modifying its base ACL:

```
$ touch myfile
$ ls -l myfile
-rw-rw-r--    1 andrew    andrew        0 Oct 13 15:57 myfile
$ setfacl -m u::---,g::---,o:--- myfile
$ ls -l myfile
----------    1 andrew    andrew        0 Oct 13 15:57 myfile
```

From this example, you can also see that multiple ACLs can be listed by separating them with commas.

You can also specify ACLs for an arbitrary number of groups or users:

```
$ touch foo
$ setfacl -m u:jlope:rwx,g:wine:rwx ,o:--- foo
$ getfacl foo
# file: foo
# owner: andrew
# group: andrew
user::rw-
user:jlope:rwx
group::---
group:wine:rwx
mask::rwx
other::---
```

Now if you changed the mask to r--, the ACLs for jlope and wine would effectively become r-- as well:

```
$ setfacl -m m:r-- foo
$ getfacl foo
# file: foo
# owner: andrew
# group: andrew
user::rw-
user:jlope:rwx                    #effective:r--
group::---
group:wine:rwx                    #effective:r--
mask::r--
other::---
```

As mentioned earlier, directories can have default ACLs that will automatically be applied to files that are created within the directory. Default ACLs are set by prepending a d: to the ACL that you want to set:

```
$ mkdir mydir
$ setfacl -m d:u:jlope:rwx mydir
$ getfacl mydir
# file: mydir
# owner: andrew
# group: andrew
user::rwx
group::---
other::---
default:user::rwx
default:user:jlope:rwx
default:group::---
default:mask::rwx
default:other::---

$ touch mydir/bar
$ getfacl mydir/bar
# file: mydir/bar
# owner: andrew
# group: andrew
```

```
user::rw-
user:jlope:rwx                    #effective:rw-
group::---
mask::rw-
other::---
```

As you may have noticed from the previous examples, you can list ACLs by using the getfacl command. This command is pretty straightforward and has only a few options. The most useful is the -R option, which allows you to list ACLs recursively and works very much like ls -R.

H A C K   Protect Your Logs from Tampering
#5   Use file attributes to prevent intruders from removing traces of their break-in.

In the course of an intrusion, an attacker will more than likely leave telltale signs of his actions in various system logs. This is a valuable audit trail that should be well protected. Without reliable logs, it can be very difficult to figure out how the attacker got in, or where the attack came from. This information is crucial in analyzing the incident and then responding to it by contacting the appropriate parties involved [Hack #100]. However, if the break-in attempt is successful and the intruder gains root privileges, what's to stop him from removing the traces of his misbehavior?

This is where file attributes come in to save the day (or at least make it a little better). Both Linux and the BSDs have the ability to assign extra attributes to files and directories. This is different from the standard Unix permissions scheme in that the attributes set on a file apply universally to all users of the system, and they affect file accesses at a much deeper level than file permissions or ACLs [Hack #4]. In Linux you can see and modify the attributes that are set for a given file by using the lsattr and chattr commands, respectively. Under the BSDs, ls -lo can be used to view the attributes, and chflags can be used to modify them. At the time of this writing, file attributes in Linux are available only when using the ext2 and ext3 filesystems. There are also kernel patches available for attribute support in XFS and reiserfs.

One useful attribute for protecting log files is append-only. When this attribute is set, the file cannot be deleted, and writes are only allowed to append to the end of the file.

To set the append-only flag under Linux, run this command:

```
# chattr +a filename
```

Under the BSDs, use this:

```
# chflags sappnd filename
```

See how the +a attribute works by creating a file and setting its append-only attribute:

```
# touch /var/log/logfile
# echo "append-only not set" > /var/log/logfile
# chattr +a /var/log/logfile
# echo "append-only set" > /var/log/logfile
bash: /var/log/logfile: Operation not permitted
```

The second write attempt failed, since it would overwrite the file. However, appending to the end of the file is still permitted:

```
# echo "appending to file" >> /var/log/logfile
# cat /var/log/logfile
append-only not set
appending to file
```

Obviously, an intruder who has gained root privileges could realize that file attributes are being used and just remove the append-only flag from our logs by running chattr -a. To prevent this, we need to disable the ability to remove the append-only attribute. To accomplish this under Linux, use its capabilities mechanism. Under the BSDs, use its *securelevel* facility.

The Linux capabilities model divides up the privileges given to the all-powerful root account and allows you to selectively disable them. In order to prevent a user from removing the append-only attribute from a file, we need to remove the CAP_LINUX_IMMUTABLE capability. When present in the running system, this capability allows the append-only attribute to be modified. To modify the set of capabilities available to the system, we will use a simple utility called lcap (*http://packetstormsecurity.org/linux/admin/lcap-0.0.3.tar.bz2*).

To unpack and compile the tool, run this command:

```
# tar xvfj lcap-0.0.3.tar.bz2 && cd lcap-0.0.3 && make
```

Then, to disallow modification of the append-only flag, run:

```
# ./lcap CAP_LINUX_IMMUTABLE
# ./lcap CAP_SYS_RAWIO
```

The first command removes the ability to change the append-only flag, and the second command removes the ability to do raw I/O. This is needed so that the protected files cannot be modified by accessing the block device they reside on. It also prevents access to */dev/mem* and */dev/kmem*, which would provide a loophole for an intruder to reinstate the CAP_LINUX_ IMMUTABLE capability. To remove these capabilities at boot, add the previous two commands to your system startup scripts (e.g., */etc/rc.local*). You should ensure that capabilities are removed late in the boot order, to prevent problems with other startup scripts. Once lcap has removed kernel capabilities, they can be reinstated only by rebooting the system.

The BSDs accomplish the same thing through the use of securelevels. The securelevel is a kernel variable that can be set to disallow certain functionality. Raising the securelevel to 1 is functionally the same as removing the two previously discussed Linux capabilities. Once the securelevel has been set to a value greater than 0, it cannot be lowered. By default, OpenBSD will raise the securelevel to 1 when in multiuser mode. In FreeBSD, the securelevel is −1 by default.

To change this behavior, add the following line to /etc/sysctl.conf:

```
kern.securelevel=1
```

Before doing this, you should be aware that adding append-only flags to your log files will most likely cause log rotation scripts to fail. However, doing this will greatly enhance the security of your audit trail, which will prove invaluable in the event of an incident.

Delegate Administrative Roles

HACK #6

Let others do your work for you without giving away root privileges.

The *sudo* utility can help you delegate some system responsibilities to other people, without giving away full root access. It is a setuid root binary that executes commands on an authorized user's behalf, after she has entered her current password.

As root, run */usr/sbin/visudo* to edit the list of users who can call *sudo*. The default *sudo* list looks something like this:

```
root ALL=(ALL) ALL
```

Unfortunately, many system administrators tend to use this entry as a template and grant unrestricted root access to all other admins unilaterally:

```
root ALL=(ALL) ALL
rob ALL=(ALL) ALL
jim ALL=(ALL) ALL
david ALL=(ALL) ALL
```

While this may allow you to give out root access without giving away the root password, this method is truly useful only when all of the *sudo* users can be completely trusted. When properly configured, the *sudo* utility provides tremendous flexibility for granting access to any number of commands, run as any arbitrary uid.

The syntax of the *sudo* line is:

```
user machine=(effective user) command
```

The first column specifies the *sudo* user. The next column defines the hosts in which this *sudo* entry is valid. This allows you to easily use a single *sudo* configuration across multiple machines.

For example, suppose you have a developer who needs root access on a development machine, but not on any other server:

```
peter beta.oreillynet.com=(ALL) ALL
```

The next column (in parentheses) specifies the effective user that may run the commands. This is very handy for allowing users to execute code as users other than root:

```
peter lists.oreillynet.com=(mailman) ALL
```

Finally, the last column specifies all of the commands that this user may run:

```
david ns.oreillynet.com=(bind) /usr/sbin/rndc,/usr/sbin/named
```

If you find yourself specifying large lists of commands (or, for that matter, users or machines), then take advantage of *sudo*'s Alias syntax. An Alias can be used in place of its respective entry on any line of the *sudo* configuration:

```
User_Alias ADMINS=rob,jim,david
User_Alias WEBMASTERS=peter,nancy
Runas_Alias DAEMONS=bind,www,smmsp,ircd
Host_Alias WEBSERVERS=www.oreillynet.com,www.oreilly.com,www.perl.com
Cmnd_Alias PROCS=/bin/kill,/bin/killall,/usr/bin/skill,/usr/bin/top
Cmnd_Alias APACHE=/usr/local/apache/bin/apachectl
WEBMASTERS WEBSERVERS=(www) APACHE
ADMINS ALL=(DAEMONS) ALL
```

It is also possible to specify system groups in place of the user specification, to allow any user who belongs to that group to execute commands. Just preface the group with a %, like this:

```
%wwwadmin WEBSERVERS=(www) APACHE
```

Now any user who is part of the wwwadmin group can execute *apachectl* as the www user on any of the web server machines.

One very useful feature is the NOPASSWD: flag. When present, the user won't have to enter a password before executing the command:

```
rob ALL=(ALL) NOPASSWD: PROCS
```

This will allow the user rob to execute *kill*, *killall*, *skill*, and *top* on any machine, as any user, without entering a password.

Finally, *sudo* can be a handy alternative to *su* for running commands at startup out of the system *rc* files:

```
(cd /usr/local/mysql; sudo -u mysql ./bin/safe_mysqld &)
sudo -u www /usr/local/apache/bin/apachectl start
```

For that to work at boot time, the default line root ALL=(ALL) ALL must be present.

Use *sudo* with the usual caveats that apply to setuid binaries. Particularly if you allow *sudo* to execute interactive commands (like editors) or any sort of compiler or interpreter, you should assume that it is possible that the *sudo* user will be able to execute arbitrary commands as the effective user. Still, under most circumstances this isn't a problem, and it's certainly preferable to giving away undue access to root privileges.

—*Rob Flickenger*

HACK #7 Automate Cryptographic Signature Verification

Use scripting and key servers to automate the chore of checking software authenticity.

One of the most important things you can do for the security of your system is to be familiar with the software you are installing. You probably will not have the time, knowledge, or resources to actually go through the source code for all of the software that you are installing. However, verifying that the software you are compiling and installing is what the authors intended it to be can go a long way toward preventing the widespread distribution of Trojan horses. Recently, several pivotal pieces of software (such as tcpdump, LibPCap, Sendmail, and OpenSSH) have had Trojaned versions distributed. Since this is an increasingly popular vector for attack, verifying your software is critically important.

Why is this even an issue? Unfortunately, it takes a little bit of effort to verify software before installing it. Either through laziness or ignorance, many system administrators overlook this critical step. This is a classic example of "false" laziness, as it will likely lead to more work for the sysadmin in the long run. This problem is difficult to solve because it relies on the programmers and distributors to get their acts together. Then there's the laziness aspect: many times, software packages don't even come with a signature to use for verifying the legitimacy of what you've downloaded. Often, signatures are available right along with the source code, but in order to verify the code, you must then hunt through the site for the public key that was used to create the signature. After finding the public key, you have to download it, verify that the key is genuine, add it to your keyring, and finally check the signature of the code.

Here is what this would look like when checking the signature for Version 1.3.28 of the Apache web server using GnuPG (*http://www.gnupg.org*):

```
# gpg -import KEYS
# gpg -verify apache_1.3.28.tar.gz.asc apache_1.3.28.tar.gz
gpg: Signature made Wed Jul 16 13:42:54 2003 PDT using DSA key ID 08C975E5
gpg: Good signature from "Jim Jagielski <jim@zend.com>"
gpg:                     aka "Jim Jagielski <jim@apache.org>"
gpg:                     aka "Jim Jagielski <jim@jaguNET.com>"
```

```
gpg: WARNING: This key is not certified with a trusted signature!
gpg:          There is no indication that the signature belongs to the
owner.
Fingerprint: 8B39 757B 1D8A 994D F243  3ED5 8B3A 601F 08C9 75E5
```

As you can see, it's not terribly difficult to do, but this step is often over-looked when you are in a hurry. This is where this hack comes to the res-cue. We'll use a little bit of shell scripting and what are known as *key servers* to reduce the number of steps to perform this process.

Key servers are a part of a public-key cryptography infrastructure that allows you to retrieve keys from a trusted third party. A nice feature of GnuPG is its ability to query key servers for a key ID and to download the result into a local keyring. To figure out which key ID to ask for, we rely on the fact that the error message generated by GnuPG tells us which key ID it was unable to find locally when trying to verify the signature.

In the previous example, if the key that GnuPG was looking for had not been imported prior to verifying the signature, it would have generated an error like this:

```
gpg: Signature made Wed Jul 16 13:42:54 2003 PDT using DSA key ID 08C975E5
gpg: Can't check signature: public key not found
```

The following script takes advantage of that error:

```
#!/bin/sh
VENDOR_KEYRING=vendors.gpg
KEYSERVER=search.keyserver.net
KEYID="0x`gpg --verify $1 $2 2>&1 | grep 'key ID' | awk '{print $NF}'`"
gpg --no-default-keyring --keyring $VENDOR_KEYRING --recv-key \
  --keyserver $KEYSERVER $KEYID
gpg --keyring $VENDOR_KEYRING --verify $1 $2
```

The first line of the script specifies the keyring in which the result from the key server query will be stored. You could use *pubring.gpg* (which is the default keyring for GnuGP), but using a separate file will make managing vendor pub-lic keys easier. The second line of the script specifies which key server to query (the script uses *search.keyserver.net*; another good one is *pgp.mit.edu*). The third line attempts (and fails) to verify the signature without first consulting the key server. It then uses the key ID it saw in the error, and prepends an 0x in order to query the key server on the next line. Finally, GnuPG attempts to ver-ify the signature, and specifies the keyring in which the query result was stored.

This script has shortened the verification process by eliminating the need to search for and import the public key that was used to generate the signature. Going back to the example of verifying the Apache 1.3.28 source code, you can see how much more convenient it is to verify the package's authenticity:

```
# checksig apache_1.3.28.tar.gz.asc apache_1.3.28.tar.gz
gpg: requesting key 08C975E5 from HKP keyserver search.keyserver.net
```

```
gpg: key 08C975E5: public key imported
gpg: Total number processed: 1
gpg:                   imported: 1
gpg: Warning: using insecure memory!
gpg: please see http://www.gnupg.org/faq.html for more information
gpg: Signature made Wed Jul 16 13:42:54 2003 PDT using DSA key ID 08C975E5
gpg: Good signature from "Jim Jagielski <jim@zend.com>"
gpg:                 aka "Jim Jagielski <jim@apache.org>"
gpg:                 aka "Jim Jagielski <jim@jaguNET.com>"
gpg: checking the trustdb
gpg: no ultimately trusted keys found
gpg: WARNING: This key is not certified with a trusted signature!
gpg:          There is no indication that the signature belongs to the
owner.
Fingerprint: 8B39 757B 1D8A 994D F243  3ED5 8B3A 601F 08C9 75E5
```

With this small and quick script, both the number steps needed to verify a source package and the amount of time needed have been reduced. As with any good shell script, it should help you to be lazy in a good way: by doing more work properly, but with less effort on your part.

Check for Listening Services

HACK #8

Find out whether unneeded services are listening and looking for possible backdoors.

One of the first things that should be done after a fresh operating system install is to see what services are running, and remove any unneeded services from the system startup process. You could use a port scanner (such as nmap [Hack #42]) and run it against the host, but if one didn't come with the operating system install, you'll likely have to connect your fresh (and possibly insecure) machine to the network to download one. Also, nmap can be fooled if the system is using firewall rules. With proper firewall rules, a service can be completely invisible to nmap unless certain criteria (such as the source IP address) also match. When you have shell access to the server itself, it is usually more efficient to find open ports using programs that were installed with the operating system. One program that will do what we need is *netstat*, a program that will display various network-related information and statistics.

To get a list of listening ports and their owning processes under Linux, run this:

```
# netstat -luntp
Active Internet connections (only servers)
Proto Recv-Q Send-Q Local Address Foreign Address  State   PID/Program name
tcp       0      0 0.0.0.0:22    0.0.0.0:*        LISTEN  1679/sshd
udp       0      0 0.0.0.0:68    0.0.0.0:*                1766/dhclient
```

From the output, you can see that this machine is probably a workstation, since it just has a DHCP client running along with an SSH daemon for remote access. The ports in use are listed after the colon in the Local Address column (22 for sshd and 68 for dhclient). The absence of any other listening processes means that this is probably a workstation, and not a network server.

Unfortunately, the BSD version of *netstat* does not let us list the processes and the process IDs (PIDs) that own the listening port. Nevertheless, the BSD netstat command is still useful for listing the listening ports on your system.

To get a list of listening ports under FreeBSD, run this command:

```
# netstat -a -n | egrep 'Proto|LISTEN'
Proto Recv-Q Send-Q  Local Address         Foreign Address      (state)
tcp4      0      0  *.587                 *.*                  LISTEN
tcp4      0      0  *.25                  *.*                  LISTEN
tcp4      0      0  *.22                  *.*                  LISTEN
tcp4      0      0  *.993                 *.*                  LISTEN
tcp4      0      0  *.143                 *.*                  LISTEN
tcp4      0      0  *.53                  *.*                  LISTEN
```

Again, the ports in use are listed in the Local Address column. Many seasoned system administrators have memorized the common port numbers for popular services, and can see that this server is running SSH, SMTP, DNS, IMAP, and IMAP+SSL services. If you are ever in doubt about which services typically run on a given port, either eliminate the -n switch from netstat (which tells *netstat* to use names but can take much longer to run when looking up DNS addresses) or manually grep the */etc/services* file:

```
# grep -w 993 /etc/services
imaps           993/udp    # imap4 protocol over TLS/SSL
imaps           993/tcp    # imap4 protocol over TLS/SSL
```

Also notice that, unlike the output of netstat on Linux, we don't get the PIDs of the daemons themselves. You might also notice that no UDP ports were listed for DNS. This is because UDP sockets do not have a LISTEN state in the same sense that TCP sockets do. In order to display UDP sockets, you must add udp4 to the argument for egrep, thus making it 'Proto|LISTEN|udp4'. However, due to the way UDP works, not all UDP sockets will necessarily be associated with a daemon process.

Under FreeBSD, there is another command that will give us just what we want. The sockstat command performs only a small subset of what netstat can do, and is limited to just listing information on both Unix domain sockets and Inet sockets.

To get a list of listening ports and their owning processes with sockstat, run this command:

```
# sockstat -4 -l
USER     COMMAND     PID    FD PROTO   LOCAL ADDRESS        FOREIGN ADDRESS
root     sendmail    1141   4 tcp4     *:25                 *:*
root     sendmail    1141   5 tcp4     *:587                *:*
root     sshd        1138   3 tcp4     *:22                 *:*
root     inetd       1133   4 tcp4     *:143                *:*
root     inetd       1133   5 tcp4     *:993                *:*
named    named       1127  20 tcp4     *:53                 *:*
named    named       1127  21 udp4     *:53                 *:*
named    named       1127  22 udp4     *:1351               *:*
```

Once again, we see that sshd, SMTP, DNS, IMAP, and IMAP+SSL services are running, but now we have the process that owns the socket plus its PID. We can now see that the IMAP services are being spawned from inetd instead of standalone daemons, and that sendmail and named are providing the SMTP and DNS services.

For most other Unix-like operating systems you can use the *lsof* utility (*http://ftp.cerias.purdue.edu/pub/tools/unix/sysutils/lsof/*). *lsof* is short for "list open files" and, as the name implies, allows you to list files that are open on a system, in addition to the processes and PIDs that have them open. Since sockets and files work the same way under Unix, *lsof* can also be used to list open sockets. This is done with the -i command-line option.

To get a list of listening ports and the processes that own them using *lsof*, run this command:

```
# lsof -i -n | egrep 'COMMAND|LISTEN'
COMMAND    PID  USER  FD TYPE     DEVICE    SIZE/OFF NODE NAME
named     1127 named  20u IPv4 0xeb401dc0       0t0  TCP *:domain (LISTEN)
inetd     1133  root  4u IPv4 0xeb401ba0       0t0  TCP *:imap (LISTEN)
inetd     1133  root  5u IPv4 0xeb401980       0t0  TCP *:imaps (LISTEN)
sshd      1138  root  3u IPv4 0xeb401760       0t0  TCP *:ssh (LISTEN)
sendmail  1141  root  4u IPv4 0xeb41b7e0       0t0  TCP *:smtp (LISTEN)
sendmail  1141  root  5u IPv4 0xeb438fa0       0t0  TCP *:submission (LISTEN)
```

Again, you can change the argument to egrep to display UDP sockets. However, this time use UDP instead of udp4, which makes the argument 'COMMAND|LISTEN|UDP'. As mentioned earlier, not all UDP sockets will necessarily be associated with a daemon process.

Prevent Services from Binding to an Interface
#9   Keep services from listening on a port instead of firewalling them.

Sometimes you might want to limit a service to listen on only a specific interface. For instance, Apache [Hack #50] can be configured to listen on a specific interface as opposed to all available interfaces. You can do this by using the Listen directive in your configuration file and specifying the IP address of the interface:

```
Listen 192.168.0.23:80
```

If you use VirtualHost entries, you can specify interfaces to bind to on a per-virtual-host basis:

```
<VirtualHost 192.168.0.23>
...
</VirtualHost>
```

You may even have services that are listening on a TCP port but don't need to be. Database servers such as MySQL are often used in conjunction with Apache, and are frequently set up to coexist on the same server when used in this way. Connections that come from the same machine that MySQL is installed on use a domain socket in the filesystem for communications. Therefore, you don't need to have MySQL listening on a TCP socket. To do this, you can either use the --skip-networking command-line option when starting MySQL or specify it in the [mysqld] section of your *my.cnf* file:

```
[mysqld]
...
skip-networking
...
```

Another program that you'll often find listening on a port is your X11 server, which listens on TCP port 6000 by default. This port is traditionally used to enable remote clients to connect to your X11 server so they can draw their windows and accept keyboard and mouse input; however, with the advent of SSH and X11 forwarding, this really isn't needed anymore. With X11 forwarding enabled in *ssh*, any client that needs to connect to your X11 server will be tunneled through your SSH connection and will bypass the listening TCP port when connecting to your X11 server. To get your X Windows server to stop listening on this port, all you need to do is add -nolisten tcp to the command that is used to start the server. This can be tricky, though—figuring out which file controls how the server is started can be a daunting task. Usually, you can find what you're looking for in */etc/X11*.

If you're using *gdm*, open your *gdm.conf* and look for a line similar to this one:

```
command=/usr/X11R6/bin/X
```

Then just add -nolisten tcp to the end of the line.

If you're using *xdm*, look for a file called *Xservers* and make sure it contains a line similar to this:

```
:0 local /usr/X11R6/bin/X -nolisten tcp
```

Alternatively, if you're not using a managed display and instead you're using startx or a similar command to start your X11 server, you can just add -nolisten tcp to the end of your startx command. To be sure that it is passed to the X server process, start it after an extra set of hyphens:

```
$ startx -- -nolisten tcp
```

Once you start X, fire up a terminal and see what is listening using *lsof* or *netstat* [Hack #8]. You should no longer see anything bound to port 6000.

HACK #10 Restrict Services with Sandboxed Environments

Mitigate system damage by keeping service compromises contained.

Sometimes keeping up with the latest patches just isn't enough to prevent a break-in. Often, a new exploit will circulate in private circles long before an official advisory is issued, during which time your servers may be open to unexpected attack. With this in mind, it's wise to take extra preventative measures to contain the aftermath of a compromised service. One way to do this is to run your services in sandbox environments. Ideally, this lets the service be compromised while minimizing the effects on the overall system.

Most Unix and Unix-like systems include some sort of system call or other mechanism for sandboxing that offers various levels of isolation between the host and the sandbox. The least restrictive and easiest to set up is a chroot( ) environment, which is available on nearly all Unix and Unix-like systems. In addition to chroot( ), FreeBSD includes another mechanism called jail( ), which provides a few more restrictions beyond those provided by chroot( ).

chroot( ) very simply changes the root directory of a process and all of its children. While this is a powerful feature, there are many caveats to using it. Most importantly, there should be no way for anything running within the sandbox to change its effective UID (EUID) to 0, which is root's UID. Naturally, this implies that you don't want to run anything as root within the jail. If an attacker is able to gain root privileges within the sandbox, then all bets are off. While the attacker will not be able to directly break out of the sandbox environment, it does not prevent him from running functions inside the exploited processes' address space that will let him break out. There are many ways to break out of a chroot( ) sandbox. However, they all rely on being able to get root privileges within the sandboxed environment. The Achilles heel of chroot( ) is possession of UID 0 inside the sandbox.

There are a few services that support chroot( ) environments by calling the function within the program itself, but many services do not. To run these services inside a sandboxed environment using chroot( ), we need to make use of the chroot command. The chroot command simply calls chroot( ) with the first command-line argument and attempts to execute the program specified in the second argument. If the program is a statically linked binary, all you have to do is copy the program to somewhere within the sandboxed environment; but if the program is dynamically linked, you will need to copy all of its supporting libraries to the environment as well.

See how this works by setting up bash in a chroot( ) environment. First we'll try to run chroot without copying any of the libraries bash needs:

```
# mkdir -p /chroot_test/bin
# cp /bin/bash /chroot_test/bin/
# chroot /chroot_test /bin/bash
chroot: /bin/bash: No such file or directory
```

Now we'll find out what libraries bash needs, which you can do with the ldd command, and attempt to run chroot again:

```
# ldd /bin/bash
libtermcap.so.2 => /lib/libtermcap.so.2 (0x4001a000)
libdl.so.2 => /lib/libdl.so.2 (0x4001e000)
libc.so.6 => /lib/tls/libc.so.6 (0x42000000)
/lib/ld-linux.so.2 => /lib/ld-linux.so.2 (0x40000000)
# mkdir -p chroot_test/lib/tls && \
> (cd /lib; \
> cp libtermcap.so.2 libdl.so.2 ld-linux.so.2 /chroot_test/lib; \
> cd tls; cp libc.so.6 /chroot_test/lib/tls)
# chroot /chroot_test /bin/bash
bash-2.05b#
bash-2.05b# echo /*
/bin /lib
```

Setting up a chroot environment mostly involves trial and error in getting permissions right and all of the library dependencies in order. Be sure to consider the implications of having other programs such as *mknod* or *mount* available in the chroot environment. If these were available, the attacker could possibly create device nodes to access memory directly or to remount filesystems, thus breaking out of the sandbox and gaining total control of the overall system. This threat can be mitigated by putting the directory on a filesystem mounted with options that prohibit the use of device files (as in "Secure Mount Points" [Hack #1]), but that isn't always convenient. It is advisable to make as many of the files and directories in the chrooted directory as possible owned by root and writable only by root, in order to make it impossible for a process to modify any supporting files (this includes files such as libraries and configuration files). In general it is best to keep permissions as restrictive as possible, and to relax them only when necessary (for example, if the permissions prevent the daemon from working properly).

The best candidates for a chroot( ) environment are services that do not need root privileges at all. For instance, MySQL listens for remote connections on port 3306 by default. Since this port is above 1024, mysqld can be started without root privileges and therefore doesn't pose the risk of being used to gain root access. Other daemons that need root privileges can include an option to drop these privileges after completing all the operations for which it needs root access (e.g., binding to a port below 1024), but care should be taken to ensure that the program drops its privileges correctly. If a program uses seteuid( ) rather than setuid( ) to drop its privileges, it is still possible to gain root access when exploited by an attacker. Be sure to read up on current security advisories for programs that will run only with root privileges.

You might think that simply not putting compilers, a shell, or utilities such as *mknod* in the sandbox environment may protect them in the event of a root compromise within the restricted environment. In reality, attackers can accomplish the same functionality by changing their code from calling system("/bin/sh") to calling any other C library function or system call that they desire. If you can mount the filesystem that the chrooted program runs from using the read-only flag **[Hack #1]**, you can make it more difficult for attackers to install their own code, but this is still not quite bulletproof. Unless the daemon you need to run within the environment can meet the criteria discussed earlier, you might want to look into using a more powerful sandboxing mechanism.

One such mechanism is available under FreeBSD and is implemented through the jail( ) system call. jail( ) provides many more restrictions in isolating the sandbox environment from the host system and provides additional features, such as assigning IP addresses from virtual interfaces on the host system. Using this functionality, you can create a full virtual server or just run a single service inside the sandboxed environment.

Just as with chroot( ), the system provides a jail command that uses the jail( ) system call. The basic form of the jail command is:

```
jail new root  hostname ipaddr command
```

where *ipaddr* is the IP address of the machine on which the jail is running. Try it out by running a shell inside a jail:

```
# mkdir -p /jail_test/bin
# cp /bin/sh /jail_test/sh
# jail /jail_test jail_test 192.168.0.40 /bin/sh
# echo /*
/bin
```

This time, no libraries needed to be copied, because FreeBSD's */bin/sh* is statically linked.

On the opposite side of the spectrum, we can build a jail that can function as a nearly full-function virtual server with its own IP address. The steps to do this basically involve building FreeBSD from source and specifying the jail directory as the install destination.

You can do this by running the following commands:

```
# mkdir /jail_test
# cd /usr/src
# make world DESTDIR=/jail_test
# cd /etc && make distribution DESTDIR=/jail_test -DNO_MAKEDEV_RUN
# cd /jail_test/dev && sh MAKEDEV jail
# cd /jail_test && ln -s dev/null kernel
```

However, if you're planning to run just one service from within the jail, this is definitely overkill. Note that in the real world you'll most likely need to create */dev/null* and */dev/log* device nodes in your sandbox environment for most daemons to work correctly.

HACK #11 Use proftp with a MySQL Authentication Source

Make sure that your database system's OS is running as efficiently as possible with these tweaks.

proftpd is a powerful FTP daemon with a configuration syntax much like Apache. It has a whole slew of options not available in most FTP daemons, including ratios, virtual hosting, and a modularized design that allows people to write their own modules.

One such module is *mod_sql*, which allows *proftpd* to use a SQL database as its back-end authentication source. Currently, *mod_sql* supports MySQL and PostgreSQL. This can be a good way to help lock down access to your server, as inbound users will authenticate against the database (and therefore not require an actual shell account on the server). In this hack, we'll get *proftpd* authenticating against a MySQL database.

First, download and build the source to *proftpd* and *mod_sql*:

```
~$ bzcat proftpd-1.2.6.tar.bz2 | tar xf -
~/proftpd-1.2.6/contrib$ tar zvxf ../../mod_sql-4.08.tar.gz
~/proftpd-1.2.6/contrib$ cd ..
~/proftpd-1.2.6$ ./configure --with-modules=mod_sql:mod_sql_mysql \
--with-includes=/usr/local/mysql/include/ \
--with-libraries=/usr/local/mysql/lib/
```

(Naturally, substitute the path to your mySQL install, if it isn't in */usr/local/ mysql/*.) Now, build the code and install it:

```
rob@catlin:~/proftpd-1.2.6$ make && sudo make install
```

Next, create a database for *proftpd* to use (assuming that you already have mysql up and running):

```
$ mysqladmin create proftpd
```

Then, permit read-only access to it from *proftpd*:

```
$ mysql -e "grant select on proftpd.* to proftpd@localhost \
    identified by 'secret';"
```

Create two tables in the database, with this schema:

```
CREATE TABLE users (
userid varchar(30) NOT NULL default '',
password varchar(30) NOT NULL default '',
uid int(11) default NULL,
gid int(11) default NULL,
homedir varchar(255) default NULL,
shell varchar(255) default NULL,
UNIQUE KEY uid (uid),
UNIQUE KEY userid (userid)
) TYPE=MyISAM;

CREATE TABLE groups (
groupname varchar(30) NOT NULL default '',
gid int(11) NOT NULL default '0',
members varchar(255) default NULL
) TYPE=MyISAM;
```

One quick way to create the tables is to save this schema to a file called *proftpd.schema* and run a command like mysql proftpd < proftpd.schema.

Now we need to tell *proftpd* to use this database for authentication. Add the following lines to */usr/local/etc/proftpd.conf*:

```
SQLConnectInfo proftpd proftpd secret
SQLAuthTypes crypt backend
SQLMinUserGID 111
SQLMinUserUID 111
```

The SQLConnectInfo line takes the form *database user password*. You could also specify a database on another host (even on another port) with something like:

```
SQLConnectInfo proftpd@dbhost:5678 somebody somepassword
```

The SQLAuthTypes line lets you create users with passwords stored in the standard Unix crypt format, or *mysql*'s PASSWORD( ) function. Be warned that if you're using *mod_sql*'s logging facilities, the password may be exposed in plain text, so keep those logs private.

The SQLAuthTypes line as specified won't allow blank passwords; if you need that functionality, also include the empty keyword. The SQLMinUserGID and SQLMinUserUID lines specify the minimum group and user ID that *proftpd* will permit on login. It's a good idea to make this greater than 0 (to prohibit root logins), but it should be as low as you need to allow proper permissions in the filesystem. On this system, we have a user and group called www, with both its uid and gid set to 111. As we'll want web developers to be able to log in with these permissions, we'll need to set the minimum values to 111.

Finally, we're ready to create users in the database. This will create the user jimbo, with effective user rights as www/www, and dump him in the */usr/local/apache/htdocs/* directory at login:

```
mysql -e "insert into users values ('jimbo',PASSWORD('sHHH'),'111', \
    '111', '/usr/local/apache/htdocs','/bin/bash');" proftpd
```

The password for jimbo is encrypted with *mysql*'s PASSWORD( ) function before being stored. The /bin/bash line is passed to *proftpd* to pass *proftpd*'s RequireValidShell directive. It has no bearing on granting actual shell access to the user jimbo.

At this point, you should be able to fire up *proftpd* and log in as user jimbo, with a password of sHHH. If you are having trouble getting connected, try running *proftpd* in the foreground with debugging on, like this:

```
# proftpd -n -d 5
```

Watch the messages as you attempt to connect, and you should be able to track down the source of difficulty. In my experience, it's almost always due to a failure to set something properly in *proftpd.conf*, usually regarding permissions.

The *mod_sql* module can do far more than I've shown here; it can connect to existing mysql databases with arbitrary table names, log all activity to the database, modify its user lookups with an arbitrary WHERE clause, and much more.

See Also

- The *mod_sql* home page at *http://www.lastditcheffort.org/~aah/proftpd/mod_sql/*
- The *proftpd* home page at *http://www.proftpd.org/*

—*Rob Flickenger (Linux Server Hacks)*

Prevent Stack-Smashing Attacks
HACK #12
Learn how to prevent stack-based buffer overflows.

In C and C++, memory for local variables is allocated in a chunk of memory called the *stack*. Information pertaining to the control flow of a program is also maintained on the stack. If an array is allocated on the stack and that array is overrun (that is, more values are pushed into the array than the available space provides), an attacker can overwrite the control flow information that is also stored on the stack. This type of attack is often referred to as a *stack-smashing attack*.

Stack-smashing attacks are a serious problem, since an otherwise innocuous service (such as a web server or FTP server) can be made to execute arbitrary commands. Several technologies have been developed that attempt to protect programs against these attacks. Some are implemented in the compiler, such as IBM's ProPolice (*http://www.trl.ibm.com/projects/security/ssp/*) and the Stackguard (*http://www.immunix.org/stackguard.html*) versions of GCC. Others are dynamic runtime solutions, such as LibSafe (*http://www.research.avayalabs.com/project/libsafe/*). While recompiling the source gets to the heart of the buffer overflow attack, runtime solutions can protect programs when the source isn't available or recompiling simply isn't feasible.

All of the compiler-based solutions work in much the same way, although there are some differences in the implementations. They work by placing a "canary" (which is typically some random value) on the stack between the control flow information and the local variables. The code that is normally generated by the compiler to return from the function is modified to check the value of the canary on the stack; if it is not what it is supposed to be, the program is terminated immediately.

The idea behind using a canary is that an attacker attempting to mount a stack-smashing attack will have to overwrite the canary to overwrite the control flow information. By choosing a random value for the canary, the attacker cannot know what it is and thus cannot include it in the data used to "smash" the stack.

When a program is distributed in source form, the developer of the program cannot enforce the use of StackGuard or ProPolice, because they are both nonstandard extensions to the GCC compiler. It is the responsibility of the person compiling the program to make use of one of these technologies.

For Linux systems, Avaya Labs's LibSafe technology is not implemented as a compiler extension, but instead takes advantage of a feature of the dynamic loader that causes a dynamic library to be preloaded with every executable. Using LibSafe does not require the source code for the programs it protects, and it can be deployed on a system-wide basis.

LibSafe replaces the implementation of several standard functions that are known to be vulnerable to buffer overflows, such as gets( ), strcpy( ), and scanf( ). The replacement implementations attempt to compute the maximum possible size of a statically allocated buffer used as a destination buffer for writing, using a GCC built-in function that returns the address of the frame pointer. That address is normally the first piece of information on the stack following local variables. If an attempt is made to write more than the estimated size of the buffer, the program is terminated.

Unfortunately, there are several problems with the approach taken by Lib-Safe. First, it cannot accurately compute the size of a buffer; the best it can do is limit the size of the buffer to the difference between the start of the buffer and the frame pointer. Second, LibSafe's protections will not work with programs that were compiled using the -fomit-frame-pointer flag to GCC, an optimization that causes the compiler not to put a frame pointer on the stack. Although relatively useless, this is a popular optimization for programmers to employ. Finally, LibSafe will not work on SUID binaries without static linking or a similar trick.

In addition to providing protection against conventional stack-smashing attacks, the newest versions of LibSafe also provide some protection against format-string attacks. The format-string protection also requires access to the frame pointer because it attempts to filter out arguments that are not pointers into either the heap or the local variables on the stack.

In addition to user-space solutions, you can also opt to patch your kernel to use nonexecutable stacks and detect buffer overflow attacks. We'll do just that in "Lock Down Your Kernel with grsecurity" [Hack #13].

HACK #13 Lock Down Your Kernel with grsecurity

Harden your system against attacks with the grsecurity kernel patch.

Hardening a Unix system can be a difficult process. It typically involves setting up all the services that the system will run in the most secure fashion possible, as well as locking down the system to prevent local compromises. However, putting effort into securing the services that you're running does little for the rest of the system and for unknown vulnerabilities. Luckily, even though the standard Linux kernel provides few features for proactively securing a system, there are patches available that can help the enterprising system administrator do so. One such patch is *grsecurity* (*http://www.grsecurity.net*).

grsecurity started out as a port of the OpenWall patch (*http://www.openwall. com*) to the 2.4.x series of Linux kernels. This patch added features such as nonexecutable stacks, some filesystem security enhancements, restrictions on access to */proc*, as well as some enhanced resource limits. These features helped to protect the system against stack-based buffer overflow attacks, prevented filesystem attacks involving race conditions on files created in */tmp*, limited a user to only seeing his own processes, and even enhanced Linux's resource limits to perform more checks. Since its inception, *grsecurity* has grown to include many features beyond those provided by the OpenWall patch. *grsecurity* now includes many additional memory address space protections to prevent buffer overflow exploits from succeeding, as well as enhanced chroot( ) jail restrictions, increased randomization of process and IP IDs, and increased auditing features that enable you to track every process executed on a system. *grsecurity* adds a sophisticated access control list (ACL) system that makes use of Linux's capabilities system. This ACL system can be used to limit the privileged operations that individual processes are able to perform on a case-by-case basis.

Configuration of ACLs is handled through the *gradm* utility. If you already have *grsecurity* installed on your machine, feel free to skip ahead to "Restrict Applications with grsecurity" [Hack #14].

To compile a kernel with *grsecurity*, you will need to download the patch that corresponds to your kernel version and apply it to your kernel using the *patch* utility.

For example, if you are running Linux 2.4.24:

```
# cd /usr/src/linux-2.4.24
# patch -p1 < ~andrew/grsecurity-1.9.13-2.4.24.patch
```

While the command is running, you should see a line for each kernel source file that is being patched. After the command has finished, you can make sure that the patch applied cleanly by looking for any files that end in *.rej*. The patch program creates these when it cannot apply the patch cleanly to a file. A quick way to see if there are any *.rej* files is to use the find command:

```
# find ./ -name \*.rej
```

If there are any rejected files, they will be listed on the screen. If the patch applied cleanly, you should be returned back to the shell prompt without any additional output.

After the patch has been applied, you can configure the kernel to enable *grsecurity*'s features by running make config to use text prompts, make menuconfig for a curses-based interface, or make xconfig to use a Tk-based GUI. If you went the graphical route and used make xconfig, you should then see a dialog similar to Figure 1-1. If you ran make menuconfig or make config, the relevant kernel options have the same name as the menu options described in this example.

To configure which *grsecurity* features will be enabled in the kernel, click the button labeled Grsecurity. After doing that, you should see a dialog similar to Figure 1-2.

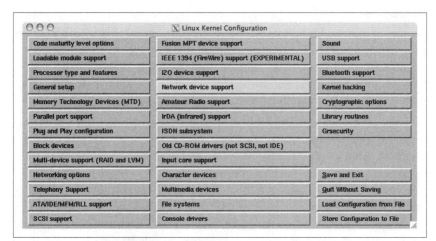

Figure 1-1. Linux kernel configuration after the grsecurity patch has been applied

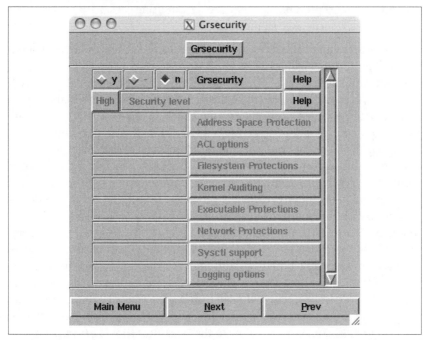

Figure 1-2. The Grsecurity configuration dialog

To enable *grsecurity,* click the y radio button. After you've done that, you can enable predefined sets of features with the Security Level drop-down list, or set it to Custom and go through the menus to pick and choose which features to enable.

Choosing Low is safe for any system and should not affect any software's normal operation. Using this setting will enable linking restrictions in directories with mode 1777. This prevents race conditions in */tmp* from being exploited, by only following symlinks to files that are owned by the process following the link. Similarly, users won't be able to write to FIFOs that they do not own if they are within a directory with permissions of 1777.

In addition to the tighter symlink and FIFO restrictions, the Low setting increases the randomness of process and IP IDs. This helps to prevent attackers from using remote detection techniques to correctly guess the operating system your machine is running (as in "Block OS Fingerprinting" [Hack #40]), and it also makes it difficult to guess the process ID of a given program. The Low security level also forces programs that use chroot( ) to change their current working directory to / after the chroot( ) call. Otherwise, if a program left its working directory outside of the chroot environment, it could be used to break out of the sandbox. Choosing the Low security level also prevents nonroot users from using dmesg, a utility that can be used to view recent kernel messages.

Choosing Medium enables all of the same features as the Low security level, but this level also includes features that make chroot( )-based sandboxed environments more secure. The ability to mount filesystems, call chroot( ), write to sysctl variables, or create device nodes within a chrooted environment are all restricted, thus eliminating much of the risk involved in running a service in a sandboxed environment under Linux. In addition, TCP source ports will be randomized, and failed fork( ) calls, changes to the system time, and segmentation faults will all be logged. Enabling the Medium security level will also restrict total access to */proc* to those who are in the wheel group. This hides each user's processes from other users and denies writing to */dev/kmem*, */dev/mem*, and */dev/port*. This makes it more difficult to patch kernel-based root kits into the running kernel. Also, process memory address space layouts are randomized, making it harder for an attacker to successfully exploit buffer overrun attacks. Because of this, information on process address space layouts is removed from */proc* as well. Because of these */proc* restrictions, you will need to run your *identd* daemon (if you are running one) as an account that belongs to the wheel group. According to the *grsecurity* documentation, none of these features should affect the operation of your software, unless it is very old or poorly written.

To enable nearly all of *grsecurity*'s features, you can choose the High security level. In addition to the features provided by the lower security levels, this level implements additional */proc* restrictions by limiting access to device and CPU information to users who are in the wheel group. Sandboxed environments are also further restricted by disallowing chmod to set the SUID or SGID bit when operating within such an environment. Additionally, applications that are running within such an environment will not be allowed to insert loadable modules, perform raw I/O, configure network devices, reboot the system, modify immutable files, or change the system's time. Choosing this security level will also cause the kernel's stack to be laid out randomly, to prevent kernel-based buffer overrun exploits from succeeding. In addition, the kernel's symbols will be hidden—making it even more difficult for an intruder to install Trojan code into the running kernel—and filesystem mounting, remounting, and unmounting will be logged.

The High security level also enables *grsecurity*'s PaX code, which enables nonexecutable memory pages. Enabling this will cause many buffer overrun exploits to fail, since any code injected into the stack through an overrun will be unable to execute. However, it is still possible to exploit a program with buffer overrun vulnerabilities, although this is made much more difficult by *grsecurity*'s address space layout randomization features. PaX can also carry with it some performance penalties on the x86 architecture, although they are said to be minimal. In addition, some programs—such as XFree86, wine, and Java™ virtual machines—will expect that the memory addresses returned by malloc( ) will be executable. Unfortunately, PaX breaks this behavior, so enabling it will cause those programs and others that depend on it to fail. Luckily, PaX can be disabled on a per-program basis with the *chpax* utility (*http://chpax.grsecurity.net*).

To disable PaX for a program, you can run a command similar to this one:

```
# chpax -ps /usr/bin/java
```

There are also other programs that make use of special GCC features, such as trampoline functions. This allows a programmer to define a small function within a function, so that the defined function is only in the scope of the function in which it is defined. Unfortunately, GCC puts the trampoline function's code on the stack, so PaX will break any programs that rely on this. However, PaX can provide emulation for trampoline functions, which can be enabled on a per-program basis with chpax, as well by using the -E switch.

If you do not like the sets of features that are enabled with any of the predefined security levels, you can just set the kernel option to "custom" and enable only the features you need.

After you've set a security level or enabled the specific options you want to use, just recompile your kernel and modules as you normally would. You can do that with commands similar to these:

```
# make dep clean && make bzImage
# make modules && make modules_install
```

Then reboot with your new kernel. In addition to the kernel restrictions already in effect, you can now use gradm to set up ACLs for your system. We'll see how to do that in "Restrict Applications with grsecurity" [Hack #14].

As you can see, *grsecurity* is a complex but tremendously useful modification of the Linux kernel. For more detailed information on installing and configuring the patches, consult the extensive documentation at *http://www.grsecurity.net/papers.php*.

Restrict Applications with grsecurity

Use Linux capabilities and grsecurity's ACLs to restrict applications on your system.

Now that you have installed the *grsecurity* patches, you'll probably want to make use of its flexible ACL system to further restrict the privileged applications on your system, beyond what *grsecurity*'s kernel security features provide. If you're just joining us and are not familiar with *grsecurity*, read "Lock Down Your Kernel with grsecurity" [Hack #13] first.

To restrict specific applications, you will need to make use of the *gradm* utility, which can be downloaded from the main *grsecurity* site (*http://www.grsecurity.net*). You can compile and install it in the usual way: unpack the source distribution, change into the directory that it creates, and then run make && make install. This will install *gradm* in */sbin*, create the */etc/grsec* directory containing a default ACL, and install the manpage.

After *gradm* has been installed, the first thing you'll want to do is create a password that *gradm* will use to authenticate itself to the kernel. You can do this by running gradm with the -P option:

```
# gradm -P
Setting up grsecurity ACL password
Password:
Re-enter Password:
Password written to /etc/grsec/pw.
```

To enable *grsecurity*'s ACL system, use this command:

```
# /sbin/gradm -E
```

Once you're finished setting up your ACLs, you'll probably want to add that command to the end of your system startup. You can do this by adding it to the end of */etc/rc.local* or a similar script that is designated for customizing your system startup.

The default ACL installed in */etc/grsec/acl* is quite restrictive, so you'll want to create ACLs for the services and system binaries you want to use. For example, after the ACL system has been enabled, ifconfig will no longer be able to change interface characteristics, even when run as root:

```
# /sbin/ifconfig eth0:1 192.168.0.59 up
SIOCSIFADDR: Permission denied
SIOCSIFFLAGS: Permission denied
SIOCSIFFLAGS: Permission denied
```

The easiest way to set up an ACL for a particular command is to specify that you want to use *grsecurity*'s learning mode, rather than specifying each ACL manually. If you've enabled ACLs, you'll need to temporarily disable them for your shell by running gradm -a. You'll then be able to access files within */etc/grsec*; otherwise, the directory will be hidden to you.

Add an entry like this to */etc/grsec/acl*:

```
/sbin/ifconfig lo {
        /                h
        /etc/grsec       h
        -CAP_ALL
}
```

This is about the most restrictive ACL possible because it hides the root directory from the process and removes any privileges that it may need. The lo next to the binary to which the ACL applies says to use learning mode and to override the default ACL. After you're done editing the ACLs, you'll need to tell *grsecurity* to reload them by running gradm -R.

Now try to run the ifconfig command again:

```
# /sbin/ifconfig eth0:1 192.168.0.59 up
# /sbin/ifconfig eth0:1
eth0:1    Link encap:Ethernet  HWaddr 00:0C:29:E2:2B:C1
          inet addr:192.168.0.59  Bcast:192.168.0.255  Mask:255.255.255.0
          UP BROADCAST RUNNING MULTICAST  MTU:1500  Metric:1
          Interrupt:10 Base address:0x10e0
```

In addition to the command succeeding, *grsecurity* will create learning log entries. You can then use gradm to generate an ACL for the program based on these logs:

```
# gradm -a
Password:
# gradm -L -O stdout
/sbin/ifconfig o {
        /usr/share/locale/locale.alias r
        /usr/lib/locale/locale-archive r
        /usr/lib/gconv/gconv-modules.cache r
        /proc/net/unix r
        /proc/net/dev r
        /proc/net r
        /lib/ld-2.3.2.so x
```

```
/lib/i686/libc-2.3.2.so rx
/etc/ld.so.cache r
/sbin/ifconfig x
/etc/grsec h
/ h
-CAP_ALL
+CAP_NET_ADMIN
}
```

Now you can replace the learning ACL for */sbin/ifconfig* in */etc/grsec/acl* with this one, and ifconfig should work. You can then follow this process for each program that needs special permissions to function. Just make sure to try out anything you will want to do with those programs, to ensure that *grsecurity*'s learning mode will detect that it needs to perform a particular system call or open a specific file.

Using *grsecurity* to lock down applications can seem like tedious work at first, but it will ultimately create a system that gives each process only the permissions it needs to do its job—no more, no less. When you need to build a highly secured platform, *grsecurity* can provide very finely grained control over just about everything the system can possibly do.

HACK #15 Restrict System Calls with Systrace

Keep your programs from performing tasks they weren't meant to do.

One of the more exciting new features in NetBSD and OpenBSD is *systrace*, a system call access manager. With *systrace*, a system administrator can specify which programs can make which system calls, and how those calls can be made. Proper use of *systrace* can greatly reduce the risks inherent in running poorly written or exploitable programs. *Systrace* policies can confine users in a manner completely independent of Unix permissions. You can even define the errors that the system calls return when access is denied, to allow programs to fail in a more proper manner. Proper use of *systrace* requires a practical understanding of system calls and what functionality programs must have to work properly.

First of all, what exactly are system calls? A *system call* is a function that lets you talk to the operating-system kernel. If you want to allocate memory, open a TCP/IP port, or perform input/output on the disk, you'll need to use a system call. System calls are documented in section 2 of the manpages.

Unix also supports a wide variety of C library calls. These are often confused with system calls but are actually just standardized routines for things that could be written within a program. For example, you could easily write a function to compute square roots within a program, but you could not write a function to allocate memory without using a system call. If you're in doubt whether a particular function is a system call or a C library function, check the online manual.

You may find an occasional system call that is not documented in the online manual, such as break( ). You'll need to dig into other resources to identify these calls (break( ) in particular is a very old system call used within *libc*, but not by programmers, so it seems to have escaped being documented in the manpages).

Systrace denies all actions that are not explicitly permitted and logs the rejection using *syslog*. If a program running under *systrace* has a problem, you can find out which system call the program wants to use and decide if you want to add it to your policy, reconfigure the program, or live with the error.

Systrace has several important pieces: policies, the policy generation tools, the runtime access management tool, and the sysadmin real-time interface. This hack gives a brief overview of policies; in "Automated Systrace Policy Creation" [Hack #16], we'll learn about the *systrace* tools.

The systrace(1) manpage includes a full description of the syntax used for policy descriptions, but I generally find it easier to look at some examples of a working policy and then go over the syntax in detail. Since *named* has been a subject of recent security discussions, let's look at the policy that Open-BSD 3.2 provides for *named*.

Before reviewing the *named* policy, let's review some commonly known facts about the name server daemon's system-access requirements. Zone trans-fers and large queries occur on port 53/TCP, while basic lookup services are provided on port 53/UDP. OpenBSD chroots *named* into */var/named* by default and logs everything to */var/log/messages*.

Each *systrace* policy file is in a file named after the full path of the program, replacing slashes with underscores. The policy file *usr_sbin_named* contains quite a few entries that allow access beyond binding to port 53 and writing to the system log. The file starts with:

```
# Policy for named that uses named user and chroots to /var/named
# This policy works for the default configuration of named.
Policy: /usr/sbin/named, Emulation: native
```

The Policy statement gives the full path to the program this policy is for. You can't fool *systrace* by giving the same name to a program elsewhere on the system. The Emulation entry shows which ABI this policy is for. Remem-ber, BSD systems expose ABIs for a variety of operating systems. *Systrace* can theoretically manage system-call access for any ABI, although only native and Linux binaries are supported at the moment.

The remaining lines define a variety of system calls that the program may or may not use. The sample policy for *named* includes 73 lines of system-call rules. The most basic look like this:

```
native-accept: permit
```

When */usr/sbin/named* tries to use the accept( ) system call to accept a connection on a socket, under the native ABI, it is allowed. Other rules are far more restrictive. Here's a rule for bind( ), the system call that lets a program request a TCP/IP port to attach to:

```
native-bind: sockaddr match "inet-*:53" then permit
```

sockaddr is the name of an argument taken by the accept( ) system call. The match keyword tells *systrace* to compare the given variable with the string inet-*:53, according to the standard shell pattern-matching (globbing) rules. So, if the variable sockaddr matches the string inet-*:53, the connection is accepted. This program can bind to port 53, over both TCP and UDP protocols. If an attacker had an exploit to make *named* attach a command prompt on a high-numbered port, this *systrace* policy would prevent that exploit from working.

At first glance, this seems wrong:

```
native-chdir: filename eq "/" then permit
native-chdir: filename eq "/namedb" then permit
```

The eq keyword compares one string to another and requires an exact match. If the program tries to go to the root directory, or to the directory */namedb*, *systrace* will allow it. Why would you possibly want to allow *named* to access the root directory? The next entry explains why:

```
native-chroot: filename eq "/var/named" then permit
```

We can use the native chroot( ) system call to change our root directory to */var/named*, but to no other directory. At this point, the */namedb* directory is actually */var/named/namedb*. We also know that *named* logs to syslog. To do this, it will need access to */dev/log*:

```
native-connect: sockaddr eq "/dev/log" then permit
```

This program can use the native connect( ) system call to talk to */dev/log* and only */dev/log*. That device hands the connections off elsewhere.

We'll also see some entries for system calls that do not exist:

```
native-fsread: filename eq "/" then permit
native-fsread: filename eq "/dev/arandom" then permit
native-fsread: filename eq "/etc/group" then permit
```

Systrace aliases certain system calls with very similar functions into groups. You can disable this functionality with a command-line switch and only use the exact system calls you specify, but in most cases these aliases are quite useful and shrink your policies considerably. The two aliases are fsread and fswrite. fsread is an alias for stat( ), lstat( ), readlink( ), and access( ) under the native and Linux ABIs. fswrite is an alias for unlink( ), mkdir( ), and rmdir( ), in both the native and Linux ABIs. As open( ) can be used to either read or write a file, it is aliased by both fsread and fswrite, depending on how it is called. So *named* can read certain */etc* files, it can list the contents of the root directory, and it can access the groups file.

Systrace supports two optional keywords at the end of a policy statement, errorcode and log. The errorcode is the error that is returned when the program attempts to access this system call. Programs will behave differently depending on the error that they receive. *named* will react differently to a "permission denied" error than it will to an "out of memory" error. You can get a complete list of error codes from the errno manpage. Use the error name, not the error number. For example, here we return an error for non-existent files:

```
filename sub "<non-existent filename>" then deny[enoent]
```

If you put the word log at the end of your rule, successful system calls will be logged. For example, if we wanted to log each time *named* attached to port 53, we could edit the policy statement for the bind( ) call to read:

```
native-bind: sockaddr match "inet-*:53" then permit log
```

You can also choose to filter rules based on user ID and group ID, as the example here demonstrates.

```
native-setgid: gid eq "70" then permit
```

This very brief overview covers the vast majority of the rules you will see. For full details on the *systrace* grammar, read the *systrace* manpage. If you want some help with creating your policies, you can also use *systrace*'s automated mode [Hack #16].

The original article that this hack is based on is available online at *http://www.onlamp.com/pub/a/bsd/2003/01/30/Big_Scary_Daemons.html*.

—*Michael Lucas*

HACK #16 Automated Systrace Policy Creation

Let Systrace's automated mode do your work for you.

In a true paranoid's ideal world, system administrators would read the source code for every application on their system and be able to build system-call access policies by hand, relying only on their intimate understanding of every feature of the application. Most system administrators don't have that sort of time, and would have better things to do with that time if they did.

Luckily, *systrace* includes a policy-generation tool that will generate a policy listing for every system call that an application makes. You can use this policy as a starting point to narrow down the access you will allow the application. We'll use this method to generate a policy for inetd.

Use the -A flag to systrace, and include the full path to the program you want to run:

```
# systrace -A /usr/sbin/inetd
```

To pass flags to inetd, add them at the end of the command line.

Then use the program for which you're developing a policy. This system has ident, daytime, and time services open, so run programs that require those services. Fire up an IRC client to trigger ident requests, and telnet to ports 13 and 37 to get time services. Once you have put inetd through its paces, shut it down. inetd has no control program, so you need to kill it by process ID.

Checking the process list will show two processes:

```
# ps -ax | grep inet
24421 ??  Ixs     0:00.00 /usr/sbin/inetd
12929 ??  Is      0:00.01 systrace -A /usr/sbin/inetd
```

Do not kill the systrace process (PID 12929 in this example)—that process has all the records of the system calls that inetd has made. Just kill the inetd process (PID 24421), and the systrace process will exit normally.

Now check your home directory for a *.systrace* directory, which will contain *systrace*'s first stab at an inetd policy. Remember, policies are placed in files named after the full path to the program, replacing slashes with underscores.

Here's the output of ls:

```
# ls .systrace
usr_libexec_identd   usr_sbin_inetd
```

systrace created two policies, not one. In addition to the expected policy for */usr/sbin/inetd*, there's one for */usr/libexec/identd*. This is because inetd implements time services internally, while ident calls a separate program to service requests. When inetd spawned identd, systrace captured the identd system calls as well.

By reading the policy, you can improve your understanding of what the program actually does. Look up each system call the program uses, and see if you can restrict access further. You'll probably want to look for ways to further restrict the policies that are automatically generated. However, these policies make for a good starting point.

Applying a policy to a program is much like creating the *systrace* policy itself; just run the program as an argument to systrace, using the -a option:

```
# systrace -a /usr/sbin/inetd
```

If the program tries to perform system calls not listed in the policy, they will fail. This may cause the program to behave unpredictably. *Systrace* will log failed entries in */var/log/messages*.

To edit a policy, just add the desired statement to the end of the rule list, and it will be picked up. You could do this by hand, of course, but that's the hard way. *Systrace* includes a tool to let you edit policies in real time, as the system call is made. This is excellent for use in a network operations center environment, where the person responsible for watching the network monitor can also be assigned to watch for system calls and bring them to the attention of the appropriate personnel. You can specify which program you wish to monitor by using systrace's -p flag. This is called *attaching* to the program.

For example, earlier we saw two processes containing inetd. One was the actual inetd process, and the other was the systrace process managing inetd. Attach to the systrace process, not the actual program (to use the previous example, this would be PID 12929), and give the full path to the managed program as an argument:

```
# systrace -p 12929 /usr/sbin/inetd
```

At first nothing will happen. When the program attempts to make an unauthorized system call, however, a GUI will pop up. You will have the options to allow the system call, deny the system call, always permit the call, or always deny it. The program will hang until you make a decision, however, so decide quickly.

Note that these changes will only take effect so long as the current process is running. If you restart the program, you must also restart the attached systrace monitor, and any changes you set in the monitor are gone. You must add those rules to the policy if you want them to be permanent.

The original article that this hack is based on is available online at *http://www.onlamp.com/pub/a/bsd/2003/02/27/Big_Scary_Daemons.html*.

—*Michael Lucas*

Control Login Access with PAM

#17

Seize fine-grained control of when and where your users can access your system.

In traditional Unix authentication there is not much granularity available in limiting a user's ability to log in. For example, how would you limit the hosts that users can come from when logging into your servers? Your first thought might be to set up TCP wrappers or possibly firewall rules [Hack #33] and [Hack #34]. But what if you wanted to allow some users to log in from a specific host, but disallow others from logging in from it? Or what if you wanted to prevent some users from logging in at certain times of the day because of daily maintenance, but allow others (i.e., administrators) to log in at any time they wish? To get this working with every service that might be running on your system, you would traditionally have to patch each of them to support this new functionality. This is where PAM enters the picture.

PAM, or pluggable authentication modules, allows for just this sort of functionality (and more) without the need to patch all of your services. PAM has been available for quite some time under Linux, FreeBSD, and Solaris, and is now a standard component of the traditional authentication facilities on these platforms. Many services that need to use some sort of authentication now support PAM.

Modules are configured for services in a stack, with the authentication process proceeding from top to bottom as the access checks complete successfully. You can build a custom stack for any service by creating a file in */etc/pam.d* with the same name as the service. If you need even more granularity, an entire stack of modules can be included by using the pam_stack module. This allows you to specify another external file containing a stack. If a service does not have its own configuration file in */etc/pam.d*, it will default to using the stack specified in */etc/pam.d/other*.

When configuring a service for use with PAM, there are several types of entries available. These types allow one to specify whether a module provides authentication, access control, password change control, or session setup and teardown. Right now, we are interested in only one of the types: the account type. This entry type allows you to specify modules that will control access to accounts that have been authenticated. In addition to the service-specific configuration files, some modules have extended configuration information that can be specified in files within the */etc/security* directory. For this hack, we'll mainly use two of the most useful modules of this type, pam_access and pam_time.

The pam_access module allows one to limit where a user or group of users may log in from. To make use of it, you'll first need to configure the service you wish to use the module with. You can do this by editing the service's PAM config file in */etc/pam.d*.

Here's an example of what */etc/pam.d/login* might look like under Red Hat 9:

```
#%PAM-1.0
auth        required    pam_securetty.so
auth        required    pam_stack.so service=system-auth
auth        required    pam_nologin.so
account     required    pam_stack.so service=system-auth
password    required    pam_stack.so service=system-auth
session     required    pam_stack.so service=system-auth
session     optional    pam_console.so
```

Notice the use of the `pam_stack` module—it includes the stack contained within the *system-auth* file. Let's see what's inside */etc/pam.d/system-auth*:

```
#%PAM-1.0
# This file is auto-generated.
# User changes will be destroyed the next time authconfig is run.
auth        required    /lib/security/$ISA/pam_env.so
auth        sufficient  /lib/security/$ISA/pam_unix.so likeauth nullok
auth        required    /lib/security/$ISA/pam_deny.so
account     required    /lib/security/$ISA/pam_unix.so
password    required    /lib/security/$ISA/pam_cracklib.so retry=3 type=
password    sufficient  /lib/security/$ISA/pam_unix.so nullok use_authtok
md5 shadow
password    required    /lib/security/$ISA/pam_deny.so
session     required    /lib/security/$ISA/pam_limits.so
session     required    /lib/security/$ISA/pam_unix.so
```

To add the `pam_access` module to the login service, you could add another account entry to the login configuration file, which would, of course, just enable the module for the login service. Alternatively, you could add the module to the *system-auth* file, which would enable it for most of the PAM-aware services on the system.

To add `pam_access` to the login service (or any other service for that matter), simply add a line like this to the service's configuration file after any pre-existing account entries:

```
account     required    pam_access.so
```

Now that we've enabled the `pam_access` module for our services, we can edit */etc/security/access.conf* to control how the module behaves. Each entry in the file can specify multiple users, groups, and hostnames to which the entry applies, and specify whether it's allowing or disallowing remote or local access. When `pam_access` is invoked by an entry in a service configuration file, it will look through the lines of *access.conf* and stop at the first match it finds. Thus, if you want to create default entries to fall back on, you'll want to put the more specific entries first, with the general entries following them.

The general form of an entry in *access.conf* is:

```
permission : users : origins
```

where *permission* can be either a + or -. This denotes whether the rule grants or denies access, respectively.

The *users* portion allows you to specify a list of users or groups, separated by whitespace. In addition to simply listing users in this portion of the entry, you can use the form *user@host*, where *host* is the local hostname of the machine being logged into. This allows you to use a single configuration file across multiple machines, but still specify rules pertaining to specific machines. The *origins* portion is compared against the origin of the access attempt. Hostnames can be used for remote origins, and the special LOCAL keyword can be used for local access. Instead of explicitly specifying users, groups, or origins, you can also use the ALL and EXCEPT keywords to perform set operations on any of the lists.

Here's a simple example of locking out the user andrew (Eep! That's me!) from a host named colossus:

```
- : andrew : colossus
```

Note that if a group that shares its name with a user is specified, the module will interpret the rule as applying to both the user and the group.

Now that we've covered how to limit where a user may log in from and how to set up a PAM module, let's take a look at how to limit what time a user may log in by using the pam_time module. To configure this module, you need to edit */etc/security/time.conf*. The format for the entries in this file are a little more flexible than that of *access.conf*, thanks to the availability of the NOT (!), AND (&), and OR (|) operators.

The general form for an entry in *time.conf* is:

```
services;devices;users;times
```

The *services* portion of the entry specifies what PAM-enabled service will be regulated. You can usually get a full list of the available services by looking at the contents of your */etc/pam.d* directory.

For instance, here's the contents of */etc/pam.d* on a RedHat Linux system:

```
$ ls -1 /etc/pam.d
authconfig
chfn
chsh
halt
internet-druid
kbdrate
```

```
login
neat
other
passwd
poweroff
ppp
reboot
redhat-config-mouse
redhat-config-network
redhat-config-network-cmd
redhat-config-network-druid
rhn_register
setup
smtp
sshd
su
sudo
system-auth
up2date
up2date-config
up2date-nox
vlock
```

To set up pam_time for use with any of these services, you'll need to add a
line like this to the file in */etc/pam.d* that corresponds to the service that you
want to regulate:

```
account     required      /lib/security/$ISA/pam_time.so
```

The *devices* portion specifies the terminal device that the service is being
accessed from. For console logins, you can use !ttyp*, which specifies all
TTY devices except for pseudo TTYs. If you want the entry to only affect
remote logins, then use ttyp*. You can restrict it to all users (console,
remote, and X11) by using tty*.

For the users portion of the entry, you can specify a single user or a list of
users by separating each one with a | character. The times portion is used to
specify the times that the rule will apply. Each time range is specified with a
combination of two character abbreviations, which denote the days that the
rule will apply, followed with a range of hours for that day. The abbreviations for the days of the week are Mo, Tu, We, Th, Fr, Sa, and Su. For convenience you can use Wk to specify weekdays and Wd to specify the weekend. In
addition, you can use Al to specify every day of the week. These last three
basically expand to the set of days that compose each time period. This is
important to remember, since repeated days are subtracted from the set of
days that the rule will apply to (e.g., WkSu would effectively be just Sa). The
range of hours is simply specified as two 24-hour times, minus the colons,
separated by a dash (e.g., 0630-1345 is 6:30 A.M. to 1:45 P.M.).

If you wanted to disallow access to the user andrew from the local console on weekends and during the week after hours, you could use an entry like this:

```
system-auth;!ttyp*;andrew;Wk1700-0800|Wd0000-2400
```

Or perhaps you want to limit remote logins through SSH during a system maintenance window lasting from 7 P.M. Friday to 7 A.M. Saturday, but want to allow a sysadmin to log in:

```
sshd;ttyp*;!andrew;Fr1900-0700
```

As you can see, there's a lot of flexibility for creating entries, thanks to the logical Boolean operators that are available. Just make sure that you remember to configure the service file in */etc/pam.d* for use with pam_time when you create entries in */etc/security/time.conf*.

HACK #18 Restricted Shell Environments
Keep your users from shooting themselves (and you) in the foot.

Sometimes a sandboxed environment [Hack #10] is overkill for your needs. If you want to set up a restricted environment for a group of users that only allows them to run a few particular commands, you'll have to duplicate all of the libraries and binaries for those commands for each user. This is where restricted shells come in handy. Many shells include such a feature, which is usually invoked by running the shell with the -r switch. While not as secure as a system call–based sandbox environment, it can work well if you trust your users not to be malicious, but worry that some might be curious to an unhealthy degree.

Some common features of restricted shells are the ability to prevent a program from changing directories, to only allow the execution of commands using absolute pathnames, and to prohibit executing commands in other subdirectories. In addition to these restrictions, all of the command-line redirection operators are disabled. With these features, restricting the commands a user can execute is as simple as picking and choosing which commands should be available and making symbolic links to them inside the user's home directory. If a sequence of commands needs to be executed, you can also create shell scripts owned by another user. These scripts will execute in a nonrestricted environment and can't be edited within the environment by the user.

Let's try running a restricted shell and see what happens:

```
$ bash -r
bash: SHELL: readonly variable
bash: PATH: readonly variable
bash-2.05b$ ls
```

```
bash: ls: No such file or directory
bash-2.05b$ /bin/ls
bash: /sbin/ls: restricted: cannot specify `/' in command names
bash-2.05b$ exit
$ ln -s /bin/ls .
$ bash -r
bash-2.05b$ ls -la
total 24
drwx------   2 andrew    andrew     4096 Oct 20 08:01 .
drwxr-xr-x   4 root      root       4096 Oct 20 14:16 ..
-rw-------   1 andrew    andrew       18 Oct 20 08:00 .bash_history
-rw-r--r--   1 andrew    andrew       24 Oct 20 14:16 .bash_logout
-rw-r--r--   1 andrew    andrew      197 Oct 20 07:59 .bash_profile
-rw-r--r--   1 andrew    andrew      127 Oct 20 07:57 .bashrc
lrwxrwxrwx   1 andrew    andrew        7 Oct 20 08:01 ls -> /bin/ls
```

Restricted ksh is a little different in that it will allow you to run scripts and
binaries that are in your PATH, which can be set before entering the shell:

```
$ rksh
$ ls -la
total 24
drwx------   2 andrew    andrew     4096 Oct 20 08:01 .
drwxr-xr-x   4 root      root       4096 Oct 20 14:16 ..
-rw-------   1 andrew    andrew       18 Oct 20 08:00 .bash_history
-rw-r--r--   1 andrew    andrew       24 Oct 20 14:16 .bash_logout
-rw-r--r--   1 andrew    andrew      197 Oct 20 07:59 .bash_profile
-rw-r--r--   1 andrew    andrew      127 Oct 20 07:57 .bashrc
lrwxrwxrwx   1 andrew    andrew        7 Oct 20 08:01 ls -> /bin/ls
$ which ls
/bin/ls
$ exit
```

This worked because /bin was in the PATH before we invoked ksh. Now let's
change the PATH and run rksh again:

```
$ export PATH=.
$ /bin/rksh
$ /bin/ls
/bin/rksh: /bin/ls: restricted
$ exit
$ ln -s /bin/ls .
$ ls -la
total 24
drwx------   2 andrew    andrew     4096 Oct 20 08:01 .
drwxr-xr-x   4 root      root       4096 Oct 20 14:16 ..
-rw-------   1 andrew    andrew       18 Oct 20 08:00 .bash_history
-rw-r--r--   1 andrew    andrew       24 Oct 20 14:16 .bash_logout
-rw-r--r--   1 andrew    andrew      197 Oct 20 07:59 .bash_profile
-rw-r--r--   1 andrew    andrew      127 Oct 20 07:57 .bashrc
lrwxrwxrwx   1 andrew    andrew        7 Oct 20 08:01 ls -> /bin/ls
```

Restricted shells are incredibly easy to set up and can provide minimal restricted access. They may not be able to keep out determined attackers, but they certainly make a hostile user's job much more difficult.

HACK #19 Enforce User and Group Resource Limits

Make sure resource-hungry users don't bring down your entire system.

Whether it's through malicious intent or an unintentional slip, having a user bring your system down to a slow crawl by using too much memory or CPU time is no fun at all. One popular way of limiting resource usage is to use the ulimit command. This method relies on a shell to limit its child processes, and it is difficult to use when you want to give different levels of usage to different users and groups. Another, more flexible way of limiting resource usage is with the PAM module pam_limits.

pam_limits is preconfigured on most systems that have PAM installed. All you should need to do is edit */etc/security/limits.conf* to configure specific limits for users and groups.

The *limits.conf* configuration file consists of single-line entries describing a single type of limit for a user or group of users. The general format for an entry is:

    domain   type   resource   value

The *domain* portion specifies to whom the limit applies. Single users may be specified here by name, and groups can be specified by prefixing the group name with an @. In addition, the wildcard character * may be used to apply the limit globally to all users except for root. The *type* portion of the entry specifies whether the limit is a soft or hard resource limit. Soft limits may be increased by the user, whereas hard limits can be changed only by root. There are many types of resources that can be specified for the *resource* portion of the entry. Some of the more useful ones are cpu, memlock, nproc, and fsize. These allow you to limit CPU time, total locked-in memory, number of processes, and file size, respectively. CPU time is expressed in minutes, and sizes are in kilobytes. Another useful limit is maxlogins, which allows you to specify the maximum number of concurrent logins that are permitted.

One nice feature of pam_limits is that it can work together with ulimit to allow the user to raise her limit from the soft limit to the imposed hard limit.

Let's try a quick test to see how it works. First we'll limit the number of open files for the guest user by adding these entries to *limits.conf*:

    guest   soft   nofile   1000
    guest   hard   nofile   2000

Now the guest account has a soft limit of 1,000 concurrently open files and a hard limit of 2,000. Let's test it out:

```
# su - guest
$ ulimit -a
core file size      (blocks, -c) 0
data seg size       (kbytes, -d) unlimited
file size        (blocks, -f) unlimited
max locked memory    (kbytes, -l) unlimited
max memory size      (kbytes, -m) unlimited
open files            (-n) 1000
pipe size       (512 bytes, -p) 8
stack size         (kbytes, -s) 8192
cpu time         (seconds, -t) unlimited
max user processes       (-u) 1024
virtual memory      (kbytes, -v) unlimited
$ ulimit -n 2000
$ ulimit -n
2000
$ ulimit -n 2001
-bash: ulimit: open files: cannot modify limit: Operation not permitted
```

There you have it. In addition to open files, you can create resource limits for any number of other resources and apply them to specific users or entire groups. As you can see, pam_limits is quite powerful and useful in that it doesn't rely upon the shell for enforcement.

Automate System Updates
Patch security holes in a timely manner to prevent intrusions.

Updating and patching a system in a timely manner is one of the most important things you can do to help protect your systems from the deluge of newly discovered security vulnerabilities. Unfortunately, this task often gets pushed to the wayside in favor of "more pressing" issues, such as performance tuning, hardware maintenance, and software debugging. In some circles, it's viewed as a waste of time and overhead that doesn't contribute to the primary function of a system. Coupled with management demands to maximize production, keeping a system up-to-date is often pushed even further down on the to-do list.

Updating a system can be very repetitive and time consuming if you're not using scripting to automate it. Fortunately, most Linux distributions make their updated packages available for download from a standard online location. We can monitor that location for changes and automatically detect and download the new updates when they're made available. To demonstrate how to do this on an RPM-based distribution, we'll use AutoRPM (*http://www.autorpm.org*).

AutoRPM is a powerful Perl script that allows you to monitor multiple FTP sites for changes. It will automatically download new or changed packages and either install them automatically or alert you so that you may do so. In addition to monitoring single FTP sites, you can also monitor a pool of mirror sites, to ensure that you still get your updates in spite of a busy FTP server. This feature is especially nice in that AutoRPM will monitor busy FTP servers and keep track of how many times a connection to them has been attempted. Using this information, it assigns internal scores to each of the FTP sites configured within a given pool, with the outcome that the server in the pool that is available most often will be checked first.

To install AutoRPM, download the latest package and install it like this:

```
# rpm -ivh autorpm-3.3-1.noarch.rpm
```

Although a tarball is also available, installation is a little more tricky than the typical make; make install, and so it is recommended that you stick to installing from the RPM package.

By default, AutoRPM is configured to monitor for updated packages for Red Hat's Linux distribution. However, you can configure it to monitor any file repository of your choosing, such as one for SuSe or Mandrake.

Windows Host Security

Hacks 21–30

This chapter shows you some ways to keep your Windows system up-to-date and secure, thereby making your network a safer place to work (and have fun). Although many may scoff at the mention of Windows and security in the same sentence, you actually can make a Windows system fairly secure without too much effort.

One of the main reasons that Windows gets a bad rap is the poorly administered state in which Windows machines seem to be kept. The recent deluge of worm and virus attacks that have brought down many a network shows this to hold true. A lot of this can be traced back to the "ease" of administration that Windows seems to provide by effectively keeping the Windows administrator out of the loop about the inner workings of her environment—effectively wresting control from the system administrator's hands.

This chapter seeks to remedy that to some degree by showing you ways to see exactly what your server is really doing. While this may seem old hat to a Unix sysadmin, getting details on open ports and running services is often a new concept to the average Windows administrator. In addition, this chapter shows you how to disable some Windows "features," such as sharing out all your files automatically and truncating log files. You'll also learn how to enable some of the auditing and logging features of Windows, to give you early warning of possible security incidents (rather than waiting for the angry phone call from someone at the wrong end of a denial-of-service attack originating from your network).

HACK #21 Check Servers for Applied Patches

Make sure your Windows servers have the latest patches installed.

Keeping a network of systems patched and up-to-date is hard enough in Unix, but it can be even more difficult on Windows systems. A lack of robust built-in scripting and remote access capabilities makes Windows unsuitable for automation. Nevertheless, before you even attempt to update your systems, you need to know which updates have been applied to each system; otherwise, you might waste time and effort updating systems that don't need it. Clearly, this problem gets more difficult as the number of systems that need to be managed increases. We can avoid much of the extra work of manually updating systems by using the *HFNetChk* tool, which was originally a standalone program from Shavlik Technologies. It is now a part of Microsoft's Baseline Security Analyzer (*http://download.microsoft.com/download/8/e/e/8ee73487-4d36-4f7f-92f2-2bdc5c5385b3/mbsasetup.msi*) and is available through its command-line interface, *mbsacli.exe*.

Not only can *HFNetChk* remotely check the status of Windows Server 2003 and Windows XP/2000/NT, but it can also check whether critical updates for IIS, SQL Server, Exchange Server, Media Player, and Internet Explorer have been applied. Although it can only check the update status of a system (and won't actually bring the system up-to-date), it is still an invaluable timesaving tool.

HFNetChk works by downloading a signed and compressed XML file from Microsoft that contains information on all currently available updates. This information includes checksums and versions of files covered by each update, as well as the registry keys modified by each update. Additional dependency information is also included. When scanning a system, *HFNetChk* will first scan the registry for the keys that are associated with the most current set of updates available for the current system configuration. If any of these registry keys are missing or do not match what is contained in the XML file, it will flag the update as not having been installed. If the registry key for an update is present and matches the information in the XML file, *HFNetChk* will then attempt to verify whether the files specified in the update information are present on the system and whether their version and checksum matches. If any of the checks fail, the update will be flagged. All flagged updates are then displayed in a report, along with a reference to the Microsoft Knowledge Base article with more information on the specific update.

To get *HFNetChk* installed on your system, you first need to download and install the Microsoft Baseline Security Analyzer. To run *HFNetChk*, open a command prompt and change to the directory that was created during the install (*C:\Program Files\Microsoft Baseline Security Analyzer* is the default).

To check the update status of the local system, run this command:

```
C:\> Program Files\Microsoft Baseline Security Analyzer> mbsacli /hf
Microsoft Baseline Security Analyzer
Version 1.1.1
Powered by HFNetChk Technology - Version 3.82.0.1
Copyright (C) Shavlik Technologies, 2001-2003
Developed for Microsoft by Shavlik Technologies, LLC
```

```
info@shavlik.com (www.shavlik.com)


Please use the -v switch to view details for
Patch NOT Found, Warning and Note messages


Attempting to get cab from http://go.microsoft.com/fwlink/?LinkId=16932


XML successfully loaded.


Scanning PLUNDER
..............................
Done scanning PLUNDER
----------------------------
PLUNDER(192.168.0.65)
----------------------------


        * WINDOWS XP SP1

        Note            MS02-008        317244
        Warning         MS02-055        323255
        Note            MS03-008        814078
        Note            MS03-030        819696
        Patch NOT Found MS03-041        823182
        Patch NOT Found MS03-044        825119
        Patch NOT Found MS03-045        824141
        Patch NOT Found MS03-049        828035
        Note            MS03-051        813360

        * INTERNET EXPLORER 6 SP1

        Patch NOT Found MS03-048        824145

        * WINDOWS MEDIA PLAYER FOR WINDOWS XP SP1

        Information
        All necessary hotfixes have been applied.
```

The first column tells why the check for a particular update failed. The second column shows which update failed the check, and the third column lists a Microsoft Knowledge Base (*http://support.microsoft.com*) article number that you can refer to for more information on the issue fixed by that particular update.

If you want more information on why a particular check failed, you can run the command with the -v (verbose) switch. Here are the results of the previous command, but this time with the verbose switch:

```
Scanning PLUNDER
..............................
```

```
Done scanning PLUNDER
----------------------------
PLUNDER(192.168.0.65)
----------------------------
```

```
    * WINDOWS XP SP1

    Note            MS02-008        317244
    Please refer to Q306460 for a detailed explanation.

    Warning         MS02-055        323255
    File C:\WINDOWS\system32\hhctrl.ocx has a file
    version [5.2.3735.0] greater than what is expected [5.2.3669.0].

    Note            MS03-008        814078
    Please refer to Q306460 for a detailed explanation.

    Note            MS03-030        819696
    Please refer to Q306460 for a detailed explanation.

    Patch NOT Found MS03-041        823182
    File C:\WINDOWS\system32\cryptui.dll has a file
    version [5.131.2600.1106] that is less than what is expected
    [5.131.2600.1243].

    Patch NOT Found MS03-044        825119
    File C:\WINDOWS\system32\itircl.dll has a file
    version [5.2.3644.0] that is less than what is expected
    [5.2.3790.80].

    Patch NOT Found MS03-045        824141
    File C:\WINDOWS\system32\user32.dll has a file
    version [5.1.2600.1134] that is less than what is expected
    [5.1.2600.1255].

    Patch NOT Found MS03-049        828035
    File C:\WINDOWS\system32\msgsvc.dll has a file
    version [5.1.2600.0] that is less than what is expected
    [5.1.2600.1309].

    Note            MS03-051        813360
    Please refer to Q306460 for a detailed explanation.


    * INTERNET EXPLORER 6 SP1

    Patch NOT Found MS03-048        824145
    The registry key **SOFTWARE\Microsoft\Internet Explorer\ActiveX
    Compatibility\{69DEAF94-AF66-11D3-BEC0-00105AA9B6AE}** does not
    exist.  It is required for this patch to be considered installed.
```

```
* WINDOWS MEDIA PLAYER FOR WINDOWS XP SP1

Information
All necessary hotfixes have been applied.
```

After applying the listed updates, you should see something like this:

```
Scanning PLUNDER
...........................
Done scanning PLUNDER
---------------------------
PLUNDER(192.168.0.65)
---------------------------

    * WINDOWS XP SP1

    Information
    All necessary hotfixes have been applied.

    * INTERNET EXPLORER 6 SP1

    Information
    All necessary hotfixes have been applied.

    * WINDOWS MEDIA PLAYER FOR WINDOWS XP SP1

    Information
    All necessary hotfixes have been applied.
```

When scanning the local system, Administrator privileges are needed. If you wish to scan a remote machine, you will need Administrator privileges on it. There are several ways to scan remote machines. To scan a single remote system, a NetBIOS name can be specified with the -h switch. Likewise, an IP address can be specified with the -i switch.

For example, to scan the machine PLUNDER from another machine, either of these two commands can be used:

```
mbsacli /hf -h PLUNDER
mbsacli /hf -i 192.168.0.65
```

You can also scan a handful of additional systems by listing them on the command line with commas separating each NetBIOS name or IP address.

Note that, in addition to having Administrator privileges on the remote machine, you must also ensure that you have not disabled the default shares [Hack #27]. If the default administrative shares have been disabled, then *HFNetChk* will not be able to check for the proper files on the remote system and, consequently, will not be able to determine whether an update was applied.

If you wish to scan a group of systems, there are several options for this as well. Using the -fh option, you can specify a file containing up to 256 NetBIOS hostnames (one on each line) that will be scanned. You can do the same thing with IP addresses, using the -fip option. Ranges of IP addresses may also be specified by using the -r option.

For example, you could run a command like this to scan from 192.168.1.23 to 192.168.1.172:

```
mbsacli /hf -r 192.168.1.123 - 192.168.1.172
```

All of these options are very flexible, and you can use them in any combination to specify which remote systems will be scanned.

In addition to specifying remote systems by NetBIOS name and IP address, you can also scan systems by domain name by using the -d option, or you can scan your entire local network segment by using the -n command-line option.

When scanning systems from a personal workstation, the -u and -p options can prove useful. These allow you to specify a username and password to use when accessing the remote systems. These switches are particularly handy if you don't normally log in using the Administrator account. The account that is specified with the -u option will of course need to have Administrator privileges on the remote machines being scanned.

Also, if you're scanning a large number of systems, you might want to use the -t option. This allows you to specify the number of threads used by the scanner, and increasing this value generally will speed up scanning. Valid values are from 1 to 128; the default value is 64.

If you are scanning more than one machine, a huge amount of data will simply be dumped to the screen. Use the -f option to specify a file to store the results of the scan in, and view it at your leisure using a text editor.

HFNetChk is a very flexible tool and can be used to check the update status of a large number of machines in a very short amount of time. It is especially useful when a new worm has come onto the scene and you need to know if all of your systems are up-to-date on their patches.

See Also

- Microsoft Network Security Hotfix Checker (*Hfnetchk.exe*) Tool: Knowledge Base Article 303215, at *http://support.microsoft.com/default. aspx?scid=kb;EN-US;303215*
- Frequently Asked Questions about the Microsoft Network Security Hotfix Checker (*Hfnetchk.exe*) Tool: Knowledge Base Article 305385, at *http:// support.microsoft.com/default.aspx?scid=kb;EN-US;305385*

Get a List of Open Files and Their Owning Processes

Look for suspicious activity by monitoring file accesses.

Suppose you're looking at the list of processes in the task manager one day after noticing some odd behavior on your workstation, and you notice a process you haven't seen before. Well, what do you do now? If you were running something other than Windows, you might try to determine what the process is doing by looking at the files it has open. Unfortunately, Windows doesn't provide a tool to do this.

Sysinternals makes an excellent tool called Handle, which is available for free at *http://www.sysinternals.com/ntw2k/freeware/handle.shtml*. Handle is a lot like lsof **[Hack #8]**, but it can list many other types of operating resources, including threads, events, and semaphores. It can also display open registry keys and IOCompletion structures.

Running handle without any command-line arguments will list all open file handles on the system. You can also specify a filename, which will list the processes that are currently accessing it, by typing this:

```
C:\> handle filename
```

Or you can list only files that are opened by a particular process—in this case Internet Explorer:

```
C:\> handle -p iexplore
Handle v2.10
Copyright (C) 1997-2003 Mark Russinovich
Sysinternals - www.sysinternals.com

------------------------------------------------------------------------
IEXPLORE.EXE pid: 688 PLUNDER\andrew
    98: Section       \BaseNamedObjects\MTXCOMM_MEMORY_MAPPED_FILE
    9c: Section       \BaseNamedObjects\MtxWndList
   12c: Section       \BaseNamedObjects\__R_0000000000d4_SMem__
   18c: File          C:\Documents and Settings\andrew\Local Settings\
Temporary Internet Files\Content.IE5\index.dat
   198: Section       \BaseNamedObjects\C:_Documents and Settings_andrew_
Local Settings_Temporary Internet Files_Content.IE5_index.dat_3194880
   1a0: File          C:\Documents and Settings\andrew\Cookies\index.dat
   1a8: File          C:\Documents and Settings\andrew\Local Settings\
History\History.IE5\index.dat
   1ac: Section       \BaseNamedObjects\C:_Documents and Settings_andrew_
Local Settings_History_History.IE5_index.dat_245760
   1b8: Section       \BaseNamedObjects\C:_Documents and Settings_andrew_
Cookies_index.dat_81920
   228: Section       \BaseNamedObjects\UrlZonesSM_andrew
   2a4: Section       \BaseNamedObjects\SENS Information Cache
   540: File          C:\Documents and Settings\andrew\Application Data\
Microsoft\SystemCertificates\My
```

```
574: File        C:\Documents and Settings\All Users\Desktop
5b4: Section     \BaseNamedObjects\mmGlobalPnpInfo
5cc: File        C:\WINNT\system32\mshtml.tlb
614: Section     \BaseNamedObjects\WDMAUD_Callbacks
640: File        C:\WINNT\system32\Macromed\Flash\Flash.ocx
648: File        C:\WINNT\system32\STDOLE2.TLB
6a4: File        \Dfs
6b4: File        C:\Documents and Settings\andrew\Desktop
6c8: File        C:\Documents and Settings\andrew\Local Settings\
Temporary Internet Files\Content.IE5\Q5USFSTO\softwareDownloadIndex[1].htm
70c: Section     \BaseNamedObjects\MSIMGSIZECacheMap
758: File        C:\WINNT\system32\iepeers.dll
75c: File        C:\Documents and Settings\andrew\Desktop
770: Section     \BaseNamedObjects\RotHintTable
```

If you want to find the Internet Explorer process that owns a resource with a partial name of handle, you could type:

```
C:\> handle -p iexplore handle
Handle v2.10
Copyright (C) 1997-2003 Mark Russinovich
Sysinternals - www.sysinternals.com

IEXPLORE.EXE     pid: 1396   C:\Documents and Settings\andrew\Local
Settings\Temporary Internet Files\Content.IE5\H1EZGFSH\handle[1].htm
```

Additionally, if you wanted to list all types of resources, you could use the -a option. Handle is quite a powerful tool, and any of its command-line options can be mixed together to quickly narrow your search and find just what you want.

HACK #23   List Running Services and Open Ports

Check for remotely accessible services the Windows way.

Unix makes it quick and easy to see which ports on a system are open, but how can you do that on Windows? Well, with FPort from Foundstone (*http://www.foundstone.com/resources/index_resources.htm*) it's as quick and easy as running good old netstat.

FPort has very few command-line options, and those deal mostly with specifying how you'd like the output sorted. For instance, if you want the output sorted by application name, you can use /a; if you want it sorted by process ID, you can use /i. While it may not be as full of features as netstat, it definitely gets the job done.

To get a listing of all ports that are open on your system, simply type fport. If you want the list to be sorted by port number, use the /p switch:

```
C:\> fport /p
FPort v2.0 - TCP/IP Process to Port Mapper
Copyright 2000 by Foundstone, Inc.
```

http://www.foundstone.com

```
Pid   Process         Port  Proto Path
432   svchost    ->   135   TCP   C:\WINNT\system32\svchost.exe
8     System     ->   139   TCP
8     System     ->   445   TCP
672   MSTask     ->   1025  TCP   C:\WINNT\system32\MSTask.exe
8     System     ->   1028  TCP
8     System     ->   1031  TCP
1116  navapw32   ->   1035  TCP   C:\PROGRA~1\NORTON~1\navapw32.exe
788   svchost    ->   1551  TCP   C:\WINNT\system32\svchost.exe
788   svchost    ->   1553  TCP   C:\WINNT\system32\svchost.exe
788   svchost    ->   1558  TCP   C:\WINNT\system32\svchost.exe
1328  svchost    ->   1565  TCP   C:\WINNT\System32\svchost.exe
8     System     ->   1860  TCP
1580  putty      ->   3134  TCP   C:\WINNT\putty.exe
772   WinVNC     ->   5800  TCP   C:\Program Files\TightVNC\WinVNC.exe
772   WinVNC     ->   5900  TCP   C:\Program Files\TightVNC\WinVNC.exe

432   svchost    ->   135   UDP   C:\WINNT\system32\svchost.exe
8     System     ->   137   UDP
8     System     ->   138   UDP
8     System     ->   445   UDP
256   lsass      ->   500   UDP   C:\WINNT\system32\lsass.exe
244   services   ->   1027  UDP   C:\WINNT\system32\services.exe
688   IEXPLORE   ->   2204  UDP   C:\Program Files\Internet Explorer\
IEXPLORE.EXE
1396  IEXPLORE   ->   3104  UDP   C:\Program Files\Internet Explorer\
IEXPLORE.EXE
256   lsass      ->   4500  UDP   C:\WINNT\system32\lsass.exe
```

Notice that there are some processes listed—such as navapw32, putty, and IEXPLORE—that don't appear to be services. These show up in the output because FPort lists all open ports, not just opened ports that are listening.

While FPort is not as powerful as some of the commands available under other operating systems, it is still a valuable, quick, and easy-to-use tool that is a great addition to Windows.

HACK #24 Enable Auditing

Log suspicious activity to help spot intrusions.

Windows 2000 includes some very powerful auditing features, but unfortunately they are all disabled by default. Windows 2003 has corrected this by enabling some features by default, but it is still wise to check that you are tracking precisely what you want to audit. Using these capabilities, you can monitor failed logins, account management events, file access, privilege use, and more. You can also log security policy changes as well as system events.

To enable auditing in any one of these areas, locate and double-click the Administrative Tools icon in the Control Panel. Now find and double-click the Local Security Policy icon. Expand the Local Policies tree node, and you should see something similar to Figure 2-1.

Local Security Settings			
Action View	Policy	Local Setting	Effective Setting
Security Settings	Audit account logon events	No auditing	No auditing
Account Policies	Audit account management	No auditing	No auditing
Local Policies	Audit directory service access	No auditing	No auditing
Audit Policy	Audit logon events	No auditing	No auditing
User Rights Assig	Audit object access	No auditing	No auditing
Security Options	Audit policy change	No auditing	No auditing
Public Key Policies	Audit privilege use	No auditing	No auditing
IP Security Policies or	Audit process tracking	No auditing	No auditing
	Audit system events	No auditing	No auditing

Figure 2-1. Audit Policy settings in the Local Security Settings applet

Now you can go through each of the audit policies and check whether to log successes or failures for each type. You can do this by double-clicking the policy you wish to modify, located in the right pane of the window. After double-clicking, you should see a dialog similar to Figure 2-2.

Leaving auditing off is akin to not logging anything at all, so you should enable auditing for all policies. Once you've enabled auditing for a particular policy, you should begin to see entries in the event logs for when a particular audit event occurs. For example, once you have enabled logon event auditing, you should begin to see entries for logon successes and failures in the system's security event log.

HACK #25 Secure Your Event Logs

Keep your system's logs from being tampered with.

Windows has some very powerful logging features. Unfortunately, by default the event logs are not protected against unauthorized access or modification. You may not realize that even though you have to view the logs through the Event Viewer, the event logs are simply regular files just like any other. To secure them, all we have to do is locate them and apply the proper ACLs.

Unless their location has been changed through the registry, you should be able to find the logs in the *%SystemRoot%\system32\config* directory.

The three files that correspond to the Application Log, Security Log, and System Log are *AppEvent.Evt*, *SecEvent.Evt*, and *SysEvent.Evt*, respectively.

Figure 2-2. The "Audit logon events" dialog

Now, apply ACLs to limit access to only Administrator accounts. You can do this by bringing up the Properties dialog for the files and clicking the Security tab. After you've done this, remove any users or groups other than Administrators and SYSTEM from the top pane.

HACK #26 Change Your Maximum Log File Sizes

Change your log properties so that they see the whole picture.

From a security point of view, logs are one of the most important assets contained on a server. After all, without logs how will you know if or when someone has gained access to your machine? Therefore, it is imperative that your logs not miss a beat. If you're trying to track down the source of an incident, having missing log entries is not much better than having no logs at all.

One common problem is that the maximum log size is set too low—the default is a measly 512KB. To change this, open the Administrative Tools control panel, and then open the Event Viewer. You should now see something similar to Figure 2-3.

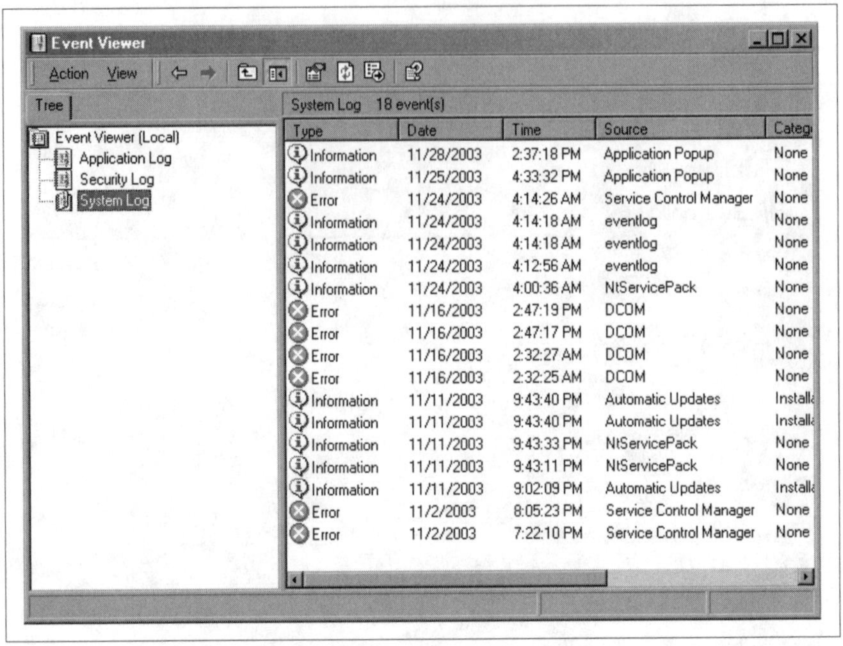

Figure 2-3. The Windows Event Viewer

After you have done this, select one of the log files from the left pane of the Event Viewer window and right-click it. Now select the Properties menu item. You should now see something similar to Figure 2-4.

Now locate the text input box with the label "Maximum log size". You can type in the new maximum size directly, or you can use the arrows next to the text box to change the value. Anything above 1MB is good to use here. It all depends on how often you want to review and archive your logs. However, keep in mind that having very large log files won't inherently slow down the machine, but can slow down the Event Viewer when you're trying to view the logs. While you're here, you may also want to change the behavior for when the log file reaches its maximum size. By default, it will start overwriting log entries that are older than seven days with newer log entries. It is recommended that you change this value to something higher—say 31 days. Alternatively, you could elect not to have logs overwritten automatically at all, in which case you'll need to clear the log manually.

HACK #27 Disable Default Shares

Stop sharing all your files with the world.

By default, Windows enables sharing for each logical disk on your system (C$ for the C drive) in addition to another share called ADMIN$ for the

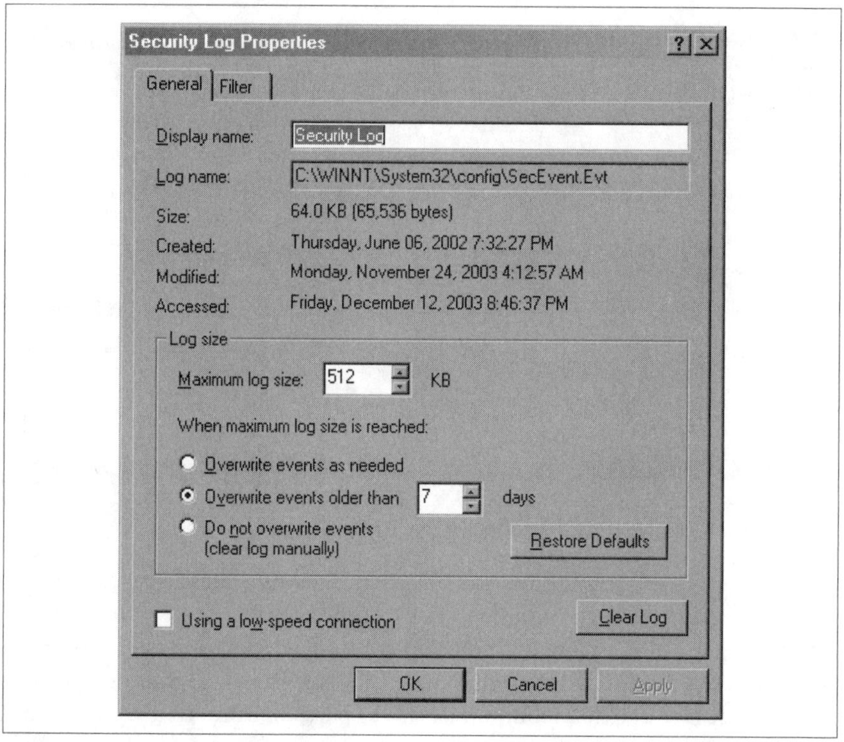

Figure 2-4. Security Log Properties

%SystemRoot% directory (e.g., *C:\WINNT*). Although this is accessible only to Administrators, it is wise to disable these shares (if at all possible) since they still present a potential security hole.

To disable these shares, open the Registry by running *regedit.exe* and then find the *HKey_Local_Machine\SYSTEM\CurrentControlSet\Services\ lanmanserver\parameters* key.

If you're using Windows 2000 workstation, add an AutoShareWks DWORD key with the value of 0 (as shown in Figure 2-5) by clicking Edit → New → DWORD Value. For Windows 2000 Server, add an AutoShareServer key with a value of 0. When you're done editing the Registry, restart Windows for the change to take effect.

After Windows has finished loading, you can verify that the default shares no longer exist by running net share:

```
C:\>net share

Share name    Resource                Remark
-------------------------------------------------------------------------
IPC$          Remote IPC              The command completed successfully.
```

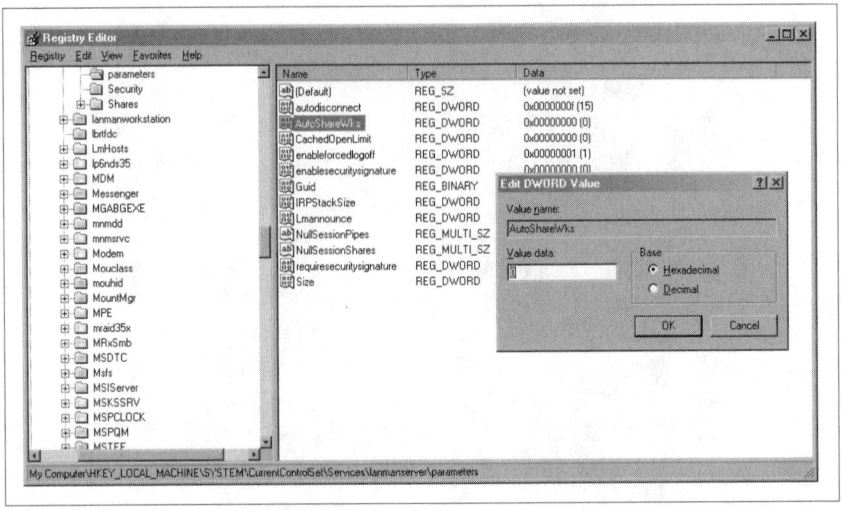

Figure 2-5. Adding an AutoShareWks registry key

Before doing this, you should be sure that disabling these shares will not negatively affect your environment. Lack of these shares can cause some system management software—such as *HFNetChk* [Hack #21] or System Management Server—to not work. This is because software like this depends on remote access to the default administrative shares in order to access the contents of the systems disks.

HACK #28 Encrypt Your Temp Folder
Keep prying eyes out of your temporary files.

Many Windows applications will create intermediary files while they do their work. They typically store these files in a temporary folder within the current user's settings directory. Most often these files are created world-readable and aren't always cleaned up when the program exits. How would you like it if your word processor left a copy of the last document you were working on for anyone to come across and read? Not a pretty thought, is it?

One way to guard against this situation is to encrypt your temporary files folder. To do this, open an Explorer window and go to the *C:\Documents and Settings\<username>\Local Settings* folder. In this folder you should see another folder called *Temp*. This is the folder that holds the temporary files. Right-click the folder and bring up its Properties dialog. Make sure the General tab is selected, and click the button labeled Advanced. This will bring up an Advanced Attributes dialog, as seen in Figure 2-6. Here you can choose to encrypt the folder.

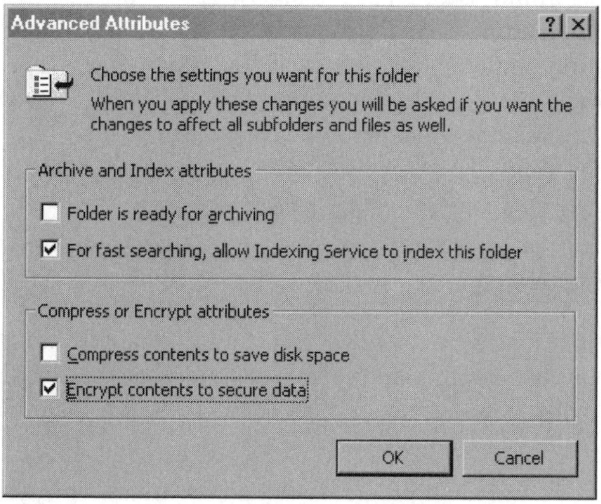

Figure 2-6. The Temp folder's Advanced Attributes dialog

Check the "Encrypt contents to secure data" box and click the OK button. When you have done that, click the Apply button in the Properties dialog. Another dialog (as seen in Figure 2-7) will open asking you whether you would like the encryption to apply recursively.

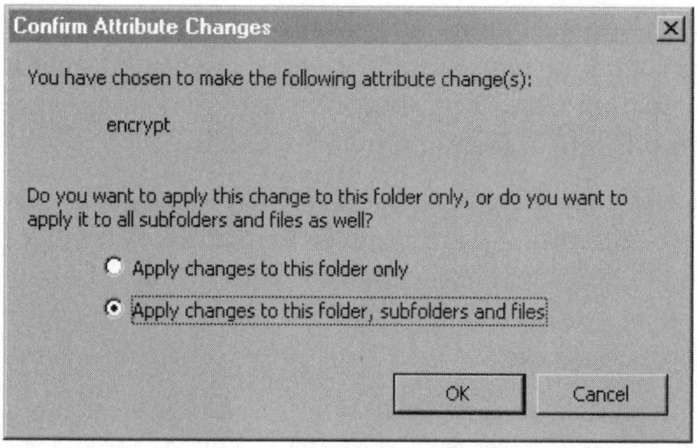

Figure 2-7. Confirm the choice of encryption and make it recursive

To apply the encryption recursively, choose the "Apply changes to this folder, subfolders and files" option. This will automatically create a public-key pair if you have never encrypted any files before. Otherwise, Windows will use the public key that it generated for you previously. When decrypting, Windows ensures that the private keys are stored in nonpaged kernel memory, so that the decryption key will never be left in the paging file. Unfortunately, the encryption algorithm used, DESX, is barely an improvement on DES and is nowhere near as strong as 3DES. However, it serves the purpose of transparently encrypting temporary files very well. If you want to encrypt other files, it is suggested you use a third-party utility such as GnuPG (*http://www.gnupg.org*), which has Windows binaries available on its web site.

HACK #29   Clear the Paging File at Shutdown

Prevent information leaks by automatically clearing the swap file before shutting down.

Virtual memory management (VMM) is truly a wonderful thing. It protects programs from one another and lets them think that they have more memory available than is physically in the system. To accomplish this, the VMM uses what is called a *paging file*.

As you run more and more programs over the course of time, you'll begin to run out of physical memory. Since things can start to go awry when this happens, the memory manager will look for the least frequently used pieces of memory owned by programs that aren't actively doing anything at the moment and write the chunks of memory out to the disk (i.e., the virtual memory). This is known as *swapping*.

However, there is one possibly bad side effect of this feature: if a program containing confidential information in its memory space is running, the memory containing such information may be written out to disk. This is fine when the operating system is running and there are safeguards to prevent the paging file from being read, but what about when the system is off or booted into a different operating system?

This is where this hack comes in handy. What we're going to do is tell the operating system to overwrite the paging file with zeros when it shuts down. Keep in mind that this will not work if the cord is pulled from the system or the system is shut down improperly, since this overwrite will only be done during a proper shutdown.

To enable this feature of Windows, we must edit the system registry. To do this, open the Registry and find the *HKEY_LOCAL_MACHINE\SYSTEM\CurrentControlSet\Control\Session Manager\Memory Management* key. You should now see something that looks like Figure 2-8.

Locate the ClearPageFileAtShutdown entry in the right pane of the window and change its value to 1. Now restart Windows for the change to take effect, and your swap file will be cleared at shutdown. The only side effect of enabling this is that Windows may take longer to shut down. However, this is very much dependent on your hardware (e.g., disk controller chipset, disk

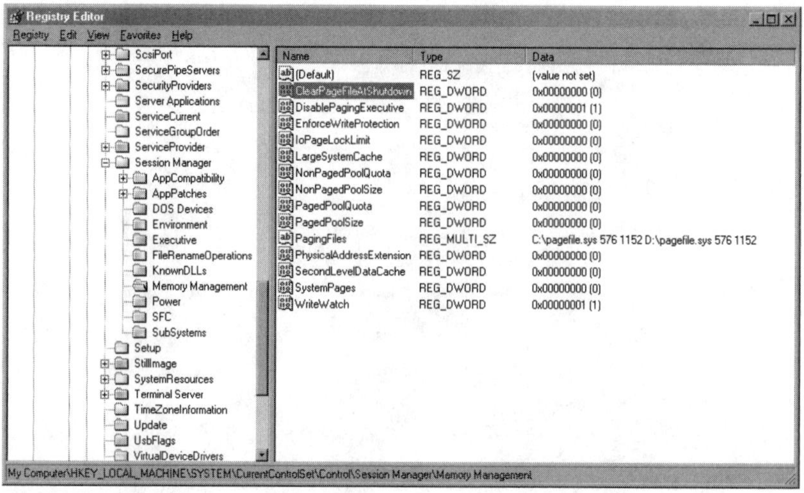

Figure 2-8. The Memory Management registry key

drive speed, processor speed, etc.), since that's what will govern how long it will take to overwrite your paging file with zeros.

Restrict Applications Available to Users

HACK #30

Prevent your users from running potentially dangerous applications.

Keeping users from running certain applications isn't so important when you're an administrator using your own workstation. But when you're dealing with regular users in an enterprise network environment, you don't want your users running any nefarious programs. Such programs include those that can break their operating system installation, introduce security holes to their system, or even attack other machines on your network.

There are a couple ways to restrict the applications available to your users. First you can modify the ACLs for a particular program so that users cannot execute it. For example, suppose you have a sniffer installed on a user's machine for network diagnostic purposes. Access to this program is fine for an administrator, but probably is not appropriate for a normal user. You can prevent normal users from running the program by removing execution permissions for the Users group. To do this, locate the program's executable file and right-click it. Now click the Properties menu item, and you should see a dialog box like the one shown in Figure 2-9.

Now click on the Security tab and select the Users group from the list at the top of the dialog. You should now see something similar to Figure 2-10.

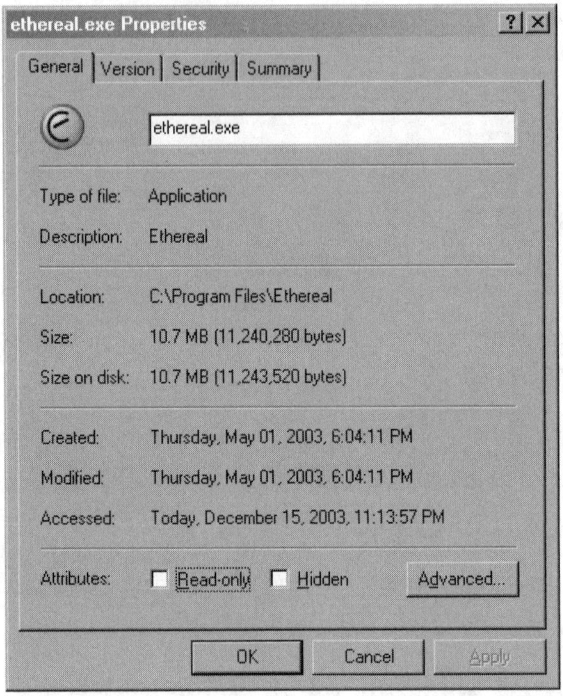

Figure 2-9. Properties dialog for ethereal.exe, the Ethernet sniffer

Now click the Deny checkbox that applies to the Read & Execute permission. After clicking the Apply button, anyone that is a member of the Users group will not be able to run the program. Alternatively, you could also modify the ACL for the directory that the program resides in and disallow read access. This approach could be useful if you want to keep all of your administrative tools under a single folder and restrict access to all of them at once.

If you are running a terminal-server version of Windows, there is another alternative to using ACLs. If you have the Microsoft Windows 2000 resource kit installed, you can use the *AppSec* program to disallow program access with just a few clicks. To use *AppSec*, locate its directory and start the program. After the program loads, you will be presented with a list of programs. If the program that you want to disallow from your terminal-service users is on the list, simply click the Disabled radio button. For instance, if you wanted to disable *cmd.exe*, you would see something similar to Figure 2-11.

If the application you want to restrict is not on the list, you can click the Add button and browse for the application. After you have made your choices, click Exit. Before these changes can fully take effect, all users will have to log off of the terminal server.

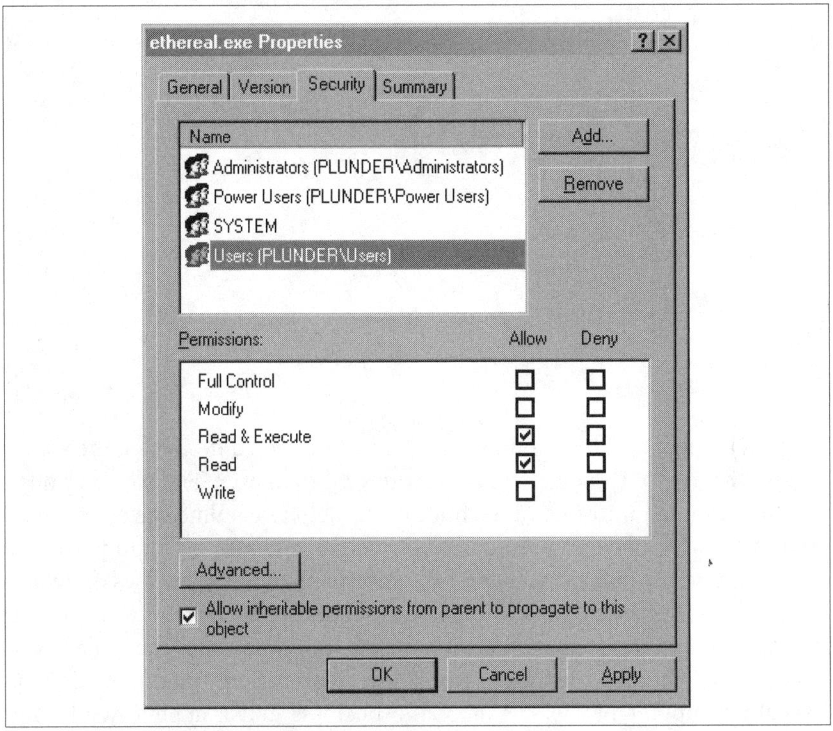

Figure 2-10. The Security tab of the ethereal.exe Properties dialog

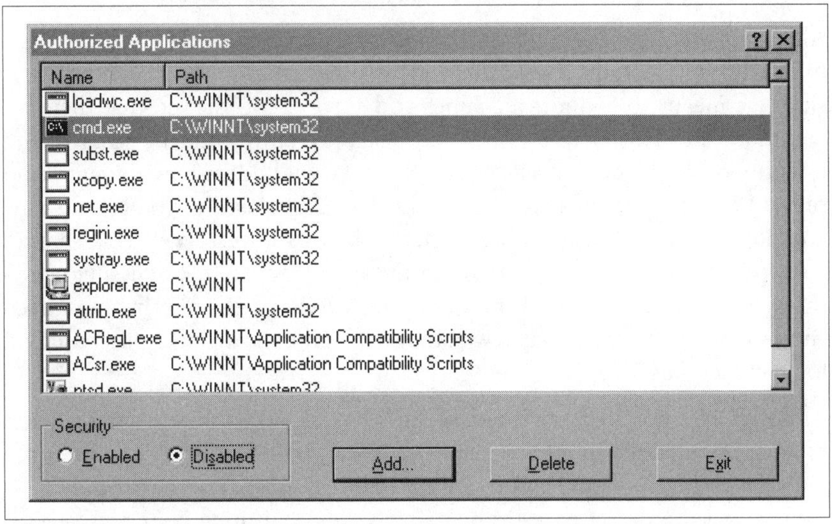

Figure 2-11. Restricting cmd.exe

## CHAPTER THREE

Network Security
Hacks 31–53

As we rely more and more on massively interconnected networks, the stability and security of these networks is more vital than ever. The world of business has adopted information technology to help streamline their processes, increase productivity, and cut costs. As such, a company's IT infrastructure is a core asset to many businesses. Because of this, many businesses would cease to function if disaster (whether natural or digital) were to disrupt their network operations in a significant way. At the same time, the widespread adoption of the Internet as a global communications medium has also brought computer networks out of the business and academic world and into our personal lives, where it is used not only for entertainment, but also as a means to keep in touch with friends, family, and loved ones.

Although this book as a whole is meant to address network security, the information it contains extends into many other areas. After all, a network is simply a means to connect machines and services together so that they can communicate. This chapter, however, deals primarily with the security and integrity of the network itself. In this chapter, you'll learn how to detect and prevent certain types of spoofing attacks that can be used to compromise the core integrity of a TCP/IP Ethernet network at its lowest level. This chapter also includes a great deal of information about firewalls, discussing everything from basic port-based firewalling to MAC-address filtering, and even shows you how to create a gateway that will authenticate machines based on login credentials.

Although it is not always a direct security threat, network reconnaissance is often a precursor to an attack. In this chapter, you'll learn how to fool those who are trying to gather information about the hosts on your network, as well as ways to detect eavesdroppers who are monitoring your network for juicy bits of information.

Detect ARP Spoofing

Find out if there's a "man in the middle" impersonating your server.

One of the biggest threats to a computer network is a rogue system pretending to be a trusted host. Once someone has successfully impersonated another host, they can do a number of nefarious things. For example, they can intercept and log traffic destined for the real host, or lay in wait for clients to connect and begin sending the rogue host confidential information. Spoofing a host has especially severe consequences in IP networks, as this opens many other avenues of attack. One technique for spoofing a host on an IP network is Address Resolution Protocol (ARP) spoofing. *ARP spoofing* is limited only to local segments and works by exploiting the way IP addresses are translated to hardware Ethernet addresses.

When an IP datagram is sent from one host to another on the same physical segment, the IP address of the destination host must be translated into a MAC address. This is the hardware address of the Ethernet card that is physically connected to the network. To accomplish this, the Address Resolution Protocol is used.

When a host needs to know another host's Ethernet address, it sends out a broadcast frame that looks like this:

```
01:20:14.833350 arp who-has 192.168.0.66 tell 192.168.0.62
```

This is called an *ARP request*. Since this is sent to the broadcast address, all Ethernet devices on the local segment should see the request. The machine that matches the requests responds by sending an *ARP reply*:

```
01:20:14.833421 arp reply 192.168.0.66 is-at 0:0:d1:1f:3f:f1
```

Since the ARP request already contained the MAC address of the sender in the Ethernet frame, the receiver can send this response without making yet another ARP request. Unfortunately, ARP's biggest weakness is that it is a *stateless protocol*. This means that it does not track responses to the requests that are sent out, and therefore will accept responses without having sent a request. If someone wanted to receive traffic destined for another host, they could send forged ARP responses matching any chosen IP address to their MAC address. The machines that receive these spoofed ARP responses can't distinguish them from legitimate ARP responses, and will begin sending packets to the attacker's MAC address.

Another side effect of ARP being stateless is that a system's ARP tables usually only use the results of the last response. In order for someone to continue to spoof an IP address, it is necessary to flood the host with ARP responses that overwrite legitimate ARP responses from the original host. This particular kind of attack is commonly known as *ARP cache poisoning*.

Several tools—such as Ettercap (*http://ettercap.sourceforge.net*), Dsniff (*http://www.monkey.org/~dugsong/dsniff/*), and Hunt (*http://lin.fsid.cvut.cz/~kra/*)—employ techniques like this to both sniff on switched networks and perform man-in-the-middle attacks. This technique can of course be used between any two hosts on a switched segment, including the local default gateway. To intercept traffic bidirectionally between hosts A and B, the attacking host C will poison host A's ARP cache, making it think that host B's IP address matches host C's MAC address. C will then poison B's cache, to make it think A's IP address corresponds to C's MAC address.

Luckily, there are methods to detect just this kind of behavior, whether you're using a shared or switched Ethernet segment. One program that can help accomplish this is Arpwatch (*ftp://ftp.ee.lbl.gov/arpwatch.tar.gz*). It works by monitoring an interface in promiscuous mode and recording MAC/IP address pairings over a period of time. When it sees anomalous behavior, such as a change to one of the MAC/IP pairs that it has learned, it will send an alert to the syslog. This can be very effective in a shared network using a hub, since a single machine can monitor all ARP traffic. However, due to the unicast nature of ARP responses, this program will not work as well on a switched network.

To achieve the same level of detection coverage in a switched environment, Arpwatch should be installed on as many machines as possible. After all, you can't know with 100% certainty what hosts an attacker will decide to target. If you're lucky enough to own one, many high-end switches allow you to designate a *monitor port* that can see the traffic of all other ports. If you have such a switch, you can install a server on that port for network monitoring, and simply run Arpwatch on it.

After downloading Arpwatch, you can compile and install it in the usual manner by running:

```
# ./configure && make && make install
```

When running Arpwatch on a machine with multiple interfaces, you'll probably want to specify the interface on the command line. This can be done by using the -i command-line option:

```
arpwatch -i iface
```

As Arpwatch begins to learn the MAC/IP pairings on your network, you'll see log entries similar to this:

```
Nov  1 00:39:08 zul arpwatch: new station 192.168.0.65 0:50:ba:85:85:ca
```

When a MAC/IP address pair changes, you should see something like this:

```
Nov  1 01:03:23 zul arpwatch: changed ethernet address 192.168.0.65 0:e0:81:
3:d8:8e (0:50:ba:85:85:ca)
```

```
Nov  1 01:03:23 zul arpwatch: flip flop 192.168.0.65 0:50:ba:85:85:ca (0:e0:
81:3:d8:8e)
Nov  1 01:03:25 zul arpwatch: flip flop 192.168.0.65 0:e0:81:3:d8:8e (0:50:
ba:85:85:ca)
```

In this case, the initial entry is from the first fraudulent ARP response that was received, and the subsequent two are from a race condition between the fraudulent and authentic responses.

To make it easier to deal with multiple Arpwatch installs on a switched environment, you can send the log messages to a central *syslogd* [Hack #54], aggregating all the output into one place. However, due to the fact that your machines can be manipulated by the same attacks that Arpwatch is looking for, it would be wise to use static ARP table entries [Hack #32] on your syslog server, as well as all the hosts running Arpwatch.

HACK #32 Create a Static ARP Table

Use static ARP table entries to combat spoofing and other nefarious activities.

As discussed in "Detect ARP Spoofing" [Hack #31], a lot of bad things can happen if someone successfully poisons the ARP table of a machine on your network. The previous hack discussed how to monitor for this behavior, but how do we prevent the effects of someone attempting to poison an ARP table?

One way to prevent the ill effects of this behavior is to create static ARP table entries for all of the devices on your local network segment. When this is done, the kernel will ignore all ARP responses for the specific IP address used in the entry and use the specified MAC address instead.

To do this, you can use the arp command, which allows you to directly manipulate the kernel's ARP table entries. To add a single static ARP table entry, run this:

```
arp -s ipaddr macaddr
```

If you know that the MAC address that corresponds to 192.168.0.65 is 00:50:BA:85:85:CA, you could add a static ARP entry for it like this:

```
# arp -s 192.168.0.65 00:50:ba:85:85:ca
```

For more than a few entries, this can be a time-consuming process. To be fully effective, you must add an entry for each device on your network on every host that allows you to create static ARP table entries.

Luckily, most versions of the arp command can take a file as input and use it to create static ARP table entries. Under Linux, this is done with the -f command-line switch. Now all you need to do is generate a file containing the MAC and IP address pairings, which you can then copy to all the hosts on your network.

To make this easier, you can use this quick-n-dirty Perl script:

```perl
#!/usr/bin/perl
#
# gen_ethers.pl <from ip> <to ip>
#

my ($start_1, $start_2, $start_3, $start_4) = split(/\./, $ARGV[0], 4);
my ($end_1, $end_2, $end_3, $end_4) = split(/\./, $ARGV[1], 4);
my $ARP_CMD="/sbin/arp -n";

for(my $oct_1 = $start_1; $oct_1 <= $end_1 && $oct_1 <= 255; $oct_1++ ){
  for(my $oct_2 = $start_2; $oct_2 <= $end_2 && $oct_2 <= 255; $oct_2++){
    for(my $oct_3 = $start_3; $oct_3 <= $end_3 && $oct_3 <= 255; $oct_3++){
      for(my $oct_4 = $start_4; $oct_4 <= $end_4 && $oct_4 < 255; $oct_4++){
      system("ping -c 1 -W 1 $oct_1.$oct_2.$oct_3.$oct_4 > /dev/null 2>&1");
              my $ether_addr = `$ARP_CMD $oct_1.$oct_2.$oct_3.$oct_4 | egrep
'HWaddress|(incomplete)' | awk '{print \$3}'`;
        chomp($ether_addr);
        if(length($ether_addr) == 17){
          print("$ether_addr\t$oct_1.$oct_2.$oct_3.$oct_4\n");
        }
      }
    }
  }
}
```

This script will take a range of IP addresses and attempt to ping each one once. In doing this, each active IP address will appear in the machine's ARP table. After an IP address is pinged, the script will then look for that IP address in the ARP table, and print out the MAC/IP address pair in a format suitable for putting into a file to load with the arp command. This script was written with Linux in mind but should work on other Unix-like operating systems as well.

For example, if you wanted to generate a file for all the IP addresses from 192.168.1.1 to 192.168.1.255 and store the results in /etc/ethers, you would run the script like this:

```
# ./gen_ethers 192.168.1.1 192.168.1.255 > /etc/ethers
```

When using arp with the -f switch, it will automatically use the /etc/ethers file to create the static entries. However, you can specify any file you prefer. For example, if you wanted to use /root/arp_entries instead, you would run this:

```
# arp -f /root/arp_entries
```

This script isn't perfect, but it can save a lot of time when creating static ARP table entries for the hosts on your network. Once you've generated the file with the MAC/IP pairings, you can copy it to the other hosts and add an arp command to the system startup scripts, to automatically load them at boot time. The main downside to using this method is that all the devices on your network need to be powered on when the script runs; otherwise, they will be missing from the list. In addition, if the machines on your network change frequently, you'll have to regenerate and distribute the file often, which may be more trouble than it's worth. But for servers and devices that never change their IP or MAC address, this method can protect your machines from ARP poisoning attacks.

HACK #33 Firewall with Netfilter

Protect your network with Linux's powerful firewalling features.

Linux has long had the capability for filtering packets, and it has come a long way since the early days in terms of both power and flexibility. The first generation of packet-filtering code was called *ipfw* (for "IP firewall") and provided basic filtering capability. Since it was somewhat inflexible and inefficient for complex configurations, *ipfw* is rarely used now. The second generation of IP filtering was called *IP chains*. It improved greatly on *ipfw* and is still in common use. The latest generation of filtering is called Netfilter and is manipulated with the `iptables` command. It is used exclusively with the 2.4.x and later series of kernels. Although Netfilter is the kernel component and *iptables* is the user-space configuration tool, these terms are often used interchangeably.

An important concept in Netfilter is the *chain*, which consists of a list of rules that are applied to packets as they enter, leave, or traverse through the system. The kernel defines three chains by default, but new chains of rules can be specified and linked to the predefined chains. The INPUT chain applies to packets that are received and are destined for the local system, and the OUTPUT chain applies to packets that are transmitted by the local system. Finally, the FORWARD chain applies whenever a packet will be routed from one network interface to another through the system. It is used whenever the system is acting as a packet router or gateway, and applies to packets that are neither originating from nor destined for this system.

The `iptables` command is used to make changes to the Netfilter chains and rulesets. You can create new chains, delete chains, list the rules in a chain, flush chains (that is, remove all rules from a chain), and set the default action for a chain. `iptables` also allows you to insert, append, delete, and replace rules in a chain.

Before we get started with some example rules, it's important to set a default behavior for all the chains. To do this we'll use the -P command-line switch, which stands for "policy":

```
# iptables -P INPUT DROP
# iptables -P FORWARD DROP
```

This will ensure that only those packets covered by subsequent rules that we specify will make it past our firewall. After all, with the relatively small number of services that will be provided by the network, it is far easier to explicitly specify all the types of traffic that we want to allow, rather than all the traffic that we don't. Note that a default policy was not specified for the OUTPUT chain; this is because we want to allow traffic to proceed out of the firewall itself in a normal manner.

With the default policy set to DROP, we'll specify what is actually allowed. Here's where we'll need to figure out what services will have to be accessible to the outside world. For the rest of these examples, we'll assume that eth0 is the external interface on our firewall and that eth1 is the internal one. Our network will contain a web server (*192.168.1.20*), a mail server (*192.168.1.21*), and a DNS server (*192.168.1.18*)—a fairly minimal setup for a self-managed Internet presence.

However, before we begin specifying rules, we should remove filtering from our loopback interface:

```
# iptables -P INPUT -i lo -j ACCEPT
# iptables -P OUTPUT -o lo -j ACCEPT
```

Now let's construct some rules to allow this traffic through. First, we'll make a rule to allow traffic on TCP port 80—the standard port for web servers—to pass to the web server unfettered by our firewall:

```
# iptables -A FORWARD -m state --state NEW -p tcp \
 -d 192.168.1.20 --dport 80 -j ACCEPT
```

And now for the mail server, which uses TCP port 25 for SMTP:

```
# iptables -A FORWARD -m state --state NEW -p tcp \
 -d 192.168.1.21 --dport 25 -j ACCEPT
```

Additionally, we might want to allow remote POP3, IMAP, and IMAP+SSL access as well:

POP3
```
# iptables -A FORWARD -m state --state NEW -p tcp \
 -d 192.168.1.21 --dport 110 -j ACCEPT
```
IMAP
```
# iptables -A FORWARD -m state --state NEW -p tcp \
 -d 192.168.1.21 --dport 143 -j ACCEPT
```
IMAP+SSL
```
# iptables -A FORWARD -m state --state NEW -p tcp \
 -d 192.168.1.21 --dport 993 -j ACCEPT
```

Unlike the other services, DNS can use both TCP and UDP port 53:

```
# iptables -A FORWARD -m state --state NEW -p tcp \
 -d 192.168.1.21 --dport 53 -j ACCEPT
```

Since we're using a default deny policy, it makes it slightly more difficult to use UDP for DNS. This is because our policy relies on the use of state tracking rules, and since UDP is a stateless protocol, there is no way to track it. In this case, we can configure our DNS server either to use only TCP, or to use a UDP source port of 53 for any response that it sends back to clients that were using UDP to query the nameserver.

If the DNS server is configured to respond to clients using UDP port 53, we can allow this traffic through with the following two rules:

```
# iptables -A FORWARD -p udp -d 192.168.1.18 --dport 53 -j ACCEPT
# iptables -A FORWARD -p udp -s 192.168.1.18 --sport 53 -j ACCEPT
```

The first rule allows traffic into our network destined for the DNS server, and the second rule allows responses from the DNS server to leave the network.

You may be wondering what the -m state and --state arguments are about. These two options allow us to use Netfilter's stateful packet-inspection engine. Using these options tells Netfilter that we want to allow only new connections to the destination IP and port pairs that we have specified. When these rules are in place, the triggering packet is accepted and its information is entered into a state table.

Now we can specify that we want to allow any outbound traffic that is associated with these connections by adding a rule like this:

```
# iptables -A FORWARD -m state --state ESTABLISHED,RELATED -j ACCEPT
```

The only thing left now is to allow traffic from machines behind the firewall to reach the outside world. To do this, we'll use a rule like the following:

```
# iptables -A FORWARD -m state --state NEW -i eth1 -j ACCEPT
```

This rule enters any outbound connections from the internal network into the state table. It works by matching packets coming into the internal interface of our firewall that are creating new connections. If we were setting up a firewall that had multiple internal interfaces, we could have used a Boolean NOT operator on the external interface (e.g., -i ! eth0). Now any traffic that comes into the firewall through the external interface that corresponds to an outbound connection will be accepted by the preceding rule, because this rule will have put the corresponding connection into the state table.

In these examples, the order in which the rules were entered does not really matter. Since we're operating with a default DENY policy, all our rules have an ACCEPT target. However, if we had specified targets of DROP or REJECT as arguments to the -j option, then we would have to take a little extra care to ensure that the order of those rules would result in the desired effect. Remember that the first rule that matches a packet is always triggered as the rule chains are traversed, so rule order can sometimes be critically important.

It should also be noted that rule order can have a performance impact in some circumstances. For example, the rule shown earlier that matches ESTABLISHED and RELATED states should be specified before any of the other rules, since that particular rule will be matched far more often than any of the rules that will match only on new connections. By putting that rule first, it will prevent any packets that are already associated with a connection from having to traverse the rest of the rule chain before finding a match.

To complete our firewall configuration, we'll want to enable packet forwarding. Run this command:

```
# echo 1 > /proc/sys/net/ipv4/ip_forward
```

This tells the kernel to forward packets between interfaces whenever appropriate. To have this done automatically at boot time, add the following line to /etc/sysctl.conf:

```
net.ipv4.ip_forward=1
```

If your system doesn't support /etc/sysctl.conf, you can put the preceding echo command in one of your startup rc scripts, such as /etc/rc.local. Another useful kernel parameter is rp_filter, which helps prevent IP spoofing. This enables source address verification by checking that the IP address for any given packet has arrived on the expected network interface. This can be enabled by running the following command:

```
# echo 1 > /proc/sys/net/ipv4/conf/default/rp_filter
```

Much like how we enabled IP forwarding, we can also enable source address verification by editing /etc/sysctl.conf on systems that support it, or else put the changes in your rc.local. To enable rp_filter in your sysctl.conf, add the following line:

```
net.ipv4.conf.all.rp_filter=1
```

To save all of our rules, we can either write all of our rules to a shell script or use our Linux distribution's particular way of saving them. We can do this in Red Hat by running the following command:

```
# /sbin/service iptables save
```

This will save all currently active filter rules to /etc/sysconfig/iptables. To achieve the same effect under Debian, edit /etc/default/iptables and set enable_iptables_initd=true.

After doing this, run the following command:

```
# /etc/init.d/iptables save_active
```

When the machine reboots, your *iptables* configuration will be automatically restored.

HACK #34 Firewall with OpenBSD's PacketFilter

Use OpenBSD's firewalling features to protect your network.

PacketFilter, commonly known as PF, is the firewalling system available in OpenBSD. While it is a relatively new addition to the operating system, it has already surpassed IPFilter, the system it has replaced, in both features and flexibility. PF shares many features with Linux's Netfilter. Although Linux's Netfilter is more easily extensible with modules, PF outshines it in its traffic normalization capabilities and enhanced logging features.

To communicate with the kernel portion of PF, we need to use the `pfctl` command. Unlike the `iptables` command that is used with Linux's Netfilter, it is not used to specify individual rules, but instead uses its own configuration and rule specification language. To actually configure PF, we must edit */etc/pf.conf*. PF's rule specification language is actually very powerful, flexible, and easy to use. The *pf.conf* file is split up into seven sections, each of which contains a particular type of rule. Not all sections need to be used—if you don't need a specific type of rule, that section can simply be left out of the file.

The first section is for macros. In this section you can specify variables to hold either single values or lists of values for use in later sections of the configuration file. Like an environment variable or a programming-language identifier, macros must start with a letter and also may contain digits and underscores.

Here are some example macros:

```
EXT_IF="de0"
INT_IF="de1"
RFC1918="{ 192.168.0.0/16, 172.16.0.0/12, 10.0.0.0/8 }"
```

A macro can be referenced later by prefixing it with the $ character:

```
block drop quick on $EXT_IF from any to $RFC1918
```

The second section allows you to specify tables of IP addresses to use in later rules. Using tables for lists of IP addresses is much faster than using a macro, especially for large numbers of IP addresses, because when a macro is used in a rule, it will expand to multiple rules, with each one matching on a single value contained in the macro. Using a table adds just a single rule when it is expanded.

Rather than using the macro from our previous example, we can define a table to hold the nonroutable RFC 1918 IP addresses:

```
table <rfc1918> const { 192.168.0.0/16, 172.16.0.0/12, 10.0.0.0/8 }
```

The const keyword ensures that this table cannot be modified once it has been created. Tables are specified in a rule in the same way that they were created:

```
block drop quick on $EXT_IF from any to <rfc1918>
```

You can also load a list of IP addresses into a table by using the file keyword:

```
table <spammers> file "/etc/spammers.table"
```

If you elect not to use the const keyword, then you can add addresses to a table by running a command such as this:

```
pfctl -t spammers -T add 10.1.1.1
```

Additionally, you can delete an address by running a command like this:

```
pfctl -t spammers -T delete 10.1.1.1
```

To list the contents of a table, you can run:

```
pfctl -t spammers -T show
```

In addition to IP addresses, hostnames may also be specified. In this case, all valid addresses returned by the resolver will be inserted into the table.

The next section of the configuration file contains options that affect the behavior of PF. By modifying options, we can control session timeouts, defragmentation timeouts, state-table transitions, statistic collection, and other behaviors. Options are specified by using the set keyword. The number of options is too numerous to discuss all of them in any meaningful detail; however, we will discuss the most pertinent and useful ones.

One of the most important options is block-policy. This option specifies the default behavior of the block keyword and can be configured to silently drop matching packets by specifying drop. Alternatively, return may be used, to specify that packets matching a block rule will generate a TCP reset or an ICMP unreachable packet, depending on whether the triggering packet is TCP or UDP. This is similar to the REJECT target in Linux's Netfilter.

For example, to have PF drop packets silently by default, add a line like this to /etc/pf.conf:

```
set block-policy drop
```

In addition to setting the block-policy, additional statistics such as packet and byte counts can be collected for an interface. To enable this for an interface, add a line similar to this to the configuration file:

```
set loginterface de0
```

However, these statistics can only be collected on a single interface at a time. If you do not want to collect any statistics, you can replace the interface name with the none keyword.

To better utilize resources on busy networks, we can also modify the session-timeout values. Setting this to a low value can help improve the performance of the firewall on high-traffic networks, but at the expense of dropping valid idle connections.

To set the session timeout (in seconds), put a line similar to this in */etc/pf.conf*:

```
set timeout interval 20
```

With this setting in place, any TCP connection that is idle for 20 seconds will automatically be reset.

PF can also optimize performance on low-end hardware by tuning its memory use regarding how many states may be stored at any one time or how many fragments may reside in memory for fragment reassembly. For example, to set the number of states to 20,000 and the number of entries used by the fragment reassembler to 15,000, we could put this in our *pf.conf*:

```
set limit states 20000
set limit frags 15000
```

Alternatively, we could combine these entries into a single one, like this:

```
set limit { states 20000, frags 15000 }
```

Moving on, the next section is for traffic normalization rules. Rules of this type ensure that packets passing through the firewall meet certain criteria regarding fragmentation, IP IDs, minimum TTLs, and other attributes of a TCP datagram. Rules in this section are all prefixed by the scrub keyword. In general, just putting scrub all is fine. However, if necessary, we can get quite detailed in specifying what we want normalized and how we want to normalize it. Since we can use PF's general filtering-rule syntax to determine what types of packets a scrub rule will match, we can normalize packets with a great deal of control.

One of the more interesting possibilities is to randomize all IP IDs in the packets leaving your network for the outside world. In doing this, we can make sure that passive operating system determination methods based on IP IDs will break when trying to figure out the operating system of a system protected by the firewall. Because such methods depend on analyzing how the host operating system increments the IP IDs in its outgoing packets, and our firewall ensures that the IP IDs in all the packets leaving our network are totally random, it's pretty hard to match them against a known pattern for an operating system. This also helps to prevent enumeration of machines in a network address translated (NAT) environment. Without random IP IDs, someone outside the network can perform a statistical analysis of the IP IDs being emitted by the NAT gateway in order to count the number of machines on the private network. Randomizing the IP IDs defeats this kind of attack.

To enable random ID generation on an interface, put a line such as this in */etc/pf.conf*:

```
scrub out on de0 all random-id
```

We can also use the scrub directive to reassemble fragmented packets before forwarding them to their destinations. This helps prevent specially frag-mented packets (such as packets that overlap) from evading intrusion-detection systems that are sitting behind the firewall.

To enable fragment reassembly on all interfaces, simply put the following line in the configuration file:

```
scrub fragment reassemble
```

If we want to limit reassembly to just a single interface, we can change this to:

```
scrub in on de0 all fragment reassemble
```

This will enable fragment reassembly for the de0 interface.

The next two sections of the *pf.conf* file involve packet queuing and address translation, but since this hack focuses on packet filtering, we'll skip these. This brings us to the last section, which contains the actual packet-filtering rules. In general, the syntax for a filter rule can be defined by the following:

```
action direction [log] [quick] on int [af] [proto protocol] \
    from src_addr [port src_port] to dst_addr [port dst_port] \
    [tcp_flags] [state]
```

In PF, a rule can have only two actions: block and pass. As discussed previ-ously, the block policy affects the behavior of the block action. However, this can be modified for specific rules by specifying it along with an action, such as block drop or block return. Additionally, block return-icmp can be used, which will return an ICMP unreachable message by default. An ICMP type can be specified as well, in which case that type of ICMP message will be returned.

For most purposes, we want to start out with a default deny policy; that way we can later add rules to allow the specific traffic that we want through the firewall.

To set up a default deny policy for all interfaces, put the following line in */etc/pf.conf*:

```
block all
```

Now we can add rules to allow traffic through our firewall. First we'll keep the loopback interface unfiltered. To accomplish this, we'll use this rule:

```
pass quick on lo0 all
```

Notice the use of the quick keyword. Normally PF will continue through our rule list even if a rule has already allowed a packet to pass, in order to see whether a more specific rule that appears later on in the configuration file will drop the packet. The use of the quick keyword modifies this behavior and causes PF to stop processing the packet at this rule if it matches the packet and to take the specified action. With careful use, this can greatly improve the performance of a ruleset.

To prevent external hosts from spoofing internal addresses, we can use the antispoof keyword:

```
antispoof quick for $INT_IF inet
```

Next we'll want to block any packets from entering or leaving our external interface that have a nonroutable RFC 1918 IP address. Such packets, unless explicitly allowed later, would be caught by our default deny policy. However, if we use a rule to specifically match these packets and use the quick keyword, we can increase performance by adding a rule like this:

```
block drop quick on $EXT_IF from any to <rfc1918>
```

If we wanted to allow traffic into our network destined for a web server at 192.168.1.20, we could use a rule like this:

```
pass in on $EXT_IF proto tcp from any to 192.168.1.20 port 80 \
    modulate state flags S/SA
```

This will allow packets destined to TCP port 80 at 192.168.1.20 only if they are establishing a new connection (i.e., the SYN flag is set), and will enter the connection into the state table. The modulate keyword ensures that a high-quality initial sequence number is generated for the session, which is important if the operating system in use at either end of the connection uses a poor algorithm for generating its ISNs.

Similarly, if we wanted to pass traffic to and from an email server at the IP address 192.168.1.21, we could use this rule:

```
pass in on $EXT_IF proto tcp from any to 192.168.1.21 \
    port { smtp, pop3, imap2, imaps } modulate state flags S/SA
```

Notice that multiple ports can be specified for a rule by separating them with commas and enclosing them in curly braces. We can also use service names, as defined in /etc/services, instead of specifying the service's port number.

To allow traffic to a DNS server at *192.168.1.18*, we can add a rule like this:

```
pass in on $EXT_IF proto tcp from any to 192.168.1.18 port 53 \
    modulate state flags S/SA
```

This still leaves the firewall blocking UDP DNS traffic. To allow this through, add this rule:

```
pass in on $EXT_IF proto udp from any to 192.168.1.18 port 53 \
    keep state
```

Notice here that even though this is a rule for UDP packets we have still used the state keyword. In this case, PF will keep track of the connection using the source and destination IP address and port pairs. Also, since UDP datagrams do not contain sequence numbers, the modulate keyword is not applicable. We use keep state instead, which is how to specify stateful inspection when not modulating ISNs. In addition, since UDP datagrams do not contain flags, we simply omit them.

Now we'll want to allow connections initiated from the internal network to pass through the firewall. To do this, we'll need to add the following rules to let the traffic into the internal interface of the firewall:

```
pass in on $INT_IF from $INT_IF:network to any
pass out on $INT_IF from any to $INT_IF:network
pass out on $EXT_IF proto tcp all modulate state flags S/SA
pass out on $EXT_IF proto { icmp, udp } all keep state
```

As you can see, OpenBSD has a very powerful and flexible firewalling system. There are too many features and possibilities to discuss here. For more information, you can look at the excellent PF documentation available online or the *pf.conf* manpage.

HACK #35   Create an Authenticated Gateway

Use PF to keep unauthorized users off the network.

Firewalling gateways have traditionally been used to block traffic from specific services or machines. Instead of watching IP addresses and port numbers, an authenticated gateway allows you to regulate traffic to or from machines based on a user's credentials. With an authenticated gateway, a user will have to log in and authenticate himself to the gateway in order to gain access to the protected network. This can be useful in many situations, such as restricting Internet access or restricting a wireless segment to be used only by authorized users.

With the release of OpenBSD 3.1, you can implement this functionality through the use of PF and the *authpf* shell. Using *authpf* also provides an audit trail by logging usernames, originating IP addresses, and the time that they authenticated with the gateway, as well as when they logged off the network.

To set up authentication with *authpf*, you'll first need to create an account on the gateway for each user. Specify */usr/sbin/authpf* as the shell, and be sure to add authpf as a valid shell to */etc/shells*. When a user logs in through SSH, *authpf* will obtain the user's name and IP address through the environment. After doing this, a template file containing NAT and filter rules is read in, and the username and IP address are applied to it. The resulting rules are then added to the running configuration. When the user logs out (i.e., types ^C), the rules that were created are unloaded from the current ruleset. For user-specific rule templates, *authpf* looks in */etc/authpf/users/$USER/authpf.rules*. Global rule templates are stored in */etc/authpf/authpf.rules*. Similarly, NAT entries are stored in *authpf.nat*, in either of these two directories. When a user-specific template is present for the user who has just authenticated, the template completely replaces the global rules, instead of just adding to them. When loading the templates, *authpf* will expand the $user_ip macro to the user's current IP address.

For example:

```
pass in quick on wi0 proto { tcp, udp } from $user_ip to any \
    keep state flags S/SA
```

This particular rule will pass in all traffic on the wireless interface from the newly authenticated user's IP address. This works particularly well with a default deny policy, where only the initial SSH connection to the gateway and DNS have been allowed from the authenticating IP address.

You could be much more restrictive and allow only HTTP-, DNS-, and email-related traffic through the gateway:

```
pass in quick on wi0 proto tcp from $user_ip to any \
    port { smtp, www, https, pop3, pop3s, imap, imaps } \
    keep state flags S/SA
pass in quick on wi0 proto udp from $user_ip to any port domain
```

After the template files have been created, you must then provide an entry point into *pf.conf* for the rules that *authpf* will create for evaluation by PF. These entry points are added to your *pf.conf* with the various anchor keywords:

```
nat-anchor authpf
rdr-anchor authpf
binat-anchor authpf
anchor authpf
```

Note that each anchor point needs to be added to the section it applies to—you cannot just put them all at the end or beginning of your *pf.conf*. Thus the nat-anchor, rdr-anchor, and binat-anchor entries must go into the address translation section of the *pf.conf*. Likewise, the anchor entry, which applies only to filtering rules, should be added to the filtering section.

When a user logs into the gateway, he should now be presented with a message like this:

```
Hello andrew, You are authenticated from host "192.168.0.61"
```

The user will also see the contents of */etc/authpf/authpf.message* if it exists and is readable.

If you examine */var/log/daemon*, you should also see log messages similar to these for when a user logs in and out:

```
Dec  3 22:36:31 zul authpf[15058]: allowing 192.168.0.61, \
   user andrew
Dec  3 22:47:21 zul authpf[15058]: removed  192.168.0.61, \
   user andrew- duration 650 seconds
```

Note that since it is present in */etc/shells*, any user that has a local account is capable of changing his shell to *authpf*. If you want to ensure that the user cannot do this, you can create a file named after his username and put it in the */etc/authpf/banned* directory. The contents of this file will be displayed when he logs into the gateway. On the other hand, you can also explicitly allow users by listing their usernames, one per line, in */etc/authpf/authpf. allow*. However, any bans that have been specified in */etc/authpf/banned* take precedence over entries in *authpf.allow*.

Since *authpf* relies on the SSH session to determine when the rules pertaining to a particular user are to be unloaded, care should be taken in configuring your SSH daemon to time out connections. Timeouts should happen fairly quickly, to revoke access as soon as possible once a connection has gone stale. This also helps prevent connections to systems outside the gateway from being held open by those conducting ARP spoof attacks.

You can set up OpenSSH to guard against this by adding these to lines to your *sshd_config*:

```
ClientAliveInterval 15
ClientAliveCountMax 3
```

This will ensure that the SSH daemon will send a request for a client response 15 seconds after it has received no data from the client. The ClientAliveCountMax option specifies that this can happen three times without a response before the client is disconnected. Thus, after a client has become unresponsive, it will be disconnected after 45 seconds. These keep-alive packets are sent automatically by the SSH client software and don't require any intervention on the part of the user.

Authpf is very powerful in its flexibility and integration with PF, OpenBSD's native firewalling system. It is easy to set up and has very little performance overhead, since it relies on SSH and the operating system to do authentication and manage sessions.

HACK #36 Firewall with Windows

Yes, you can use Windows as a firewall.

You may not know it, but Windows has a very capable firewall built right in. To access it, run the Microsoft Management Console. You can do this by opening up a Run dialog, typing mmc, and clicking the OK button. After the program loads, you should see something similar to Figure 3-1.

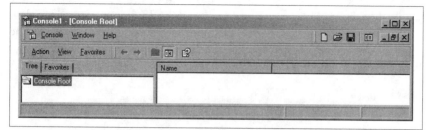

Figure 3-1. The Microsoft Management Console

Click on the Console menu and select the "Add/Remove Snap-in..." menu item. Next you should be presented with a dialog that has an Add button at the bottom. After clicking the Add button, you should see a dialog box with a list of available snap-ins. Scroll through the list and locate the item titled IP Security Policy Management. After you've selected this, the dialog box should look like Figure 3-2.

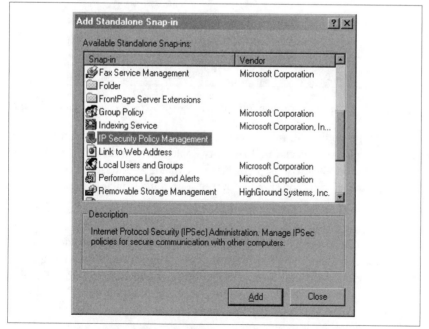

Figure 3-2. Adding the IP Security Policy Management snap-in

Now click the Add button. You'll be presented with a dialog asking whether you want the snap-in to manage the local computer or a domain. Determine whether you want to apply the filtering settings to just the local computer or the entire domain, and click the Finish button. Click the Close button in the Add Standalone Snap-in list dialog as shown in Figure 3-2. You should now see the IP Security Policies snap-in listed in the Add/Remove Snap-in dialog, as shown in Figure 3-3. Click the OK button and you'll be returned to the original Management Console window. You should now see the IP Security Policies snap-in listed in the window.

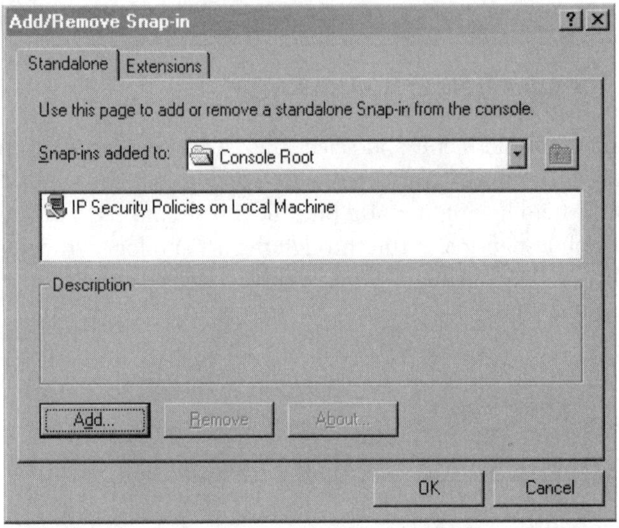

Figure 3-3. The Add/Remove Snap-in dialog with the IP Security Policies snap-in loaded

Before setting up firewall rules, you'll need to create a block action for them to use. To do this, right-click the IP Security Policies icon and select the "Manage IP filter lists and filter actions" item. After the dialog appears, click on the Manage Filter Actions tab. You should now see something similar to Figure 3-4.

If the Use Add Wizard checkbox is not checked, be sure to check it. Now click the Add button. Click the Next button after the wizard dialog opens. Then type "Block" for name of the new filter action. For the description, type "Blocks Access" or something similarly appropriate. After filling those in, click the Next button. Now click the Block radio button, and then click the Next button once again. After that, click the Finish button. You should now see the new filter action in the list that was shown in Figure 3-3. You may now click the Close button.

Now you can set up the firewall rules. Right-click the security policy icon and select the Create IP Security Policy item. This will bring up a wizard. Click the Next button and fill in the Name and Description; a good choice for both of them would be "Firewall". After filling those in, click the Next

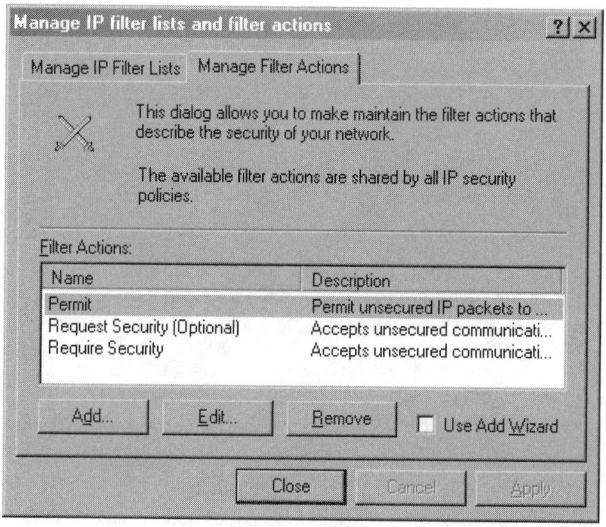

Figure 3-4. The Manage Filter Actions tab

button. You should now see a checkbox labeled "Activate the default
response rule". Uncheck this box and then click the Next button. After that,
click the Finish button. You should now see a dialog called Firewall Properties, as shown in Figure 3-5.

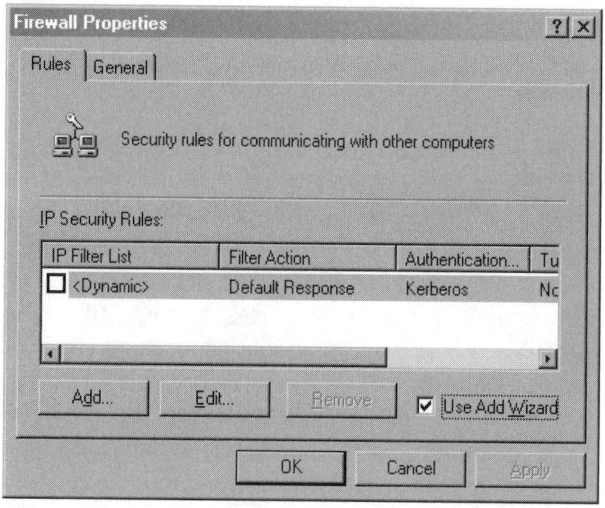

Figure 3-5. The Firewall Properties dialog

To create a new filtering rule, uncheck the Use Add Wizard box and click
the Add button. You should now see a dialog box that looks like Figure 3-6.

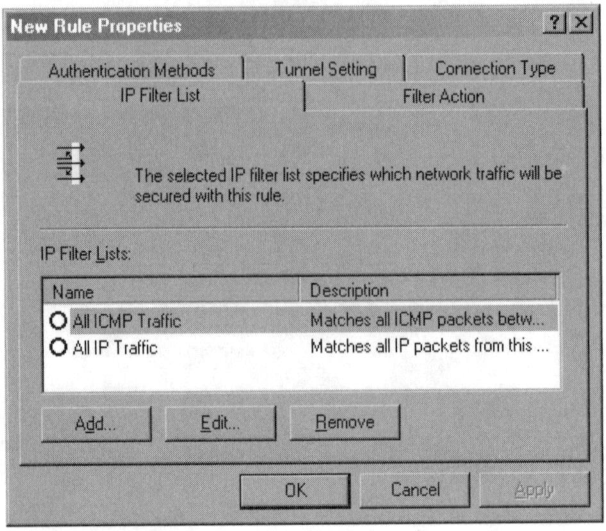

Figure 3-6. Adding a new rule

To select the IP addresses to match on, click the Add button in the IP Filter List tab. This will also let you define ports and protocols to match on. After you have selected the IP addresses and ports you want the rule to apply to, click the Filter Action tab and choose your selections from the list of actions.

HACK #37   Keep Your Network Self-Contained

Use egress filtering to mitigate attacks and information leaks coming from your network.

You're probably familiar with the concept of firewalling as it applies to blocking traffic coming into your network. Have you considered the benefits of filtering traffic that leaves your network? For instance, what would happen if someone compromised a host on your network and used it as a platform to attack other networks? What if a worm somehow made it onto your network and tried to infect hosts across the Internet? At the very least, you would probably receive some angry phone calls and emails. Luckily, filtering your outbound traffic—otherwise known as *egress filtering*—can help to contain such malicious behavior. Egress filtering can not only protect others from attacks originating from your network, but can also be used to enforce network usage policies and make sure information doesn't leak out of your network onto the wider Internet. In many situations, egress filtering is just as important as filtering inbound traffic.

The general guideline when crafting egress-filtering rules is the same as when constructing any inbound-filtering rule—devices should only be allowed to do what they were meant to do. That is, a mail server should only be allowed to serve and relay mail, a web server should only be allowed to serve web content, a DNS server should only service DNS requests, and so on. By ensuring that this policy is implemented, you can better contain the threats mentioned earlier.

It may also be a good idea to force users to use internal services rather than Internet services wherever possible. For example, if you are using your own DNS servers, clients shouldn't be able to connect to external DNS servers to resolve hostnames. If a client is allowed to do this, you risk the chance that they will reveal intranet hostnames to outside parties when the client attempts to resolve an internal hostname through an external DNS server.

For instance, this restriction can be accomplished in OpenBSD with a rule like this:

```
rdr on $INT_IF inet proto { tcp, udp } from $INT_IF:network to any port 53
-> $DNS_SERVER port 53
```

Of course, you'll need to set INT_IF to the interface facing your internal network and set DNS_SERVER to the IP address of your internal DNS server.

Similarly, if you're running an internal mail server, then company email need never cross the Internet. If you have gone to the trouble of setting up an internal email server, do you really want your employees to be able to connect to servers outside your network?

You can do this with a similar rule:

```
rdr on $INT_IF inet proto tcp from $INT_IF:network to any port 25 -> $SMTP_
HOST port 25
```

Egress filtering can also prevent IP spoofing. By filtering on your external interface at the border of your network, you can verify that packets leaving your network have source addresses that match your address space. By filtering all other traffic, you can ensure that any IP spoofing attack performed from your network or routed through it will be dropped before the packets are able to leave.

Test Your Firewall
HACK #38   Find out if your firewall really works the way you think it should.

So you've set up a firewall and done a few cursory tests to make sure it's working, but have you tested the firewall to be sure that it's blocking everything that it's supposed to? You may not have done this because you think it will take too long or be too difficult. Luckily there's *ftester (http:// ftester.sourceforge.net)*, a free tool for doing extensive firewall tests.

Ftester consists of three Perl scripts. The *ftest* script is used for injecting custom packets as defined in the configuration file *ftest.conf*. If you are testing how the firewall behaves with ingress traffic, you should run this script on a machine outside of your firewalled network. If you want to test your firewall's behavior toward egress traffic, you will need to run *ftest* from a machine within your firewall's protected network. One of the other scripts is *ftestd*, which listens for the packets injected with *ftest* that come through the firewall that you are testing. This script should be run on a machine within your internal network if you are testing the firewall's ingress behavior. If you are testing egress behavior, you'll need to run it on a machine external to your network. Both of these scripts keep a log of what they send or receive. After a test run, their respective logs can be compared using the *freport* script, to quickly see what packets were able to get through the firewall.

Before you can use *Ftester*, you will need the `Net::RawIP`, `Net::PcapUtils`, and `NetPacket` Perl modules. You will also need the `Net::Pcap` module if it is not already installed, since the `Net::PcapUtils` module depends on it. If you have the CPAN Perl module available, you can install these modules with the following commands:

```
# perl -MCPAN -e "install Net::RawIP"
# perl -MCPAN -e "install Net::PcapUtils"
# perl -MCPAN -e "install NetPacket"
```

Once these modules are available on the systems you will be using to conduct your firewall test, you will need to create a configuration file to tell *ftest* what packets it should generate.

The general form for a TCP or UDP packet in *ftest.conf* is:

```
source addr:source port:dest addr:dest port:flags:proto:tos
```

where `source addr` and `source port` are the source IP address and port, and `dest addr` and `dest port` are the destination IP address and port. Address ranges can be specified in the `low-high` format or by using CIDR notation. Port ranges can be specified using the `low-high` format as well. The *flags* field is where you specify the TCP that you want set for the packet. Valid values for this field are S for SYN, A for ACK, P for PSH, U for URG, R for RST, and F for FIN. The *proto* field specifies which protocol to use (either `TCP` or `UDP`), and *tos* contains the number to set the Type-of-Service (ToS) field in the IP header to. Sometimes routers will use the contents of this field to make decisions about traffic prioritization. You can get more information on the ToS field by reading RFC 791 (*http://www.ietf.org/rfc/rfc0791.txt*), which defines Internet Protocol.

ICMP packets can be defined in a similar manner. Here's the general form for one:

```
source addr::dest addr:::ICMP:type:code
```

Here you can see that the main difference between the two forms is the omission of port numbers and flags. This is because ICMP does not use port numbers and does not make use of flags. Instead, it uses types and codes, hence the addition of the *type* and *code* fields. Currently, there are over 40 ICMP types. Some that may be familiar to you are the ones used by the ping utility, echo (type 8) and echo reply (type 0), or the type used by the traceroute command (type 30). ICMP codes are like subclassifications of an ICMP type. Not all ICMP types have ICMP codes associated with them, although there are roughly the same number of ICMP codes as there are types. You can find out more about ICMP types and codes by reading the IANA's assignments for them (see *http://www.iana.org/assignments/icmp-parameters*).

Here's an *ftest.conf* that will check all of the unprivileged TCP ports on a machine with the IP address 10.1.1.1:

```
192.168.1.10:1025:10.1.1.1:1-1025:S:TCP:0
stop_signal=192.168.1.10:1025:10.1.1.1:22:S:TCP:0
```

The stop_signal creates a payload for the packet that will tell *ftestd* that the testing is over.

Before starting *ftest*, you should start *ftestd*:

```
# ./ftestd -i eth0
```

Now, to run *ftest*:

```
# ./ftest -f ftest.conf
```

This will create a log file called *ftest.log* containing an entry for every packet *ftest* sent. When *ftestd* receives the signal to stop, it will exit. You can then find its log of what packets it received in *ftestd.log*. Now you can copy the logs to the same machine and run them through *freport*. If you used a configuration file like the one shown earlier and were allowing SSH, SMPTP, and HTTP traffic, you might get a report similar to this:

```
# ./freport ftest.log ftestd.log

Authorized packets:
-------------------

22 - 192.168.1.10:1025 > 10.1.1.1:22 S TCP 0
25 - 192.168.1.10:1025 > 10.1.1.1:25 S TCP 0
80 - 192.168.1.10:1025 > 10.1.1.1:80 S TCP 0

Modified packets (probably NAT):
-------------------------------

Filtered or dropped packets:
---------------------------
```

```
1 - 192.168.1.10:1025 > 10.1.1.1:1 S TCP 0
2 - 192.168.1.10:1025 > 10.1.1.1:2 S TCP 0
3 - 192.168.1.10:1025 > 10.1.1.1:3 S TCP 0
```

If you are using a stateful firewall and want to test this functionality, you can also specify packets that have flags other than SYN set. For instance, if the previous example had used ACK or some other flag instead of SYN, it would be dropped by the firewall since only packets with the SYN flag set are used to initiate connections.

It's a good idea to run *ftest* each time you make changes to your firewall, or periodically just to make sure that your firewall works as you expect it to. While complex rulesets on your firewall can sometimes make it difficult to predict exactly how it will behave, *ftest* will tell you with good authority exactly what kind of traffic is permitted.

HACK #39   MAC Filtering with Netfilter

Keep unwanted machines off your network with MAC address whitelisting

Media Access Control (MAC) address filtering is a well-known method for protecting wireless networks. This type of filtering works on the default deny principle: you specify the hosts that are allowed to connect, while leaving unknown ones behind. MAC addresses are unique 48-bit numbers that have been assigned to every Ethernet device that has ever been manufactured, including 802.11 devices, and are usually written as six 8-bit hexadecimal digits separated by colons.

In addition to Linux's native IP packet filtering system, Netfilter also contains MAC address filtering functionality. While many of the wireless access points on the market today already support this, there are many older ones that do not. MAC filtering is also important if your access point is actually the Linux machine itself, using a wireless card. If you have a Linux-based firewall already set up, it's a trivial modification to enable it to filter at the MAC level. MAC address filtering with *iptables* is very much like IP-based filtering, and is just as easy to do.

This example demonstrates how to allow a particular MAC address if your firewall policy is set to DROP [Hack #33]:

```
iptables -A FORWARD -m state --state NEW \
   -m mac --mac-source 00:DE:AD:BE:EF:00 -j ACCEPT
```

This command will allow any traffic sent from the network interface with the address 00:DE:AD:BE:EF:00. Using rules like this one along with a default deny policy enables you to create a whitelist of the MAC addresses that you want to allow through your gateway. To create a blacklist, you can employ a default accept policy and change the MAC address matching rule's target to DENY.

This is all pretty straightforward if you already know the MAC addresses for which you want to create rules, but what if you don't? If you have access to the system, you can find out the MAC address of an interface by using the ifconfig command:

```
$ ifconfig eth0
eth0      Link encap:Ethernet  HWaddr 00:0C:29:E2:2B:C1
          inet addr:192.168.0.41  Bcast:192.168.0.255  Mask:255.255.255.0
          UP BROADCAST RUNNING MULTICAST  MTU:1500  Metric:1
          RX packets:132893 errors:0 dropped:0 overruns:0 frame:0
          TX packets:17007 errors:0 dropped:0 overruns:0 carrier:0
          collisions:0 txqueuelen:100
          RX bytes:46050011 (43.9 Mb)  TX bytes:1601488 (1.5 Mb)
          Interrupt:10 Base address:0x10e0
```

Here you can see that the MAC address for this interface is 00:0C:29:E2:2B:C1. The output of ifconfig is somewhat different on other operating systems, but they are all similar to some degree (this output was from a Linux system).

Finding the MAC address of a system remotely is slightly more involved and can be done by using the arp and ping commands. By pinging the remote system, its IP address will be resolved to a MAC address, which can then be looked up using the arp command.

For example, to look up the MAC address that corresponds to the IP address 192.168.0.61, you could run the following commands:

```
$ ping -c 1 192.168.0.61
$ /sbin/arp 192.168.0.61 | awk '{print $3}'
```

Or you could use this very small and handy shell script:

```
#!/bin/sh
ping -c $1 >/dev/null && /sbin/arp $1 | awk '{print $3}' \
   | grep -v Hwaddress
```

When implementing MAC address filtering, please be aware that it is not foolproof. Under many circumstances, it is quite trivial to change the MAC address that an interface uses by simply instructing the driver to do so. It is also possible to send out link-layer frames with forged MAC addresses by using raw link-layer sockets. Thus, MAC address filtering should only be considered as an additional measure that you can use to protect your network. Treat MAC filtering more as a "Keep Out" sign, rather than a good deadbolt.

Block OS Fingerprinting

HACK #40

Keep outsiders on a need-to-know basis regarding your operating systems.

When performing network reconnaissance, one very valuable piece of information for would-be attackers is the operating system running on each system discovered in their scans. From an attacker's point of view, this is very helpful in figuring out what vulnerabilities the system might have or which exploits may work on a system. Combined with the knowledge of open ports found during a port-scan, this information can be devastating. After all, an RPC exploit for SPARC Solaris isn't very likely to work for x86 Linux—the code for the portmap daemon isn't common to both systems, and they have different processor architectures. Armed with the knowledge of a given server's platform, attackers can very efficiently try the techniques most likely to grant them further access without wasting time on exploits that cannot work.

Traditionally, individuals performing network reconnaissance would simply connect to any services detected by their port-scan, to see which operating system the remote system is running. This works because many daemons, such as Sendmail, Telnet, and even FTP, readily announce the underlying operating system, as well as their own version numbers. Even though this method is easy and straightforward, it is now seen as intrusive since it's easy to spot someone connecting in the system log files. Additionally, most services can be configured not to disclose this sensitive information. In response, more sophisticated methods were developed that do not require a full connection to the target system to determine which operating system it is running. These methods rely on the eccentricities of the host operating system's TCP/IP stack and its behavior when responding to certain types of packets. Since individual operating systems respond to these packets in a particular way, it is possible to make a very good guess at what OS a particular server is running based on how it responds to *probe packets*, which normally don't show up in log files. Luckily, such probe packets can be blocked at the firewall to circumvent any operating system detection attempts that deploy methods like this.

One popular tool that employs such OS detection methods is Nmap (*http://www.insecure.org/nmap/*), which not only allows you to detect the operating system running on a remote system, but also perform various types of port-scans.

Attempting to detect an operating system with Nmap is as simple as running it with the -O switch. Here are the results of scanning an OpenBSD 3.3 system:

```
# nmap -O puffy

Starting nmap 3.48 ( http://www.insecure.org/nmap/ ) at 2003-12-02 19:14 MST
Interesting ports on puffy (192.168.0.42):
(The 1653 ports scanned but not shown below are in state: closed)
PORT     STATE SERVICE
13/tcp   open  daytime
22/tcp   open  ssh
37/tcp   open  time
113/tcp  open  auth
```

```
Device type: general purpose
Running: OpenBSD 3.X
OS details: OpenBSD 3.0 or 3.3

Nmap run completed -- 1 IP address (1 host up) scanned in 24.873 seconds
```

To thwart Nmap's efforts, we can employ firewall rules that block packets used for operating-system probes. These are fairly easy to spot, since several of them have invalid combinations of TCP flags. Some of the tests that Nmap performs cannot be blocked by PF by simply adding block rules, but they can be blocked if stateful filtering and a default deny policy have been implemented in the ruleset. This is because some of the tests make use of TCP options, which cannot be filtered with PF.

To block these fingerprinting attempts with OpenBSD's PF, we can put rules similar to these in our */etc/pf.conf*:

```
set block-policy  return

block in log quick proto tcp flags FUP/WEUAPRSF
block in log quick proto tcp flags WEUAPRSF/WEUAPRSF
block in log quick proto tcp flags SRAFU/WEUAPRSF
block in log quick proto tcp flags /WEUAPRSF
block in log quick proto tcp flags SR/SR
block in log quick proto tcp flags SF/SF
```

This also has the side effect of logging any attempts to the pflog0 interface. Even if we can't block all of Nmap's tests, we can at least log some of the more unique attempts, and possibly confuse it by providing an incomplete picture of our operating system's TCP stack behavior. Packets that have triggered these rules can be viewed with *tcpdump* by running the following commands:

```
# ifconfig pflog0 up
# tcpdump -n -i pflog0
```

Now let's look at the results of an Nmap scan after enabling these rules:

```
# nmap -O puffy

Starting nmap 3.48 ( http://www.insecure.org/nmap/ ) at 2003-12-02 22:56 MST
Interesting ports on puffy (192.168.0.42):
(The 1653 ports scanned but not shown below are in state: closed)
PORT    STATE SERVICE
13/tcp  open  daytime
22/tcp  open  ssh
37/tcp  open  time
113/tcp open  auth
No exact OS matches for host (If you know what OS is running on it, see
http://www.insecure.org/cgi-bin/nmap-submit.cgi).
TCP/IP fingerprint:
SInfo(V=3.48%P=i686-pc-linux-gnu%D=12/2%Time=3FCD7B3F%O=13%C=1)
TSeq(Class=TR%IPID=RD%TS=2HZ)
```

```
T1(Resp=Y%DF=Y%W=403D%ACK=S++%Flags=AS%Ops=MNWNNT)
T2(Resp=Y%DF=Y%W=0%ACK=S%Flags=AR%Ops=)
T3(Resp=Y%DF=Y%W=0%ACK=0%Flags=AR%Ops=)
T4(Resp=Y%DF=Y%W=4000%ACK=0%Flags=R%Ops=)
T5(Resp=Y%DF=Y%W=0%ACK=S++%Flags=AR%Ops=)
T6(Resp=Y%DF=Y%W=0%ACK=0%Flags=R%Ops=)
T7(Resp=Y%DF=Y%W=0%ACK=S++%Flags=AR%Ops=)
PU(Resp=Y%DF=N%TOS=0%IPLEN=38%RIPTL=134%RID=E%RIPCK=F%UCK=E%ULEN=134%DAT=E)
```

```
Nmap run completed -- 1 IP address (1 host up) scanned in 27.028 seconds
```

As you can see, this time the attempt was unsuccessful. But if you are feeling particularly devious, simply confusing Nmap attempts may not be enough. What if you want to actually trick would-be attackers into believing that a server is running a different OS entirely? For example, this could be useful when setting up a honeypot [Hack #94] to attract miscreants away from your critical servers. If this sounds like fun to you, read on.

HACK #41 Fool Remote Operating System Detection Software

Evade remote OS detection attempts by disguising your TCP/IP stack.

Another method to thwart operating system detection attempts is to modify the behavior of your system's TCP/IP stack and make it emulate the behavior of another operating system. This may sound difficult, but can be done fairly easily in Linux by patching your kernel with code available from the IP Personality project (*http://ippersonality.sourceforge.net*). This code extends the kernel's built-in firewalling system, Netfilter, as well as its user-space component, the iptables command.

To set up IP Personality, download the package that corresponds to your kernel. If you can't find the correct one, visit the SourceForge patches page for the project (*http://sourceforge.net/tracker/?group_id=7557&atid=307557*), which usually has more recent kernel patches available.

To patch your kernel, unpack the IP Personality source distribution and go to the directory containing your kernel source; then run the patch command:

```
# cd /usr/src/linux
# patch -p1 < \
../ippersonality-20020819-2.4.19/patches/ippersonality-20020819-linux-2.4.
19.diff
```

If you are using a patch downloaded from the patches page, just substitute it in your patch command. To verify that the patch has been applied correctly, you can run this command:

```
# find ./ -name \*.rej
```

If the patch was applied correctly, this command should not find any files.

Now that the kernel is patched, you will need to configure the kernel for IP Personality support. As mentioned in "Lock Down Your Kernel with grsecurity" [Hack #13], running make xconfig, make menuconfig, or even make config while you are in the kernel source's directory will allow you to configure your kernel. Regardless of the method you choose, the menu options will remain the same.

First, be sure that "Prompt for development and/or incomplete code/drivers" is enabled under "Code maturity level options". Under Networking Options, find and enable the option for Netfilter Configuration.

The list displayed by make xconfig is shown in Figure 3-7. Find the option labeled IP "Personality Support", and either select y to statically compile it into your kernel, or select m to create a dynamically loaded module.

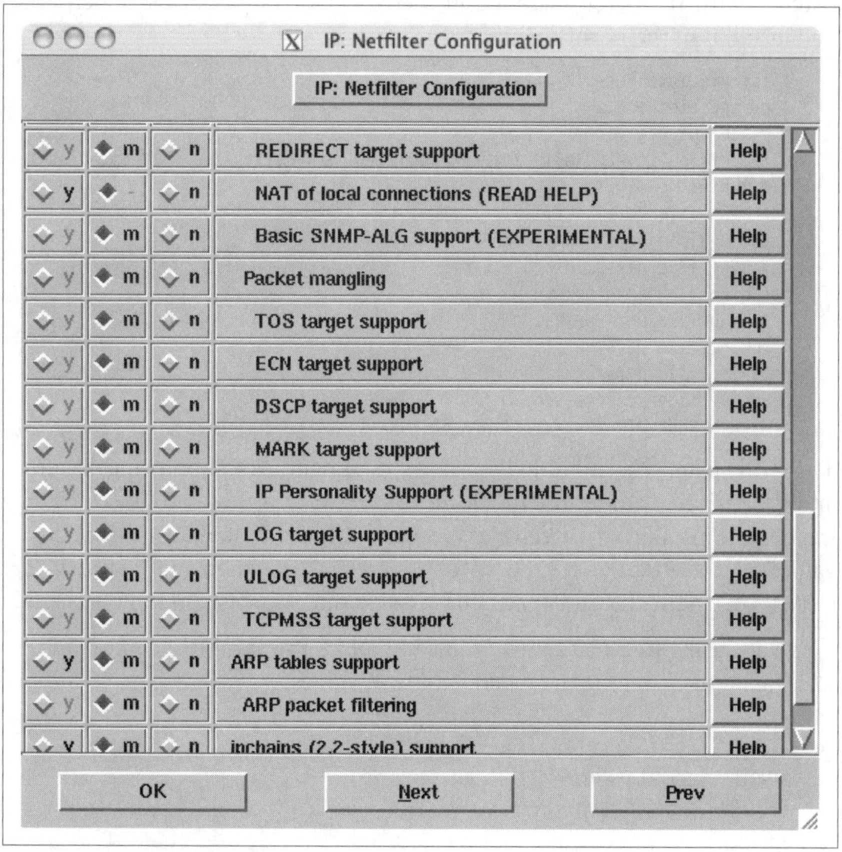

Figure 3-7. Enable IP Personality Support

After you have configured in support for IP Personality, save your configuration. Now compile the kernel and modules, and install them by running commands similar to these:

```
# make dep && make clean
# make bzImage && make modules
# cp arch/i386/boot/bzImage /boot/vmlinuz
# make modules_install
```

Now reboot with your new kernel. In addition to patching your kernel, you'll also need to patch the user-space portion of Netfilter, the iptables command. To do this, go to the Netfilter web site (*http://www.netfilter.org*) and download the version specified by the patch that came with your IP Personality package. For instance, the iptables patch included in *ippersonality-20020819-2.4.19.tar.gz* is for Netfilter Version 1.2.2.

After downloading the proper version and unpacking it, you will need to patch it with the patch included in the IP Personality package. Then build and install it in the normal way:

```
# tar xfj iptables-1.2.2.tar.bz2
# cd iptables-1.2.2
# patch -p1 < \
../ippersonality-20020819-2.4.19/patches/ippersonality-20020427-iptables-\
1.2.2.diff
patching file pers/Makefile
patching file pers/example.conf
patching file pers/libipt_PERS.c
patching file pers/pers.h
patching file pers/pers.l
patching file pers/pers.y
patching file pers/pers_asm.c
patching file pers/perscc.c
# make KERNEL_DIR=/usr/src/linux && make install
```

This will install the modified iptables command, its supporting libraries, and the manpage under the */usr/local* hierarchy. If you would like to change the default installation directories, you can edit the Makefile and change the values of the BINDIR, LIBDIR, MANDIR, and INCDIR macros. Be sure to set KERNEL_DIR to the directory containing the kernel sources you built earlier.

If you are using Red Hat Linux, you can replace the iptables command that is installed by changing the macros to these values:

```
LIBDIR:=/lib
BINDIR:=/sbin
MANDIR:=/usr/share/man
INCDIR:=/usr/include
```

In addition to running make install, you may also want to create a directory for the operating system personality configuration files. These files are located in the *samples/* directory within the IP Personality distribution. For example, you could create a directory called */etc/personalities* and copy them there.

Before setting up IP Personality, try running Nmap against the machine to see which operating system it detects:

```
# nmap -O colossus

Starting nmap 3.48 ( http://www.insecure.org/nmap/ ) at 2003-12-12 18:36 MST
Interesting ports on colossus (192.168.0.64):
(The 1651 ports scanned but not shown below are in state: closed)
PORT     STATE SERVICE
22/tcp   open  ssh
25/tcp   open  smtp
111/tcp  open  rpcbind
139/tcp  open  netbios-ssn
505/tcp  open  mailbox-lm
631/tcp  open  ipp
Device type: general purpose
Running: Linux 2.4.X|2.5.X
OS details: Linux Kernel 2.4.0 - 2.5.20
Uptime 3.095 days (since Tue Dec 9 16:19:55 2003)

Nmap run completed -- 1 IP address (1 host up) scanned in 7.375 seconds
```

If your machine has an IP address of 192.168.0.64 and you want it to pretend that it's running Mac OS 9, you can run iptables commands like these:

```
# iptables -t mangle -A PREROUTING -d 192.168.0.64 -j PERS \
  --tweak dst --local --conf /etc/personalities/macos9.conf
# iptables -t mangle -A OUTPUT -s 192.168.0.64 -j PERS \
  --tweak src --local --conf /etc/personalities/macos9.conf
```

Now run Nmap again:

```
# nmap -O colossus

Starting nmap 3.48 ( http://www.insecure.org/nmap/ ) at 2003-12-12 18:47 MST
Interesting ports on colossus (192.168.0.64):
(The 1651 ports scanned but not shown below are in state: closed)
PORT     STATE SERVICE
22/tcp   open  ssh
25/tcp   open  smtp
111/tcp  open  rpcbind
139/tcp  open  netbios-ssn
505/tcp  open  mailbox-lm
631/tcp  open  ipp
Device type: general purpose
Running: Apple Mac OS 9.X
OS details: Apple Mac OS 9 - 9.1
Uptime 3.095 days (since Tue Dec 9 16:19:55 2003)

Nmap run completed -- 1 IP address (1 host up) scanned in 5.274 seconds
```

You can of course emulate other operating systems that aren't provided with the IP Personality package. All you need is a copy of Nmap's operating system fingerprints file, *nmap-os-fingerprints*, and then you can construct your own IP Personality configuration file for any operating system Nmap knows about.

HACK #42 Keep an Inventory of Your Network

Use Nmap to keep track of the devices and services on your network.

As we saw in "Block OS Fingerprinting" [Hack #40], Nmap (*http://www. insecure.org/nmap/*) is free a tool that can be used to conduct various sorts of scans on networks. Normally when people think of using Nmap, they assume it's used to conduct some sort of nefarious network reconnaissance in preparation for an attack. But as with all powerful tools, Nmap can be used for far more than breaking into networks.

For example, simple TCP connect scans can be conducted without needing root privileges:

```
$ nmap rigel

Starting nmap 3.48 ( http://www.insecure.org/nmap/ ) at 2003-12-15 17:42 MST
Interesting ports on rigel (192.168.0.61):
(The 1595 ports scanned but not shown below are in state: filtered)
PORT       STATE  SERVICE
7/tcp      open   echo
9/tcp      open   discard
13/tcp     open   daytime
19/tcp     open   chargen
21/tcp     open   ftp
22/tcp     open   ssh
23/tcp     open   telnet
25/tcp     open   smtp
37/tcp     open   time
79/tcp     open   finger
111/tcp    open   rpcbind
512/tcp    open   exec
513/tcp    open   login
514/tcp    open   shell
587/tcp    open   submission
4045/tcp   open   lockd
7100/tcp   open   font-service
32771/tcp open   sometimes-rpc5
32772/tcp open   sometimes-rpc7
32773/tcp open   sometimes-rpc9
32774/tcp open   sometimes-rpc11
32775/tcp open   sometimes-rpc13
32776/tcp open   sometimes-rpc15
32777/tcp open   sometimes-rpc17

Nmap run completed -- 1 IP address (1 host up) scanned in 75.992 seconds
```

This is tremendously useful for checking on the state of your own machines. You could probably guess that this scan was performed on a Solaris machine, and one that needs to have some services disabled at that.

Nmap can also scan ranges of IP addresses by specifying the range or using CIDR notation:

```
nmap 192.168.0.1-254
nmap 192.168.0.0/24
```

Nmap can provide much more information if it is run as root. When run as root, it can use special packets to determine the operating system of the remote machine by using the -O flag. Additionally, you can do half-open TCP scanning by using the -sS flag. When doing a half-open scan, Nmap will send a SYN packet to the remote host and wait to receive the ACK from it; if it receives an ACK, it knows that the port is open. This is different from a normal three-way TCP handshake, where the client will send a SYN packet and then send an ACK back to the server once it has received the initial server ACK. Attackers typically use this option to avoid having their scans logged on the remote machine.

Try it out for yourself:

```
# nmap -sS -O rigel

Starting nmap V. 3.00 ( www.insecure.org/nmap/ )
Interesting ports on rigel.nnc (192.168.0.61):
(The 1578 ports scanned but not shown below are in state: filtered)
Port        State    Service
7/tcp       open     echo
9/tcp       open     discard
13/tcp      open     daytime
19/tcp      open     chargen
21/tcp      open     ftp
22/tcp      open     ssh
23/tcp      open     telnet
25/tcp      open     smtp
37/tcp      open     time
79/tcp      open     finger
111/tcp     open     sunrpc
512/tcp     open     exec
513/tcp     open     login
514/tcp     open     shell
587/tcp     open     submission
7100/tcp    open     font-service
32771/tcp   open     sometimes-rpc5
32772/tcp   open     sometimes-rpc7
32773/tcp   open     sometimes-rpc9
32774/tcp   open     sometimes-rpc11
32775/tcp   open     sometimes-rpc13
32776/tcp   open     sometimes-rpc15
```

```
32777/tcp  open        sometimes-rpc17
Remote operating system guess: Solaris 9 Beta through Release on SPARC
Uptime 44.051 days (since Sat Nov  1 16:41:50 2003)

Nmap run completed -- 1 IP address (1 host up) scanned in 166 seconds
```

With OS detection enabled, Nmap has confirmed that the operating system is Solaris, but now you also know that it's probably Version 9 running on a SPARC processor.

One powerful feature that can be used to help keep track of your network is Nmap's XML output capabilities. This is activated by using the -oX command-line switch:

```
# nmap -sS -O -oX scandata.xml rigel
```

This is especially useful when scanning a range of IP addresses or your whole network, because you can put all the information gathered from the scan into a single XML file that can be parsed and inserted into a database. Here's what an XML entry for an open port looks like:

```
<port protocol="tcp" portid="22">
<state state="open" />
<service name="ssh" method="table" conf="3"  />
</port>
```

Nmap is a powerful tool. By using its XML output capabilities, a little bit of scripting, and a database, you can create an even more powerful tool that can monitor your network for unauthorized services and machines.

HACK #43   Scan Your Network for Vulnerabilities

Use Nessus to quickly and easily scan your network for services that are vulnerable to attack.

As a network administrator, you not only need to know which hosts are on your network and the services they are running, but also if those services are vulnerable to exploits. While Nmap [Hack #40] can only show you what machines and ports are reachable on your network, a security scanner such as *Nessus* (*http://www.nessus.org*) can tell you if those machines are vulnerable to known exploits.

Unlike a regular port scanner, a security scanner first locates listening services, and then connects to those services and attempts to execute all known exploits. It then records whether the exploit was successful and continues scanning until all available services have been tested. The key benefit here is that you'll know at a glance how your systems perform against the most recent exploits, and thus know whether they truly are vulnerable to attack.

If you're feeling a bit adventurous, *Nessus* can be installed by simply typing the following command:

```
$ lynx -source http://install.nessus.org | sh
```

This will completely automate the installation of *Nessus*, but isn't really a good idea since you don't know what you'll be executing on your system until you actually run it. A better way to install *Nessus* that retains the benefits of the automated installer is to download the *nessus-installer.sh* script and execute it manually. After you've downloaded the installer script and run it, you will be asked where you want to install *Nessus* (the default is */usr/local*) and prompted for your root password. The script will then create a temporary SUID shell that is accessible only through your user account. This may sound alarming at first, but it tells you the filename for the shell, so you can verify that it is indeed accessible only to you and make sure that it is deleted when the installation has completed.

After installation has finished, you'll need to create a *Nessus* user (not the same thing as a Unix account). Since *Nessus* uses a client-server model, you'll also need to generate a certificate so that all communications can be encrypted.

To create a new *Nessus* user, run nessus-adduser. It will then prompt you for a name and a password. To create a certificate, you can run nessus-mkcert, or if you have your own Certificate Authority (CA) **[Hack #45]**, you can use that to create a certificate for *Nessus* to use. If you do use your own CA, you'll need to edit *nessus.conf* to tell it where to look for the CA certificate and the certificate and key that you generated.

The configuration file usually lives in */etc* or */usr/local/etc*. To tell *Nessus* where its certificates are, add lines similar to the following:

```
cert_file=/etc/ssl/nessus.key
key_file=/etc/ssl/nessus.crt
ca_file=/etc/ssl/ca.crt
```

If you generated a certificate-key pair and used a password, you can specify that password here as well:

```
pem_password=mypassword
```

After you've done all of that, you can start the *Nessus* daemon. This is the business end of *Nessus* and is what will actually perform the scans against the hosts on your network.

You can start it by running something similar to this command:

```
# /usr/local/sbin/nessusd -D
```

Now you can start the *Nessus* client and connect to the server. There are several *Nessus* clients available, including a command-line interface, an X11 application, and a Windows client. The figures in this hack show the X11 interface. You can start the client by simply typing nessus. After you've done that, you should see a window like the one shown in Figure 3-8.

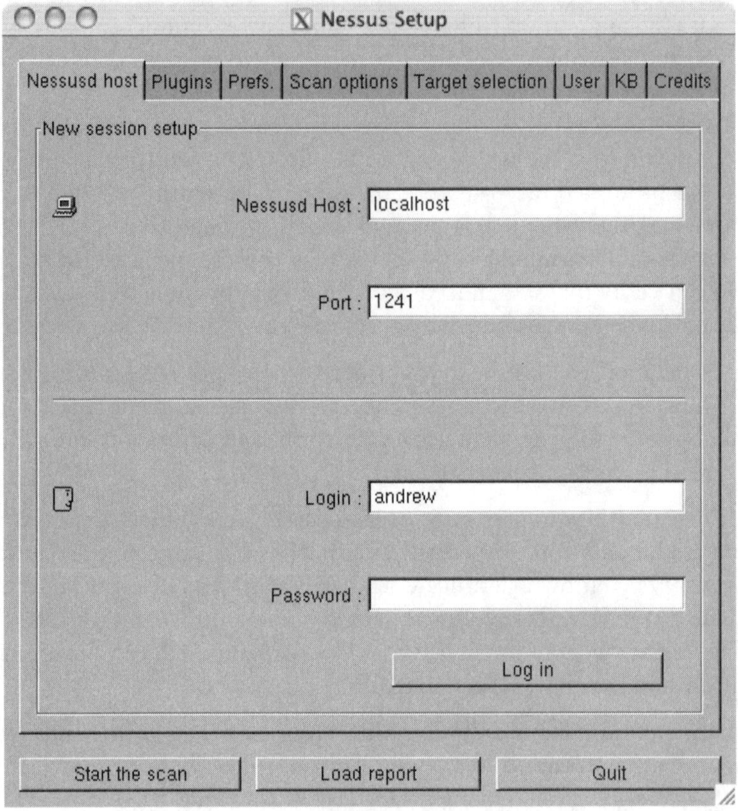

Figure 3-8. Nessus client setup

You'll need to fill in the information for the user that you created and click the "Log In" button. After that, you'll be presented with a dialog that allows you to verify the information contained in the server's certificate.

To select which types of vulnerabilities to scan for, click on the Plugins tab, and you'll see something similar to Figure 3-9.

In the top pane you can enable or disable types of scans, and in the bottom pane you can disable individual vulnerability checks that belong to the category selected in the top pane. One thing to note: scans listed in the bottom pane that have an exclamation icon next to them will potentially crash the server that they are run against. If you want to enable all scans except for

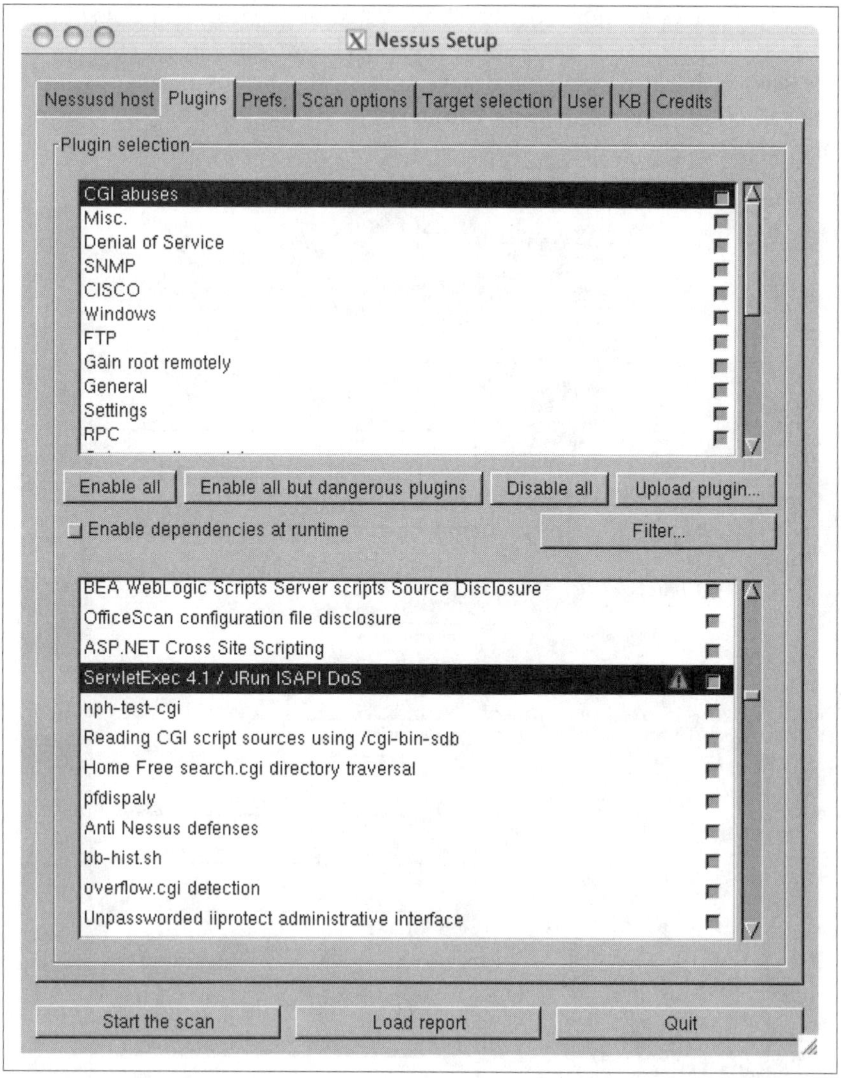

Figure 3-9. Nessus plugin selection

these, you can click the "Enable all but dangerous plugins" button. If you're running *Nessus* on a noncritical machine, you can probably leave these scans on, but you have been warned! You'll probably want to disable several types of scans unless you need to scan a machine or group of machines that run a wide variety of services; otherwise, you'll waste time having *Nessus* scan for services that you aren't running. For instance, if you wanted to scan a Solaris system, you might disable CGI abuses, CISCO, Windows, Peer-To-Peer File Sharing, Backdoors, Firewalls, Windows User Management, and Netware plug-ins.

In order for *Nessus* to more thoroughly test your services, you can supply it with login information for various services. This way, it can actually log into the service that it is testing and have access just like any normal user. You can tell *Nessus* about the accounts to use with the Prefs tab, as shown in Figure 3-10.

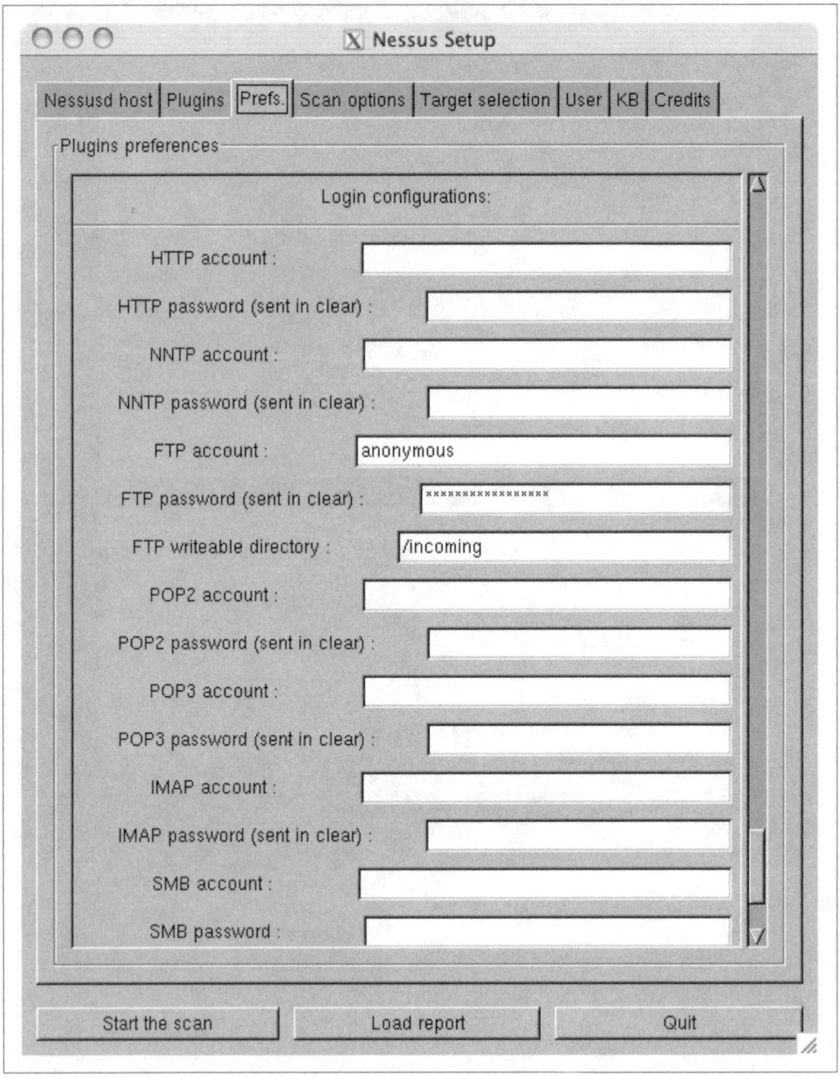

```
┌────────────────────────────────────────────────────────────────────────┐
│ ○ ○ ○                    X Nessus Setup                                  │
│                                                                          │
│ Nessusd host │ Plugins │ Prefs. │ Scan options │ Target selection │ User │ KB │ Credits │
│ ┌Plugins preferences──────────────────────────────────────────────────┐ │
│ │                     Login configurations:                          △ │ │
│ │                                                                      │ │
│ │       HTTP account :        [                                   ]    │ │
│ │   HTTP password (sent in clear) :  [                          ]      │ │
│ │       NNTP account :        [                                   ]    │ │
│ │   NNTP password (sent in clear) :  [                          ]      │ │
│ │        FTP account :        [ anonymous                        ]     │ │
│ │   FTP password (sent in clear) :   [ ***************** ]             │ │
│ │     FTP writeable directory :      [ /incoming                 ]     │ │
│ │       POP2 account :        [                                   ]    │ │
│ │   POP2 password (sent in clear) :  [                          ]      │ │
│ │       POP3 account :        [                                   ]    │ │
│ │   POP3 password (sent in clear) :  [                          ]      │ │
│ │       IMAP account :        [                                   ]    │ │
│ │   IMAP password (sent in clear) :  [                          ]      │ │
│ │        SMB account :        [                                   ]    │ │
│ │        SMB password :       [                                   ] ▽  │ │
│ └──────────────────────────────────────────────────────────────────────┘ │
│                                                                          │
│ │  Start the scan   │  │   Load report   │  │      Quit      │          │
└────────────────────────────────────────────────────────────────────────┘
```

Figure 3-10. Nessus's Prefs tab

In addition, you can tell *Nessus* to attempt brute-force logins to the services it is scanning. This can be a good test—not only of the services themselves, but also of your intrusion detection system (IDS) **[Hack #82]** and your system logs.

The "Scan options" tab lets you configure how *Nessus* will conduct its port-scans. Most of these settings can be left at their default value, unless you are also checking to see whether *Nessus* can evade detection by the hosts that you are scanning. For instance, *Nessus* is configured by default to perform full TCP connect scans and to ping the remote host that it is scanning. You can change this behavior by going to the "Scan options" tab, enabling "SYN scans" instead of "TCP connect", and disabling the ping. To specify which hosts you want to scan, you can use the "Target selection" tab.

After you've made your selections, try scanning a host by clicking "Start the scan" at the bottom of the window. You should now see a window similar to Figure 3-11. In this case, *Nessus* is performing a scan against a Solaris machine.

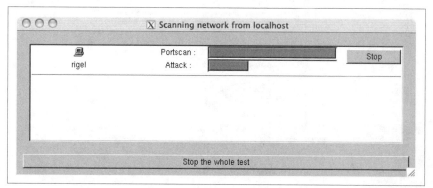

Figure 3-11. Performing a vulnerability scan

The results of the scan are shown in Figure 3-12.

If you scanned multiple subnets, you can select those in the Subnet pane. Any hosts that are in the selected subnet will then appear in the Host pane. Similarly, when you select a host, the list of open ports on it will appear in the Port pane. You can select these to view the warnings, notes, and possible security holes that were found regarding the selected port. You can view the information that *Nessus* provides for these by clicking on them in the Severity pane. Don't be too alarmed by most of *Nessus's* security notes and warnings; they are designed mainly to let you know what services you are running and to tell you if that service might present a potential vulnerability. Security holes are far more serious and should be investigated.

To save the report that you are viewing, click the "Save report" button. *Nessus* will let you save reports in a variety of formats. If you want to view the report in *Nessus* again at a later date, you should use *Nessus's* own report format (NBE). Reports in this format can be viewed by using the "Load report" button in the main *Nessus* client window. Additionally, you can save reports in XML, HTML, ASCII, and even LaTeX format.

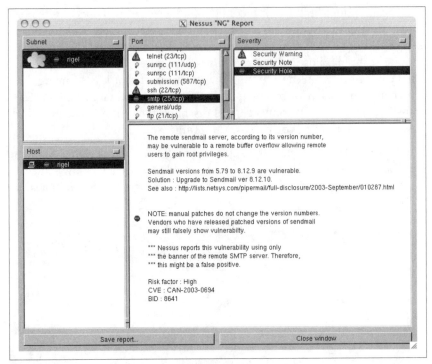

Figure 3-12. The vulnerability scan results

While Nmap is probably the champion of host and port detection, *Nessus* goes even further to demonstrate whether your own services are vulnerable to known attacks. Of course, new exploits surface all of the time, so it is important to keep your *Nessus* plug-ins up-to-date. Using *Nessus*, you can protect your own services by attempting to break into them before the bad boys do.

HACK #44   Keep Server Clocks Synchronized

Make log analysis easier by keeping the time on your systems in sync.

Correlating events that occurred on multiple servers can be a chore if there are discrepancies between the machines' clocks. Keeping the clocks on your systems synchronized can save valuable time when analyzing router, firewall, and host logs after a compromise, or when debugging everyday networking issues. Luckily, it's not that hard to do this with a little help from NTP, the Network Time Protocol.

NTP is a peer-to-peer protocol designed to provide subsecond precision and accuracy between host clocks. To get this going, all you need is the NTP distribution (*http://www.ntp.org/downloads.html*), which contains a daemon for performing clock synchronization, plus other supporting tools. While NTP might not be installed on your system, it usually comes with the various Linux distributions, FreeBSD, and OpenBSD as an optional package or port, so poke around your installation media or the ports tree if it's not already installed. If it isn't available with your OS of choice, you can still download and compile it yourself.

Configuring ntpd as a client is a fairly simple process. However, first you'll need to find out whether you have a local time server, either on your network or at your ISP. If you don't, you'll have to locate an NTP server that will let you query from it. Don't worry, though—a list of all the publicly accessible time servers is available at *http://www.eecis.udel.edu/~mills/ntp/servers.html*. One new term you will encounter when looking for a server is *stratum* (e.g., stratum 1 or stratum 2). This refers to the hierarchy of the server within the public NTP infrastructure. Stratum 1 servers are usually machines that have a direct time-sync source, such as a GPS or atomic clock signal that provides updates to the daemon running on that machine. Stratum 2 servers obtain their time sync from stratum 1 servers. Using stratum 2 servers helps to reduce the load on stratum 1 servers and is still accurate enough for our purposes. In addition, you'll want to find servers that are as geographically close to you as possible.

With this in mind, let's look for some NTP servers that we can use (using more than one is generally a good idea, in case one fails). I live in Colorado, so after following the link to the stratum 2 server list (*http://www.eecis.udel.edu/~mills/ntp/clock2a.html*), I find two entries:

```
# US CO ntp1.linuxmedialabs.com
Location: Linux Media Labs LLC, Colorado Springs, CO
Service Area: US
Synchronization: NTP Secondary (stratum 2), i686/Linux
Access Policy: open access
Contact: ntp@linuxmedialabs.com
Note: ntp1 is an alias and the IP address may change, please use DNS

# US CO ntp1.tummy.com
Location: tummy.com, ltd., Fort Collins, CO
Service Area: US
Synchronization: NTP Secondary (stratum 2), i686/Linux
Access Policy: open access.
Contact: ntp@tummy.com
Note: ntp1 is an alias and the IP address may change, please use DNS.
```

Since they're both listed as open access, I can just add them to */etc/ntp.conf*:

```
server ntp1.linuxmedialabs.com
server ntp1.tummy.com
```

In addition, ntpd can automatically correct for the specific clock frequency drift of your machine. It does this by learning the average drift over time as it receives sync messages. To enable this, add a line similar to the following to your *ntp.conf*:

```
driftfile /etc/ntp.drift
```

Of course, if you're keeping all of your ntpd configuration files in */etc/ntp*, you'll want to use a directory similar to */etc/ntp/ntp.drift* instead.

That's it. Simply add ntpd to your startup scripts, start it up, and you're ready to go.

HACK #45   Create Your Own Certificate Authority

Sign your own certificates to use in securing your network.

SSL certificates are usually thought of as being used for secure communications over the HTTP protocol. However, they are also useful in providing both a means for authentication and a means for initiating key exchange for a myriad of other services where encryption is desired, such as POP and IMAP [Hack #47], SMTP [Hack #48], IPSec (see Chapter 6), and, of course, SSL tunnels [Hack #76]. To make the best use of SSL, you will need to properly manage your own certificates.

If an SSL client needs to verify the authenticity of an SSL server, the cert used by the server needs to be signed by a Certificate Authority (CA) that is already trusted by the client. Well-known Certificate Authorities (such as Thawte and VeriSign) exist to serve as an authoritative, trusted third party for authentication. They are in the business of signing SSL certificates that are used on sites dealing with sensitive information (such as account numbers or passwords). If a site's SSL certificate is signed by a trusted authority, then presumably it is possible to verify the identity of a server supplying that cert's credentials. However, for anything other than e-commerce applications, a self-signed certificate is usually sufficient for gaining all of the security advantages that SSL provides. But even a self-signed cert must be signed by an authority that the client recognizes.

OpenSSL, a free SSL implementation, is perfectly capable of generating everything you need to run your own Certificate Authority. The *CA.pl* utility makes the process very simple.

In these examples, you'll need to type anything in boldface, and enter passwords wherever appropriate (they don't echo to the screen). To establish your new Certificate Authority, first change to the *misc/* directory under wherever OpenSSL is installed (*/System/Library/OpenSSL/* on OpenBSD; */usr/ssl/* or */usr/local/ssl/* on most Linux systems). Then use these commands:

```
$ ./CA.pl -newca
CA certificate filename (or enter to create)
```

```
Making CA certificate ...
Generating a 1024 bit RSA private key
..........++++++
....................++++++
writing new private key to './demoCA/private/cakey.pem'
Enter PEM pass phrase:
Verifying - Enter PEM pass phrase:
-----
You are about to be asked to enter information that will be incorporated
into your certificate request.
What you are about to enter is what is called a Distinguished Name or a DN.
There are quite a few fields but you can leave some blank
For some fields there will be a default value,
If you enter '.', the field will be left blank.
-----
Country Name (2 letter code) []:US
State or Province Name (full name) []:Colorado
Locality Name (eg, city) []:Denver
Organization Name (eg, company) []:NonExistant Enterprises
Organizational Unit Name (eg, section) []:IT Services
Common Name (eg, fully qualified host name) []:ca.nonexistantdomain.com
Email Address []:certadmin@nonexistantdomain.com
```

Note that you don't necessarily need root permissions, but you will need write permissions on the current directory.

Congratulations! You're the proud owner of your very own Certificate Authority. Take a look around:

```
$ ls -l demoCA/
total 16
-rw-r--r--  1 andrew  andrew  1399  3 Dec 19:52 cacert.pem
drwxr-xr-x  2 andrew  andrew    68  3 Dec 19:49 certs
drwxr-xr-x  2 andrew  andrew    68  3 Dec 19:49 crl
-rw-r--r--  1 andrew  andrew     0  3 Dec 19:49 index.txt
drwxr-xr-x  2 andrew  andrew    68  3 Dec 19:49 newcerts
drwxr-xr-x  3 andrew  andrew   102  3 Dec 19:49 private
-rw-r--r--  1 andrew  andrew     3  3 Dec 19:49 serial
```

The public key for your new Certificate Authority is contained in *cacert.pem*, and the private key is in *private/cakey.pem*. You can now use this private key to sign other SSL certs.

By default, *CA.pl* will create keys that are good for only one year. To change this behavior, edit *CA.pl* and change the line that reads:

```
$DAYS="-days 365";
```

Alternatively, you can forego *CA.pl* altogether and generate the public and private keys manually with a command like this:

```
$ openssl req -new -x509 -keyout cakey.pem -out \
  cakey.pem -days 3650
```

This will create a key pair that is good for the next 10 years, which can of course be changed by using a different argument to the -days switch. Additionally, you should change the private key's permissions to 600, to ensure that it is protected from being read by anyone.

So far, we have only created the Certificate Authority. To actually create keys that you can use with your services, you need to create a certificate-signing request and a key. Again, this can be done easily with *CA.pl*. First, a certificate-signing request is created:

```
$ ./CA.pl -newreq-nodes
Generating a 1024 bit RSA private key
...++++++
.................................................++++++
writing new private key to 'newreq.pem'
-----
You are about to be asked to enter information that will be incorporated
into your certificate request.
What you are about to enter is what is called a Distinguished Name or a DN.
There are quite a few fields but you can leave some blank
For some fields there will be a default value,
If you enter '.', the field will be left blank.
-----
Country Name (2 letter code) [AU]:US
State or Province Name (full name) [Some-State]:Colorado
Locality Name (eg, city) []:Denver
Organization Name (eg, company) [Internet Widgits Pty Ltd]:NonExistant
Enterprises
Organizational Unit Name (eg, section) []:IT Services
Common Name (eg, YOUR name) []:mail.nonexistantdomain.com
Email Address []:postmaster@nonexistantdomain.com

Please enter the following 'extra' attributes
to be sent with your certificate request
A challenge password []:
An optional company name []:NonExistant Enterprises
Request (and private key) is in newreq.pem
```

If you wish to encrypt the private key, you can use the -newreq switch in place of -newreq-nodes. However, if you encrypt the private key, you will have to enter the password for it each time the service that uses it is started. If you decide not to use an encrypted private key, be extremely cautious with your private key, as anyone who can obtain a copy of it can impersonate your server.

Now, to actually sign the request and generate the signed certificate:

```
$ ./CA.pl -sign
Using configuration from /System/Library/OpenSSL/openssl.cnf
Enter pass phrase for ./demoCA/private/cakey.pem:
Check that the request matches the signature
Signature ok
```

```
Certificate Details:
        Serial Number: 1 (0x1)
        Validity
            Not Before: Dec  3 09:05:08 2003 GMT
            Not After : Dec  3 09:05:08 2004 GMT
        Subject:
            countryName               = US
            stateOrProvinceName       = Colorado
            localityName              = Denver
            organizationName          = NonExistant Enterprises
            organizationalUnitName    = IT Services
            commonName                = mail.nonexistantdomain.com
            emailAddress              = postmaster@nonexistantdomain.com
        X509v3 extensions:
            X509v3 Basic Constraints:
            CA:FALSE
            Netscape Comment:
            OpenSSL Generated Certificate
            X509v3 Subject Key Identifier:
            94:0F:E9:F5:22:40:2C:71:D0:A7:5C:65:02:3E:BC:D8:DB:10:BD:88
            X509v3 Authority Key Identifier:
            keyid:7E:AF:2D:A4:39:37:F5:36:AE:71:2E:09:0E:49:23:70:61:28:5F:4A
            DirName:/C=US/ST=Colorado/L=Denver/O=NonExistant Enterprises/
OU=IT Services/CN=Certificate Administration/
emailAddress=certadmin@nonexistantdomain.com
            serial:00

Certificate is to be certified until Dec  7 09:05:08 2004 GMT (365 days)
Sign the certificate? [y/n]:y


1 out of 1 certificate requests certified, commit? [y/n]y
Write out database with 1 new entries
Data Base Updated
Signed certificate is in newcert.pem
```

Now you can set up keys in this manner for each server that needs to provide an SSL-encrypted service. It is easier to do this if you designate a single workstation to maintain the certificate authority and all the files associated with it. Don't forget to distribute your CA cert to programs that need to trust it [Hack #46].

HACK #46 Distribute Your CA to Clients

Be sure all of your clients trust your new Certificate Authority.

Once you have created a Certificate Authority (CA) [Hack #45], any certificates that are signed by your CA will be trusted by any program that trusts your CA. To establish this trust, you need to distribute your CA's certificate to each program that needs to trust it. This could include email programs, IPSec installations, or web browsers.

Since SSL uses public key cryptography, there is no need to keep the certificate a secret. You can simply install it on a web server and download it to your clients over plain old HTTP. While the instructions for installing a CA cert are different for every program, this hack will show you a quick and easy way to install your CA on web browsers.

There are two possible formats that browsers will accept for new CA certs: *pem* and *der*. You can generate a *der* from your existing *pem* with a single openssl command:

```
$ openssl x509 -in demoCA/cacert.pem -outform DER -out cacert.der
```

Also, add the following line to the *conf/mime.types* file in your Apache installation:

```
application/x-x509-ca-cert     der pem crt
```

Now restart Apache for the change to take effect. You should now be able to place both the *cacert.der* and *demoCA/cacert.pem* files anywhere on your web server and have clients install the new cert by simply clicking on either link.

Early versions of Netscape expected *pem* format, but recent versions will accept either. Internet Explorer is just the opposite (early IE would accept only *der* format, but recent versions will take both). Other browsers will generally accept either format.

You will get a dialog box in your browser when downloading the new Certificate Authority, asking if you'd like to continue. Accept the certificate, and that's all there is to it. Now SSL certs that are signed by your CA will be accepted without warning the user.

Keep in mind that Certificate Authorities aren't to be taken lightly. If you accept a new CA in your browser, you had better trust it completely—a mischievous CA manager could sign all sorts of certs that you should never trust, but your browser would never complain (since you claimed to trust the CA when you imported it). Be very careful about who you extend your trust to when using SSL-enabled browsers. It's worth looking around in the CA cache that ships with your browser to see exactly who you trust by default.

For example, did you know that AOL/Time Warner has its own CA? How about GTE? Or VISA? CA certs for all of these entities (and many others) ship with Netscape 7.0 for Linux, and are all trusted authorities for web sites, email, and application add-ons by default. Keep this in mind when browsing to SSL-enabled sites: if any of the default authorities have signed online content, your browser will trust it without requiring operator acknowledgment.

If you value your browser's security (and, by extension, the security of your client machine), then make it a point to review your trusted CA relationships.

—*Rob Flickenger (Linux Server Hacks)*

Encrypt IMAP and POP with SSL

HACK
#47

Keep your email safe from prying eyes while also protecting your POP and
IMAP passwords.

Having your email available on an IMAP server is invaluable when you have
to access your email from multiple locations. Unlike POP, IMAP stores all
your email and any folders you create on the server, so you can access all of
your email from whatever email client you decide to use. You can even set
up a web-based email client so that messages can be accessed from literally
any machine with an Internet connection and a web browser. But more than
likely, you will need to cross untrusted networks along the way. How do
you protect your email account password and email from others with less
than desirable intentions? You use encryption, of course!

If you already have an IMAP or POP daemon installed that does not have
the ability to use SSL natively, you can use *stunnel* [Hack #76] to wrap the service in an SSL tunnel. If you're starting from scratch, you have the luxury of
choosing a daemon that has SSL support compiled directly into the binary.

One daemon that supports SSL out of the box is the University of Washing-
ton's IMAP daemon, otherwise known as UW-IMAP (*http://www.
washington.edu/imap/*). The IMAP daemon is included with their IMAP software distribution.

To compile and install the IMAP daemon, download the compressed tar
archive and run commands similar to these:

```
$ tar xfz imap.tar.Z
$ cd imap-2002e
$ make lnp SSLDIR=/usr SSLCERTS=/usr/share/ssl/certs
```

The Makefile target specifies what type of system you are building for. In
this case, lnp stands for Linux-PAM. Other popular Makefile targets are bsf
for FreeBSD, bso for OpenBSD, osx for Mac OS X, sol for Solaris, and gso
for Solaris with GCC. The SSLDIR variable is used to set the base directory
for your OpenSSL installation. By default, the Makefile is set to use */usr/
local/ssl*, which would cause it to look for the libraries in */usr/local/ssl/lib* and
the headers in */usr/local/ssl/include*. If a version of OpenSSL came installed
with your operating system and you want to use that, you will most likely
need to use SSLDIR=/usr as shown in the example. The SSLCERTS variable is
used to tell the *imapd* and *popd* where to find their SSL certificates.

If the compile aborts due to errors, look for a message similar to this:

```
In file included from /usr/include/openssl/ssl.h:179,
                 from osdep.c:218:
/usr/include/openssl/kssl.h:72:18: krb5.h: No such file or directory
```

```
In file included from /usr/include/openssl/ssl.h:179,
              from osdep.c:218:
```

This means that the compiler cannot find the Kerberos header files, a known issue with newer versions of Red Hat Linux. This happens because the files are located in */usr/kerberos/include*, which is a nonstandard directory on the system.

To tell the compiler where to find the headers, use the EXTRACFLAGS variable. The make command from the previous example will now look like this:

```
$ make lnp SSLDIR=/usr SSLCERTS=/usr/share/ssl/certs \
EXTRACFLAGS=-I/usr/kerberos/include
```

After the binaries have been built, become root and copy them to a suitable place:

```
# cp imapd/imapd ipopd/ipopd /usr/local/bin
```

Next, to create self-signed certificates, run these two commands:

```
$ openssl req -new -x509 -nodes \
 -out /usr/share/ssl/certs/imapd.pem \
 -keyout /usr/share/ssl/certs/imapd.pem -days 3650
$ openssl req -new -x509 -nodes \
 -out /usr/share/ssl/certs/ipopd.pem \
 -keyout /usr/share/ssl/certs/ipopd.pem -days 3650
```

Alternatively, you can sign the certificates with your own Certificate Authority [Hack #45]. However, if you go this route, you must change the certificates' names to *imapd.pem* and *ipopd.pem*.

All that's left to do now is edit your */etc/inetd.conf* file so that *inetd* will listen on the correct ports and spawn *imapd* and *ipopd* when a client connects. To do this, add the following lines at the end of the file:

```
imaps stream tcp nowait root /usr/libexec/tcpd /usr/local/bin/imapd
pop3s stream tcp nowait root /usr/libexec/tcpd /usr/local/bin/ipop3d
```

Now tell *inetd* to reload its configuration:

```
# kill -HUP `ps -ax | grep inetd | grep -v grep \
 | awk '{print $1}'`
```

That's the final task for the server end of things. All you need to do now is configure your email clients to connect to the secure version of the service that you were using. Usually, there will be a Use Encryption, Use SSL, or some other similarly named checkbox in the incoming mail settings for your client. Just check the box, reconnect, and you should be using SSL now. Be sure your client trusts your CA cert, or you will be nagged with annoying (but important!) trust warnings.

Set Up TLS-Enabled SMTP

Protect your users' in-transit email from eavesdroppers.

If you have set up encrypted POP and IMAP services [Hack #47], your users' incoming email is protected from others once it reaches your servers, but what about their outgoing email? You can protect outgoing email quickly and easily by setting up your MTA to use Transport Layer Security (TLS) encryption. Virtually all modern email clients support TLS—enable it by simply checking a box in the email account preferences.

If you're using Sendmail, you can check to see if it has TLS support compiled-in by running this command:

```
$ sendmail -bt -d0.1
```

This will print out the options that your sendmail binary was compiled with. If you see a line that says STARTTLS, then all you need to do is supply some additional configuration information to get TLS support working. However, if you don't see this line, you'll need to recompile sendmail.

Before recompiling sendmail, you will need to go into the directory containing sendmail's source code and add the following lines to *devtools/Site/site.config.m4*:

```
APPENDDEF(`conf_sendmail_ENVDEF', `-DSTARTTLS')
APPENDDEF(`conf_sendmail_LIBS', `-lssl -lcrypto')
```

If this file doesn't exist, simply create it. The build process will automatically include the file once you create it. The first line in the example will cause TLS support to be compiled into the sendmail binary, and the second line will link the binary with *libssl.so* and *libcrypto.so*.

After adding these lines, you can recompile and reinstall sendmail by running this command:

```
# ./Build -c && ./Build install
```

After you've done this, you will need to create a certificate and key pair to use with sendmail [Hack #45]. Then you'll need to reconfigure sendmail to use the certificate and key that you created. You can do this by editing the file your *sendmail.cf* file is generated from, which is usually */etc/mail/sendmail.mc*. Once you've located the file, add lines, similar to the following, that point to your Certificate Authority's certificate as well as the certificate and key you generated earlier:

```
define(`confCACERT_PATH', `/etc/mail/certs')
define(`confCACERT', `/etc/mail/certs/cacert.pem')
define(`confSERVER_CERT', `/etc/mail/certs/cert.pem')
define(`confSERVER_KEY', `/etc/mail/certs/key.pem')
```

```
define(`confCLIENT_CERT', `/etc/mail/certs/cert.pem')
define(`confCLIENT_KEY', `/etc/mail/certs/key.pem')
```

The first line tells sendmail where your Certificate Authority is located, and the second one tells it where to find the CA certificate itself. The next two lines tell sendmail which certificate and key to use when it is acting as a server (i.e., accepting mail from a MUA or another mail server). The last two lines tell sendmail which certificate and key to use when it is acting as a client (i.e., relaying mail to another mail server). Usually you can then rebuild your *sendmail.cf* by typing make sendmail.cf while inside the */etc/mail* directory. Now kill sendmail and then restart it.

After you've restarted sendmail, you can check whether TLS is set up correctly by connecting to it:

```
# telnet localhost smtp
Trying 127.0.0.1...
Connected to localhost.
Escape character is '^]'.
220 mail.example.com ESMTP Sendmail 8.12.9/8.12.9; Sun, 11 Jan 2004 12:07:43
-0800 (PST)
ehlo localhost
250-mail.example.com Hello IDENT:6l4ZhaGP3Qczqknqm/KdTFGsrBe2SCYC@localhost
[127.0.0.1], pleased to meet you
250-ENHANCEDSTATUSCODES
250-PIPELINING
250-EXPN
250-VERB
250-8BITMIME
250-SIZE
250-DSN
250-ETRN
250-AUTH DIGEST-MD5 CRAM-MD5
250-STARTTLS
250-DELIVERBY
250 HELP
QUIT
221 2.0.0 mail.example.com closing connection
Connection closed by foreign host.
```

When sendmail relays mail to another TLS-enabled mail server, your mail will be encrypted. Now all you need to do is configure your mail client to use TLS when connecting to your mail server, and your users' email will be protected all the way to the MTA.

While there isn't enough room in this hack to cover every MTA available, nearly all support some variant of TLS. If you are running Exim (*http://www.exim.org*) or Courier (*http://www.courier-mta.org*), you can build TLS support straight out of the box. Postfix (*http://www.postfix.org*) has TLS support and is designed to be used in conjunction with Cyrus-SASL (see the HOWTO at *http://postfix.state-of-mind.de/patrick.koetter/smtpauth/*). Qmail has an RFC 2487 (TLS) patch available at *http://inoa.net/qmail-tls/*. With TLS support in virtually all MTAs and email clients, there is no longer any good reason to send email "in the clear."

HACK #49 Detect Ethernet Sniffers Remotely

Detect potential spies on your network without having to trust compromised machines.

Ethernet sniffers are one of the most powerful tools in your network security arsenal. However, in the wrong hands they can be one of the biggest threats to the security of your network. It may be an insider or it could be a malicious intruder, but, nevertheless, once a system has been detected they will most likely begin sniffing the local network. This network reconnaissance will help these "spies" find their next target, or simply collect juicy bits of information (such as usernames and passwords, email, or other sensitive data).

Not too long ago, it was commonly thought that only shared-medium Ethernet networks were vulnerable to being sniffed. These networks employed a central hub, which would rebroadcast every transmitted packet to each port on the hub. In this type of setup, every frame sent by any network node is received by every other node on the local network segment. Each node's network interface then performs a quick check to see if it is the node that the frame is destined for. If it is not, the frame is discarded. If it is, the frame is passed up through the operating system's protocol stack and is eventually processed by an application. Because of this, sniffing other systems' traffic on the network was trivial. After all, since all the traffic was reaching each system, one only needed to disable the check that the network interface performs, and the system would have access to the traffic meant for others. This is usually referred to as putting the network interface into *promiscuous mode*, which usually can be done only by a privileged user.

Eventually, switched Ethernet networks became prevalent and the shared-medium aspect no longer applied. Thus, the main facilitator of sniffing was removed. Unlike hubs, Ethernet switches will only send traffic to the device that it is destined for. To do this, an Ethernet switch learns which network device's MAC address corresponds to what port on the switch as traffic passes through the switch. When the switch sees an Ethernet frame with a certain destination MAC address, it will look up which port on the switch corresponds to it and forward the frame to only that port. In doing this, the switch effectively creates a virtual dedicated connection from the sending station to the receiving station every time an Ethernet frame is transmitted on the network. Thus, only the machine that the frame was originally intended for is able to see it. This would be fine, but certain aspects of the Ethernet specification and the TCP/IP can cause problems.

One problem is that switches can memorize only a limited number of MAC addresses. The maximum number will often be several orders of magnitude higher than the number of ports that the switch has, which allows switches to be connected to each other hierarchically. In order to do this efficiently, each switch must memorize the MAC addresses available on the switches to which it is connected. For example, suppose you have a 24-port switch (switch A) with 23 machines plugged into it, and the 24th port is occupied by another switch. This other switch (switch B) has 48 ports, with the 47 other ports being occupied by machines. In this situation, switch A will learn the MAC addresses of the 47 systems on switch B and associate it with its 24th port, and switch B will learn the MAC addresses of the 23 systems connected directly to switch A and associate it with its own 48th port. Even though the average switch can memorize upwards of several thousand MAC addresses, it is still possible to overflow the switch's MAC address table by generating large amounts of traffic with fake MAC addresses. This tactic is desirable for a malicious user because many switches will revert to behaving like a hub once their MAC address tables have been filled. Once this happens, the network is no different than a shared-medium segment using a hub. A malicious user will then be able to sniff the network by simply putting her network interface into promiscuous mode.

Luckily this approach is fairly invasive—in order for it to work, the network will need to be flooded with bogus traffic, which is something that can be detected passively with tools such as Arpwatch [Hack #31]. A flood of bogus MAC and IP address pairings would cause Arpwatch to likewise flood your system logs. As long as you're good about monitoring your logs, this attack should be fairly easy to spot. As mentioned in "Detect ARP Spoofing" [Hack #31], Arpwatch is also capable of detecting ARP table poisoning. That makes it an effective tool for detecting the two most common types of ARP attacks that are usually precursors to data logging: ARP flooding and targeted ARP poisoning.

Another way to monitor switched networks is to simply change the MAC address of the Ethernet card in the system that is going to be used for sniffing. In Linux and many other Unix and Unix-like operating systems, this can be done with the ifconfig command:

```
# /sbin/ifconfig eth1
eth1      Link encap:Ethernet  HWaddr 00:E0:81:03:D8:8F
          BROADCAST MULTICAST  MTU:1500  Metric:1
          RX packets:0 errors:0 dropped:0 overruns:0 frame:0
          TX packets:0 errors:0 dropped:0 overruns:0 carrier:0
          collisions:0 txqueuelen:100
```

```
        RX bytes:0 (0.0 b)  TX bytes:0 (0.0 b)
        Interrupt:11 Base address:0x1c80

# /sbin/ifconfig eth0 hw ether 00:DE:AD:BE:EF:00
# /sbin/ifconfig eth1
eth1      Link encap:Ethernet  HWaddr 00:DE:AD:BE:EF:00
          BROADCAST MULTICAST  MTU:1500  Metric:1
          RX packets:0 errors:0 dropped:0 overruns:0 frame:0
          TX packets:0 errors:0 dropped:0 overruns:0 carrier:0
          collisions:0 txqueuelen:100
          RX bytes:0 (0.0 b)  TX bytes:0 (0.0 b)
          Interrupt:11 Base address:0x1c80
```

The purpose of doing this is to trick the switch into forwarding the traffic to two different nodes on the segment. This is sometimes a hit-or-miss deal, since different switches will behave differently when there are duplicate MAC addresses in use on the same network. The switch may forward traffic to both ports, distribute the traffic unpredictably between them, stop passing traffic altogether, or raise an error. All of these methods can be detected and stopped with more expensive managed switches, which allow you to specify what MAC addresses are allowed on each individual port. This feature is sometimes called *port security*.

However, even if attackers choose not to employ these methods, they can still gather quite a bit of information by just putting the network interface into promiscuous mode. For example, broadcast traffic such as DHCP and ARP requests will still be sent to every port on the switch. This traffic is not as easy to detect, unless you already have the infrastructure in place to do so.

One tool that can help to detect promiscuous interfaces on both switched and unswitched networks is *sniffdet* (*http://sniffdet.sourceforge.net*). For a tool that really only serves a single purpose, *sniffdet* is fairly versatile, as it can detect sniffers in several ways. The main difference between *sniffdet* and a tool like Arpwatch is that *sniffdet* actively scans for sniffers. That is, if you suspect that a machine may be running a sniffer, you can simply run *sniffdet* and point it at that machine to determine whether its network device is in promiscuous mode.

To build and install *sniffdet*, you will first have to obtain the libnet packet injection library (*http://www.packetfactory.net/projects/libnet/*). Make sure to download the latest 1.0.x version—the 1.1 versions of libnet are incompatible with programs written for the 1.0.x versions.

To compile libnet, unpack the source distribution and go into the directory that it creates. Then run this command:

```
$ ./configure && make
```

After it has finished compiling, become root and type make install.

Building *sniffdet* is a similar affair. Like libnet, you will need to unpack the source distribution and change to the directory that it creates. Then, to build and install it, do the same thing you did for libnet.

sniffdet has several methods for determining whether a target machine is running a sniffer. However, only two of the methods that it employs will work with repeatable and predictable results. These are the ARP and DNS tests.

The ARP test relies on how the sniffing system's protocol stack deals with ARP queries while in promiscuous mode. When running this test against a target machine, *sniffdet* will send out an ARP query to the target machine. This request has fake source and destination MAC addresses but uses the correct IP addresses of the machine being checked. If the target machine is in promiscuous mode, the ARP query with the fake MAC address will be passed up the protocol stack, and the target machine will send a reply. If the machine is not in promiscuous mode, this ARP query will be quietly discarded. This method is effective on both switched and unswitched networks.

Let's look at a *sniffdet* scan against sirius (192.168.0.2) from colossus (192.168.0.64), two machines that are on the same switched network.

Here are the results of running *sniffdet* against sirius:

```
colossus # sniffdet -i eth0 -t arp sirius
------------------------------------------------------------
Sniffdet Report
Generated on: Wed Dec 31 03:49:28 2003
------------------------------------------------------------
Tests Results for target sirius
------------------------------------------------------------
Test: ARP Test (single host)
      Check if target replies a bogus ARP request (with wrong MAC)
Validation: OK
Started on: Wed Dec 31 03:49:08 2003
Finished on: Wed Dec 31 03:49:28 2003
Bytes Sent: 252
Bytes Received: 0
Packets Sent: 6
Packets Received: 0
------------------------------------------------------------
RESULT: NEGATIVE
------------------------------------------------------------


------------------------------------------------------------
Number of valid tests: #1
Number of tests with positive result: #0
------------------------------------------------------------
```

Now start a sniffer on sirius and run the scan again:

```
sirius # tcpdump -i le0 arp
tcpdump: listening on le0
```

```
06:58:00.458836 arp who-has sirius.nnc tell colossus.nnc
06:58:00.458952 arp reply sirius.nnc is-at 8:0:20:81:a4:a3
06:58:00.466601 arp who-has sirius.nnc (ff:0:0:0:0:0) tell colossus.nnc
06:58:00.466928 arp reply sirius.nnc is-at 8:0:20:81:a4:a3
```

Let's look at the results of the scan:

```
-------------------------------------------------------------
Sniffdet Report
Generated on: Wed Dec 31 06:58:01 2003
-------------------------------------------------------------
Tests Results for target sirius
-------------------------------------------------------------
Test: ARP Test (single host)
      Check if target replies a bogus ARP request (with wrong MAC)
Validation: OK
Started on: Wed Dec 31 06:58:00 2003
Finished on: Wed Dec 31 06:58:01 2003
Bytes Sent: 84
Bytes Received: 60
Packets Sent: 2
Packets Received: 1
-------------------------------------------------------------
RESULT: POSITIVE
-------------------------------------------------------------


-------------------------------------------------------------
Number of valid tests: #1
Number of tests with positive result: #1
-------------------------------------------------------------
```

The DNS test works very well, particularly on shared-medium networks such as hubs or wireless LANs. However, it does rely on name resolution being enabled in the sniffer. When performing DNS tests, *sniffdet* will send bogus packets that contain IP addresses that are not in use on the local network segment. If name resolution is enabled, the sniffer will attempt to do a reverse lookup in order to determine the hostname that corresponds to the IP addresses. Since these addresses are not in use, *sniffdet* will determine that the target machine is in promiscuous mode when it sees the DNS queries.

This test can be performed just as the ARP test, but instead of using -t arp, use -t dns.

Install Apache with SSL and suEXEC

HACK #50

Help secure your web applications with mod_ssl and suEXEC.

Web server security is a very important issue these days, especially since people are always finding new and creative ways to put the Web to use. If you're using any sort of web application that needs to handle authentication or provides some sort of restricted information, you should seriously consider installing a web server with SSL capabilities. Without SSL, any authentication information your users send to the web server is sent over the network in the clear, and any information that clients can access can be viewed by anyone with a sniffer. If you are already using Apache, you can easily add SSL capabilities with mod_ssl (*http://www.modssl.org*).

In addition, if your web server serves up dynamic content for multiple users, you may want to enable Apache's suEXEC functionality. suEXEC allows your web server to execute server-side scripts as the user that owns them, rather than as the account under which the web server is running. Otherwise, any user could create a script and run code as the account the web server is running under. This is a bad thing, particularly on a multiuser web server. If you don't review the scripts that your users write before allowing them to be run, they could very well write code that allows them to access other users' data or other sensitive information, such as database accounts and passwords.

To compile Apache with mod_ssl, download the appropriate mod_ssl source distribution for the version of Apache that you'll be using. (If you don't want to add mod_ssl to an existing Apache source tree, you will also need to download and unpack the Apache source.) After you've done that, unpack the mod_ssl distribution and go into the directory that it created. Then run a command like this:

```
# ./configure \
--with-apache=../apache_1.3.29 \
--with-ssl=SYSTEM \
--prefix=/usr/local/apache \
--enable-module=most \
--enable-module=mmap_static \
--enable-module=so \
--enable-shared=ssl \
--disable-rule=SSL_COMPAT \
--server-uid=www \
--server-gid=www \
--enable-suexec \
--suexec-caller=www \
--suexec-uidmin=500 \
--suexec-gidmin=500
```

This will both patch the Apache source tree with extensions provided with mod_ssl and configure Apache for the build process.

You will probably need to change a number of options in order to build Apache. The directory specified in the --with-apache switch should point to the directory that contains the Apache source code for the version that you are building. In addition, if you want to use a version of OpenSSL that has not been installed yet, specify the location of its build tree with the --with-ssl switch. If you elect to do that, you should configure and build OpenSSL in the specified directory before attempting to build Apache and mod_ssl. The --server-uid and --server-gid switches are used to specify what user and group the web server will run under. Apache defaults to the "nobody" account. However, many programs that can be configured to drop their privileges also default to the nobody account; if you end up accepting these defaults with every program, the nobody account can become quite privileged. So, it is recommended that you create a separate account for every program that provides this option.

The remaining options enable and configure Apache's suEXEC. To provide the suEXEC functionality, Apache uses a SUID wrapper program to execute users' scripts. This wrapper program makes several checks before it will allow a program to execute. One thing that the wrapper checks is the UID of the process that invoked it. If it is not the account that was specified with the --suexec-caller option, then execution of the user's script will abort. Since the suEXEC wrapper will be called by the web server, this option should be set to the same value as --server-uid. Additionally, since most privileged accounts and groups on a system usually all have a UID and GID beneath a certain value, the suEXEC wrapper will check to see if the UID or GID of the process invoking it is less than this threshold. For this to work, you must specify the appropriate value for your system. In this example, Apache and mod_ssl are being built on a Red Hat system, which starts regular user accounts and groups at UID and GID 500. In addition to these checks, suEXEC performs a multitude of other checks, such as ensuring that the script is writable only by the owner, that the owner is not root, and that the script is not SUID or SGID.

After the configure script completes, change to the directory that contains the Apache source code and run make and make install. You can run make certificates if you would like to generate an SSL certificate to test out your installation. You can also run make certificate TYPE=custom to generate a certificate signing request to be signed by either a commercial Certificate Authority or your own CA. See "Create Your Own Certificate Authority" [Hack #45] if you would like to run your own Certificate Authority.

After installing Apache, you can start it by running this command:

```
# /usr/local/apache/bin/apachectl startssl
```

If you want to start out by testing it without SSL, run this:

```
# /usr/local/apache/bin/apacectl start
```

You can then verify that suEXEC support is enabled by running this command:

```
# grep suexec /usr/local/apache/logs/error_log
[Thu Jan  1 16:48:17 2004] [notice] suEXEC mechanism enabled (wrapper: /usr/
local/apache/bin/suexec)
```

Now add a `Directory` entry similar to this to enable CGI scripts for user directories:

```
<Directory /home/*/public_html>
    AllowOverride FileInfo AuthConfig Limit
    Options MultiViews Indexes SymLinksIfOwnerMatch Includes ExecCGI
    <Limit GET POST OPTIONS PROPFIND>
        Order allow,deny
        Allow from all
    </Limit>
    <LimitExcept GET POST OPTIONS PROPFIND>
        Order deny,allow
        Deny from all
    </LimitExcept>
</Directory>
```

In addition, add this line to enable CGI scripts outside of the *ScriptAlias* directories:

```
AddHandler cgi-script .cgi
```

After you've done that, you can restart Apache by running this:

```
# /usr/local/apache/bin/apachectl restart
```

Now test out suEXEC with a simple script that runs the `id` command, which will print out information about the user the script is executed as:

```
#!/bin/sh

echo -e "Content-Type: text/plain\r\n\r\n"
/usr/sbin/id
```

Put this script in a directory such as */usr/local/apache/cgi-bin*, name it *suexec-test.cgi*, and make it executable. Now enter the URL for the script (i.e., *http://webserver/cgi-bin/suexec-test.cgi*) into your favorite web browser. You should see something like this:

```
uid=80(www) gid=80(www) groups=80(www)
```

As you can see, it is being executed as the same user that the web server runs as.

Now copy the script into a user's *public_html* directory:

```
$ mkdir public_html && chmod 711 ~/ ~/public_html
$ cp /usr/local/apache/cgi-bin/suexec-test.cgi .
```

After you've done that, enter the URL for the script (i.e., *http://webserver/ ~user/suexec-test.cgi*) in your web browser. You should see something similar to this:

```
uid=500(andrew) gid=500(andrew) groups=500(andrew)
```

In addition to handling scripts in users' private HTML directories, suEXEC can also execute scripts as another user within a virtual host. However, to do this, you will need to create all of your virtual host's directories beneath the web server's document root (i.e., */usr/local/apache/htdocs*). When doing this, you can configure what user and group the script will execute as by using the User and Group configuration directives within the VirtualHost statement.

For example:

```
<VirtualHost>
    User myuser
    Group mygroup
    DocumentRoot /usr/local/apache/htdocs/mysite
    ...
</VirtualHost>
```

Unfortunately, suEXEC is incompatible with mod_perl and mod_php because the modules run within the Apache process itself instead of a separate program. Since the Apache process is running as a nonroot user it cannot change the UID under which the scripts execute. suEXEC works by having Apache call a special SUID wrapper (e.g., */usr/local/apache/bin/suexec*) that can only be invoked by Apache processes. If you care to make the security/ performance trade-off by using suEXEC but still need to run Perl scripts, you can do so through the standard CGI interface. Just as with Perl, you can also run PHP programs through the CGI interface, but you'll have to create a php binary and specify it as the interpreter in all the PHP scripts you wish to execute through suEXEC. You can also execute your scripts through mod_ perl or mod_php by locating them outside the directories where suEXEC will work.

HACK #51 Secure BIND

Lock down your BIND setup to help contain potential security problems.

Due to BIND's not-so-illustrious track record with regard to security, you'll probably want to spend some time hardening your setup if you want to continue using it. One way to make running BIND a little safer is to run it inside a sandboxed environment. This is easy to do with recent versions of BIND, since it natively supports running as a nonprivileged user within a chroot( ) jail. All you need to do is set up the directory you're going to have it chroot( ) to, and then change the command you're using to start *named* to reflect this.

To begin, create a user and group to run *named* as (e.g., named). To prepare the sandboxed environment, you'll need to create the appropriate directory structure. You can create the directories for such an environment within */named_chroot* by running the following commands:

```
# mkdir /named_chroot
# cd /named_chroot
# mkdir -p dev etc/namedb/slave var/run
```

Next, you'll need to copy your *named.conf* and *namedb* directory to the sandboxed environment:

```
# cp /etc/named.conf /named_chroot/etc
# cp -a /var/namedb/* /named_chroot/etc/namedb
```

This assumes that you store your zone files in */var/namedb*. If you're setting up BIND as a secondary DNS server, you will need to make the */named_chroot/etc/namedb/slave* directory writable so that *named* can update the records it contains when it performs a domain transfer from the master DNS node. You can do this by running a command similar to the following:

```
# chown -R named:named /named_chroot/etc/namedb/slave
```

In addition, *named* will need to write its process ID (PID) file to */named_chroot/var/run*, so you'll need to make this directory writable by the named user as well:

```
# chown named:named /named_chroot/var/run
```

Now you'll need to create some device files that *named* will need to access after it has called chroot( ):

```
# cd /named_chroot/dev
# ls -la /dev/null /dev/random
crw-rw-rw-  1 root    root    1,  3 Jan 30  2003 /dev/null
crw-r--r--  1 root    root    1,  8 Jan 30  2003 /dev/random
# mknod null c 1 3
# mknod random c 1 8
# chmod 666 null random
```

You'll also need to copy your time zone file from */etc/localtime* to */named_chroot/etc/localtime*. Additionally, *named* usually uses */dev/log* to communicate its log messages to *syslogd*. Since this doesn't exist inside the sandboxed environment, you will need to tell *syslogd* to create a socket that the chrooted named process can write to. You can do this by modifying your *syslogd* startup command and adding -a /named_chroot/dev/log to it. Usually you can do this by modifying an existing file in */etc*.

For instance, under Red Hat Linux you would edit */etc/sysconfig/syslogd* and modify the SYSLOGD_OPTIONS line to read:

```
SYSLOGD_OPTIONS="-m 0 -a /named_chroot/dev/log"
```

Or if you're running FreeBSD, you would modify the syslogd_flags line in */etc/rc.conf*:

```
syslogd_flags="-s -a /named_chroot/dev/log"
```

After you restart *syslogd*, you should see a log socket in */named_chroot/dev*.

Now to start *named* all you need to do is run this command:

```
# named -u named -t /named_chroot
```

Other tricks for increasing the security of your BIND installation include limiting zone transfers to your slave DNS servers and altering the response to BIND version queries. Restricting zone transfers ensures that random attackers will not be able to request a list of all the hostnames for the zones hosted by your name servers. You can globally restrict zone transfers to certain hosts by putting an allow-transfer section within the options section in your *named.conf*.

For instance, if you wanted to restrict transfers on all zones hosted by your DNS server to only 192.168.1.20 and 192.168.1.21, you could use an allow-transfer section like this:

```
allow-transfer {
    192.168.1.20;
    192.168.1.21;
};
```

If you don't want to limit zone transfers globally and instead want to specify the allowed hosts on a zone-by-zone basis, you can put the allow-transfer section inside the zone section.

Before an attacker attempts to exploit a BIND vulnerability, they will often scan for vulnerable versions of BIND by connecting to name servers and performing a version query. Since you should never need to perform a version query on your own name server, you can modify the reply BIND sends to the requester. To do this, add a version statement to the options section in your *named.conf*.

For example:

```
version "SuperHappy DNS v1.5";
```

Note that this really doesn't provide extra security, but if you don't want to advertise what software and version you're running to the entire world, you don't have to.

See Also

- The section "Securing BIND" in *Building Secure Servers with Linux*, by Michael D. Bauer (O'Reilly)

Secure MySQL

#52   Basic steps you can take to harden your MySQL installation.

MySQL (*http://www.mysql.com*), one of the most popular open source database systems available today, is often used in conjunction with both the Apache web server and the PHP scripting language to drive dynamic content on the Web. However, MySQL is a complex piece of software internally and, given the fact that it often has to interact both locally and remotely with a broad range of other programs, special care should be taken to secure it as much as possible.

Some steps you can take are running MySQL in a chrooted environment [Hack #10], running it as a nonroot user, and disabling MySQL's ability to load data from local files. Luckily, none of these are as hard to do as they may sound. To start with, let's look at how to chroot( ) MySQL.

First create a user and group for MySQL to run as. Next, you'll need to download the MySQL source distribution. After you've done that, unpack it and go into the directory that it created. Run this command to build MySQL and set up its directory structure for chrooting:

```
$ ./configure --prefix=/mysql --with-mysqld-ldflags=-all-static && make
```

This configures MySQL to be installed in */mysql* and statically links the mysqld binary. This will make setting up the chroot environment much easier, since you won't need to copy any additional libraries to the environment.

After the compilation finishes, become root and then run these commands to install MySQL:

```
# make install DESTDIR=/mysql_chroot && ln -s /mysql_chroot/mysql /mysql
# scripts/mysql_install_db
```

The first command installs MySQL, but instead of placing the files in */mysql*, it places them in */mysql_chroot/mysql*. In addition, it creates a symbolic link from that directory to */mysql*, which makes administering MySQL much easier after installation. The second command creates MySQL's default databases. If you hadn't created the symbolic link prior to running this command, the *mysql_install_db* script would have failed. This is because it expected to find MySQL installed beneath */mysql*. Many other scripts and programs will expect this, too, so creating the symbolic link will make your life easier.

Now you need to set up the correct directory permissions so that MySQL will be able to function properly. To do this, run these commands:

```
# chown -R root:mysql /mysql
# chown -R mysql /mysql/var
```

Now try running MySQL:

```
# /mysql/bin/mysqld_safe&
Starting mysqld daemon with databases from /mysql/var
# ps -aux | grep mysql | grep -v grep
root     10137 0.6 0.5  4156   744 pts/2   S   23:01   0:00 /bin/sh /
mysql/bin/mysqld_safe
mysql    10150 7.0 9.3 46224 11756 pts/2   S   23:01   0:00 [mysqld]
mysql    10151 0.0 9.3 46224 11756 pts/2   S   23:01   0:00 [mysqld]
mysql    10152 0.0 9.3 46224 11756 pts/2   S   23:01   0:00 [mysqld]
mysql    10153 0.0 9.3 46224 11756 pts/2   S   23:01   0:00 [mysqld]
mysql    10154 0.0 9.3 46224 11756 pts/2   S   23:01   0:00 [mysqld]
mysql    10155 0.3 9.3 46224 11756 pts/2   S   23:01   0:00 [mysqld]
mysql    10156 0.0 9.3 46224 11756 pts/2   S   23:01   0:00 [mysqld]
mysql    10157 0.0 9.3 46224 11756 pts/2   S   23:01   0:00 [mysqld]
mysql    10158 0.0 9.3 46224 11756 pts/2   S   23:01   0:00 [mysqld]
mysql    10159 0.0 9.3 46224 11756 pts/2   S   23:01   0:00 [mysqld]
# /mysql/bin/mysqladmin shutdown
040103 23:02:45  mysqld ended

[1]+  Done                    /mysql/bin/mysqld_safe
```

Now that you know MySQL is working outside of its chroot environment, you can create the additional files and directories it will need to work inside the chroot environment:

```
# mkdir /mysql_chroot/tmp /mysql_chroot/dev
# chmod 1777 /mysql_chroot/tmp
# ls -l /dev/null
crw-rw-rw-   1 root     root      1,   3 Jan 30  2003 /dev/null
# mknod /mysql_chroot/dev/null c 1 3
```

Now try running mysqld in the chrooted environment:

```
# /usr/sbin/chroot /mysql_chroot /mysql/libexec/mysqld -u 100
```

Here the UID of the user you want mysqld to run as is specified with the -u option. This should correspond to the UID of the user created earlier.

To ease management, you may want to modify the *mysqld_safe* shell script to chroot mysqld for you. You can accomplish this by finding the lines where mysqld is called and modifying them to use the chroot program.

To do this, open up */mysql/bin/mysqld_safe* and locate block of lines that looks like this:

```
if test -z "$args"
  then
    $NOHUP_NICENESS $ledir/$MYSQLD $defaults \
      --basedir=$MY_BASEDIR_VERSION  \
      --datadir=$DATADIR $USER_OPTION \
      --pid-file=$pid_file --skip-locking >> $err_log 2>&1
  else
    eval "$NOHUP_NICENESS $ledir/$MYSQLD $defaults \
      --basedir=$MY_BASEDIR_VERSION \
```

```
    --datadir=$DATADIR $USER_OPTION \
    --pid-file=$pid_file --skip-locking $args >> $err_log 2>&1"
fi
```

Change them to look like this:

```
if test -z "$args"
  then
    $NOHUP_NICENESS /usr/sbin/chroot /mysql_chroot \
    $ledir/$MYSQLD $defaults \
    --basedir=$MY_BASEDIR_VERSION \
    --datadir=$DATADIR $USER_OPTION  \
    --pid-file=$pid_file  --skip-locking >> $err_log 2>&1
  else
    eval "$NOHUP_NICENESS /usr/sbin/chroot /mysql_chroot \
    $ledir/$MYSQLD $defaults \
    --basedir=$MY_BASEDIR_VERSION \
    --datadir=$DATADIR $USER_OPTION \
    --pid-file=$pid_file --skip-locking $args >> $err_log 2>&1"
  fi
```

Now you can start MySQL by using the *mysqld_safe* wrapper script, like this:

```
# /mysql/bin/mysqld_safe --user=100
```

In addition, you may want to create a separate *my.conf* file for the MySQL utilities and server. For instance, in */etc/my.cnf* you could specify socket = /mysql_chroot/tmp/mysql.sock in the [client] section so you do not have to manually specify the socket every time you run a MySQL-related program.

You'll also probably want to disable MySQL's ability to load data from local files. To do this, you can add set-variable=local-infile=0 to the [mysqld] section of your */mysql_chroot/etc/my.cnf*. This disables MySQL's LOAD DATA LOCAL INFILE command. Alternatively, you can disable it from the command line by using the --local-infile=0 option.

HACK #53 Share Files Securely in Unix

Use SFS to help secure your remote filesystems.

If you are using Unix systems and sharing files on your network, you are most likely using NFS. However, there are a lot of security problems, not only with individual implementations, but also with the design of the protocol itself. For instance, if a user can spoof an IP address and mount an NFS share that is only meant for a certain computer, she essentially has root access to all the files on that share. In addition, NFS employs secret file handles that are used with each file request. Since NFS does not encrypt its traffic, this makes it very easy for attackers to guess these file handles. If they guess correctly, they essentially get total root access to the remote filesystem.

SFS (*http://www.fs.net*), the Self-certifying File System, fixes all of these problems by employing a drastically different design philosophy. NFS was created with the notion that you can (and should) trust your network. SFS has been designed from the beginning with the idea that no network should ever be trusted until it can definitively prove its identity. To accomplish this, SFS makes use of public keys on both the client and server ends. It uses these keys to verify the identity of servers and clients, and also provides access control on the server side. One particularly nice side effect of such strong encryption is that SFS provides a much finer grained level of access control than NFS. With NFS, you are limited to specifying which hosts can or cannot connect to a given exported filesystem. In order to access an SFS server, a user must create a key pair and then authorizes the key by logging into the SFS server and registering the key manually.

Building SFS can take up quite a lot of disk space. Before you attempt to build SFS, make sure you have at least 550MB of disk space available on the filesystem on which you'll be compiling SFS. You will also need to make sure that you have GMP (*http://www.swox.com/gmp/*), the GNU multiple precision math library, installed. Before you begin to build SFS, you will also need to create a user and group for SFS's daemons. By default, these are both called sfs. If you want to use a different user or group, you can do this by passing options to the configure script.

Once your system is ready, you can build SFS by simply typing this command:

```
$ ./configure && make
```

Once that process is finished, become root and type make install.

If you want to use a user and group other than sfs, you can specify these with the --with-sfsuser and --with-sfsgroup options:

```
$ ./configure --with-sfsuser=nobody --with-sfsgroup=nobody
```

Building SFS can take quite a bit of time, so you may want to take the opportunity to enjoy a cup of coffee, a snack, or maybe even a full meal, depending on the speed of your machine and the amount of memory it has.

After SFS has finished building and you have installed it, you can test it out by connecting to the SFS project's public server. You can do this by starting the SFS client daemon, *sfscd*, and then changing to the directory that the SFS server will be mounted under:

```
# sfscd
# cd /sfs/@sfs.fs.net,uzwadtctbjb3dg596waiyru8cx5kb4an
# ls
CONGRATULATIONS  cvs  pi0  reddy  sfswww
```

```
# cat CONGRATULATIONS
You have set up a working SFS client.
#
```

sfscd automatically creates the */sfs* directory and the directory for the SFS server. Note that SFS relies on the operating system's portmap daemon and NFS mounter; you'll need to have those running before running the client.

To set up an SFS server, first log into your server and generate a public and private key pair:

```
# mkdir /etc/sfs
# sfskey gen -P /etc/sfs/sfs_host_key
```

sfskey will then ask you to bang on the keys for a little while in order to gather entropy for the random number generator.

Now you will need to create a configuration file for *sfssd*, the SFS server daemon. To do this, create a file in */etc/sfs* called *sfsrwsd_config*, which is where you configure the filesystem namespace that SFS will export to other hosts.

If you wanted to export the */home* filesystem, you would create a configuration file like this:

```
Export /var/sfs/root /
Export /home /home
```

Then you would need to create the */var/sfs/root* and */var/sfs/home* directories. After that, you would create NFS exports so that the */home* filesystem could be mounted under */var/sfs/root/home*. These are then reexported by *sfssd*. The NFS exports need only to allow mounting from localhost.

Here's what */etc/exports* looks like for exporting */home*:

```
/var/sfs/root    localhost(rw)
/home        localhost(rw)
```

This *exports* file is for Linux. If you are running the SFS server on another operating system (such as Solaris or OpenBSD), consult your operating system's *mountd* manpage for the proper way to add these shares.

Now start your operating system's NFS server. Once NFS has started, you can then start *sfssd*. After attempting to connect to the *sfssd* server, you should see some messages in your logs like these:

```
Dec 12 12:29:14 colossus : sfssd: version 0.7.2, pid 3503
Dec 12 12:29:14 colossus : rexd: version 0.7.2, pid 3505
Dec 12 12:29:14 colossus : sfsauthd: version 0.7.2, pid 3506
Dec 12 12:29:14 colossus : rexd: serving @colossus.
nnc,fd82m36uwxj6m3q8tawp56ztgsvu7g77
Dec 12 12:29:14 colossus : rexd: spawning /usr/local/lib/sfs-0.7.2/ptyd
Dec 12 12:29:15 colossus rpc.mountd: authenticated mount request from
localhost.localdomain:715 for /var/sfs/root (/var/sfs/root)
```

```
Dec 12 12:29:15 colossus rpc.mountd: authenticated mount request from
localhost.localdomain:715 for /home (/home)
Dec 12 12:29:15 colossus : sfsauthd: serving @colossus.
nnc,fd82m36uwxj6m3q8tawp56ztgsvu7g77
Dec 12 12:29:16 colossus : sfsrwsd: version 0.7.2, pid 3507
Dec 12 12:29:16 colossus : sfsrwsd: serving /sfs/@colossus.
nnc,fd82m36uwxj6m3q8tawp56ztgsvu7g77
```

The last log entry shows the path that users can use to mount your filesystem. Before mounting any filesystems on your server, users will have to create a key pair and register it with your server. They can do this by logging into your server and running the sfskey command:

```
$ sfskey register
sfskey: /home/andrew/.sfs/random_seed: No such file or directory
sfskey: creating directory /home/andrew/.sfs
sfskey: creating directory /home/andrew/.sfs/authkeys
/var/sfs/sockets/agent.sock: No such file or directory
sfskey: sfscd not running, limiting sources of entropy
Creating new key: andrew@colossus.nnc#1 (Rabin)
        Key Label: andrew@colossus.nnc#1
Enter passphrase:
        Again:

sfskey needs secret bits with which to seed the random number generator.
Please type some random or unguessable text until you hear a beep:
DONE
UNIX password:
colossus.nnc: New SRP key: andrew@colossus.nnc/1024
wrote key: /home/andrew/.sfs/authkeys/andrew@colossus.nnc#1
```

Alternatively, if you already have an existing key pair on another server, you can type sfskey *user@otherserver* instead. This will retrieve the key from the remote machine and register it with the server you are currently logged into.

Now that you have registered a key with the server, you can log into the SFS server from another machine. This is also done with the *sfskey* program:

```
$ sfskey login andrew@colossus.nnc
Passphrase for andrew@colossus.nnc/1024:
SFS Login as andrew@colossus.nnc
```

Now try to access the remote server:

```
$ cd /sfs/@colossus.nnc,fd82m36uwxj6m3q8tawp56ztgsvu7g77
$ ls
home
```

As you can see, SFS is a very powerful tool for sharing files across a network, and even across the Internet. Not only does it provide security, but it also provides a unique and universal method for referencing a remote host and its exported filesystems. You can even put your home directory on an SFS server, simply by linking the universal pathname of the exported filesystem */home*.

## CHAPTER FOUR

Logging
Hacks 54–60

Keeping logs is a very important aspect of maintaining the security of your network, as logs can assist in everything from alerting you to an impending attack to debugging network problems. After an incident has occurred, good logs can help you track down how the attacker got in, fix the security hole, and figure out which machines were affected. In addition, logs can help with tracing the attack back to its source, so you can identify or take legal action against the intruder. In short, log files are worth their weight in gold (just pretend that bits and bytes weigh a lot). As such, they should be given at least as much protection as any other information that's stored on your servers—even the patent schematics for your perpetual motion machine.

This chapter deals mostly with various ways to set up remote logging, whether it be a simple central *syslogd* that your servers are logging to, setting up your Windows machines to send to a *syslogd*, or using *syslog-ng* to collect logs from remote sites through an encrypted TCP connection. Using these methods, you can ensure that your logs are sitting safely on a dedicated server that's running minimal services, to decrease the chance that the logs will be compromised.

Once you have all your logs collected in a central place, what can you do with them? This chapter also covers ways to summarize your logs into reports that are easy to read and understand, so you can quickly spot the most pertinent information. If that's not fast enough for you, you'll also learn how to set up real-time alerts that will notify you as soon as a critical event occurs. In some circumstances, responding immediately to an event—rather than waiting around for it to end up in a report that you read the next morning—can save hours of effort.

HACK #54 Run a Central Syslog Server

Keep your logs safe from attackers by storing them remotely.

Once an intruder has gained entry into one of your systems, how are you to know when or if this has happened? By checking your logs, of course. What if the intruder modified the logs? In this situation, centralized logging definitely saves the day. After all, if a machine is compromised but the log evidence isn't kept on that machine, it's going to be much more difficult for the attacker to cover his tracks. In addition to providing an extra level of protection, it's also much easier to monitor the logs for a whole network of machines when they're all in one place.

To quickly set up a central syslog server, just start your *syslogd* with the switch that causes it to listen for messages from remote machines on a UDP port.

This is done under Linux by specifying the -r command-line option:

```
# /usr/sbin/syslogd -m 0 -r
```

Under FreeBSD, run *syslogd* without the -s command-line option:

```
# /usr/sbin/syslogd
```

The -s option causes FreeBSD's *syslogd* to not listen for remote connections. FreeBSD's *syslogd* also allows you to restrict what hosts it will receive messages from. To set these restrictions, use the -a option, which has the following forms:

```
ipaddr/mask[:service]
domain[:service]
*domain[:service]
```

The first form allows you to specify a single IP address or group of IP addresses by using the appropriate netmask. The *service* option allows you to specify a source UDP port. If nothing is specified, it defaults to port 514, which is the default for the syslog service. The next two forms allow you to restrict access to a specific domain name, as determined by a reverse lookup of the IP address of the connecting host. The difference between the second and third is the use of the * wildcard character, which specifies that all machines ending in *domain* may connect.

Moving on, OpenBSD uses the -u option to listen for remote connections:

```
# /usr/sbin/syslogd -a /var/empty/dev/log -u
```

whereas Solaris's *syslogd* uses -T:

```
# /usr/sbin/syslogd -T
```

Now let's set up the clients. If you want to forward all logging traffic from a machine to your central log host, simply put the following in your */etc/syslog.conf*:

```
*.*            @loghost
```

You can either make this the only line in the configuration file, in which case messages will be logged only to the remote host, or add it to what is already there, in which case logs will be stored both locally and remotely for safe-keeping.

One drawback to remote logging is that the stock *syslogd* for most operating systems fails to provide any measure of authentication or access control with regard to who may write to a central log host. Firewalls can provide some protection, keeping out everyone but those who are determined to undermine your logging infrastructure; however, someone who has already gained access to your local network can easily spoof his network connection and bypass any firewall rules that you set up. If you've determined that this is a concern for your network, take a look at "Aggregate Logs from Remote Sites" **[Hack #59]**, which discusses one method for setting up remote logging using public-key authentication and SSL-encrypted connections.

Steer Syslog
#55 Make syslog work harder, and spend less time looking through huge log files.

The default syslog installation on many distributions doesn't do a very good job of filtering classes of information into separate files. If you see a jumble of messages from Sendmail, sudo, BIND, and other system services in */var/log/messages*, then you should probably review your */etc/syslog.conf*.

There are a number of facilities and priorities that syslog can filter on. These facilities include auth, auth-priv, cron, daemon, kern, lpr, mail, news, syslog, user, uucp, and local0 through local7. In addition, each facility can have one of eight priorities: debug, info, notice, warning, err, crit, alert, and emerg.

Note that applications decide for themselves at what facility and priority to log (and the best apps let you choose), so they may not be logged as you expect. Here's a sample */etc/syslog.conf* that attempts to shuffle around what gets logged where:

```
auth.warning                    /var/log/auth
mail.err                        /var/log/maillog
kern.*                          /var/log/kernel
cron.crit                       /var/log/cron
*.err;mail.none                 /var/log/syslog
*.info;auth.none;mail.none      /var/log/messages
```

```
#*.=debug                      /var/log/debug

local0.info                    /var/log/cluster
local1.err                     /var/log/spamerica
```

All of the lines in this example will log the specified priority (or higher) to the respective file. The special priority none tells syslog not to bother logging the specified facility at all. The local0 through local7 facilities are supplied for use with your own programs, however you see fit. For example, the */var/log/spamerica* file fills with *local1.err* (or higher) messages that are generated by our spam processing job. It's nice to have those messages separate from the standard mail delivery log (which is in */var/log/maillog*).

The commented *.=debug line is useful when debugging daemonized services. It tells syslog to specifically log only debug priority messages of any facility, and generally shouldn't be running (unless you don't mind filling your disks with debug logs). Another approach is to log debug information to a fifo. This way, debug logs take up no space, but they will disappear unless a process is watching it. To log to a fifo, first create it in the filesystem:

```
# mkfifo -m 0664 /var/log/debug
```

Then amend the debug line in *syslog.conf* to include a |, like this:

```
*.=debug          |/var/log/debug
```

Now debug information is constantly logged to the fifo and can be viewed with a command like less -f /var/log/debug. A fifo is also handy if you want a process to constantly watch all system messages and perhaps notify you via email about a critical system message. Try making a fifo called */var/log/monitor*, and add a rule like this to your *syslog.conf*:

```
*.*               |/var/log/monitor
```

Now every message (at every priority) is passed to the */var/log/monitor* fifo, and any process watching it can react accordingly, all without taking up any disk space.

Mark Who?

Do you notice a bunch of lines like this in */var/log/messages*?

```
Dec 29 18:33:35 catlin -- MARK --
Dec 29 18:53:35 catlin -- MARK --
Dec 29 19:13:35 catlin -- MARK --
Dec 29 19:33:35 catlin -- MARK --
Dec 29 19:53:35 catlin -- MARK --
Dec 29 20:13:35 catlin -- MARK --
Dec 29 20:33:35 catlin -- MARK --
Dec 29 20:53:35 catlin -- MARK --
Dec 29 21:13:35 catlin -- MARK --
```

These are generated by the mark functionality of syslog, as a way of "touch-ing base" with the system, so that you can (theoretically) tell if syslog has unexpectedly died. Most times, this only serves to fill your log files, and unless you are having problems with syslog, you probably don't need it. To turn this off, pass the -m 0 switch to *syslogd* (after first killing any running *syslogd*), like this:

```
# killall syslogd; /usr/sbin/syslogd -m 0
```

If all of this fiddling about with facilities and priorities strikes you as arcane Unix speak, you're not alone. These examples are provided for systems that include the default (and venerable) *syslogd* daemon. If you have the opportu-nity to install a new *syslogd*, you will likely want to look into *syslog-ng*. This new implementation of *syslogd* allows much more flexible filtering and a slew of new features. We take a look at some of what is possible with *syslog-ng* in "Aggregate Logs from Remote Sites" [Hack #59].

—Rob Flickenger

HACK #56 Integrate Windows into Your Syslog Infrastructure
Keep track of all of your Windows hosts the Unix way.

It's hard enough to keep tabs on all the Event Logs for all your Windows hosts, but it's even more difficult if your propensities predispose you to Unix. After all, Unix systems keep their logs in plain text files that are easily searchable with common shell commands. This is a world apart from the binary logs that Windows keeps in its Event Log. Wouldn't it be nice if you could have your Windows machines work more like the Unix machines that you're used to? Someone has already thought of it and has written a free Windows service that lets us do just that.

Ntsyslog (*http://ntsyslog.sourceforge.net/*) is a freely available service written for Windows that allows you to log to a remote *syslogd*. To set it up, just download and extract the ZIP file, and then copy the *NTSyslogCtrl.exe* and *ntsyslog.exe* files into your *%SystemRoot%\system32* directory.

To install the service, open up a command prompt and run this:

```
C:\> ntsyslog –install
```

To verify that it was installed, open up the Administrative Tools Control Panel applet and double-click the Services icon. Then scroll around and look for the NTsyslog service. You should see something similar to Figure 4-1.

By default, NTsyslog installs itself to run under the Local System account, which has complete access to the resources of the local host. This is

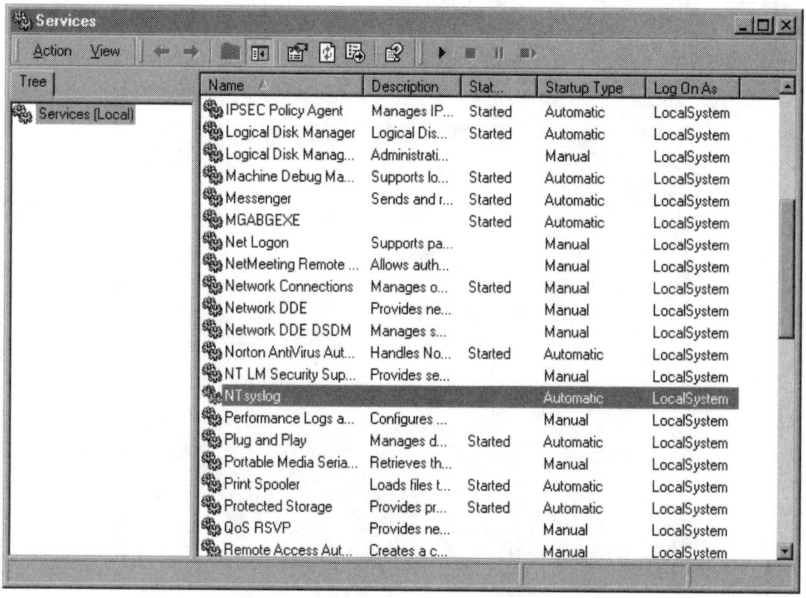

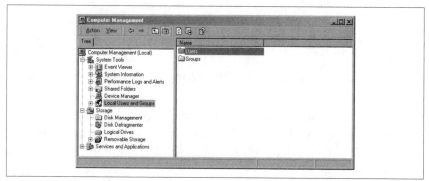

Figure 4-1. The Services Control Panel applet with the NTsyslog service shown

obviously not the optimal configuration, since the NTsyslog service needs access to the Event Log and nothing else. You can change this by double-clicking the NTsyslog line in the Services Control Panel applet as shown in Figure 4-1. This will bring up the Properties dialog for the service. However, before you do this, you might want to create an account specifically for the NTsyslog service that has only the necessary privileges for NTsyslog to run properly. To do this, go back to the Administrative Tools window and double-click the Computer Management icon. After clicking the Local Users and Groups icon, you should see something similar to Figure 4-2.

Figure 4-2. The Computer Management Control Panel applet with the Users folder shown

Right-click the Users folder and click New User. You should now see a dialog where you can enter the information for the new user. Enter information similar to that shown in Figure 4-3, and make sure you pick a strong password.

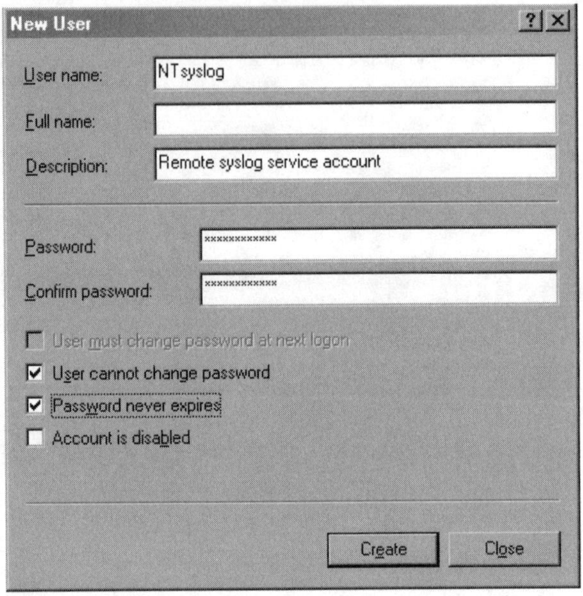

Figure 4-3. Creating a new user for NTsyslog

Now we need to give our new user the rights it needs to do its job. Locate the Local Security Policy icon in the Administrative Tools window and double-click it. Click the Local Policies folder in the left pane of the Local Security Settings window, and then double-click the User Rights Assignment folder in the right pane of the window. You should now see something similar to Figure 4-4.

The access right that we are looking for is "Manage auditing and security log". Locate this in the Policy list and double-click it. You should then see a dialog like Figure 4-5.

Click the Add button, select the name of the user from the list, and then click OK.

We have the account and we've given it the proper access rights, so let's go back to the Services window and double-click the NTsyslog service to bring up its Properties dialog. Click the Log On tab and you should see something like Figure 4-6.

Click the "This account" radio button to enable the Browse... button. Now click the Browse... button and locate and select the account that you

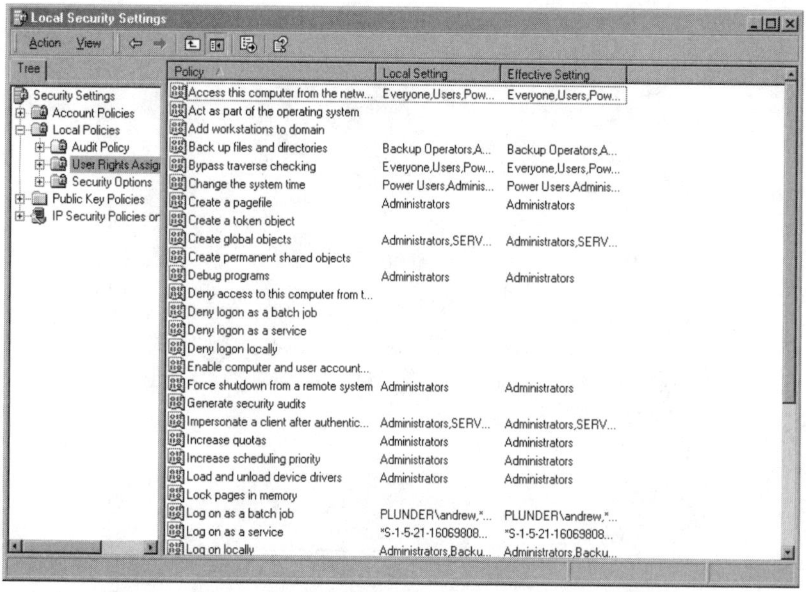

Figure 4-4. Viewing the User Rights Assignments settings in the Local Security Settings Control Panel applet

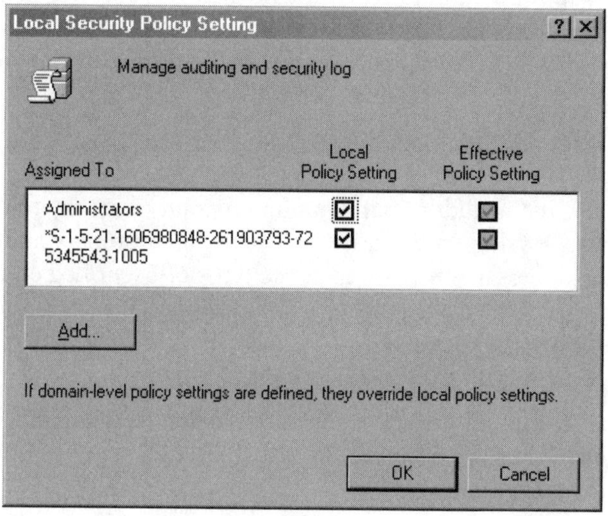

Figure 4-5. Settings for the "Manage auditing and security log" user right

created. Then click the OK button. You should now see the account name in the text box to the right of the "This account" radio button. Enter the password you set for the account and confirm it. After clicking the Apply button,

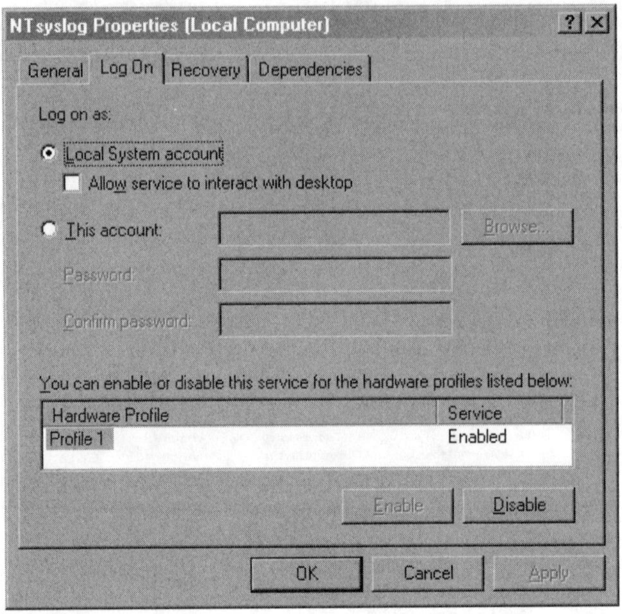

Figure 4-6. The Log On tab for the NTsyslog service Properties dialog

a dialog will appear confirming that the Log On As A Service right has been granted to the account. Click the OK button, then click the General tab in the Properties dialog. To start the service as the new user that you created, click the Start button. If you get an error dialog, you will need to change the ACL for the *ntsyslog.exe* file and add Read and Execute permissions for the new account.

Now we'll use the included configuration program to configure the settings particular to NTsyslog. You can use this to set up a primary and secondary *syslogd* to send messages to, as well as the types of Event Log events to send and their mappings to syslog facilities and severities. You can also start and stop the NTsyslog service from this screen. To use the configuration program, run *NTSyslogCtrl.exe*. You should see a window like Figure 4-7.

To start the service, click the Start Service button; to stop the service, click the Stop Service button. Clicking the Syslog Daemons button brings up the dialog shown in Figure 4-8.

Again, this is pretty straightforward. Just put in the host you want to log to, and if you have a secondary syslog host, put that in the appropriate field.

The most difficult part of the configuration is setting up the mappings of the Event Log entry types to the syslog facilities and severity levels, but even this is fairly easy. In the drop-down list (as seen in Figure 4-7) you can select

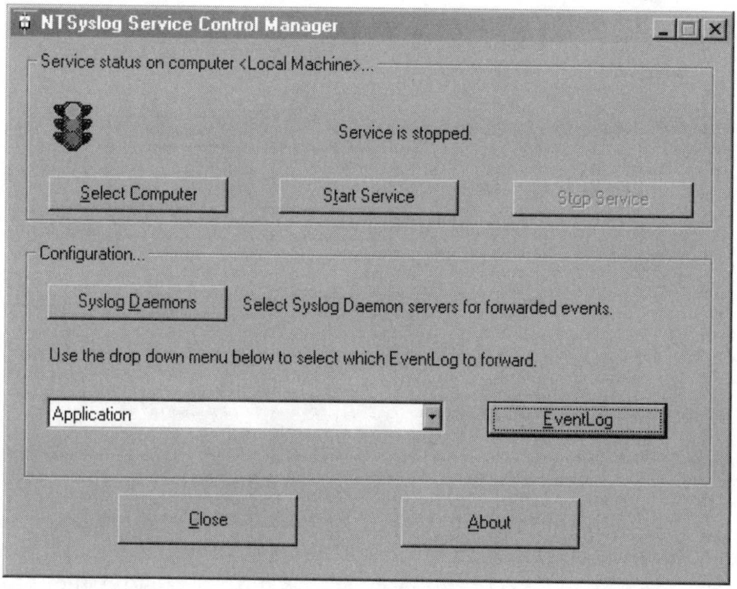

Figure 4-7. The NTSyslog configuration program

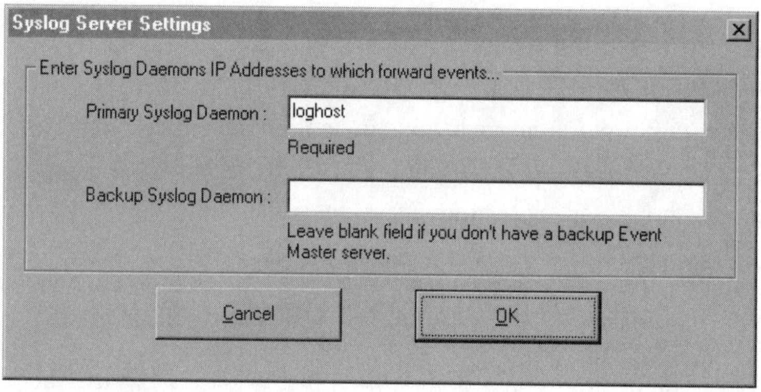

Figure 4-8. Specifying a primary and backup syslog server

between the Application, Security, and System Event Logs. To configure one, simply select it in the drop-down list and click the EventLog button. If you select the Security log and click the EventLog button, you should see something similar to Figure 4-9.

To enable the forwarding of a particular type of event, click the checkbox next to it. Using the drop-down listboxes, you can also configure the facility and severity mappings for each type. Since this is the security log, you should probably pick one of the security/auth syslog facilities. For the

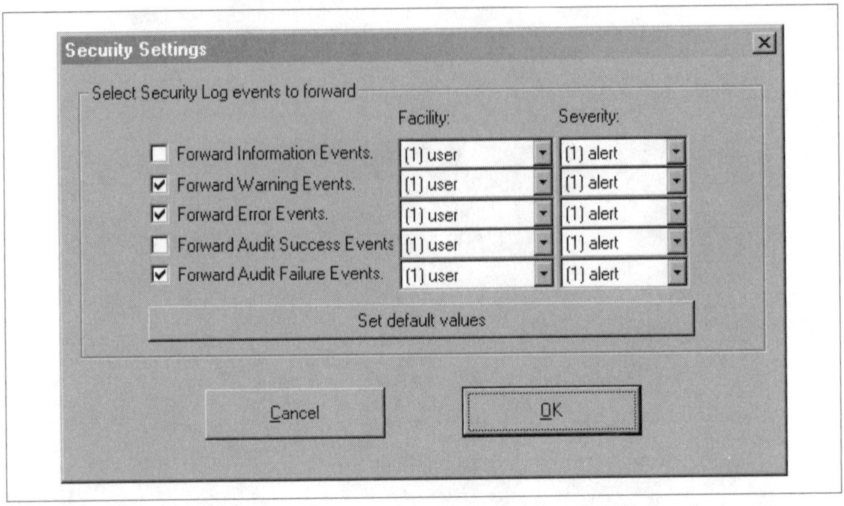

Figure 4-9. Mapping Security Event Log entries to syslog facilities and severities

severity, choose something that sounds similar to the Event Log type. For example, I selected (4)security/auth1 and (6)information for the Information type for the Security Event Log. You could, however, pick a facility and severity that's not used on any of your Unix servers, and have your *syslogd* log all Windows events to a common file separate from your Unix logs. Of course, if you're using *syslog-ng* [Hack #59], you can use any facility you like and filter out your Windows hosts by IP address.

Once you have it working, try logging in and out a few times using an incorrect password so that you can see that everything is working.

If it is, you should see login failure messages similar to this:

```
Oct 29 17:19:04 plunder security[failure] 529 NT AUTHORITY\\SYSTEM  Logon
Failure:  Reason:Unknown user name or bad password  User Name:andrew
Domain:PLUNDER  Logon Type:2  Logon Process:User32    Authentication
Package:Negotiate  Workstation Name:PLUNDER
```

One of the best things about doing this is that now you can use the wealth and flexibility of Unix log-monitoring tools to help monitor all your Windows systems.

Automatically Summarize Your Logs

HACK
#57

Wade through that haystack of logs to find the proverbial needle.

If you're logging almost every piece of information you can from all services and hosts on your network, no doubt you're drowning in a sea of information. One way to keep abreast of the real issues affecting your systems is summarizing your logs. This easy with the *logwatch* tool (*http://www.logwatch.org*).

Logwatch analyzes your system logs over a given period of time and automatically generates reports, and it can easily be run from *cron* so that it can email you the results. *Logwatch* is available with most Red Hat Linux distributions. You can also download RPM packages from the project's web site if you are using another RPM-based Linux distribution.

To compile *logwatch* from source, you can download the source code package. Since it is a script there is no need to compile anything. Thus installing it is as simple as copying the *logwatch* script to a directory.

You can install it by running commands similar to these:

```
# tar xfz logwatch-5.0.tar.gz
# cd logwatch-5.0
# mkdir /etc/log.d
# cp -R conf lib scripts /etc/log.d
```

You can also install the manpage and, for added convenience, create a link from the *logwatch.pl* script to */usr/sbin/logwatch*:

```
# cp logwatch.8 /usr/share/man/man8
# (cd /usr/sbin && \
ln -s ../../etc/log.d/scripts/logwatch.pl logwatch)
```

Running the following command will give you a taste of the summaries *logwatch* creates:

```
# logwatch --print | less
################### LogWatch 4.3.1 (01/13/03) ###################
        Processing Initiated: Sat Dec 27 21:12:26 2003
        Date Range Processed: yesterday
       Detail Level of Output: 0
          Logfiles for Host: colossus
 ################################################################

 -------------------- SSHD Begin ------------------------

Users logging in through sshd:
   andrew logged in from kryten.nnc (192.168.0.60) using password: 2 Time(s)

 --------------------- SSHD End -------------------------


###################### LogWatch End #########################
```

If you have an */etc/cron.daily* directory, you can simply make a symbolic link from the *logwatch.pl* script to */etc/cron.daily/logwatch.pl*, and the script will be run daily. Alternatively, you can create an entry in root's crontab, in which case you can also modify *logwatch*'s behavior by passing it command-line switches. For instance, you can change the email address that *logwatch* sends reports to by using the --mailto command-line option. They are sent to the local root account by default, which is probably not what you want.

Logwatch supports most standard log files without any additional configuration, but you can add support for any type of log file. To do this, you first need to create a logfile group configuration for the new file type in */etc/log.d/ conf/logfiles*. This file just needs to contain an entry pointing *logwatch* to the logfile for the service and another entry specifying a globbing pattern for any archived log files for that service.

For example, if you had a service called myservice, you could create */etc/log.d/ conf/logfiles/myservice.conf* with these contents:

```
LogFile = /var/log/myservice
Archive = /var/log/myservice.*
```

Next, you need to create a service definition file. This should be called */etc/ log.d/conf/services/myservice.conf* and should contain the following line:

```
LogFile = myservice
```

Finally, since *logwatch* is merely a framework for generating log file summaries, you'll also need to create a script in */etc/log.d/scripts/services* called *myservice*. When *logwatch* executes, it will strip all time entries from the logs and pass the rest of the log entry through standard input to the *myservice* script. Therefore, you must write your script to read from standard input, parse out the pertinent information, and then print it to standard out.

This just scratches the surface of how to get *logwatch* running on your system. There is a great deal of information in the HOWTO-Make-Filter, which is included with the *logwatch* distribution.

HACK #58   Monitor Your Logs Automatically

Use swatch to alert you to possible problems as they happen.

Automatically generated log file summaries are fine for keeping abreast of what's happening with your systems and networks, but if you want to know about events as they happen, you'll need to look elsewhere. One tool that can help keep you informed in real time is *swatch* (*http://swatch.sourceforge.net*), the "Simple WATCHer."

Swatch is a highly configurable log file monitor that can watch a file for user-defined triggers and dispatch alerts in a variety of ways. It consists of a Perl program, a configuration file, and a library of actions to take when it sees a trigger in the file it is monitoring.

To install *swatch*, download the package, unpack it, and go into the directory that it creates. Then run these commands:

```
# perl Makefile.PL
# make && make install
```

Before *swatch* will build, the Date::Calc, Date::Parse, File::Tail, and Time:
:HiRes Perl CPAN modules must be installed. If you get an error message
like the following when you run perl Makefile.PL, then you will need to
install those modules:

```
Warning: prerequisite Date::Calc 0 not found.
Warning: prerequisite Date::Parse 0 not found.
Warning: prerequisite Time::HiRes 1.12 not found.
Writing Makefile for swatch
```

If you already have Perl's CPAN module installed, simply run these commands:

```
# perl -MCPAN -e "install Date::Calc"
# perl -MCPAN -e "install Date::Parse"
# perl -MCPAN -e "Time::HiRes"
```

By default, *swatch* looks for its configuration in a file called *.swatchrc* in the
current user's home directory. This file contains regular expressions to watch
for in the file that you are monitoring with *swatch*. If you want to use a different configuration file, tell *swatch* by using the -c command-line switch.

For instance, to use */etc/swatch/messages.conf* to monitor */var/log/messages*,
you could invoke *swatch* like this:

```
# swatch -c /etc/swatch/messages.conf -t /var/log/messages
```

The general format for entries in this file is the following:

```
watchfor /<regex>/
<action1>
[action2]
[action3]
...
```

Alternatively, you can ignore specific log messages that match a regular
expression by using the ignore keyword:

```
ignore /<regex>/
```

You can also specify multiple regular expressions by separating them with
the | character.

Swatch is very configurable in what actions it can take when a string
matches a regular expression. Some useful actions that you can specify in
your *.swatchrc* are echo, write, exec, mail, pipe, and throttle.

The echo action simply prints the matching line to the console; additionally,
you can specify what text mode it will use. Thus, lines can be printed to the
console as bold, underlined, blinking, inverted, or colored text.

For instance, if you wanted to print a matching line in red, blinking text, you
could use the following action:

```
echo blink,red
```

The `write` action is similar to the `echo` action, except it does not support text modes. It can, however, write the matching line to any specified user's TTY:

```
write user:user2:...
```

The `exec` action allows you to execute any command:

```
exec <command>
```

You can use the $0 or $* variables to pass the entire matching line to the command that you execute, $1 to pass the first field in the line, $2 for the second, and so on. So, if you wanted to pass only the second and third fields from the matching line to the command *mycommand*, you could use an action like this:

```
exec "mycommand $2 $3"
```

The `mail` action is especially useful if you have an email-enabled or text messaging–capable cell phone or pager. When using the `mail` action, you can list as many recipient addresses as you like, in addition to specifying a subject line. *Swatch* will send the line that matched the regular expression to these addresses with the subject you set.

Here is the general form of the `mail` action:

```
mail addresses=address:address2:...,subject=mysubject
```

When using the `mail` action, be sure to escape the @ characters in the email addresses (i.e., @ becomes \@). If you have any spaces in the subject of the email, you should escape those as well.

In addition to the exec action, *swatch* can execute external commands with the pipe action as well. The only difference is that instead of passing arguments to the command, *swatch* will execute the command and pipe the matching line to it. To use this action, just put the `pipe` keyword followed by the command you want to use.

Alternatively, to increase performance, you can use the `keep_open` option to keep the pipe to the program open until *swatch* exits or needs to perform a different pipe action:

```
pipe mycommand,keep_open
```

One problem with executing commands or sending emails whenever a specific string occurs in a log message is that sometimes the same log message may be generated over and over again very rapidly. Clearly, if this were to happen, you wouldn't want to get paged or emailed 100 times within a 10-minute period. To alleviate this problem, *swatch* provides the `throttle` action. This action lets you suppress a specific message or any message that matches a particular regular expression for a specified amount of time.

The general form of the `throttle` action is:

```
throttle h:m:s
```

The throttle action will throttle based on the contents of the message by default. If you would like to throttle the actions based on the regular expression that caused the match, you can add a ,use=regex to the end of your throttle statement.

Swatch is an incredibly useful tool, but it can take some work to create a good *.swatchrc*. The best way to figure out what to look for is to examine your log files for behavior that you want to monitor closely.

Aggregate Logs from Remote Sites

Integrate collocated and other remote systems or networks into your central syslog infrastructure.

Monitoring the logs of a remote site or just a collocated server can often be overlooked when faced with the task of monitoring activity on your local network. You could use the traditional syslog facilities to send logging information from the remote network or systems, but since the syslog daemon uses UDP for sending to remote systems, this is not the ideal solution. UDP provides no reliability in its communications, and so you risk losing logging information. In addition, the traditional syslog daemon has no means to encrypt the traffic that it sends, so your logs might being viewable by anyone with access to the intermediary networks between you and your remote hosts or networks.

To get around these issues, you'll have to look beyond the syslog daemon that comes with your operating system and find a replacement. One such replacement syslog daemon is *syslog-ng* (*http://www.balabit.com/products/syslog_ng/*). *syslog-ng* is not only a fully functional replacement for the traditional syslog daemon, but also adds flexible message filtering capabilities, as well as support for logging to remote systems over TCP (in addition to support for the traditional UDP protocol). With the addition of TCP support, you can also employ *stunnel* or *ssh* to securely send the logs across untrusted networks.

To build *syslog-ng*, you will need the *libol* library package (*http://www.balabit.com/downloads/syslog-ng/libol/*) in addition to the *syslog-ng* package. After downloading these packages, unpack them and then build *libol*:

```
$ tar xfz libol-0.3.9.tar.gz
$ cd libol-0.3.9
$ ./configure && make
```

When you build *syslog-ng* you can have it statically link to *libol*, so there is no need to fully install the library.

And now to build *syslog-ng*:

```
$ tar xfz syslog-ng-1.5.26.tar.gz
$ cd syslog-ng-1.5.26
```

```
$ ./configure --with-libol=../libol-0.3.9
$ make
```

If you want to compile in TCP wrappers support, you can add the `--enable-tcp-wrapper` flag to the configure script. After *syslog-ng* is finished compiling, become root and run `make install`. This will install the *syslog-ng* binary and manpages. To configure the daemon, create the */usr/local/etc/syslog-ng* directory and then create a *syslog-ng.conf* to put in it. To start off with, you can use one of the sample configuration files in the *doc* directory of the *syslog-ng* distribution.

There are five types of configuration file entries for *syslog-ng*, each of which begins with a specific keyword. The `options` entry allows you to tweak the behavior of the daemon, such as how often the daemon will sync the logs to the disk, whether the daemon will create directories automatically, and hostname expansion behavior. `source` entries tell *syslog-ng* where to collect log entries from. A source can include Unix sockets, TCP or UDP sockets, files, or pipes. `destination` entries allow you to specify possible places for *syslog-ng* to send logs to. You can specify files, pipes, Unix sockets, TCP or UDP sockets, TTYs, or programs. Sources and destinations are then combined with filters (using the `filter` keyword), which let you select syslog facilities and log levels. Finally, these are all used together in a `log` entry to define precisely where the information is logged. Thus you can arbitrarily combine any source, select what syslog facilities and levels you want from it, and then route it to any destination. This is what makes *syslog-ng* an incredibly powerful and flexible tool.

To set up *syslog-ng* on the remote end so that it can replace the *syslogd* on the system and send traffic to a remote *syslog-ng*, you'll first need to translate your *syslog.conf* to equivalent `source`, `destination`, and `log` entries.

Here's the *syslog.conf* for a FreeBSD system:

```
*.err;kern.debug;auth.notice;mail.crit          /dev/console
*.notice;kern.debug;lpr.info;mail.crit;news.err /var/log/messages
security.*                                      /var/log/security
auth.info;authpriv.info                         /var/log/auth.log
mail.info                                       /var/log/maillog
lpr.info                                        /var/log/lpd-errs
cron.*                                          /var/log/cron
*.emerg                                         *
```

First you'll need to configure a source. Under FreeBSD, */dev/log* is a link to */var/run/log*. The following source entry tells *syslog-ng* to read entries from this file:

```
source src { unix-dgram("/var/run/log"); internal(); };
```

If you were using Linux, you would specify unix-stream and /dev/log like this:

```
source src { unix-stream("/dev/log"); internal() };
```

The internal() entry is for messages generated by *syslog-ng* itself. Notice that you can include multiple sources in a source entry. Next, include destination entries for each of the actual log files:

```
destination console { file("/dev/console"); };
destination messages { file("/var/log/messages"); };
destination security { file("/var/log/security"); };
destination authlog { file("/var/log/auth.log"); };
destination maillog { file("/var/log/maillog"); };
destination lpd-errs { file("/var/log/lpd-errs"); };
destination cron { file("/var/log/cron"); };
destination slip { file("/var/log/slip.log"); };
destination ppp { file("/var/log/ppp.log"); };
destination allusers { usertty("*"); };
```

In addition to these destinations, you'll also want to specify one for remote logging to another *syslog-ng* process. This can be done with a line similar to this:

```
destination loghost { tcp("192.168.0.2" port(5140)); };
```

The port number can be any available TCP port.

Defining the filters is straightforward. You can simply create one for each syslog facility and log level, or you can create them according to those used in your *syslog.conf*. If you do the latter, you will only have to specify one filter in each log statement, but it will still take some work to create your filters.

Here are example filters for the syslog facilities:

```
filter f_auth { facility(auth); };
filter f_authpriv { facility(authpriv); };
filter f_console { facility(console); };
filter f_cron { facility(cron); };
filter f_daemon { facility(daemon); };
filter f_ftp { facility(ftp); };
filter f_kern { facility(kern); };
filter f_lpr { facility(lpr); };
filter f_mail { facility(mail); };
filter f_news { facility(news); };
filter f_security { facility(security); };
filter f_user { facility(user); };
filter f_uucp { facility(uucp); };
```

and examples for the log levels:

```
filter f_emerg { level(emerg); };
filter f_alert { level(alert..emerg); };
filter f_crit { level(crit..emerg); };
```

```
filter f_err { level(err..emerg); };
filter f_warning { level(warning..emerg); };
filter f_notice { level(notice..emerg); };
filter f_info { level(info..emerg); };
filter f_debug { level(debug..emerg); };
```

Now you can combine the source with the proper filter and destination within the log entries:

```
# *.err;kern.debug;auth.notice;mail.crit              /dev/console
log { source(src); filter(f_err); destination(console); };
log { source(src); filter(f_kern); filter(f_debug); destination(console); };
log { source(src); filter(f_auth); filter(f_notice); destination(console); };
log { source(src); filter(f_mail); filter(f_crit); destination(console); };

# *.notice;kern.debug;lpr.info;mail.crit;news.err     /var/log/messages
log { source(src); filter(f_notice); destination(messages); };
log { source(src); filter(f_kern); filter(f_debug); destination(messages); };
log { source(src); filter(f_lpr); filter(f_info); destination(messages); };
log { source(src); filter(f_mail); filter(f_crit); destination(messages); };
log { source(src); filter(f_news); filter(f_err); destination(messages); };

# security.*                                          /var/log/security
log { source(src); filter(f_security); destination(security); };

# auth.info;authpriv.info                             /var/log/auth.log
log { source(src); filter(f_auth); filter(f_info); destination(authlog); };
log { source(src); filter(f_authpriv); filter(f_info); destination(authlog); };

# mail.info                                           /var/log/maillog
log { source(src); filter(f_mail); filter(f_info); destination(maillog); };

# lpr.info                                            /var/log/lpd-errs
log { source(src); filter(f_lpr); filter(f_info); destination(lpd-errs); };

# cron.*                                              /var/log/cron
log { source(src); filter(f_cron); destination(cron); };

# *.emerg                                                            *
log { source(src); filter(f_emerg); destination(allusers); };
```

You can set up the machine that will be receiving the logs in much the same way as if you were replacing the currently used *syslogd*.

To configure *syslog-ng* to receive messages from a remote host, you must specify a source entry:

```
source r_src { tcp(ip("192.168.0.2") port(5140)); };
```

Alternatively, you can dump all the logs from the remote machines into the same destinations that you use for your local log entries. This is not really recommended, because it can be a nightmare to manage, but can be done by including multiple source drivers in the source entry that you use for your local logs:

```
source src {
    unix-dgram("/var/run/log");
    tcp(ip("192.168.0.2") port(5140));
    internal();
};
```

Now logs gathered from remote hosts will appear in any of the destinations that were combined with this source.

If you would like all logs from remote hosts to go into a separate file named for each host in /var/log, you could use a destination like this:

```
destination r_all { file("/var/log/$HOST"); };
```

syslog-ng will expand the $HOST macro to the hostname of the system sending it logs and create a file named after it in /var/log. An appropriate log entry to use with this would be:

```
log { source(r_src); destination(r_all); };
```

However, an even better method is to recreate all of the remote syslog-ng log files on your central log server. For instance, a destination for a remote machine's messages file would look like this:

```
destination fbsd_messages { file("/var/log/$HOST/messages"); };
```

Notice here that the $HOST macro is used in place of a directory name. If you are using a destination entry like this, be sure to create the directory beforehand, or use the create_dirs() option:

```
options { create_dirs(yes); };
```

syslog-ng's macros are a very powerful feature. For instance, if you wanted to separate logs by hostname and day, you could use a destination like this:

```
destination fbsd_messages {
    file("/var/log/$HOST/$YEAR.$MONTH.$DAY/messages");
};
```

You can combine the remote source with the appropriate destinations for the logs coming in from the network just as you did when configuring syslog-ng for local logging—just specify the remote source with the proper destination and filters.

Another neat thing you can do with syslog-ng is collect logs from a number of remote hosts and then send all of those to yet another syslog-ng daemon. You can do this by combining a remote source and a remote destination with a log entry:

```
log { source(r_src); destination(loghost); };
```

Since *syslog-ng* is now using TCP ports, you can use any encrypting tunnel you like to secure the traffic between your *syslog-ng* daemons. You can use SSH port forwarding **[Hack #72]** or *stunnel* **[Hack #76]** to create an encrypted channel between each of your servers. By limiting connections on the listening port to include only localhost (using firewall rules, as in "Firewall with Netfilter" **[Hack #33]** or "Firewall with OpenBSD's PacketFilter" **[Hack #34]**), you can eliminate the possibility of bogus log entries or denial-of-service attacks.

Server logs are among the most critical information that a system administrator needs to do her job. Using new tools and strong encryption, you can keep your valuable log data safe from prying eyes.

H A C K   Log User Activity with Process Accounting
#60   Keep a detailed audit trail of what's being done on your systems.

Process accounting allows you to keep detailed logs of every command a user runs, including CPU time and memory used. From a security standpoint, this means the system administrator can gather information about what user ran which command and at what time. This is not only very useful in assessing a break-in or local root compromise, but can also be used to spot attempted malicious behavior by normal users of the system. (Remember that intrusions don't always come from the outside.)

To enable process accounting, run these commands:

```
# mkdir /var/account
# touch /var/account/pacct && chmod 660 /var/account/pacct
# /sbin/accton /var/account/pacct
```

Alternatively, if you are running Red Hat or SuSE Linux and have the process accounting package installed, you can run a startup script to enable process accounting. On Red Hat, try this:

```
# chkconfig psacct on
# /sbin/service psacct start
```

On SuSE, use these commands:

```
# chkconfig acct on
# /sbin/service acct start
```

The process accounting package provides several programs to make use of the data that is being logged. The *ac* program analyzes total connect time for users on the system.

Running it without any arguments prints out the number of hours logged by the current user:

```
[andrew@colossus andrew]$ ac
        total      106.23
```

If you want to display connect time for all users who have logged onto the system, use the -p switch:

```
# ac -p
        root                            0.07
        andrew                        106.05
        total        106.12
```

The lastcomm command lets you search the accounting logs by username, command name, or terminal:

```
# lastcomm andrew
ls                      andrew    ??      0.01 secs Mon Dec 15 05:58
rpmq                    andrew    ??      0.08 secs Mon Dec 15 05:58
sh                      andrew    ??      0.03 secs Mon Dec 15 05:44
gunzip                  andrew    ??      0.00 secs Mon Dec 15 05:44

# lastcomm bash
bash             F      andrew    ??      0.00 secs Mon Dec 15 06:44
bash             F      root      stdout  0.01 secs Mon Dec 15 05:20
bash             F      root      stdout  0.00 secs Mon Dec 15 05:20
bash             F      andrew    ??      0.00 secs Mon Dec 15 05:19
```

To summarize the accounting information, you can use the sa command. By default it will list all the commands found in the accounting logs and print the number of times that each one has been executed:

```
# sa
        14        0.04re      0.03cp      0avio      1297k    troff
         7        0.03re      0.03cp      0avio       422k    lastcomm
         2       63.90re      0.01cp      0avio       983k    info
        14       34.02re      0.01cp      0avio       959k    less
        14        0.03re      0.01cp      0avio      1132k    grotty
        44        0.02re      0.01cp      0avio       432k    gunzip
```

You can also use the -u flag to output per-user statistics:

```
# sa -u
root        0.01 cpu       344k mem     0 io which
root        0.00 cpu      1094k mem     0 io bash
root        0.07 cpu      1434k mem     0 io rpmq
andrew      0.02 cpu       342k mem     0 io id
andrew      0.00 cpu       526k mem     0 io bash
andrew      0.01 cpu       526k mem     0 io bash
andrew      0.03 cpu       378k mem     0 io grep
andrew      0.01 cpu       354k mem     0 io id
andrew      0.01 cpu       526k mem     0 io bash
andrew      0.00 cpu       340k mem     0 io hostname
```

You can peruse the output of these commands every so often to look for suspicious activity, such as increases in CPU usage or commands that are known to be used for mischief.

## CHAPTER FIVE

Monitoring and Trending
Hacks 61–66

While the importance of reliable system logs can't be overestimated, logs only tell part of the story of what is happening on your network. When something out of the ordinary happens, the event is duly logged to the appropriate file, where it waits for a human to notice and take the appropriate action. But logs are valuable only if someone actually reads them. When log files add to the deluge of information that most network administrators already wade through each day, many log files may go unread for days or weeks. This situation is made worse when log files are clogged with irrelevant information. For example, a cry for help from an overburdened mail server can easily be lost if it is surrounded by innocuous entries about failed spam attempts. All too often, logs are used as a resource to figure out "what happened" when systems fail, rather than as a guide to what is happening now.

Another important aspect of log entries is that they only provide a "spot check" of your system at a particular moment. Without a history of what normal performance looks like, it can be difficult to tell the difference between ordinary network traffic, a DoS attack, and a visitation from Slashdot readers. While you can easily build a report on how many times the */var* partition filled up, how can you easily know what usage looks like over time? Is the mail spool clogged due to one inconsiderate user, or is it part of an attack by an adversary? Or is it simply a general trend that is the result of trying to serve too many users on too small a disk?

This chapter describes a number of methods for tracking the availability of services and resources over time. Rather than having to watch system logs manually, it is usually far better to have the systems notify you when there is a problem—and *only* when there is a problem. There are also a number of suggestions about how to recognize trends in your network traffic by monitoring flows and plotting the results on a graph. Sure, you may know what your average outbound Internet traffic looks like, but how much of that traffic is made up of HTTP versus SMTP? You may know roughly how much is being used by each server on your network, but what if you want to break the traffic down by protocol? The hacks in this chapter will show you how.

HACK #61 Monitor Availability

Use Nagios to keep tabs on your network.

Since remote exploits can often crash the service that is being broken into or cause its CPU use to skyrocket, you should monitor the services that are running on your network. Just looking for an open port (such as by using Nmap [Hack #42]) isn't enough. The machine may be able to respond to a TCP connect request, but the service may be unable to respond (or worse, could be replaced by a different program entirely!). One tool that can help you verify your services at a glance is Nagios (*http://www.nagios.org*).

Nagios is a network-monitoring application that monitors not only the services running on the hosts on your network, but also the resources on each host, such as CPU usage, disk space, memory usage, running processes, log files, and much more. In the advent of a problem it can notify you through email, pager, or any other method that you define, and you can check the status of your network at a glace by using the web GUI. Nagios is also easily extensible through its plug-in API.

To install Nagios, download the source distribution from the Nagios web site. Then, unpack the source distribution and go into the directory it creates:

```
$ tar xfz nagios-1.1.tar.gz
$ cd nagios-1.1
```

Before running Nagios's configure script, you should create a user and group for Nagios to run as (e.g., nagios). Then run the configure script with a command similar to this:

```
$ ./configure --with-nagios-user=nagios --with-nagios-grp=nagios
```

This will install Nagios in */usr/local/nagios*. As usual, you can modify this behavior by using the --prefix switch. After the configure script finishes, compile Nagios by running make all. Then become root and run make install to install it. In addition, you can optionally install Nagios's initialization scripts by running make install-init.

If you take a look into the */usr/local/nagios* directory right now, you will see that there are four directories. The *bin* directory contains a single file, *nagios*, that is the core of the package. This application does the actual monitoring. The *sbin* directory contains the CGI scripts that will be used in the web-based interface. Inside the *share* directory, you'll find the HTML files and documentation. Finally, the *var* directory is where Nagios will store its information once it starts running.

Before you can use Nagios, you will need a couple of configuration files. These files go into the *etc* directory, which will be created when you run `make install-config`. This command also creates a sample copy of each required configuration file and puts them into the *etc* directory.

At this point the Nagios installation is complete. However, it is not very useful in its current state, because it lacks the actual monitoring applications. These applications, which check whether a particular monitored service is functioning properly, are called *plug-ins*. Nagios comes with a default set of plug-ins, but they must be downloaded and installed separately.

Download the latest Nagios Plugins package and decompress it. You will need to run the provided configure script to prepare the package for compilation on your system. You will find that the plug-ins are installed in a fashion similar to the actual Nagios program.

To compile the plug-ins, run commands similar to these:

```
$ ./configure --prefix=/usr/local/nagios \
--with-nagios-user=nagios --with-nagis-grp=nagios
$ make all
```

You might get notifications about missing programs or Perl modules while the script is running. These are mostly fine, unless you specifically need the mentioned applications to monitor a service.

After compilation is finished, become root and run `make install` to install the plug-ins. The plug-ins will be installed in the *libexec* directory of your Nagios base directory (e.g., */usr/local/nagios/libexec*).

There are a few rules that all Nagios plug-ins should implement, making them suitable for use by Nagios. All plug-ins provide a `--help` option that displays information about the plug-in and how it works. This feature is very helpful when you're trying to monitor a new service using a plug-in you haven't used before.

For instance, to learn how the `check_ssh` plug-in works, run the following command:

```
$ /usr/local/nagios/libexec/check_ssh
check_ssh (nagios-plugins 1.4.0alpha1) 1.13
The nagios plugins come with ABSOLUTELY NO WARRANTY. You may redistribute
copies of the plugins under the terms of the GNU General Public License.
For more information about these matters, see the file named COPYING.
Copyright (c) 1999 Remi Paulmier <remi@sinfomic.fr>
Copyright (c) 2000-2003 Nagios Plugin Development Team
        <nagiosplug-devel@lists.sourceforge.net>
```

Try to connect to SSH server at specified server and port

Usage: check_ssh [-46] [-t <timeout>] [-p <port>] <host>
       check_ssh (-h | --help) for detailed help
       check_ssh (-V | --version) for version information

Options:
 -h, --help
    Print detailed help screen
 -V, --version
    Print version information
 -H, --hostname=ADDRESS
    Host name or IP Address
 -p, --port=INTEGER
    Port number (default: 22)
 -4, --use-ipv4
    Use IPv4 connection
 -6, --use-ipv6
    Use IPv6 connection
 -t, --timeout=INTEGER
    Seconds before connection times out (default: 10)
 -v, --verbose
    Show details for command-line debugging (Nagios may truncate output)

Send email to nagios-users@lists.sourceforge.net if you have questions
regarding use of this software. To submit patches or suggest improvements,
send email to nagiosplug-devel@lists.sourceforge.net

Now that both Nagios and the plug-ins are installed, we are almost ready to
begin monitoring our servers. However, Nagios will not even start before it's
configured properly.

The sample configuration files provide a good starting point:

```
$ cd /usr/local/nagios/etc
$ ls -1
cgi.cfg-sample
checkcommands.cfg-sample
contactgroups.cfg-sample
contacts.cfg-sample
dependencies.cfg-sample
escalations.cfg-sample
hostgroups.cfg-sample
hosts.cfg-sample
misccommands.cfg-sample
nagios.cfg-sample
resource.cfg-sample
services.cfg-sample
timeperiods.cfg-sample
```

Since these are sample files, the Nagios authors added a *.cfg-sample* suffix to
each file. First, we need to copy or rename each one to end in *.cfg*, so that

the software can use them properly. (If you don't change the configuration filenames, Nagios will not be able to find them.)

You can either rename each file manually or use the following command to take care of them all at once. Type the following script on a single line:

```
# for i in *cfg-sample; do mv $i `echo $i | \
    sed -e s/cfg-sample/cfg/`; done;
```

First there is the main configuration file, *nagios.cfg*. You can pretty much leave everything as is—the Nagios installation process will make sure the file paths used in the configuration file are correct. There's one option, however, that you might want to change: check_external_commands, which is set to 0 by default. If you would like to be able to directly run commands through the web interface, you will want to set this to 1. Depending on your network environment, this may or may not be an acceptable security risk, as enabling this option will permit the execution of scripts from the web interface. Other options you need to set in *cgi.cfg* configure which usernames are allowed to run external commands.

To get Nagios running, you must modify all but a few of the sample configuration files. Configuring Nagios to monitor your servers is not as difficult as it looks. To help you, you can use the verbose mode of the Nagios binary by running:

```
#  /usr/local/nagios/bin/nagios -v /usr/local/nagios/etc/nagios.cfg
```

This command will go through the configuration files and report any errors. Start fixing the errors one by one, and run the command again to find the next error. For testing purposes, it is easiest to disable all hosts and services definitions in the sample configuration files and merely use the files as templates for your own hosts and services. You can keep most of the files as is, but remove the following, which will be created from scratch:

```
hosts.cfg
services.cfg
contacts.cfg
contactgroups.cfg
hostgroups.cfg
```

Start by configuring a host to monitor. We first need to add our host definition and configure some options for that host. You can add as many hosts as you like, but we will stick with one for the sake of simplicity.

Here are the contents of *hosts.cfg*:

```
# Generic host definition template
define host{
  # The name of this host template - referenced i
  name                    generic-host
```

```
n other host definitions, used for template recursion/resolution
# Host notifications are enabled
notifications_enabled            1
# Host event handler is enabled
event_handler_enabled            1
# Flap detection is enabled
flap_detection_enabled           1
# Process performance data
process_perf_data                1
# Retain status information across program restarts
retain_status_information        1
# Retain non-status information across program restarts
retain_nonstatus_information     1
# DONT REGISTER THIS DEFINITION - ITS NOT A REAL HOST,
# JUST A TEMPLATE!
register                         0
}


# Host Definition
define host{
# Name of host template to use
use                     generic-host
host_name               freelinuxcd.org
alias                   Free Linux CD Project Server
address                 www.freelinuxcd.org
check_command           check-host-alive
max_check_attempts      10
notification_interval   120
notification_period     24x7
notification_options    d,u,r
}
```

The first host defined is not a real host but a template from which other host definitions are derived. This mechanism can be seen in other configuration files and makes configuration based on a predefined set of defaults a breeze.

With this setup we are monitoring only one host, *www.freelinuxcd.org*, to see if it is alive. The host_name parameter is important because other configuration files will refer to this server by this name. Now the host needs to be added to a hostgroup, so that the application knows which contact group to send notifications to.

Here's what *hostgroups.cfg* looks like:

```
define hostgroup{
hostgroup_name  flcd-servers
alias           The Free Linux CD Project Servers
contact_groups  flcd-admins
members         freelinuxcd.org
}
```

This defines a new hostgroup and associates the flcd-admins contact_group with it. Now you'll need to define that contact group in *contactgroups.cfg*:

```
define contactgroup{
contactgroup_name       flcd-admins
alias                   FreeLinuxCD.org Admins
members                 oktay, verty
}
```

Here the flcd-admins contact_group is defined with two members, oktay and verty. This configuration ensures that both users will be notified when something goes wrong with a server that flcd-admins is responsible for. The next step is to set the contact information and notification preferences for these users.

Here are the definitions for those two members in *contacts.cfg*:

```
define contact{
contact_name                        oktay
alias                               Oktay Altunergil
service_notification_period         24x7
host_notification_period            24x7
service_notification_options        w,u,c,r
host_notification_options           d,u,r
service_notification_commands       notify-by-email,notify-by-epager
host_notification_commands          host-notify-by-email,host-notify-by-epager
email                               oktay@freelinuxcd.org
pager                               dummypagenagios-admin@localhost.localdomain
}

define contact{
contact_name                        Verty
alias                               David 'Verty' Ky
service_notification_period         24x7
host_notification_period            24x7
service_notification_options        w,u,c,r
host_notification_options           d,u,r
service_notification_commands       notify-by-email,notify-by-epager
host_notification_commands          host-notify-by-email
email                               verty@flcd.org
}
```

In addition to providing contact details for a particular user, the contact_ name in the *contacts.cfg* file is also used by the CGI scripts (i.e., the web interface) to determine whether a particular user is allowed to access a particular resource. Now that your hosts and contacts are configured, you can start to configure monitoring for individual services on your server.

This is done in *services.cfg*:

```
# Generic service definition template
define service{
# The 'name' of this service template, referenced in other service definitions
```

```
name    generic-service
# Active service checks are enabled
active_checks_enabled  1
# Passive service checks are enabled/accepted
passive_checks_enabled  1
# Active service checks should be parallelized
# (disabling this can lead to major performance problems)
parallelize_check  1
# We should obsess over this service (if necessary)
obsess_over_service  1
# Default is to NOT check service 'freshness'
check_freshness   0
# Service notifications are enabled
notifications_enabled  1
# Service event handler is enabled
event_handler_enabled  1
# Flap detection is enabled
flap_detection_enabled  1
# Process performance data
process_perf_data  1
# Retain status information across program restarts
retain_status_information 1
# Retain non-status information across program restarts
retain_nonstatus_information 1
# DONT REGISTER THIS DEFINITION - ITS NOT A REAL SERVICE, JUST A TEMPLATE!
register   0
}

# Service definition
define service{
# Name of service template to use
use    generic-service
host_name   freelinuxcd.org
service_description  HTTP
is_volatile   0
check_period   24x7
max_check_attempts  3
normal_check_interval  5
retry_check_interval  1
contact_groups   flcd-admins
notification_interval  120
notification_period  24x7
notification_options  w,u,c,r
check_command   check_http
}

# Service definition
define service{
# Name of service template to use
use    generic-service
host_name   freelinuxcd.org
service_description  PING
is_volatile   0
```

```
check_period    24x7
max_check_attempts  3
normal_check_interval  5
retry_check_interval  1
contact_groups    flcd-admins
notification_interval  120
notification_period  24x7
notification_options  c,r
check_command    check_ping!100.0,20%!500.0,60%
}
```

This setup configures monitoring for two services. The first service definition, which has been called HTTP, will monitor whether the web server is up and will notify you if there's a problem. The second definition monitors the ping statistics from the server and notifies you if the response time or packet loss become too high. The commands used are check_http and check_ping, which were installed into the *libexec* directory during the plug-in installation. Please take your time to familiarize yourself with all other available plug-ins and configure them similarly to the previous example definitions.

Once you're happy with your configuration, run Nagios with the -v switch one last time to make sure everything checks out. Then run it as a daemon by using the -d switch:

```
# /usr/local/nagios/bin/nagios -d /usr/local/nagios/etc/nagios.cfg
```

That's all there is to it. Give Nagios a couple of minutes to generate some data, and then point your browser to the machine and look at the pretty service warning lights.

HACK #62 Graph Trends
Use RRDtool to easily generate graphs for just about anything.

You may be familiar with graphing bandwidth usage with tools such as MRTG. From a security standpoint it's useful to graph bandwidth usage, since it can help you spot anomalous behavior. Having a history of typical bandwidth usage gives you a baseline to judge what's going on. This can make it easier to determine if somebody is performing a DoS attack on your site, or if a machine on your network is acting as a Warez depot.

RRDtool (http://people.ee.ethz.ch/~oetiker/webtools/rrdtool/) provides similar functionality to MRTG, but it is much more flexible. *RRDtool* is basically a tool for storing data in a general-purpose database that will never grow in size. RRD stands for *round-robin database*, which is a special type of database that maintains a fixed number of entries—the oldest entry is constantly being replaced by the newest data. *RRDtool* also has the ability to generate graphs of the data contained in a round-robin database.

The most common use of *RRDtool* is to make pretty bandwidth graphs. This is easily done with *RRDtool* and *snmpget*, a utility that queries devices managed with SNMP. First, you'll need to create a round-robin database by running a command similar to this one:

```
$ rrdtool create zul.rrd --start N \
DS:de0_in:COUNTER:600:U:U \
DS:de0_out:COUNTER:600:U:U \
RRA:AVERAGE:0.5:1:600 \
RRA:AVERAGE:0.5:6:700 \
RRA:AVERAGE:0.5:24:775 \
RRA:AVERAGE:0.5:288:797 \
RRA:MAX:0.5:1:600 \
RRA:MAX:0.5:6:700 \
RRA:MAX:0.5:24:775 \
RRA:MAX:0.5:288:797
```

This command creates a database containing entries for two separate counters, de0_in and de0_out. These will store samples of interface statistics collected every five minutes from an SNMP daemon on a router. In addition, it contains several fields for automatically maintaining running averages.

You can populate the database by running a command like this:

```
$ rrdtool update zul.rrd N:\
`snmpget -Oqv zul public interfaces.ifTable.ifEntry.ifInOctets.4`:\
`snmpget -Oqv zul public interfaces.ifTable.ifEntry.ifOutOctets.4`
```

This command queries the input and output statistics for the de0 interface on a computer named zul. To schedule it to run every five minutes, you could make a crontab entry similar to the following:

```
0-55/5 * * * * rrdtool update /home/andrew/rrdbs/zul.rrd N:`snmpget -Oqv zul
public interfaces.ifTable.ifEntry.ifInOctets.4`:`snmpget -Oqv zul public
interfaces.ifTable.ifEntry.ifOutOctets.4`
```

However, you can use whatever methods you want to collect the data. To generate hourly graphs of the data, you could run a command like this:

```
rrdtool graph zul_de0-hourly.png -t "Hourly Bandwidth" --start -3600 \
        DEF:inoctets=zul.rrd:de0_in:AVERAGE \
        DEF:outoctets=zul.rrd:de0_out:AVERAGE \
        AREA:inoctets#00FF00:"de0 In" \
        LINE1:outoctets#0000FF:"de0 Out"
```

This would create an image like the one shown in Figure 5-1.

The -3600 in the command tells rrdtool that you want to graph the data collected over the last hour (there are 3,600 seconds in an hour). Likewise, if you wanted to create a graph over the course of a day, you would use -86400.

But that's just the beginning. After collecting multiple data sources, you can combine them all into a single graph that gives you a great deal of information at a glance. Figure 5-2 shows the relative outbound usage of several

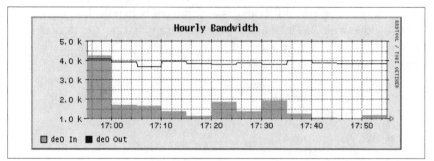

Figure 5-1. A graph generated by RRDtool

servers simultaneously, with the total average for all servers just below it. While this figure is in grayscale, the actual graph uses a different color for each server, making it easy to tell at a glance which one is hogging all of the bandwidth.

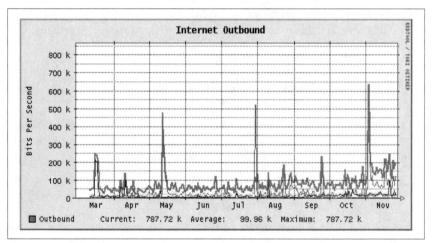

Figure 5-2. Multiple servers on a single graph

As you can see, *RRDtool* is a very flexible tool. All you need to do is tell it how much data you want to store and then set up some method to collect the data at a regular interval. Then you can easily generate a graph of the data whenever you want it.

HACK #63   Run ntop for Real-Time Network Stats

See who's doing what on your network over time with ntop.

If you're looking for real-time network statistics, check out the terrific *ntop* tool (*http://www.ntop.org*). It is a full-featured protocol analyzer with a web frontend, complete with SSL and graphing support. Unfortunately, *ntop* isn't exactly lightweight (the precise amount of resources required depend on the size of your network and the volume of network traffic), but it can give you a very nice picture of who's talking to whom on your network.

ntop needs to run initially as root (to throw your interfaces into promiscuous mode and start capturing packets), but then releases its privileges to a user that you specify. If you decide to run *ntop* for long periods of time, you'll probably be happiest running it on a dedicated monitoring box (with few other services running on it, for security and performance reasons).

Here's a quick reference on how to get *ntop* up and running. First, create an ntop user and group:

```
# groupadd ntop
# useradd -c "ntop user" -d /usr/local/etc/ntop \
  -s /bin/true -g ntop ntop
```

Then unpack and build *ntop* per the instructions in *docs/BUILD-NTOP.txt*. I assume that you have the source tree unpacked in */usr/local/src/ntop-2.1.3/*.

Create a directory for *ntop* to keep its capture database in:

```
# mkdir /usr/local/etc/ntop
```

Note that it should be owned by root, and not by the ntop user.

If you'd like to use SSL for HTTPS (instead of standard HTTP), then copy the default SSL key to */usr/local/etc/ntop*. Assuming that you have unpacked *ntop* into */usr/local/src/ntop-2.1.3/*, you can do this by running this command:

```
# cp /usr/local/src/ntop-2.1.3/ntop/*pem /usr/local/etc/ntop
```

Note that the default SSL key will not be built with the correct hostname for your server. So, you'll probably want to generate your own SSL certificate and key pair [Hack #45]. Now you'll need to initialize the *ntop* databases and set an administrative password:

```
# ntop -A -u ntop -P /usr/local/etc/ntop
21/Sep/2002 20:30:23 Initializing GDBM...
21/Sep/2002 20:30:23 Started thread (1026) for network packet analyser.
21/Sep/2002 20:30:23 Started thread (2051) for idle hosts detection.
21/Sep/2002 20:30:23 Started thread (3076) for DNS address resolution.
21/Sep/2002 20:30:23 Started thread (4101) for address purge.

Please enter the password for the admin user:
Please enter the password again:
21/Sep/2002 20:30:29 Admin user password has been set.
```

Finally, run *ntop* as a daemon, and start the SSL server on your favorite port (4242, for example):

```
# ntop -u ntop -P /usr/local/etc/ntop -W4242 -d
```

By default, *ntop* also runs a standard HTTP server on port 3000. You should seriously consider locking down access to these ports, either at your firewall or by using command-line iptables rules **[Hack #33]**.

Let *ntop* run for a while, then connect to *https://your.server.here:4242/*. You can find out all sorts of details about what traffic has been seen on your network, as shown in Figure 5-3.

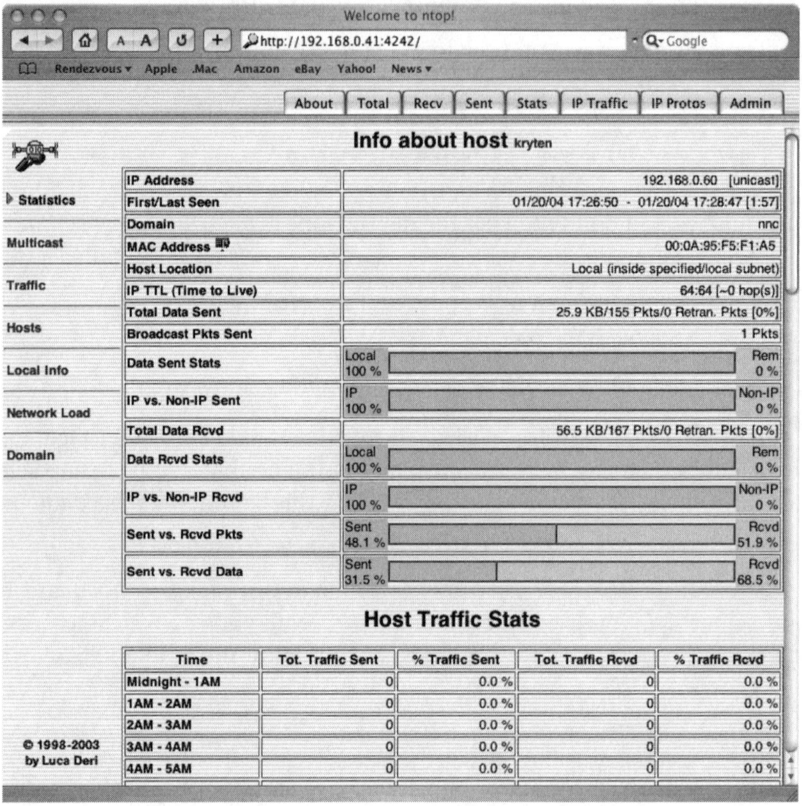

Figure 5-3. Displaying a host's statistics in ntop's web interface

While tools like tcpdump and Ethereal give you detailed, interactive analysis of network traffic, *ntop* delivers a wealth of statistical information in a very slick and easy-to-use web interface. When properly installed and locked down, it will likely become a favorite tool in your network analysis tool chest

—*Rob Flickenger (Linux Server Hacks)*

HACK #64 Audit Network Traffic

Use Argus to monitor your network and to keep an audit trail of your traffic.

Wouldn't it be nice if you could keep a complete record of everything that happened on your network? It would certainly help to track down problems and would be invaluable in the event of a security incident, but it would just take up too much space to keep all of that data around. The next best thing would be to keep a log of all the packets, but not actually keep the data. You can do this with *Argus* (*http://www.qosient.com/argus/*).

Argus, or the Audit Record Generation and Utilization System, is a tool that can log network transactions in a variety of ways and can even collect performance metrics on every connection that it is able to see. *Argus* also contains several utilities that can make queries against the logs, so you can easily extract the information you need. These tools allow you to generate ASCII-, RMON-, or XML-formatted information from an *Argus* log file. *Argus* also provides a Perl interface for accessing its log files, so you can easily write custom scripts to make use of the data it collects.

To set up *Argus*, you'll first need to download the source distribution and unpack it. Then change into the directory that it creates:

```
$ tar xfz argus-2.0.5.tar.gz
$ cd argus-2.0.5
```

To compile *Argus*, run this command:

```
$ ./configure && make
```

After compilation has finished, you can install *Argus* by becoming root and running this command:

```
# make install
```

To get a quick demo of *Argus*, run it and then let it collect some data for a little while:

```
# argus -d -e `hostname` -w /tmp/arguslog
```

This command will start argus in daemon mode and have it write its logs to */tmp/argus*.

After letting it collect some data, try querying it with the ra command. This will show you an ASCII representation of the packets that argus has logged:

```
$ ra -r /tmp/arguslog
12 Jan 04 05:42:48 udp plunder.nnc.netbios-ns -> 192.168.0.255.netbios-ns INT
12 Jan 04 05:43:09 udp 192.168.0.250.snmptrap -> 255.255.255.255.snmptrap INT
12 Jan 04 05:43:15 udp print.nnc.netbios-dgm -> 192.168.0.255.netbios-dgm INT
12 Jan 04 05:43:28 llc 0:c0:2:57:98:79.null -> Broadcast.null INT
12 Jan 04 05:43:28 nvl 0:c0:2:57:98:79 -> Broadcast INT
12 Jan 04 05:43:28 llc 0:c0:2:57:98:79.null -> Broadcast.null INT
```

```
12 Jan 04 05:43:28 llc 0:c0:2:57:98:79.null -> Broadcast.null INT
12 Jan 04 05:44:19 udp kryten.nnc.56581 -> 255.255.255.255.2222 TIM
12 Jan 04 05:43:34 udp sunder.nnc.netbios-ns -> 192.168.0.255.netbios-ns INT
12 Jan 04 05:44:08 arp plunder.nnc who-has sirius.nnc INT
12 Jan 04 05:44:08 udp plunder.nnc.netbios-ns -> 192.168.0.255.netbios-ns INT
12 Jan 04 05:44:15 udp print.nnc.netbios-dgm -> 192.168.0.255.netbios-dgm INT
12 Jan 04 05:45:06 udp sunder.nnc.netbios-dgm -> 192.168.0.255.netbios-dgm TIM
12 Jan 04 05:40:26 man pkts 734 bytes 75574 drops 0 CON
12 Jan 04 05:44:28 nvl 0:c0:2:57:98:79 -> Broadcast INT
12 Jan 04 05:44:28 llc 0:c0:2:57:98:79.null -> Broadcast.null INT
12 Jan 04 05:44:28 llc 0:c0:2:57:98:79.null -> Broadcast.null INT
12 Jan 04 05:44:28 llc 0:c0:2:57:98:79.null -> Broadcast.null INT
12 Jan 04 05:45:08 udp plunder.nnc.netbios-ns -> 192.168.0.255.netbios-ns INT
12 Jan 04 05:45:09 tcp kryten.nnc.54176 ?> colossus.nnc.ssh EST
12 Jan 04 05:45:15 udp print.nnc.netbios-dgm -> 192.168.0.255.netbios-dgm INT
```

This is just a few minutes of logs from one host, but it is stored in a very compact manner. In fact, during testing, a whole day's worth of logs consumed only 1.4 MB!

The ra command can also take tcpdump-style filters so that you can query the logs for packets that match a specific host, protocol, port, or any number of other characteristics.

For instance, if you wanted to query the logs for all packets sent either to or from the host named kryten, you could used a command similar to this one:

```
$ ra -r /tmp/argus - "host kryten"
12 Jan 04 09:26:34  udp  kryten.nnc.55689  ->  255.255.255.255.2222  TIM
12 Jan 04 09:26:36  tcp  kryten.nnc.54176  ?>  linux-vmm.nnc.ssh  EST
12 Jan 04 09:27:37  tcp  kryten.nnc.54176  ?>  linux-vmm.nnc.ssh  EST
12 Jan 04 09:28:34  udp  kryten.nnc.55691  ->  255.255.255.255.2222  TIM
12 Jan 04 09:28:05  icmp kryten.nnc  <->  linux-vmm.nnc  ECO
12 Jan 04 09:28:06  icmp kryten.nnc  <->  linux-vmm.nnc  ECO
12 Jan 04 09:29:06  tcp  kryten.nnc.54176  ?>  linux-vmm.nnc.ssh  EST
12 Jan 04 09:30:34  udp  kryten.nnc.55692  ->  255.255.255.255.2222  TIM
12 Jan 04 09:32:34  udp  kryten.nnc.55693  ->  255.255.255.255.2222  TIM
12 Jan 04 09:33:06  tcp  kryten.nnc.54176  ?>  linux-vmm.nnc.ssh  EST
12 Jan 04 09:34:34  udp  kryten.nnc.55694  ->  255.255.255.255.2222
12 Jan 04 09:53:44  tcp  kryten.nnc.54176  ?>  linux-vmm.nnc.ssh  EST
```

You can also generate a new *Argus* log file containing only the results of your query by using the -w option to ra and specifying a file to write the results to.

To get XML output from *Argus*, you can use the *raxml* utility to make queries, much in the same way as you can with ra. For instance, here's the first record returned by using the previous query for all packets that matched the hostname of kryten:

```
$ raxml -r /tmp/arguslog - "host kryten"
<ArgusFlowRecord  ArgusSourceId = "192.168.0.41" SequenceNumber = "3"
 Cause = "Status" StartDate = "2004-01-12" StartTime = "09:25:26"
 StartTimeusecs = "319091" LastDate  = "2004-01-12"
```

```
LastTime = "09:25:32"  LastTimeusecs = "521982"
Duration = "6.202891" TransRefNum = "0">
   <MACAddrs SrcAddr = "0:a:95:c7:2b:10" DstAddr = "0:c:29:e2:2b:c1" />
   <Flow> <IP SrcIPAddr = "192.168.0.60" DstIPAddr = "192.168.0.41"
    Proto = "tcp" Sport = "56060" Dport = "22" IpId = "27b8" /> </Flow>
   <FlowAttrs SrcTTL = "64" DstTTL = "64" SrcTOS = "10" DstTOS = "10" />
   <ExtFlow> <TCPExtFlow TCPState = "EST" TCPOptions = "TIME"
   SynAckuSecs = "0" AckDatauSecs = "0" >
                <TCPExtMetrics  SrcTCPSeqBase = "4204580547"
                SrcTCPAckBytes = "527" SrcTCPBytes = "528"
                SrcTCPRetrans = "0" SrcTCPWin = "65535" SrcTCPFlags = "PA"
                DstTCPSeqBase = "3077608383" DstTCPAckBytes = "1135"
                DstTCPBytes = "992" DstTCPRetrans = "0" DstTCPWin = "9792"
                DstTCPFlags = "PA" />
              </TCPExtFlow>
   </ExtFlow>
   <Metrics SrcCount = "24" DstCount = "17" SrcBytes = "2112"
    DstBytes = "2258"  SrcAppBytes = "528" DstAppBytes = "1136" />
 </ArgusFlowRecord>
```

As you can see, Argus keeps track of much more information than it would seem if you were just going by the output generated by ra. This is where Argus really shines, because it can store such a large amount of information about your network traffic in a small amount of space. In addition, Argus makes it easy to convert this information into other formats, such as XML, which makes it easy to write applications that can understand the data.

Collect Statistics with Firewall Rules
#65

Make your firewall ruleset do the work for you when you want to collect statistics.

If you want to start collecting statistics on your network traffic but dread setting up SNMP, you don't have to worry. You can use the firewalling code in your operating system to collect statistics for you.

For instance, if you were using Linux, you could use iptables commands similar to the following to keep track of bandwidth consumed by a particular machine that passes traffic through your firewall:

```
# iptables -N KRYTEN && iptables -A KRYTEN -j ACCEPT
# iptables -N KRYTEN_IN && iptables -A KRYTEN_IN -j KRYTEN
# iptables -N KRYTEN_OUT && iptables -A KRYTEN_OUT -j KRYTEN
# iptables -A FORWARD -s 192.168.0.60 -j KRYTEN_OUT
# iptables -A FORWARD -d 192.168.0.60 -j KRYTEN_IN
```

This leverages the packet and byte counters associated with each iptables rule to provide input and output bandwidth statistics for traffic forwarded through the firewall. It works by first defining a chain named KRYTEN, which is named after the host that the statistics will be collected on. This chain contains an unconditional accept rule and will be used to quickly add up the total bandwidth that kryten consumes. To itemize the downstream bandwidth kryten is using, another chain is created called `KRYTEN_IN`. This chain contains only one rule, which is to unconditionally jump to the `KRYTEN` chain in order for the inbound bandwidth to be added with the outbound bandwidth being consumed. Similarly, the `KRYTEN_OUT` chain tallies outbound bandwidth being consumed and then jumps to the `KRYTEN` chain so that the outbound bandwidth will be added to the inbound bandwidth being consumed. Finally, rules are added to the `FORWARD` chain that direct the packet to the correct chain, depending on whether it's coming from or going to kryten.

After applying these rules, you can then view the total bandwidth (inbound and outbound) consumed by kryten by running a command like this:

```
# iptables -vx -L KRYTEN
Chain kryten (2 references)
  pkts   bytes target   prot opt in   out   source    destination
   442   46340 ACCEPT   all  --  any  any   anywhere anywhere
```

You can easily parse out the bytes field, and thereby generate graphs with *RRDtool* [Hack #62], by using a command like this:

```
# iptables -vx -L KRYTEN | egrep -v 'Chain|pkts' | awk '{print $2}'
```

To get the inbound or outbound bandwidth consumed, just replace `KRYTEN` with `KRYTEN_IN` or `KRYTEN_OUT`, respectively. Of course, you don't have to limit your statistic collection criteria to just per-computer bandwidth usage. You can collect statistics on anything that you can create an iptables rule for, including ports, MAC addresses, or just about anything else that passes through your network.

HACK #66 Sniff the Ether Remotely
Monitor your networks remotely with rpcapd.

If you've ever wanted to monitor network traffic from another segment and use a graphical protocol analyzer like Ethereal (*http://www.ethereal.com*), you know how time-consuming it can be. First you have to capture the data. Then you have to get it onto the workstation that you're running the analyzer from, and then you have to load the file into the analyzer itself. This creates a real problem because it increases the time between performing an experiment and seeing the results, which makes diagnosing and fixing network problems take much longer than they should.

One tool that solves this problem is *rpcapd*, a program included with Win-Pcap (*http://winpcap.polito.it*). *rpcapd* is a daemon that monitors network interfaces in promiscuous mode and sends the data that it collects back to a sniffer running on a remote machine. You can run *rpcapd* either from the command line or as a service. To start *rpcapd*, you will probably want to use the -n flag, which tells the daemon to use null authentication. Using this option, you will be able to monitor the data stream that *rpcapd* produces with any program that uses the WinPcap capture interface. Otherwise, special code will have to be added to the program that you are using that will allow it to authenticate itself with *rpcapd*. Since the -n option allows anyone to connect to the daemon, you'll also want to use the -l option, which allows you to specify a comma-separated list of hosts that can connect.

So, to run *rpcapd* from the command line, use a command similar to this:

```
C:\Program Files\WinPcap>rpcapd -l obsidian -n
Press CTRL + C to stop the server...
```

When run as a service, *rpcapd* uses the *rpcapd.ini* file for its configuration information. This file resides in the same directory as the executable and is easily created by running *rpcapd* with the -s switch, which instructs *rpcapd* to save its configuration to the file you specify.

To create a *pcap.ini*, run a command like this:

```
C:\Program Files\WinPcap>rpcapd -l obsidian -n -s rpcapd.ini
Press CTRL + C to stop the server...
```

Now press Ctrl-C and see what the file contains:

```
C:\Program Files\WinPcap>type rpcapd.ini
# Configuration file help.

# Hosts which are allowed to connect to this server (passive mode)
# Format: PassiveClient = <name or address>

PassiveClient = obsidian

# Hosts to which this server is trying to connect to (active mode)
# Format: ActiveClient = <name or address>, <port | DEFAULT>

# Permit NULL authentication: YES or NOT

NullAuthPermit = YES
```

To start the service, you can either use the Services control panel applet or use the net command from the command line:

```
C:\Program Files\WinPcap>net start rpcapd

The Remote Packet Capture Protocol v.0 (experimental) service was started
successfully.
```

Now, to connect to the daemon you will need to find out the name that Win-Pcap uses to refer to the network device you want to monitor. To do this, you can use either WinDump, a command-line packet sniffer for Windows, or Ethereal. WinDump is available from the same web site as WinPcap.

To get the device name with WinDump simply run it with the -D flag:

```
C:\Program Files\WinPcap>windump -D
1.\Device\NPF_{EE07A5AE-4D19-4118-97CE-3BF656CD718F} (NDIS 5.0 driver)
```

You can use Ethereal to obtain the device name by starting up Ethereal, going to the Capture menu, and clicking Start. After you do that, a dialog will open that has a list of the available adapters on the system, much like the one seen in Figure 5-4. The device names in the list are those that you will later specify when connecting to *rpcapd* from a remote system.

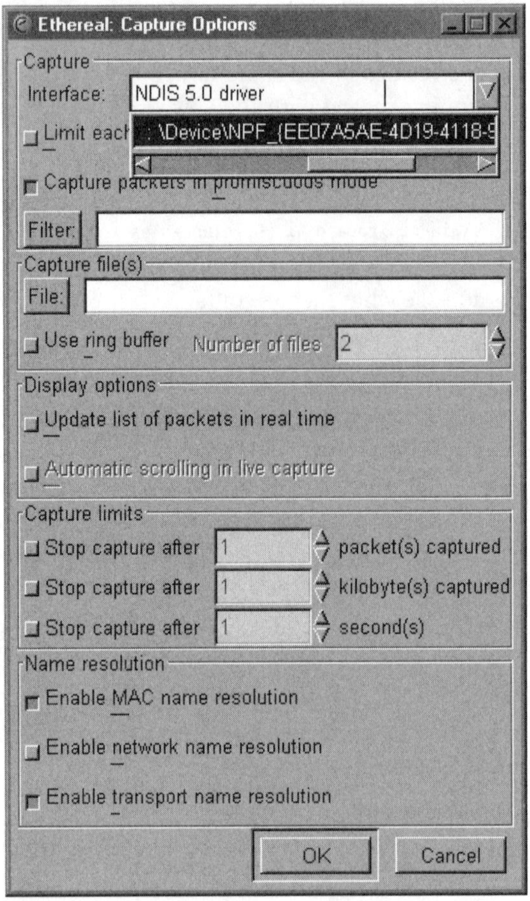

Figure 5-4. Ethereal Capture Options dialog

When you connect to a remote machine with your favorite sniffer, simply put the device name for the interface you want to monitor prefixed by rpcap and the hostname, like this:

```
rpcap://plunder/\Device\NPF_{EE07A5AE-4D19-4118-97CE-3BF656CD718F}
```

You can see an example of this with Ethereal in Figure 5-5.

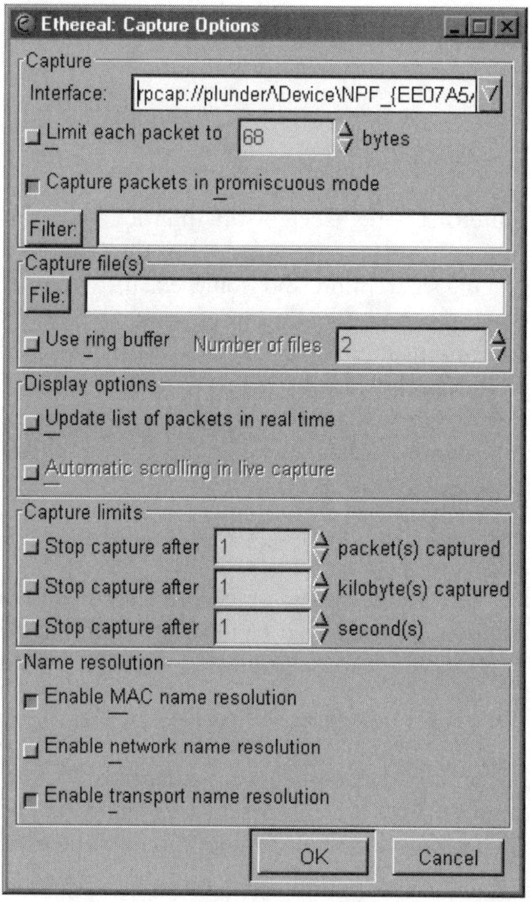

Figure 5-5. Using a remote capture source with Ethereal

If you've set up everything correctly, you should see traffic streaming from the remote end into your sniffer just as if it were being captured from a local interface.

## CHAPTER SIX

Secure Tunnels
Hacks 67–81

Untrusted computer networks (such as the Internet and public wireless networks) can be pretty hostile environments, but they can be tamed to some degree. By leveraging encryption and some encapsulation tricks, you can build more trustworthy networks on top of whatever network you choose, even if it is full of miscreants trying to watch or otherwise manipulate your data. This chapter primarily deals with how to set up secure, encrypted communications over networks that you don't completely trust. Some of the hacks focus mainly on providing a secure and encrypted transport mechanism, while others discuss how to create a virtual private network (VPN).

In reading this chapter, you'll learn how to set up Ipsec-based encrypted links on several operating systems, how to create virtual network interfaces that can be tunneled through an encrypted connection, and how to forward TCP connections over an encrypted channel. In addition, you'll also learn how to set up a cross-platform VPN solution.

The beauty of most of these hacks is that after reading them, you can mix and match transport-layer encryption solutions with whatever virtual network–oriented approach that best meets your needs. In this way, you can safely build vast, powerful private networks leveraging the public Internet as infrastructure. You can use these techniques for anything from securely connecting two remote offices to building a completely routed private network enterprise on top of the Internet.

HACK #67 Set Up IPsec Under Linux
Secure your traffic in Linux with FreeS/WAN.

The most popular way of configuring IPsec connections under Linux is to use the *FreeS/WAN* (*http://www.freeswan.org*) package. *FreeS/WAN* is made up of two components, KerneL IP Security (KLIPS) and *pluto*. KLIPS is the kernel-level code that actually encrypts and decrypts the data; it also manages the Security Policy Database (SPD). *pluto* is a user-land daemon that controls IKE negotiation.

The *FreeS/WAN* build process builds a new kernel and the required management utilities. Download the latest *FreeS/WAN* source from the project's web site and unpack the source tree in */usr/src*. The documentation that comes with *FreeS/WAN* is very extensive and can help you tailor the installation to suit your needs. The kernel component can be either installed as a kernel-loadable module or statically compiled directly into your kernel. In order to compile *FreeS/WAN*, the kernel source must be installed on your machine. During the compilation process, the kernel configuration utility will launch. This is normal. Compile *FreeS/WAN* using your kernel configuration method of choice (such the menu-based or X11-based options). Once the compilation is complete, install the kernel and user-land tools per the *FreeS/WAN* documentation (typically a make install will suffice).

FreeS/WAN configuration is controlled by two configuration files: */etc/ipsec.conf* and */etc/ipsec.secrets*. The examples given in this hack are very limited in scope and apply only to a wireless network. The manpages for both files are quite informative and useful for more complicated connection requirements. Another excellent resource for more information is the book *Building Linux Virtual Private Networks (VPNs)*, by Oleg Kolesnikov and Brian Hatch (New Riders).

The *ipsec.conf* file breaks a VPN connection into right- and lefthand segments. This difference is merely a logical division. The lefthand side can be either the internal or external network; this allows the same configuration file to be used for both ends of a VPN network-to-network tunnel. Unfortunately, in our case, there will be differences between the client and gateway configurations.

The file is broken up into a configuration section (config) and a connection section (conn). The config section specifies basic parameters for Ipsec, such as available interfaces and specific directives to be passed to *pluto*. The conn section describes the various connections that are available to the VPN. There is a global conn section (conn %default) where you can specify values that are common to all connections, such as the lifetime of a key and the method of key exchange.

The following *ipsec.conf* encrypts all information to the Internet with a VPN endpoint on your gateway:

```
# /etc/ipsec.conf
# Set configuration options
config setup
    interfaces=%defaultroute
    # Debug parameters.  Set either to "all" for more info
```

```
        klipsdebug=none
        plutodebug=none
        # standard Pluto configuration
        plutoload=%search
        plutostart=%search
        # make sure there are no PMTU Discovery problems
        overridemtu=1443
# default configuration settings
conn %default
        # Be aggressive in rekeying attempts
        keyingtries=0
        # use IKE
        keyexchange=ike
        keylife=12h
        # use shared secrets
        authby=secret
# setup the VPN to the Internet
conn wireless_connection1
        type=tunnel
        # left is the client side
        left=192.168.0.104
        # right is the internet gateway
        right=192.168.0.1
        rightsubnet=0.0.0.0/0
        # automatically start the connection
        auto=start
```

Now add the shared secret to *ipsec.secrets*:

```
192.168.0.104 192.168.0.1: PSK "supersecret"
```

That's it. Once your gateway is configured, try to ping your default gateway. *pluto* will launch automatically and the connection should come up. If you have a problem reaching the gateway, check the syslog messages on both the client and gateway.

The gateway configuration is largely the same as the client configuration. Given the intelligence of the *ipsec.conf* file, very few changes need to be made. Since your gateway has more than one Ethernet interface, you should hard-set the IPsec configuration to use the right interface:

```
# assume internal ethernet interface is eth0
interfaces="ipsec0=eth0"
```

You will then need to add a connection for each internal client. This can be handled in different ways as your network scales, but the following configuration should work for a reasonable number of clients:

```
...
conn wireless_connection2
        type=tunnel
        left=192.168.0.105
        right=192.168.0.1
```

```
        rightsubnet=0.0.0.0/0
        auto=start
conn wireless_connection3
        type=tunnel
        left=192.168.0.106
        right=192.168.0.1
        rightsubnet=0.0.0.0/0
        auto=start
...
```

Finally, add the shared secrets for all the clients to ipsec.secrets:

```
192.168.0.105 192.168.0.1: PSK "evenmoresecret"
192.168.0.106 192.168.0.1: PSK "notsosecret"
```

Clients should now be connecting to the Internet via a VPN tunnel to the gateway. Check the log files or turn up the debug level if the tunnel does not come up.

HACK #68 Set Up IPsec Under FreeBSD

Use FreeBSD's built-in IPsec support to secure your traffic.

Using IPsec with IKE under FreeBSD requires enabling IPsec in the kernel and installing a user-land program, racoon, to handle the IKE negotiations.

You'll need to make sure that your kernel has been compiled with the following options:

```
options        IPSEC              #IP security
options        IPSEC_ESP          #IP security (crypto; define w/ IPSEC)
options        IPSEC_DEBUG        #debug for IP security
```

If it hasn't, you'll need to define them and then rebuild and install the kernel. After you've done that, reboot to verify that it works.

racoon can be installed using the network section of the ports tree, or it can be downloaded from *ftp://ftp.kame.net/pub/kame/misc/*. Install raccoon per the instructions provided with the distribution.

On the client, you should first configure racoon. You will need to modify this example *racoon.conf* to suit your needs:

```
path include "/usr/local/etc/racoon" ;
path pre_shared_key "/usr/local/etc/racoon/psk.txt" ;
remote anonymous
{
        exchange_mode aggressive,main;
        my_identifier user_fqdn "user1@domain.com";
        lifetime time 1 hour;
        initial_contact on;

        proposal {
                encryption_algorithm 3des;
```

```
                    hash_algorithm sha1;
                    authentication_method pre_shared_key ;
                    dh_group 2 ;
            }
}
sainfo anonymous
{
        pfs_group 1;
        lifetime time 30 min;
        encryption_algorithm 3des ;
        authentication_algorithm hmac_sha1;
        compression_algorithm deflate ;
}
```

In your firewall configuration, be sure you allow IKE connections to your machine (UDP port 500). racoon needs to be configured to start at boot time. Save the following script in *usr/local/etc/rc.d/racoon.sh*:

```sh
#!/bin/sh
# This script will start racoon in FreeBSD
case "$1" in
start)
# start racoon
    echo -n 'starting racoon'
    /usr/local/sbin/racoon
    ;;

stop)
# Delete the MAC address from the ARP table
    echo 'stopping racoon'
    killall racoon
    ;;
*)
# Standard usage statement
    echo "Usage: `basename $0` {start|stop}" >&2
    ;;
esac

exit 0
```

Make sure the file is executable by performing this command:

```
# chmod 755 /usr/local/etc/rc.d/racoon.sh
```

The *usr/local/etc/racoon/psk.txt* file contains your credentials. This file must be readable only by root. If the permissions are not set correctly, racoon will not function. For a shared-secret IPsec connection, the file contains your identification (in this case your email address) and the secret. For instance, you can set up a *psk.txt* as the following:

```
user1@domain.com     supersecret
```

Finally, you must set up the security policy, using the *setkey* utility to add entries to the kernel SPD. Create the following *client.spd* that can be loaded by *setkey*. For this setup, the station IP is 192.168.0.104 and the gateway is 192.168.0.1:

```
# spdadd 192.168.0.104/32 0.0.0.0/0 any -P out ipsec \
esp/tunnel/192.168.0.104-192.168.0.1/require ;
# spdadd 0.0.0.0/0 192.168.0.104/32 any -P in ipsec \
esp/tunnel/192.168.0.1-192.168.0.104/require ;
```

The first entry creates a security policy that sends all traffic to the VPN endpoint. The second entry creates a security policy that allows all traffic back from the VPN endpoint. Note that in this configuration the client is unable to talk to any hosts on the local subnet, except for the VPN gateway. In a wireless network where the client is a prime target for attack, this is probably a good thing for your workstation.

Load the SPD by running:

```
# setkey -f client.spd
```

The gateway *racoon.conf* is the same as the file for the client side. This allows any client to connect. The *psk.txt* file must contain all the identification and shared secrets of all clients who may connect. For instance:

```
user1@domain.com      supersecret
user2@domain.com      evenmoresecret
user3@domain.com      notsosecret
```

Again, make sure *psk.txt* is readable only by root. Start racoon and make sure there are no errors. Finally, set up a *gateway.spd* that creates an SPD for each client. The following example assumes your clients are at 192.168.0.10[4-6]:

```
# spdadd 0.0.0.0/0 192.168.0.104/32 any -P out ipsec \
esp/tunnel/192.168.0.1-192.168.0.104/require ;
# spdadd 192.168.0.104/32 0.0.0.0/0 any -P in ipsec \
esp/tunnel/192.168.0.104-192.168.0.1/require ;
# spdadd 0.0.0.0/0 192.168.0.105/32 any -P in ipsec \
esp/tunnel/192.168.0.1-192.168.0.105/require ;
# spdadd 192.168.0.105/32 0.0.0.0/0 any -P out \
ipsec esp/tunnel/192.168.0.105-192.168.0.1/require ;
# spdadd 0.0.0.0/0 192.168.0.106/32 any -P in ipsec \
esp/tunnel/192.168.0.1-192.168.0.106/require ;
# spdadd 192.168.0.106/32 0.0.0.0/0 any -P out ipsec \
esp/tunnel/192.168.0.106-192.168.0.1/require ;
```

Load the SPD by issuing setkey -f gateway.spd. Verify the SPD entries using the spddump command in setkey. At this point, you should be able to ping a client from the gateway. It may take a packet or two for the VPN negotiation to complete, but the connection should be solid after that. If you are unable to ping, examine your syslog output for errors and warnings.

HACK #69 Set Up IPsec in OpenBSD

Use IPsec the OpenBSD way.

Setting up IPsec in OpenBSD is fairly easy since it's compiled into the kernel that ships with each release and is enabled by default. All that is left to do is to create the appropriate */etc/isakmpd/isakmpd.conf* and */etc/isakmpd/isakmpd.policy* files and start *isakmpd* (the IPsec key-management daemon). This may sound daunting, but OpenBSD's outstanding documentation and example configuration files make it easier.

First of all, you'll need to put something similar to this in your */etc/isakmpd/isakmpd.policy*:

```
KeyNote-Version: 2
Authorizer: "POLICY"
Licensees: "passphrase:mypassword"
Conditions: app_domain == "IPsec policy" &&
            esp_present == "yes" &&
            esp_enc_alg == "aes" &&
            esp_auth_alg == "hmac-sha" -> "true";
```

This sets a password to use for the IPsec connection.

Now you'll need to edit your */etc/isakmpd/isakmpd.conf* to contain the following:

```
[General]
Listen-on=               192.168.1.1
Shared-SADB=             Defined

[Phase 1]
Default=                 ISAKMP-peer-remote
#Default=                ISAKMP-peer-remote-aggressive

[Phase 2]
Passive-Connections=IPsec-local-remote

[ISAKMP-peer-remote]
Phase=                   1
Transport=               udp
Local-address=           192.168.1.1
Configuration=           Default-main-mode
Authentication=          mypassword

[ISAKMP-peer-remote-aggressive]
Phase=                   1
Transport=               udp
Local-address=           192.168.1.1
Configuration=           Default-aggressive-mode
Authentication=          mypassword

[IPsec-local-remote]
```

```
Phase=                          2
ISAKMP-peer=                    ISAKMP-peer-remote
Configuration=                  Default-quick-mode
Local-ID=                       Net-local
Remote-ID=                      Net-remote

[Net-remote]
ID-type=                        IPV4_ADDR
Address=                        0.0.0.0

[Net-local]
ID-type=                        IPV4_ADDR
Address=                        0.0.0.0

[Default-main-mode]
DOI=                            IPSEC
EXCHANGE_TYPE=                  ID_PROT
Transforms=                     3DES-SHA

[Default-aggressive-mode]
DOI=                            IPSEC
EXCHANGE_TYPE=                  AGGRESSIVE
Transforms=                     3DES-SHA-RSA

[Default-quick-mode]
DOI=                            IPSEC
EXCHANGE_TYPE=                  QUICK_MODE
Suites=                         QM-ESP-AES-SHA-PFS-SUITE
```

This configuration will allow anyone to connect with the password mypassword.

After you've edited the configuration files, you can start *isakmpd* by running this command:

```
# /sbin/isakmpd
```

To have *isakmpd* start up with each system boot, you should edit your */etc/rc.conf.local* (or create one if it doesn't exist) and put the following line in it:

```
isakmpd_flags=""
```

That should do it. As usual, check your system logs if your tunnel has trouble connecting.

HACK #70   PPTP Tunneling

Set up quick and easy VPN access using the Point-to-Point Tunneling Protocol.

The Point-to-Point Tunneling Protocol (PPTP) is basically a means to set up PPP tunnels [Hack #81] automatically without needing to manually start a PPP daemon on the remote machine. The main benefit of using PPTP is that both

Windows and Mac OS X natively support the creation of VPN connections, and both provide easy-to-use GUIs for setting up the connections on the client side. Thus, you can provide a VPN solution without much effort on your users' part.

To set up the server end, you can use *PoPToP* (*http://www.poptop.org*), an open source PPTP server. You can get a very simple PPTP VPN going with minimal effort—just download the source distribution and unpack it, then go into the directory it created.

After you've done that, you can run this command to compile it:

```
$ ./configure && make
```

Then become root and run this command to install *PoPToP*:

```
# make install
```

The PPTP daemon that this installs is called *pptpd*. Now you'll need to create a configuration file for *pptpd* (i.e., */etc/pptpd.conf*) and a *pppd* options file to use with it.

Here's a suitable */etc/pptpd.conf* to start out with:

```
option /etc/ppp/options.pptpd
localip 10.0.0.1
remoteip 10.0.0.2-100
```

This defines the IP address of the local end of the PPTP connection as 10.0.0.1 and creates a pool of addresses to be dynamically allocated to clients (i.e., 10. 0.0.2-100). When you create your *pptpd.conf* file, you should use addresses from the range used by your internal network. In addition, this configuration file tells *pptpd* to set up the PPP interface using */etc/ppp/options.pptpd* when it starts *pppd*. Otherwise it would use the default of */etc/ppp/options*, which probably isn't what you want.

Now you'll need to create the aforementioned */etc/ppp/options.pptpd*:

```
lock
name pptpd
auth
```

These options basically tell *pppd* to use authentication (auth), and indicate what entries in the */etc/ppp/chap-secrets* file correspond to this instance of *pppd* (name pptpd). So, to finish configuring authentication for *pptpd*, you'll need to create an entry for each client in the */etc/ppp/chap-secrets* file.

Here's a simple entry that allows someone with the username of andrew to connect with the password mypassword from any remote IP address:

```
# Secrets for authentication using CHAP
# client      server  secret          IP addresses
andrew        pptpd   mypassword       *
```

The pptpd in the server field should be replaced with whatever you used in the name directive in your */etc/ppp/options.pptpd* file (if you didn't use pptpd). You can of course limit the client to specific IP addresses by listing them.

Now that you have a basic setup for *PoPToP*, you can try it out by connecting to it with a Windows machine. Go to your Network Connections folder and click "Create a new connection" (this is for Windows XP; for Windows 2000, look for "Make New Connection"). After you click this, a wizard dialog should appear that looks similar to Figure 6-1.

Figure 6-1. Windows XP's New Connection Wizard

Click Next and then select the "Connect to the network at my workplace" radio button, as shown in Figure 6-2.

After you've done that, click Next again and then click the "Virtual Private Network connection" radio button. You should now see something similar to Figure 6-3.

Click Next and fill in a name for the newly created connection (e.g., PoP-ToP Test). After you've done that, click Next once again and then enter the external IP address of the server running *pptpd*. Now click Next and then Finish. You'll then be presented with a login dialog similar to the one shown in Figure 6-4.

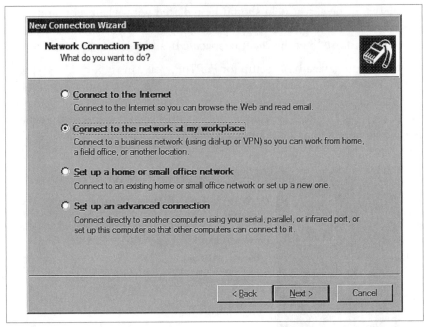

Figure 6-2. Choosing the connection type

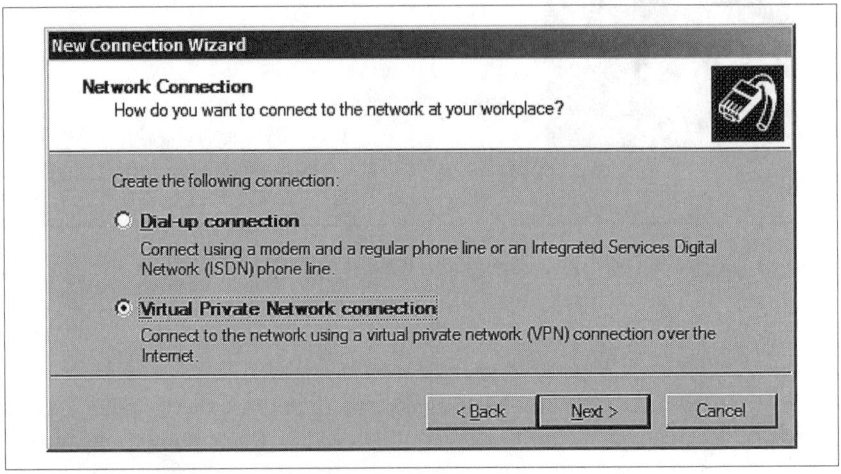

Figure 6-3. Selecting a VPN connection

Before entering the username and password that you specified in the */etc/ppp/chap-secrets* file, you'll need to click Properties and locate the Security tab. After you've done that, locate the "Require data encryption" checkbox and uncheck it. You should now see something similar to Figure 6-5.

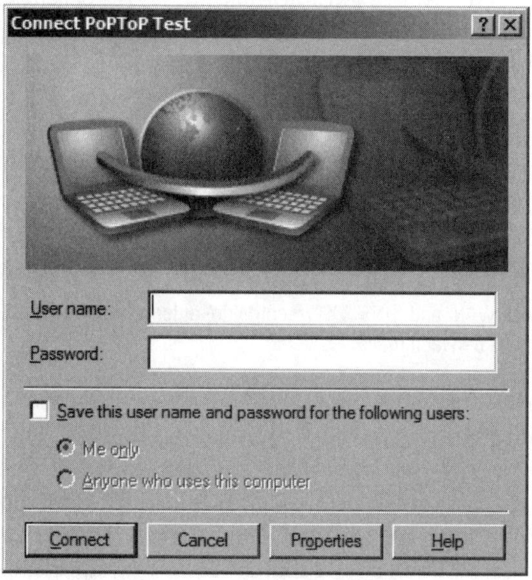

Figure 6-4. The connection login dialog

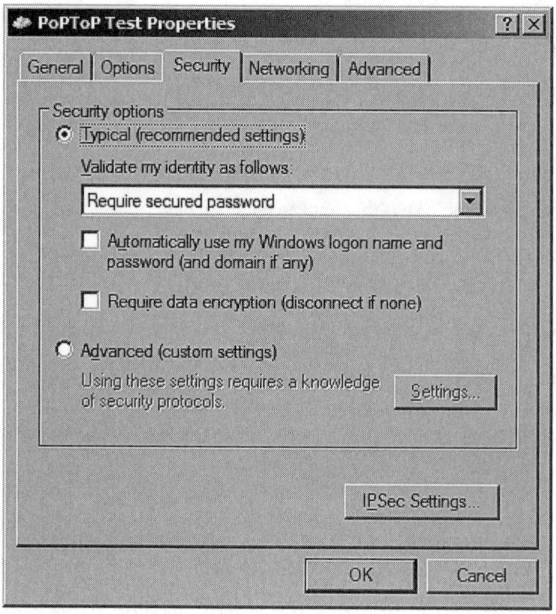

Figure 6-5. Changing the security properties

Now click OK, enter your login information, and then click Connect. In a few seconds you should be connected to the PPTP server and will be allocated an IP address from the pool that you specified. You should now test the connection by pinging the remote end of the tunnel. With the PPTP connection active, all traffic leaving the client side will be encrypted and sent to the *PoPToP* server. From there, traffic will make its way to its ultimate destination.

HACK #71   Opportunistic Encryption with FreeS/WAN

Use FreeS/WAN and DNS TXT records to automatically create encrypted connections between machines.

One particularly cool feature supported by *FreeS/WAN* **[Hack #67]** is opportunistic encryption with other hosts running *FreeS/WAN*. This allows *FreeS/WAN* to transparently encrypt traffic between all hosts that also support opportunistic encryption. To do this, each host must have a public key generated to use with *FreeS/WAN*. This key can then be stored in a DNS TXT record for that host. When a host that is set up for opportunistic encryption wishes to initiate an encrypted connection with another host, it will look up the host's public key through DNS and use it to initiate the connection.

To begin, you'll need to generate a key for each host that you want to use this feature with. You can do that by running this command:

```
# ipsec newhostkey --output /tmp/`hostname`.key
```

Now you'll need to add the contents of the file that was created by that command to */etc/ipsec.secrets*:

```
# cat /tmp/`hostname`.key >> /etc/ipsec.secrets
```

Next, you'll need to generate a TXT record to put into your DNS zone. You can do this by running a command similar to this one:

```
# ipsec showhostkey --txt @colossus.nnc
; RSA 2192 bits   colossus   Mon Jan 12 03:02:07 2004
        IN      TXT     "X-IPsec-Server(10)=@colossus.nnc" "
AQOR7rM7ZMBXu2ej/1vtzhNnMayZO1jwVHUyAIubTKpd/
PyTMogJBAdbb3IOxzGLaxadPGfiqPN2AQn76zLIsYFMJnoMbBTDY/2xK1X/
pWFRUUIHzJUqCBIijVWEMLNrIhdZbei1s5/
MgYIPaX2OUL+yAdxV4RUU3JJQhV7adVzQqEmdaNUnCjZOvZG6m4zv6dGROrVEZmJFP54v6WhckYf
qSkQu3zkctfFgzJ/rMTB6Y38yObyBg2HuWZMtWI"
        "8VrTQqi7IGGHK+mWk+wSoXer3iFD7JxRTzPOxLk6ihAJMibtKna3j7QP9ZHGOnm7NZ/
L5M9VpK+Rfe+evUUMUTfAtSdlpus2BIeXGWcPfz6rw3O5H9"
```

Now add this record to your zone and reload it. You can verify that DNS is working correctly by running this command:

```
# ipsec verify
Checking your system to see if IPsec got installed and started correctly
```

```
Version check and ipsec on-path                          [OK]
Checking for KLIPS support in kernel                     [OK]
Checking for RSA private key (/etc/ipsec.secrets)        [OK]
Checking that pluto is running                           [OK]
DNS checks.
Looking for TXT in forward map: colossus                 [OK]
Does the machine have at least one non-private address   [OK]
```

Now just restart *FreeS/WAN* by running a command similar to this:

```
# /etc/init.d/ipsec restart
```

You should now be able to connect to any other host that supports opportunistic encryption. But what if other hosts want to connect to you? To allow this, you'll need to create a TXT record for your machine in your reverse DNS zone.

You can generate the record by running a command similar to this:

```
# ipsec showhostkey --txt 192.168.0.64
; RSA 2192 bits    colossus    Tue Jan 13 03:02:07 2004
        IN      TXT      "X-IPsec-Server(10)=192.168.0.64" "
AQOR7rM7ZMBXu2ej/1vtzhNnMayZO1jwVHUyAIubTKpd/
PyTMogJBAdbb3IOxzGLaxadPGfiqPN2AQn76zLIsYFMJnoMbBTDY/2xK1X/
pWFRUUIHzJUqCBIijVWEMLNrIhdZbei1s5/
MgYIPaX2OUL+yAdxV4RUU3JJQhV7adVzQqEmdaNUnCjZOvZG6m4zv6dGROrVEZmJFP54v6WhckYf
qSkQu3zkctfFgzJ/rMTB6Y38yObyBg2HuWZMtWI"
"8VrTQqi7IGGHK+mWk+wSoXer3iFD7JxRTzPOxLk6ihAJMibtKna3j7QP9ZHGOnm7NZ/
L5M9VpK+Rfe+evUUMUTfAtSdlpus2BIeXGWcPfz6rw305H9"
```

Add this record to the reverse zone for your subnet, and other machines will be able to initiate opportunistic encryption with your machine. With opportunistic encryption in use, all traffic between the hosts will be automatically encrypted, protecting all services simultaneously. Pretty neat, huh?

Forward and Encrypt Traffic with SSH
Keep network traffic to arbitrary ports secure with ssh port forwarding.

In addition to providing remote shell access and command execution, OpenSSH can also forward arbitrary TCP ports to the other end of your connection. This can be extremely handy for protecting email, web, or any other traffic that you need to keep private (at least, all the way to the other end of the tunnel).

ssh accomplishes local forwarding by binding to a local port, performing encryption, sending the encrypted data to the remote end of the *ssh* connection, then decrypting it and sending it to the remote host and port you specify. Start an *ssh* tunnel with the -L switch (short for *Local*):

```
# ssh -f -N -L 110:mailhost:110 user@mailhost
```

Naturally, substitute *user* with your username, and *mailhost* with your mail server's name or IP address. Note that you will have to be root for this example, since you'll be binding to a privileged port (110, the POP3 port). You should also disable any locally running POP3 daemon (look in */etc/inetd.conf*) or it will get in the way.

Now, to encrypt all of your POP3 traffic, configure your mail client to connect to localhost port 110. It will happily talk to mailhost as if it were connected directly, except that the entire conversation will be encrypted. Alternatively, you could tell *ssh* to listen on a port above 1024 and eliminate the need to run it as root; however, you would have to configure your email client to also use this port, rather than port 110.

-f forks *ssh* into the background, and -N tells it not to actually run a command on the remote end (just do the forwarding). One interesting feature is that when using the -N switch you can still forward a port, even if you do not have a valid login shell on the remote server. However, for this to work you'll need to set up public key authentication with the account beforehand. If your *ssh* server supports it, you can also try the -C switch to turn on compression. This can significantly reduce the time it takes to download email. In addition, connections can be sped up even more by using the blowfish cipher, which is generally faster than 3des (the default). To use the blowfish cipher, type -c blowfish. You can specify as many -L lines as you like when establishing the connection. To also forward outbound email traffic, try this:

```
# ssh -f -N -L 110:mailhost:110 -L 25:mailhost:25 user@mailhost
```

Now set your outbound email host to localhost, and your email traffic will be encrypted as far as mailhost. Generally, this is useful only if the email is bound for an internal host, or if you can't trust your local network connection (as is the case with most wireless networks). Obviously, once your email leaves mailhost, it will be transmitted in the clear, unless you've encrypted the message with a tool such as *pgp* or *gpg*.

If you're already logged into a remote host and need to forward a port quickly, try this:

1. Press Enter.
2. Type ~C.
3. You should be at an ssh> prompt; enter the -L line as you would from the command line.

For example:

```
rob@catlin:~$
rob@catlin:~$ ~C     (it doesn't echo)
```

```
ssh> -L8080:localhost:80
Forwarding port.
```

Your current shell will then forward local port 8000 to catlin's port 80, as if you had entered it in the first place.

You can also allow other (remote) clients to connect to your forwarded port, with the -g switch. If you're logged into a remote gateway that serves as a NAT for a private network, then use a command like this:

```
$ ssh -f -g -N -L8000:localhost:80 10.42.4.6
```

This will forward all connections from the gateway's port 8000 to internal host 10.42.4.6's port 80. If the gateway has a live Internet address, this will allow anyone from the Net to connect to the web server on 10.42.4.6 as if it were running on port 8000 of the gateway.

One last point worth mentioning: the forwarded host doesn't have to be localhost; it can be any host that the machine you're connecting to can access directly. For example, to forward local port 5150 to a web server somewhere on an internal network, try this:

```
$ ssh -f -N -L5150:intranet.insider.nocat:80 gateway.nocat.net
```

Assuming that you're running a private domain called *.nocat*, and that *gateway.nocat.net* also has a connection to the private network, all traffic to port 5150 of remote will be obligingly forwarded to *intranet.insider.nocat:80*. The address *intranet.insider.nocat* doesn't have to resolve in DNS to remote; it isn't looked up until the connection is made to *gateway.nocat.net*, and then it's gateway that does the lookup. To securely browse that site from remote, try connecting to *http://localhost:5150/*.

—*Rob Flickenger (Linux Server Hacks)*

HACK #73 Quick Logins with SSH Client Keys

Use SSH keys instead of password authentication to speed up and automate logins.

When you're an admin on more than a few machines, being able to navigate quickly to a shell on any given server is critical. Having to type ssh my.server.com (followed by a password) is not only tedious, but it also breaks your concentration. Suddenly having to shift from "where's the problem?" to "getting there" and then back to "what's all this, then?" has led more than one admin to premature senility. It promotes the digital equivalent of "Why did I come into this room, anyway?"

At any rate, more effort spent logging into a machine means less effort spent solving problems. Recent versions of SSH offer a secure alternative to endlessly entering a password: public key exchange.

For these examples, I assume that you're using OpenSSHv3.4p1 or later. To use public keys with an SSH server, you'll first need to generate a public/private key pair:

```
$ ssh-keygen -t rsa
```

You can also use -t dsa for DSA keys, or -t rsa1 if you're using Protocol v1. (And shame on you if you are using v1! Upgrade to v2 as soon as you can!) If at all possible, use RSA keys—there are some problems with DSA keys, although they are very rare.

After you enter the command, you should see something like this:

```
Generating public/private rsa key pair.
Enter file in which to save the key (/home/rob/.ssh/id_rsa):
```

Just press Enter there. It will then ask you for a passphrase; just press Enter twice (but read the following section, "Security Concerns"). Here's what the results should look like:

```
Enter passphrase (empty for no passphrase):
Enter same passphrase again:
Your identification has been saved in /home/rob/.ssh/id_rsa.
Your public key has been saved in /home/rob/.ssh/id_rsa.pub.
The key fingerprint is:
a6:5c:c3:eb:18:94:0b:06:a1:a6:29:58:fa:80:0a:bc rob@localhost
```

This created two files: ~/.ssh/id_rsa and ~/.ssh/id_rsa.pub. To use this key pair on a server, try this:

```
$ cat .ssh/id_rsa.pub | \
ssh server "mkdir .ssh && chmod 0700 .ssh && cat > .ssh/authorized_keys2"
```

Of course, substitute your server name for *server*. Now, simply ssh *server* and it should log you in automatically, without a password. And yes, it will use your shiny new public key for scp, too.

If this didn't work for you, check your file permissions on both ~/.ssh/* and *server*:~/.ssh/*. Your private key (*id_rsa*) should be mode 0600 (and be present only on your local machine), and everything else should be mode 0655 or better. In addition, your home directory on the server will need to be mode 755 or better. If it is group writable, someone that belongs to the group that owns your home directory could remove ~/.ssh, even if ~/.ssh is not writable by that group. This might not seem obvious at first, but if they can do that, then they can create their own ~/.ssh and an *authorized_keys2* file, which could contain whatever keys they wish. Luckily, the SSH daemon will catch this and deny public key authentication until your permissions are fixed.

Security Concerns

Some consider the use of public keys a potential security risk. After all, one only has to steal a copy of your private key to obtain access to your servers. While this is true, the same is certainly true of passwords.

Ask yourself, how many times a day do you enter a password to gain shell access to a machine (or scp a file)? How frequently is it the same password on many (or all) of those machines? Have you ever used that password in a way that might be questionable (on a web site, a personal machine that isn't quite up-to-date, or possibly with an SSH client on a machine that you don't directly control)? If any of these possibilities sound familiar, then consider that an SSH key in the same setting would make it virtually impossible for an attacker to later gain unauthorized access (providing, of course, that you keep your private key safe).

Another way to balance ease of use with security is to use a passphrase on your key, but use the SSH agent to manage your keys for you. When you start the agent, it will ask you for your passphrase once, and will cache it until you kill the agent. Some people even go as far as to store their SSH keys on removable media (such as a USB key chain), and take their keys with them wherever they go. However you choose to use SSH keys, you'll almost certainly find that they're a very useful alternative to traditional passwords.

—Rob Flickenger (Linux Server Hacks)

Squid Proxy over SSH
#74
Secure your web traffic from prying eyes—and improve performance in the process.

Squid (http://www.squid-cache.org) is normally used as an HTTP accelerator. It is a large, well-managed, and full-featured caching HTTP proxy that is finding its way into many commercial web platforms. Best of all, *squid* is open source and freely available. Since it performs all of its magic on a single TCP port, it is an ideal candidate for use with an SSH tunnel. This not only helps to secure your web browser when using wireless networks, but also potentially makes your browser run even faster.

First, choose a server on which to host your *squid* cache. Typically, this will be a Linux or BSD machine on your local wired network—although *squid* also runs in Windows, under Cygwin (*http://www.cygwin.com/*). You want to have a fast connection to your cache, so choosing a *squid* cache at the other end of a dial-up connection is probably a bad idea (unless you enjoy simulating what the Internet was like in 1995). On a home network, this is typically the same machine you use as a firewall or DNS server. Fortunately, *squid* isn't very demanding when it supports only a few simultaneous users, so it can happily share a box that runs other services.

It is beyond the scope of this hack to include full *squid* installation instructions, but configuration isn't especially difficult. Just be sure to check your access rules and set a password for the management interface. If you have trouble getting it to run, check out Jennifer Vesperman's "Installing and Configuring Squid" (*http://linux.oreillynet.com/pub/a/linux/2001/07/26/squid.html*).

When *squid* is installed and running, it binds to TCP port 3128 by default. Once you have it running, you should test it manually by setting your HTTP proxy to the server. For example, suppose your server is running *proxy. example.com*. In Mozilla, go to Preferences → Advanced → Proxies, as in Figure 6-6.

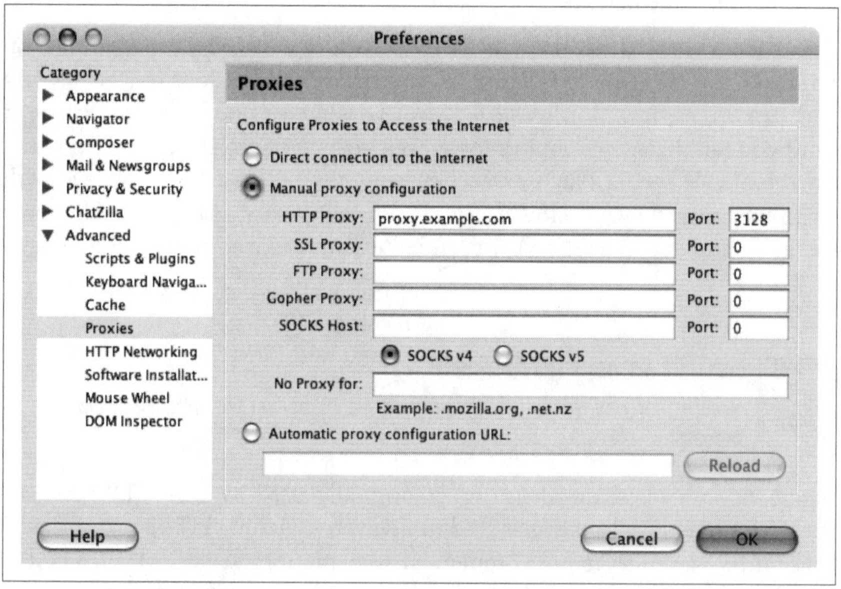

Figure 6-6. Testing your squid using the HTTP Proxy field in Mozilla

Enter "proxy.example.com" as the HTTP Proxy host and "3128" for the port. Click OK, and try to load any web page. You should immediately see the page you requested. If you see an Access Denied error, look over the http_access lines in your *squid.conf*, and restart *squid* if necessary.

Once you are satisfied that you have a happy *squid*, then you need only forward your connection to it over SSH. Set up a local listener on port 3128, forwarding to proxy.example.com:3128 like this:

```
rob@caligula:~$ ssh -L 3128:localhost:3128 proxy.example.com -f -N
```

This will set up an SSH tunnel and fork into the background automatically. Next, change the HTTP Proxy host in your browser to localhost, and reload your page. As long as your SSH tunnel is running, your web traffic will be encrypted all the way to *proxy.example.com*, where it is decrypted and sent on to the Internet.

The biggest advantage of this technique (compared to using the SSH SOCKS 4 proxy **[Hack #75]**) is that virtually all browsers support the use of HTTP proxies, while not every browser supports SOCKS 4. Also, if you are using Mac OS X, there is support for HTTP proxies built into the OS itself. This means that every properly written application will use your proxy settings transparently.

Note that HTTP proxies have the same difficulties with DNS as a SOCKS 4 proxy, so keep those points in mind when using your proxy. Typically, your *squid* proxy is used from a local network, so you don't usually run into the DNS schizophrenia issue. But your *squid* can theoretically run anywhere (even behind a remote firewall), so be sure to check out the notes on DNS in "Use SSH as a SOCKS Proxy" **[Hack #75]**.

Running *squid* takes a little bit of preparation, but it can both secure and accelerate your web traffic when using wireless. Of course, *squid* will support as many simultaneous wireless users as you care to throw at it, so be sure to set it up for all of your regular wireless users, and keep your web traffic private

—Rob Flickenger (Wireless Hacks)

Use SSH as a SOCKS Proxy

#75 Protect your web traffic using the basic VPN functionality built into SSH itself.

In the search for the perfect way to secure their wireless networks, many people overlook one of the most useful features of SSH: the -D switch. This simple little switch is buried within the SSH manpage, toward the bottom. Here is a direct quote from the manpage:

> -D port
>
> Specifies a local "dynamic" application-level port forwarding. This works by allocating a socket to listen to port on the local side, and whenever a connection is made to this port, the connection is forwarded over the secure channel, and the application protocol is then used to determine where to connect to from the remote machine. Currently the SOCKS 4 protocol is supported, and SSH will act as a SOCKS 4 server. Only root can forward privileged ports. Dynamic port forwardings can also be specified in the configuration file.

This turns out to be an insanely useful feature if you have software that is capable of using a SOCKS 4 proxy. It effectively gives you an instant encrypted proxy server to any machine that you can SSH to. It does this without the need for further software, either on your machine or on the remote server.

Just as with SSH port forwarding [Hack #72], the -D switch binds to the specified local port and encrypts any traffic to that port, sends it down the tunnel, and decrypts it on the other side. For example, to set up a SOCKS 4 proxy from local port 8080 to *remote*, type the following:

```
rob@caligula:~$ ssh -D 8080 remote
```

That's all there is to it. Now you simply specify localhost:8080 as the SOCKS 4 proxy in your application, and all connections made by that application will be sent down the encrypted tunnel. For example, to set your SOCKS proxy in Mozilla, go to Preferences → Advanced → Proxies, as shown in Figure 6-7.

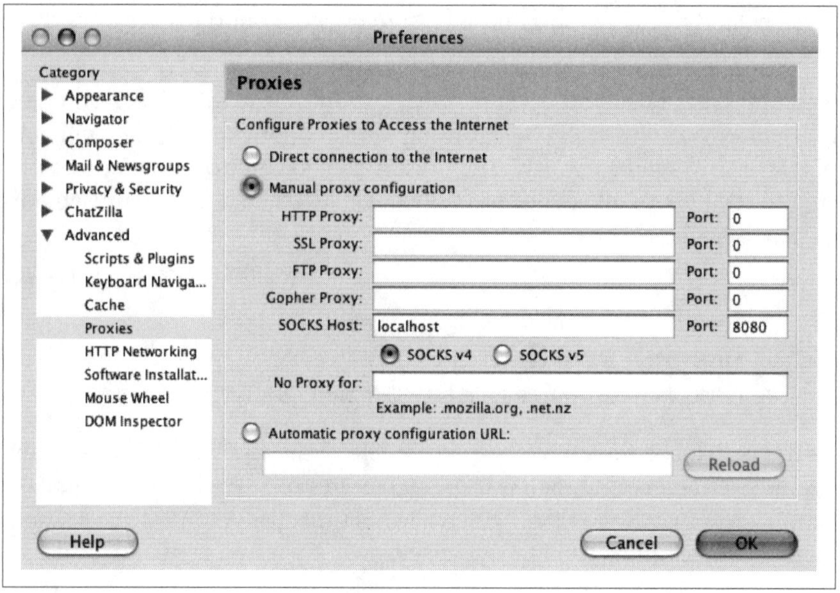

Figure 6-7. Proxy settings in Mozilla.

Select "Manual proxy configuration", then type in localhost as the SOCKS host. Enter the port number that you passed to the -D switch, and be sure to check the SOCKSv4 button.

Click OK, and you're finished. All of the traffic that Mozilla generates is now encrypted and appears to originate from the remote machine that you logged into with SSH. Anyone listening to your wireless traffic now sees a large volume of encrypted SSH traffic, but your actual data is well protected.

One important point to keep in mind is that SOCKS 4 has no native support for DNS traffic. This has two important side effects to keep in mind when using it to secure your wireless transmissions.

First of all, DNS lookups are still sent in the clear. This means that anyone listening in can still see the names of sites that you browse to, although the actual URLs and data are obscured. This is rarely a security risk, but it is worth keeping in mind.

Second, you are still using a local DNS server, but your traffic originates from the remote end of the proxy. This can have interesting (and undesirable) side effects when attempting to access private network resources.

To illustrate the subtle problems that this can cause, consider a typical corporate network with a web server called *intranet.example.com*. This web server uses the private address 192.168.1.10 but is accessible from the Internet through the use of a forwarding firewall. The DNS server for *intranet.example.com* normally responds with different IP addresses depending on where the request comes from, perhaps using the views functionality in BIND 9. When coming from the Internet, you would normally access *intranet.example.com* with the IP address 208.201.239.36, which is actually the IP address of the outside of the corporate firewall.

Now suppose that you are using the SOCKS proxy example just shown, and *remote* is actually a machine behind the corporate firewall. Your local DNS server returns 208.201.239.36 as the IP address for *intranet.mybusiness.com* (since you are looking up the name from outside the firewall). But the HTTP request actually comes from *remote* and attempts to go to 208.201.239.36. Many times, this is forbidden by the firewall rules, as internal users are supposed to access the intranet by its internal IP address, 192.168.1.10. How can you work around this DNS schizophrenia?

One simple method to avoid this trouble is to make use of a local *hosts* file on your machine. Add an entry like this to */etc/hosts* (or the equivalent on your operating system):

```
192.168.1.10    intranet.example.com
```

Likewise, you can list any number of hosts that are reachable only from the inside of your corporate firewall. When you attempt to browse to one of those sites, the local *hosts* file is consulted before DNS, so the private IP address is used. Since this request is actually made from *remote*, it finds its way to the internal server with no trouble. Likewise, responses arrive back at the SOCKS proxy on *remote*, are encrypted and forwarded over your SSH tunnel, and appear in your browser as if they came in from the Internet.

SOCKS 5 support is planned for an upcoming version of SSH, which will also make tunneled DNS resolution possible. This is particularly exciting for Mac OS X users, as there is support in the OS for SOCKS 5 proxies. Once SSH supports SOCKS 5, every native OS X application will automatically be able to take advantage of encrypting SSH socks proxies. In the meantime, we'll just have to settle for encrypted HTTP proxies [Hack #74].

—*Rob Flickenger (Wireless Hacks)*

HACK #76   Encrypt and Tunnel Traffic with SSL

Use stunnel to add SSL encryption to any network service.

Stunnel (*http://www.stunnel.org*) is a powerful and flexible program that, using SSL, encrypts traffic to and from any TCP port in several different ways. It can tunnel connections, much like SSH can, by providing a local port to connect to. It will encrypt the traffic sent to this port, forward it to a remote system, decrypt the traffic, and finally forward it to a local port on that system. *Stunnel* can also provide transparent SSL support for *inetd*-compatible services.

To install *stunnel*, simply run ./configure from the directory that was created when you unpacked the archive file that you downloaded. Since *stunnel* requires OpenSSL (*http://www.openssl.org*), download and install that first if it is not already installed. If you would like to compile *stunnel* with TCP wrappers support or install OpenSSL in a nonstandard location, you'll probably want to make use of the --with-tcp-wrappers or --with-ssl command-line options for configure.

For example, this will configure *stunnel* to include TCP wrapper support, using the OpenSSL installation under */opt/*:

```
$ ./configure --with-tcp-wrappers --with-ssl=/opt/openssl
```

After the script runs, you'll need to run make to actually compile *stunnel*. You will then be prompted for information to create a self-signed certificate. Not only will this certificate be self-signed, but it is valid for only one year. If this is not what you want, you should create your own certificate and Certificate Authority [Hack #45].

With the older 3.x versions of *stunnel,* it was possible to configure all options from the command line. The newer 4.x versions make use of a configuration file, *stunnel.conf.* A sample configuration file can usually be found in either */etc/stunnel/stunnel.conf-sample* or */usr/local/etc/stunnel/stunnel.conf-sample.*

Let's take a look at the basic form of a configuration file used to forward a local port to a remote port with *stunnel*.

The client side:

```
pid =
client = yes

[<server port>]
accept = <forwarded port>
connect = <remote address>:<server port>
```

The server side:

```
cert = /etc/stunnel/stunnel.pem
pid =
client = no

[<forwarded port>]
accept = <server port>
connect = <forwarded port>
```

You can use the default configuration file or choose another file. If you want to use the default configuration file, you can start *stunnel* without any arguments. Otherwise, you can specify the configuration file as the first argument to *stunnel*.

With this setup, a program will be able to connect to <forwarded port> on the client side. Then *stunnel* will encrypt the traffic it receives on this port and send it to <server port> on the remote system specified by <remote address>. On the remote system, *stunnel* will decrypt the traffic that it receives on this port and forward it to the program that is listening on <forwarded port> on the remote system.

The equivalent *ssh* port-forwarding command would be:

```
ssh -f -N -L <forwarded port>:<remote address>:<forwarded port> \
<remote address>
```

If you wish to specify a PID file, you can set the pid variable to whatever filename you wish. Leaving the pid variable in the configuration file without giving it a value causes *stunnel* to not create a PID file. However, if you leave out the pid variable completely, *stunnel* will try to create either */var/run/stunnel.pid* or */usr/local/var/run/stunnel.pid* (i.e., *$prefix/var/run/stunnel.pid*), depending on how you configured it at compile time.

In addition to providing SSH-style port forwarding, *stunnel* can also be used to add SSL capabilities to inetd-style services. This is perfect for adding SSL capabilities to email or other services that don't have native SSL functionality.

Here's an *inetd.conf* entry for SWAT, Samba's web-based configuration tool:

```
swat stream tcp nowait.400 root /usr/local/samba/bin/swat swat
```

To add SSL support to SWAT, you first need to create a configuration file for *stunnel* to use. Let's call it *swat.conf* and put it in */etc/stunnel*:

```
cert = /etc/stunnel/swat.pem
exec = /usr/local/samba/bin/swat
execargs = swat
```

Now modify the entry in *inetd.conf* to look like this:

```
swat stream tcp nowait.400 root /usr/sbin/stunnel stunnel \
/etc/stunnel/swat.conf
```

Now you can access SWAT securely with your favorite SSL-enabled web browser.

Alternatively, you can do away with inetd altogether and have *stunnel* listen for connections from clients and then spawn the service process itself. To do this, create a configuration file with contents similar to this:

```
cert = /etc/stunnel/swat.pem

[swat]
accept = 901
exec = /usr/local/samba/bin/swat
execargs = swat
```

Then start *stunnel* with the path to the configuration file:

```
# stunnel /etc/stunnel/swat.conf
```

In addition, you can start it at boot time by putting the previous command in your startup scripts (i.e., */etc/rc.local*).

Stunnel is a very powerful tool: not only can it forward connections through an encrypted tunnel, but it can also be used to add SSL capabilities to common services. This is especially nice when clients with SSL support for these services already exist. Thus, you can use *stunnel* solely on the server side, enabling encryption for the service with no need for the client to install any extra software.

Tunnel Connections Inside HTTP

HACK #77   Break through draconian firewalls by using httptunnel.

If you've ever been on the road and found yourself in a place where the only connectivity to the outside world is through an incredibly restrictive firewall, you probably know the pain of trying to do anything other than sending and receiving email or basic web browsing.

Here's where *httptunnel* (*http://www.nocrew.org/software/httptunnel.html*) comes to the rescue. *Httptunnel* is a program that allows you to tunnel arbitrary connections through the HTTP protocol to a remote host. This is especially useful in situations like the one mentioned earlier, when web access is allowed but all other services are denied. Of course, you could just use any kind of tunneling software and configure it to use port 80, but where would that leave you if the firewall is actually a web proxy? This is roughly the same as an application-layer firewall, and will accept only valid HTTP requests. Fortunately, *httptunnel* can deal with these as well.

To compile *httptunnel,* download the tarball and run `configure` and `make`:

```
$ tar xfz httptunnel-3.3.tar.gz
$ cd httptunnel-3.3
$ ./configure && make
```

Install it by running `make install`, which will install everything under */usr/local*. If you want to install it somewhere else, you can use the standard `--prefix=` option to the `configure` script.

The *httptunnel* client program is called `htc`, and the server is `hts`. As with *ssh* [Hack #76], *httptunnel* can be used to listen on a local TCP port for connections, forward the traffic that it receives on this port to a remote server, and then decrypt and forward the traffic to another port outside of the tunnel.

Try tunneling an SSH connection over HTTP. On the server, run a command like this:

```
# hts -F localhost:22 80
```

Now, run a command like this on the client:

```
# htc -F 2222 colossus:80
```

In this case, `colossus` is the remote server, and `htc` is listening on port 2222. You can use the standard port 22 if you aren't running a local *sshd*. If you're curious, you can verify that `htc` is now listening on port 2222 by using `lsof`:

```
# /usr/sbin/lsof -i | grep htc
htc      2323   root    6u  IPv4 0x02358a30      0t0   TCP *:2222 (LISTEN)
```

And now to try out the tunnel:

```
[andrew@kryten andrew]$ ssh -p 2222 localhost
andrew@localhost's password:
[andrew@colossus andrew]$
```

You can also forward connections to machines other than the one that you're running `hts` on. To do this, just replace the `localhost` in the `hts` command with whatever remote host you wish to forward to.

For instance, to forward the connection to `oceana.ingsoc.net` instead of `colossus`, you could run this command:

```
# hts -F oceana.ingsoc.net:22 80
```

If you're curious to see what an SSH connection tunneled through the HTTP protocol looks like, you can take a look at it with a packet sniffer. Here's the initial portion of the TCP stream that is sent to the *httptunnel* server by the client:

```
POST /index.html?crap=1071364879 HTTP/1.1
Host: linux-vm:80
Content-Length: 102400
Connection: close

SSH-2.0-OpenSSH_3.6.1p1+CAN-2003-0693
```

If your tunnel needs to go through a web proxy, no additional configuration is needed as long as the proxy is transparent and does not require authentication. If the proxy is not transparent, you can specify it with the -P switch. Additionally, if you do need to authenticate with the proxy, you'll want to make use of the -A or --proxy-authorization options, which allow you to specify a username and password to authenticate with.

Here's how to use these options:

```
htc -P myproxy:8000 -A andrew:mypassword -F 22 colossus:80
```

If the port that the proxy listens on is the standard web proxy port (8080), then you can just specify the proxy by using its IP address or hostname.

HACK #78   Tunnel with VTun and SSH

Connect two networks using VTun and a single SSH connection.

VTun is a user-space tunnel server, allowing entire networks to be tunneled to each other using the tun universal tunnel kernel driver. An encrypted tunnel such as VTun allows roaming wireless clients to secure all of their IP traffic using strong encryption. It currently runs under Linux, BSD, and Mac OS X. The examples in this hack assume that you are using Linux.

The procedure described next will allow a host with a private IP address (10.42.4.6) to bring up a new tunnel interface with a real, live, routed IP address (208.201.239.33) that works as expected, as if the private network weren't even there. Do this by bringing up the tunnel, dropping the default route, and then adding a new default route via the other end of the tunnel.

To begin with, here is the (pretunneled) network configuration:

```
root@client:~# ifconfig eth2
eth2 Link encap:Ethernet HWaddr 00:02:2D:2A:27:EA
inet addr:10.42.3.2 Bcast:10.42.3.63 Mask:255.255.255.192
UP BROADCAST RUNNING MULTICAST MTU:1500 Metric:1
RX packets:662 errors:0 dropped:0 overruns:0 frame:0
TX packets:733 errors:0 dropped:0 overruns:0 carrier:0
collisions:0 txqueuelen:100
RX bytes:105616 (103.1 Kb) TX bytes:74259 (72.5 Kb)
Interrupt:3 Base address:0x100
```

```
root@client:~# route
Kernel IP routing table
Destination Gateway Genmask Flags Metric Ref Use Iface
10.42.3.0 * 255.255.255.192 U 0 0 0 eth2
loopback * 255.0.0.0 U 0 0 0 lo
default 10.42.3.1 0.0.0.0 UG 0 0 0 eth2
```

As you can see, the local network is 10.42.3.0/26, the IP is 10.42.3.2, and the default gateway is 10.42.3.1. This gateway provides network address translation (NAT) to the Internet. Here's what the path looks like to *yahoo.com*:

```
root@client:~# traceroute -n yahoo.com
traceroute to yahoo.com (64.58.79.230), 30 hops max, 40 byte packets
 1 10.42.3.1 2.848 ms 2.304 ms 2.915 ms
 2 209.204.179.1 16.654 ms 16.052 ms 19.224 ms
 3 208.201.224.194 20.112 ms 20.863 ms 18.238 ms
 4 208.201.224.5 213.466 ms 338.259 ms 357.7 ms
 5 206.24.221.217 20.743 ms 23.504 ms 24.192 ms
 6 206.24.210.62 22.379 ms 30.948 ms 54.475 ms
 7 206.24.226.104 94.263 ms 94.192 ms 91.825 ms
 8 206.24.238.61 97.107 ms 91.005 ms 91.133 ms
 9 206.24.238.26 95.443 ms 98.846 ms 100.055 ms
10 216.109.66.7 92.133 ms 97.419 ms 94.22 ms
11 216.33.98.19 99.491 ms 94.661 ms 100.002 ms
12 216.35.210.126 97.945 ms 93.608 ms 95.347 ms
13 64.58.77.41 98.607 ms 99.588 ms 97.816 ms
```

In this example, we are connecting to a tunnel server on the Internet at 208.201.239.5. It has two spare live IP addresses (208.201.239.32 and 208.201.239.33) to be used for tunneling. We'll refer to that machine as the *server*, and our local machine as the *client*.

Now let's get the tunnel running. To begin with, load the tun driver on both machines:

```
# modprobe tun
```

It is worth noting that the tun driver will sometimes fail if the server and client kernel versions don't match. For best results, use a recent kernel (and the same version, e.g., 2.4.20) on both machines.

On the server machine, save this file to */usr/local/etc/vtund.conf*:

```
options {
    port 5000;
    ifconfig /sbin/ifconfig;
    route /sbin/route;
    syslog auth;
}

default {
    compress no;
    speed 0;
```

```
    }

home {
    type tun;
    proto tcp;
    stat yes;
    keepalive yes;

    pass sHHH; # Password is REQUIRED.

    up {
        ifconfig "%% 208.201.239.32 pointopoint 208.201.239.33";
        program /sbin/arp "-Ds 208.201.239.33 %% pub";
        program /sbin/arp "-Ds 208.201.239.33 eth0 pub";
        route "add -net 10.42.0.0/16 gw 208.201.239.33";
    };

    down {
        program /sbin/arp "-d 208.201.239.33 -i %%";
        program /sbin/arp "-d 208.201.239.33 -i eth0";
        route "del -net 10.42.0.0/16 gw 208.201.239.33";
    };
}
```

Launch the *vtund* server like so:

```
root@server:~# vtund -s
```

Now you'll need a *vtund.conf* file for the client side. Try this one, again in */usr/ local/etc/vtund.conf*:

```
options {
    port 5000;
    ifconfig /sbin/ifconfig;
    route /sbin/route;
}

default {
    compress no;
    speed 0;
}

home {
    type tun;
    proto tcp;
    keepalive yes;

    pass sHHH; # Password is REQUIRED.

    up {
        ifconfig "%% 208.201.239.33 pointopoint 208.201.239.32 arp";
        route "add 208.201.239.5 gw 10.42.3.1";
        route "del default";
        route "add default gw 208.201.239.32";
    };
```

```
down {
    route "del default";
    route "del 208.201.239.5 gw 10.42.3.1";
    route "add default gw 10.42.3.1";
};
}
```

Finally, run this command on the client:

```
root@client:~# vtund -p home server
```

Presto! Not only do you have a tunnel up between client and server, but also a new default route via the other end of the tunnel. Take a look at what happens when we traceroute to *yahoo.com* with the tunnel in place:

```
root@client:~# traceroute -n yahoo.com
traceroute to yahoo.com (64.58.79.230), 30 hops max, 40 byte packets
1 208.201.239.32 24.368 ms 28.019 ms 19.114 ms
2 208.201.239.1 21.677 ms 22.644 ms 23.489 ms
3 208.201.224.194 20.41 ms 22.997 ms 23.788 ms
4 208.201.224.5 26.496 ms 23.8 ms 25.752 ms
5 206.24.221.217 26.174 ms 28.077 ms 26.344 ms
6 206.24.210.62 26.484 ms 27.851 ms 25.015 ms
7 206.24.226.103 104.22 ms 114.278 ms 108.575 ms
8 206.24.238.57 99.978 ms 99.028 ms 100.976 ms
9 206.24.238.26 103.749 ms 101.416 ms 101.09 ms
10 216.109.66.132 102.426 ms 104.222 ms 98.675 ms
11 216.33.98.19 99.985 ms 99.618 ms 103.827 ms
12 216.35.210.126 104.075 ms 103.247 ms 106.398 ms
13 64.58.77.41 107.219 ms 106.285 ms 101.169 ms
```

This means that any server processes running on the client are now fully available to the Internet, at IP address 208.201.239.33. This has all happened without making a single change (e.g., port forwarding) on the gateway 10.42.3.1.

Here's what the new tunnel interface looks like on the client:

```
root@client:~# ifconfig tun0
tun0 Link encap:Point-to-Point Protocol
inet addr:208.201.239.33 P-t-P:208.201.239.32 Mask:255.255.255.255
UP POINTOPOINT RUNNING MULTICAST MTU:1500 Metric:1
RX packets:39 errors:0 dropped:0 overruns:0 frame:0
TX packets:39 errors:0 dropped:0 overruns:0 carrier:0
collisions:0 txqueuelen:10
RX bytes:2220 (2.1 Kb) TX bytes:1560 (1.5 Kb)
```

And here's the updated routing table (note that we still need to keep a host route to the tunnel server's IP address via our old default gateway; otherwise, the tunnel traffic can't get out):

```
root@client:~# route
Kernel IP routing table
Destination Gateway Genmask Flags Metric Ref Use Iface
208.201.239.5 10.42.3.1 255.255.255.255 UGH 0 0 0 eth2
```

```
208.201.239.32 * 255.255.255.255 UH 0 0 0 tun0
10.42.3.0 * 255.255.255.192 U 0 0 0 eth2
10.42.4.0 * 255.255.255.192 U 0 0 0 eth0
loopback * 255.0.0.0 U 0 0 0 lo
default 208.201.239.32 0.0.0.0 UG 0 0 0 tun0
```

To bring down the tunnel, simply kill the vtund process on client. This restores all network settings back to their original states.

This method works fine if you trust VTun to use strong encryption and to be free from remote exploits. Personally, I don't think you can be too paranoid when it comes to machines connected to the Internet. To use VTun over SSH (and therefore rely on the strong authentication and encryption that SSH provides), simply forward port 5000 on the client to the same port on the server. Give this a try:

```
root@client:~# ssh -f -N -c blowfish -C -L5000:localhost:5000 server
root@client:~# vtund -p home localhost
root@client:~# traceroute -n yahoo.com
traceroute to yahoo.com (64.58.79.230), 30 hops max, 40 byte packets
 1 208.201.239.32 24.715 ms 31.713 ms 29.519 ms
 2 208.201.239.1 28.389 ms 36.247 ms 28.879 ms
 3 208.201.224.194 48.777 ms 28.602 ms 44.024 ms
 4 208.201.224.5 38.788 ms 35.608 ms 35.72 ms
 5 206.24.221.217 37.729 ms 38.821 ms 43.489 ms
 6 206.24.210.62 39.577 ms 43.784 ms 34.711 ms
 7 206.24.226.103 110.761 ms 111.246 ms 117.15 ms
 8 206.24.238.57 112.569 ms 113.2 ms 111.773 ms
 9 206.24.238.26 111.466 ms 123.051 ms 118.58 ms
10 216.109.66.132 113.79 ms 119.143 ms 109.934 ms
11 216.33.98.19 111.948 ms 117.959 ms 122.269 ms
12 216.35.210.126 113.472 ms 111.129 ms 118.079 ms
13 64.58.77.41 110.923 ms 110.733 ms 115.22 ms
```

In order to discourage connections to *vtund* on port 5000 of the server, add a net filter rule to drop connections from the outside world:

```
root@server:~# iptables -A INPUT -t filter -i eth0 \
  -p tcp --dport 5000 -j DROP
```

This allows local connections to get through (since they use loopback), and therefore requires an SSH tunnel to the server before accepting a connection.

As you can see, this can be an extremely handy tool to have around. In addition to giving live IP addresses to machines behind a NAT, you can effectively connect any two networks if you can obtain a single SSH connection between them (originating from either direction).

If your head is swimming from this *vtund.conf* configuration or you're feeling lazy and don't want to figure out what to change when setting up your own client's *vtund.conf* file, take a look at the automatic *vtund.conf* generator [Hack #79].

—*Rob Flickenger (Linux Server Hacks)*

Automatic vtund.conf Generator

#79 Generate a vtund.conf on the fly to match changing network conditions.

If you've just come from "Tunnel with VTun and SSH" [Hack #78], then the following script will generate a working *vtund.conf* for the client side automatically.

If you haven't read the previous hack (or if you've never used VTun), then go back and read it before attempting to grok this bit of Perl. Essentially, it attempts to take the guesswork out of changing the routing table around on the client side by auto-detecting the default gateway and building the *vtund.conf* accordingly.

To configure the script, take a look at the Configuration section. The first line of $Config contains the addresses, port, and secret that we used in the VTun hack. The second line simply serves as an example of how to add more.

To run the script, either call it as vtundconf home or set $TunnelName to the one you want to default to. Better yet, make symlinks to the script, like this:

```
# ln -s vtundconf home
# ln -s vtundconf tunnel2
```

Then you can generate the appropriate *vtund.conf* by calling the symlink directly:

```
# vtundconf home > /usr/local/etc/vtund.conf
```

You might be wondering why anyone would go to all of the trouble to make a *vtund.conf*-generating script in the first place. Once you get the settings right, you'll never have to change them, right?

Well, usually that is the case. But consider the case of a Linux laptop that uses many different networks in the course of the day (say, a DSL line at home, Ethernet at work, and maybe a wireless connection at the local coffee shop). By running vtundconf once at each location, you will have a working configuration instantly, even if your IP and gateway is assigned by DHCP. This makes it easy to get up and running quickly with a live, routable IP address, regardless of the local network topology.

Incidentally, VTun currently runs well on Linux, FreeBSD, Mac OS X, Solaris, and others.

Save this file as *vtundconf*, and run it each time you use a new wireless network to generate an appropriate *vtund.conf* for you on the fly:

```
#!/usr/bin/perl -w
#
# vtund wrapper in need of a better name.
#
```

```perl
# (c)2002 Schuyler Erle & Rob Flickenger
#
############### CONFIGURATION

# If TunnelName is blank, the wrapper will look at @ARGV or $0.
#
# Config is TunnelName, LocalIP, RemoteIP, TunnelHost, TunnelPort, Secret
#
my $TunnelName = "";
my $Config    = q{
  home     208.201.239.33 208.201.239.32 208.201.239.5   5000   sHHH
  tunnel2   10.0.1.100        10.0.1.1        192.168.1.4      6001   foobar
};

############### MAIN PROGRAM BEGINS HERE

use POSIX 'tmpnam';
use IO::File;
use File::Basename;
use strict;

# Where to find things...
#
$ENV{PATH}   = "/bin:/usr/bin:/usr/local/bin:/sbin:/usr/sbin:/usr/local/
[RETURN]sbin";
my $IP_Match = '((?:\d{1,3}\.){3}\d{1,3})';        # match xxx.xxx.xxx.xxx
my $Ifconfig = "ifconfig -a";
my $Netstat  = "netstat -rn";
my $Vtund    = "/bin/echo";
my $Debug    = 1;

# Load the template from the data section.
#
my $template = join( "", );

# Open a temp file -- adapted from Perl Cookbook, 1st Ed., sec. 7.5.
#
my ( $file, $name ) = ("", "");
$name = tmpnam( )
  until $file = IO::File->new( $name, O_RDWR|O_CREAT|O_EXCL );
END { unlink( $name ) or warn "Can't remove temporary file $name!\n"; }

# If no TunnelName is specified, use the first thing on the command line,
# or if there isn't one, the basename of the script.
# This allows users to symlink different tunnel names to the same script.
#
$TunnelName ||= shift(@ARGV) || basename($0);
die "Can't determine tunnel config to use!\n" unless $TunnelName;

# Parse config.
#
my ($LocalIP, $RemoteIP, $TunnelHost, $TunnelPort, $Secret);
for (split(/\r*\n+/, $Config)) {
```

```
  my ($conf, @vars) = grep( $_ ne "", split( /\s+/ ));
  next if not $conf or $conf =~ /^\s*#/o; # skip blank lines, comments
  if ($conf eq $TunnelName) {
    ($LocalIP, $RemoteIP, $TunnelHost, $TunnelPort, $Secret) = @vars;
    last;
  }
}

die "Can't determine configuration for TunnelName '$TunnelName'!\n"
  unless $RemoteIP and $TunnelHost and $TunnelPort;

# Find the default gateway.
#
my ( $GatewayIP, $ExternalDevice );

for (qx{ $Netstat }) {
  # In both Linux and BSD, the gateway is the next thing on the line,
  # and the interface is the last.
  #
  if ( /^(?:0.0.0.0|default)\s+(\S+)\s+.*?(\S+)\s*$/o ) {
    $GatewayIP = $1;
    $ExternalDevice = $2;
    last;
  }
}

die "Can't determine default gateway!\n" unless $GatewayIP and
$ExternalDevice;

# Figure out the LocalIP and LocalNetwork.
#
my ( $LocalNetwork );
my ( $iface, $addr, $up, $network, $mask ) = "";

sub compute_netmask {
  ($addr, $mask) = @_;
  # We have to mask $addr with $mask because linux /sbin/route
  # complains if the network address doesn't match the netmask.
  #
  my @ip = split( /\./, $addr );
  my @mask = split( /\./, $mask );
  $ip[$_] = ($ip[$_] + 0) & ($mask[$_] + 0) for (0..$#ip);
  $addr = join(".", @ip);
  return $addr;
}

for (qx{ $Ifconfig }) {
  last unless defined $_;

  # If we got a new device, stash the previous one (if any).
  if ( /^([^\s:]+)/o ) {
    if ( $iface eq $ExternalDevice and $network and $up ) {
      $LocalNetwork = $network;
```

```
    last;
  }
  $iface = $1;
  $up = 0;
}

# Get the network mask for the current interface.
if ( /addr:$IP_Match.*?mask:$IP_Match/io ) {
  # Linux style ifconfig.
  compute_netmask($1, $2);
  $network = "$addr netmask $mask";
} elsif ( /inet $IP_Match.*?mask 0x([a-f0-9]{8})/io ) {
  # BSD style ifconfig.
  ($addr, $mask) = ($1, $2);
  $mask = join(".", map( hex $_, $mask =~ /(..)/gs ));
  compute_netmask($addr, $mask);
  $network = "$addr/$mask";
}

# Ignore interfaces that are loopback devices or aren't up.
$iface = "" if /\bLOOPBACK\b/o;
$up++     if /\bUP\b/o;
}

die "Can't determine local IP address!\n" unless $LocalIP and $LocalNetwork;

# Set OS dependent variables.
#
my ( $GW, $NET, $PTP );
if ( $^O eq "linux" ) {
  $GW = "gw"; $PTP = "pointopoint"; $NET = "-net";
} else {
  $GW = $PTP = $NET = "";
}

# Parse the config template.
#
$template =~ s/(\$\w+)/$1/gee;

# Write the temp file and execute vtund.
#
if ($Debug) {
  print $template;
} else {
  print $file $template;
  close $file;
  system("$Vtund $name");
}

__DATA__

options {
  port $TunnelPort;
```

```
  ifconfig /sbin/ifconfig;
  route /sbin/route;
}

default {
  compress no;
  speed 0;
}

# 'mytunnel' should really be `basename $0` or some such
# for automagic config selection
$TunnelName {
  type tun;
  proto tcp;
  keepalive yes;

  pass $Secret;

  up {
   ifconfig "%% $LocalIP $PTP $RemoteIP arp";
   route "add $TunnelHost $GW $GatewayIP";
   route "delete default";
   route "add default $GW $RemoteIP";
   route "add $NET $LocalNetwork $GW $GatewayIP";
  };

  down {
   ifconfig "%% down";
   route "delete default";
   route "delete $TunnelHost $GW $GatewayIP";
   route "delete $NET $LocalNetwork";
   route "add default $GW $GatewayIP";
  };
}
```

—Rob Flickenger (Linux Server Hacks)

HACK #80   Create a Cross-Platform VPN

Use OpenVPN to easily tie your networks together.

Creating a VPN can be quite difficult, especially when dealing with clients using multiple platforms. Quite often, a single VPN implementation isn't available for all of them. As an administrator, you can be left with trying to get different VPN implementations to operate on all the different platforms that you need to support, which can become a nightmare.

Luckily, someone has stepped in to fill the void in cross-platform VPN packages and has written OpenVPN (*http://openvpn.sourceforge.net*). It supports Linux, Solaris, OpenBSD, FreeBSD, NetBSD, Mac OS X, and Windows 2000/XP. OpenVPN achieves this by implementing all of the encryption, key-management, and connection-setup functionality in a user-space daemon, leaving the actual tunneling portion of the job to the host operating system.

To accomplish the tunneling, OpenVPN makes use of the host operating system's virtual TUN or TAP device. These devices export a virtual network interface, which is then managed by the *openvpn* process to provide a point-to-point interface between the hosts participating in the VPN. Instead of traffic being sent and received on these devices, it's sent and received from a user-space program. Thus, when data is sent across the virtual device, it is relayed to the *openvpn* program, which then encrypts it and sends it to the *openvpn* process running on the remote end of the VPN link. When the data is received on the other end, the *openvpn* process decrypts it and relays it to the virtual device on that machine. It is then processed just like a packet being received on any other physical interface.

OpenVPN uses SSL and relies on the OpenSSL library (*http://www.openssl.org*) for encryption, authentication, and certification functionality. Tunnels created with OpenVPN can either use preshared static keys or take advantage of TLS dynamic keying and digital certificates. Since OpenVPN makes use of OpenSSL, it can support any cipher that OpenSSL supports. The main advantage of this is that OpenVPN will be able to transparently support any new ciphers as they are added to the OpenSSL distribution.

If you're using a Windows-based operating system, all you need to do is download the executable installer and configure OpenVPN. On all other platforms, you'll need to compile OpenVPN yourself. Before you compile and install OpenVPN, make sure that you have OpenSSL installed. You can also install the LZO compression library (*http://www.oberhumer.com/opensource/lzo/*), which is generally a good idea. Using LZO compression can make much more efficient use of your bandwidth, and even greatly improve performance in some circumstances. To compile and install OpenVPN, download the tarball and type something similar to this:

```
$ tar xfz openvpn-1.5.0.tar.gz
$ cd openvpn-1.5.0
$ ./configure && make
```

If you installed the LZO libraries and header files somewhere other than */usr/lib* and */usr/include*, you will probably need to use the --with-lzo-headers and --with-lzo-lib configure script options.

For example, if you have installed LZO under the */usr/local* hierarchy, you'll want to run the configure script like this:

```
$ ./configure --with-lzo-headers=/usr/local/include \
  --with-lzo-lib=/usr/local/lib
```

If the configure script cannot find the LZO libraries and headers, it will print out a warning that looks like this:

```
LZO library and headers not found.
LZO library available from http://www.oberhumer.com/opensource/lzo/
configure: error: Or try ./configure --disable-lzo
```

If the script does find the LZO libraries, you should see output on your terminal that is similar to this:

```
configure: checking for LZO Library and Header files...
checking lzo1x.h usability... yes
checking lzo1x.h presence... yes
checking for lzo1x.h... yes
checking for lzo1x_1_15_compress in -llzo... yes
```

Now that that's out of the way, you can install OpenVPN by running the usual make install. If you are running Solaris or Mac OS X, you'll also need to install a TUN/TAP driver. The other Unix-based operating systems already include one, and the Windows installer installs the driver for you. You can get the source code to the Solaris driver from the SourceForge project page (*http://vtun.sourceforge.net/tun/*). The Mac OS X driver is available in both source and binary form from *http://chrisp.de/en/projects/tunnel.html*.

Once you have LZO, OpenSSL, the TUN/TAP driver, and OpenVPN all installed, you can test everything by setting up a rudimentary VPN from the command line.

On machine A (kryten in this example), run a command similar to this one:

```
# openvpn --remote zul --dev tun0 --ifconfig 10.0.0.19 10.0.0.5
```

The command that you'll need to run on machine B (zul) is a lot like the previous command, except the arguments to --ifconfig are swapped:

```
# openvpn --remote kryten --ifconfig 10.0.0.5 10.0.0.19
```

The first IP address is the local end of the tunnel, and the second is for the remote end; this is why you need to swap the IP addresses on the other end. When running these commands, you should see a warning about not using encryption, as well as some status messages. Once OpenVPN starts, run ifconfig to see that the point-to-point tunnel device has been set up:

```
[andrew@kryten andrew]$ /sbin/ifconfig tun0
tun0: flags=51<UP,POINTOPOINT,RUNNING> mtu 1300
        inet 10.0.0.19 --> 10.0.0.5 netmask 0xffffffff
```

Now try pinging the remote machine, using its tunneled IP address:

```
[andrew@kryten andrew]$ ping -c 4 10.0.0.5
PING 10.0.0.5 (10.0.0.5): 56 data bytes
64 bytes from 10.0.0.5: icmp_seq=0 ttl=255 time=0.864 ms
64 bytes from 10.0.0.5: icmp_seq=1 ttl=255 time=1.012 ms
64 bytes from 10.0.0.5: icmp_seq=2 ttl=255 time=0.776 ms
```

```
64 bytes from 10.0.0.5: icmp_seq=3 ttl=255 time=0.825 ms

--- 10.0.0.5 ping statistics ---
4 packets transmitted, 4 packets received, 0% packet loss
round-trip min/avg/max = 0.776/0.869/1.012 ms
```

Now that you have verified that OpenVPN is working properly, it is time to create a configuration that's a little more useful in the real world. First you will need to create SSL certificates [Hack #45] for each end of the connection. After you've done this, you'll need to create configuration files and connection setup and teardown scripts for each end of the connection.

Let's look at the configuration files first. For these examples, zul will be the gateway into the private network and kryten will be the external client.

The configuration file for zul that is used for kryten is stored in */etc/openvpn/openvpn.conf*. Here are the contents:

```
dev tun0
ifconfig 10.0.0.5 10.0.0.19
up /etc/openvpn/openvpn.up
down /etc/openvpn/openvpn.down
tls-server
dh /etc/openvpn/dh1024.pem
ca /etc/ssl/ca.crt
cert /etc/ssl/zul.crt
key /etc/ssl/private/zul.key
ping 15
verb 0
```

You can see that the dev and ifconfig options are used in the same way as they are on the command line. The up and down options specify scripts that will be executed when the VPN connection is initiated or terminated. The tls-server option enables TLS mode and specifies that you want to designate this side of the connection as the server during the TLS handshaking process. The dh option specifies the Diffie-Hellman parameters to use during key exchange. These are encoded in a *.pem* file and can be generated with the following openssl command:

```
# openssl dhparam -out dh1024.pem 1024
```

The next few configuration options deal with the SSL certificates. The ca option specifies the Certificate Authority's public certificate, and the cert option specifies the public certificate to use for this side of the connection. Similarly, the key option specifies the private key that corresponds to the public certificate. To help ensure that the VPN tunnel doesn't get dropped from any intervening firewalls that are doing stateful filtering, the ping option is used. This causes OpenVPN to ping the remote host every *n* seconds so that the tunnel's entry in the firewall's state table does not time out.

On kryten, the following configuration file is used:

```
dev tun0
remote zul
ifconfig 10.0.0.19 10.0.0.5
up /etc/openvpn/openvpn.up
down /etc/openvpn/openvpn.down
tls-client
ca /etc/ssl/ca.crt
cert /etc/ssl/kryten.crt
key /etc/ssl/private/kryten.key
ping 15
verb 0
```

The main differences with this configuration file are that the remote and tls-client options have been used. Other than that, the arguments to the ifconfig option have been swapped, and the file uses kryten's public and private keys instead of zul's. To turn on compression, add the comp-lzo option to the configuration files on both ends of the VPN.

Finally, create the *openvpn.up* and *openvpn.down* scripts on both hosts participating in the tunnel. These scripts set up and tear down the actual routes and other networking requirements.

The *openvpn.up* scripts are executed whenever a VPN connection is established. On kryten it looks like this:

```
#!/bin/sh

/sbin/route add -net 10.0.0.0 gw $5 netmask 255.255.255.0
```

This sets a route telling the operating system to send all traffic destined for the 10/24 network to the remote end of our VPN connection. From there it will be routed to the interface on zul that has been assigned an address from the 10/24 address range. The $5 in the script is replaced by the IP address used by the remote end of the tunnel. In addition to adding the route, you might want to set up nameservers for the network you are tunneling into in this script. Unless you are doing something fancy, the *openvpn.down* script on kryten is empty, since the route is automatically dropped by the kernel when the connection ends.

No additional routes are needed on zul, because it already has a route to the network that kryten is tunneling into. In addition, since tun0 on zul is a point-to-point link between itself and kryten, there is no need to add a route to pass traffic to kryten—by virtue of having a point-to-point link, a host route will be created for kryten.

The only thing that needs to be in the *openvpn.up* script on zul is this:

```
#!/bin/sh

arp -s $5 00:00:d1:1f:3f:f1 permanent pub
```

This causes zul to answer ARP queries for kryten, since otherwise the ARP traffic will not be able to reach kryten. This sort of configuration is popularly called *proxy arp*. In this particular example, zul is running OpenBSD. If you are running Linux, simply remove the permanent keyword from the arp command. Again, the $5 is replaced by the IP address that is used at the remote end of the connection, which in this case is kryten's.

The *openvpn.down* script on zul simply deletes the ARP table entry:

```
#!/bin/sh

arp -d kryten
```

Unfortunately, since scripts run through the down configuration file option are not passed an argument telling them what IP address they should be dealing with, you have to explicitly specify the IP address or hostname to delete from the ARP table. Now the only thing to worry about is firewalling. You'll want to allow traffic coming through your tun0 device, as well as UDP port 5000.

Finally, you are ready to run openvpn on both sides, using a command like this:

```
# openvpn --config /etc/openvpn/openvpn.conf --daemon
```

Setting up OpenVPN under Windows is even easier. Simply run the installer, and everything you need will be installed onto your system. This includes OpenSSL, the TUN/TAP driver, and OpenVPN itself. The installer will also associate the *.ovpn* file extension with OpenVPN. Simply put your configuration information in a *.ovpn* file, double-click it, and you're ready to go.

This should get you started using OpenVPN, but it has far too many configuration options to discuss here. Be sure to look at the OpenVPN web site for more information.

Tunnel PPP
HACK #81
Use PPP and SSH to create a secure VPN tunnel.

There are so many options to choose from when creating a VPN or tunneled connection that it's mind-boggling. You may not be aware that all the software you need to create a VPN is probably already installed on your Unix machines—namely PPP and SSH daemons.

You might have used PPP back in the day to connect to the Internet over a dial-up connection, so you may be wondering how the same PPP can operate over SSH. Well, when you used PPP in conjunction with a modem, it was talking to the modem through what the operating system presented as a

TTY interface, which is, in short, a regular terminal device. The PPP daemon on your end would send its output to the TTY, which the operating system would send out the modem and across the telephone network until it reached the remote end, where the same thing would happen in reverse.

The terminals that you use to run shell commands on (e.g., the console, an xterm, etc.) use pseudo-TTY interfaces, which are designed to operate similarly to TTYs. Because of this, PPP daemons can also operate over pseudo-TTYs. So, you can replace the serial TTYs with pseudo-TTYs, but you still need a way to connect the local pseudo-TTY to the remote one. Here's where SSH comes into the picture.

You can create the actual PPP connection in one quick command. For instance, if you wanted to use the IP 10.1.1.20 for your local end of the connection and 10.1.1.1 on the remote end, you could run a command similar to this:

```
# /usr/sbin/pppd updetach noauth silent nodeflate \
pty "/usr/bin/ssh root@colossus /usr/sbin/pppd nodetach notty noauth" \
ipparam 10.1.1.20:10.1.1.1
root@colossus's password:
local  IP address 10.1.1.20
remote IP address 10.1.1.1
```

The first line of the command starts the pppd process on the local machine and tells it to fork into the background once the connection has been established (updetach). It also tells pppd to not do any authentication (noauth)—the SSH daemon already provides very strong authentication. The pppd command also turns off deflate compression (nodeflate). The second line of the command tells pppd to run a program and to communicate with it through the program's standard input and standard output. This is used to log into the remote machine and run a pppd process there. Finally, the last line specifies the local and remote IP addresses that are to be used for the PPP connection.

After the command returns you to the shell, you should be able to see a ppp interface in the output of ifconfig:

```
$ /sbin/ifconfig ppp0
ppp0      Link encap:Point-to-Point Protocol
          inet addr:10.1.1.20  P-t-P:10.1.1.1  Mask:255.255.255.255
          UP POINTOPOINT RUNNING NOARP MULTICAST  MTU:1500  Metric:1
          RX packets:58 errors:0 dropped:0 overruns:0 frame:0
          TX packets:50 errors:0 dropped:0 overruns:0 carrier:0
          collisions:0 txqueuelen:3
          RX bytes:5372 (5.2 Kb)  TX bytes:6131 (5.9 Kb)
```

Now to try pinging the remote end's IP address:

```
$ ping 10.1.1.1
PING 10.1.1.1 (10.1.1.1) 56(84) bytes of data.
64 bytes from 10.1.1.1: icmp_seq=1 ttl=64 time=4.56 ms
```

```
64 bytes from 10.1.1.1: icmp_seq=2 ttl=64 time=4.53 ms
64 bytes from 10.1.1.1: icmp_seq=3 ttl=64 time=5.45 ms
64 bytes from 10.1.1.1: icmp_seq=4 ttl=64 time=4.51 ms

--- 10.1.1.1 ping statistics ---
4 packets transmitted, 4 received, 0% packet loss, time 3025ms
rtt min/avg/max/mdev = 4.511/4.765/5.451/0.399 ms
```

And finally, the ultimate litmus test—actually using the tunnel for something other than ping:

```
$ ssh 10.1.1.1
The authenticity of host '10.1.1.1 (10.1.1.1)' can't be established.
RSA key fingerprint is 56:36:db:7a:02:8b:05:b2:4d:d4:d1:24:e9:4f:35:49.
Are you sure you want to continue connecting (yes/no)? yes
Warning: Permanently added '10.1.1.1' (RSA) to the list of known hosts.
andrew@10.1.1.1's password:
[andrew@colossus andrew]$
```

Before deciding to keep this setup, you may want to generate login keys to use with ssh [Hack #73], so that you don't need to type in a password each time. In addition, you may want to create a separate user for logging in on the remote machine and starting pppd. However, pppd needs to be started as root, so you'll have to make use of sudo [Hack #6]. Also, you can enable SSH's built-in compression by adding a -C to the ssh command. In some circumstances, SSH compression can greatly improve the speed of the link. Finally, to tear down the tunnel, simply kill the ssh process that pppd spawned.

Although it's ugly and might not be as stable and full of features as actual VPN implementations, the PPP and SSH combination can help you create an instant encrypted network without the need to install additional software.

See Also

- The section "Creating a VPN with PPP and SSH" in *Virtual Private Networks*, Second Edition, by Charlie Scott, Paul Wolfe, and Mike Erwin (O'Reilly)

Network Intrusion Detection
Hacks 82–95

One class of tools that's come to the forefront in network security in recent years is network intrusion detection systems (NIDS). These systems can be deployed on your network and monitor the traffic until they detect suspicious behavior, when they spring into action and notify you of what is going on. They are excellent tools to use in addition to your logs, since a network IDS can often spot an attack before it reaches the intended target or has a chance to end up in your logs.

Currently, there are two main types of NIDS. The first type detects intrusions by monitoring the traffic for specific byte patterns that are similar to known attacks. A NIDS that operates in this manner is known as a signature-based intrusion detection system. The other type of network IDS is a statistical monitor. These monitor the traffic on the network, but instead of looking for a particular pattern or signature, they maintain a statistical history of the packets that pass through your network, and report when they see a packet that falls outside of the normal network traffic pattern. NIDS that employ this method are known as *anomaly-based* intrusion detection systems.

In this chapter you'll learn how to set up Snort, a signature-based IDS. You'll also learn how to set up Snort with SPADE, which adds anomaly-detection capabilities to Snort, giving you the best of both worlds. This chapter also demonstrates how to set up several different applications that can help you to monitor and manage your NIDS once you have it deployed.

Finally, you'll see how to set up a system that appears vulnerable to attackers, but is actually quietly waiting and monitoring everything it sees. These systems are called *honeypots*, and the last few hacks will show you how to quickly and easily set one up, and how to monitor intruders that have been fooled and trapped by it.

HACK #82   Detect Intrusions with Snort

Use one of the most powerful (and free) network intrusion detection systems available to help you keep an eye on your network.

Monitoring your logs can take you only so far in detecting intrusions. If the logs are being generated by a service that has been compromised, welcome to the security admin's worst nightmare: you can no longer trust your logs. This is where NIDS come into play. They can alert you to intrusion attempts, or even intrusions in progress.

The undisputed champion of open source NIDS is Snort (*http://www.snort. org*). Some of the features that make Snort so powerful are its signature-based rule engine and its easy extensibility through plug-ins and preprocessors. These features allow you to extend Snort in whichever direction you need. Consequently, you don't have to depend on anyone else to provide you with rules when a new exploit comes to your attention: with a basic knowledge of TCP/IP, you can write your own rules quickly and easily. This is probably Snort's most important feature, since new attacks are invented and reported all the time. Additionally, Snort has a very flexible reporting mechanism that allows you to send alerts to a *syslogd*, flat files, or even a database.

To compile and install a plain-vanilla version of Snort, download the latest version and unpack it. Run the configure script and then make:

```
$ ./configure && make
```

Then become root and run:

```
# make install
```

Note that all the headers and libraries for libpcap (*http://www.tcpdump.org*) must be installed before you start building Snort, or else compilation will fail. Additionally, you may need to make use of the --with-libpcap-includes and --with-libpcap-libraries configure options to tell the compiler where it can find the libraries and headers. However, you should only need to do this if you have installed the libraries and headers in a nonstandard location (i.e., somewhere other than the */usr* or */usr/local* hierarchy).

For example, if you have installed libpcap within the */opt* hierarchy, you would use this:

```
$ ./configure --with-libpcap-includes=/opt/include\
  --with-libpcap-libraries=/opt/lib
```

Snort has the ability to respond to the host that has triggered one of its rules. This capability is called *flexible response*. To enable this functionality, you'll also need to use the --enable-flexresp option, which requires the libnet packet injection library (*http://www.packetfactory.net/projects/libnet/*). After ensuring that this package is installed on your system, you can use the `--with-libnet-includes` and `--with-libnet-libraries` switches to specify its location.

If you want to include support for sending alerts to a database, you will need to make use of either the `--with-mysql`, `--with-postgresql`, or `--with-oracle` options. To see the full list of configure script options, you can type `./configure --help`.

After you have installed Snort, test it out by using it in sniffer mode. You should immediately see some traffic:

```
# ./snort -evi eth0
Running in packet dump mode
Log directory = /var/log/snort

Initializing Network Interface eth0

        --== Initializing Snort ==--
Initializing Output Plugins!
Decoding Ethernet on interface eth0

        --== Initialization Complete ==--

-*> Snort! <*-
Version 2.0.5 (Build 98)
By Martin Roesch (roesch@sourcefire.com, www.snort.org)
12/14-16:25:17.874711 0:A:95:C7:2B:10 -> 0:C:29:E2:2B:C1 type:0x800 len:0x42
192.168.0.60:53179 -> 192.168.0.41:22 TCP TTL:64 TOS:0x10 ID:56177 IpLen:20
DgmLen:52 DF
***A**** Seq: 0x67E53951  Ack: 0x2BA09FF7  Win: 0xFFFF  TcpLen: 32
TCP Options (3) => NOP NOP TS: 3426501948 469087
=+=+=+=+=+=+=+=+=+=+=+=+=+=+=+=+=+=+=+=+=+=+=+=+=+=+=+=+=+=+=+=+

12/14-16:25:17.874828 0:C:29:E2:2B:C1 -> 0:A:95:C7:2B:10 type:0x800 len:
0x252
192.168.0.41:22 -> 192.168.0.60:53179 TCP TTL:64 TOS:0x10 ID:50923 IpLen:20
DgmLen:580 DF
***AP*** Seq: 0x2BA09FF7  Ack: 0x67E53951  Win: 0x2200  TcpLen: 32
TCP Options (3) => NOP NOP TS: 469100 3426501948
=+=+=+=+=+=+=+=+=+=+=+=+=+=+=+=+=+=+=+=+=+=+=+=+=+=+=+=+=+=+=+=+
```

Some configuration files are provided with the Snort source distribution in the *etc/* directory, but they are not installed when running make install. You can create a directory to hold these in */etc* or */usr/local/etc* and copy the pertinent files to it by running something similar to this:

```
# mkdir /usr/local/etc/snort &&\
  cp etc/[^Makefile]* /usr/local/etc/snort
```

You'll probably want to copy the *rules* directory to there as well.

Now you need to edit the *snort.conf* file. Snort's sample *snort.conf* file lists a number of variables. Some are defined with default values, and all are accompanied by comments that make this section mostly self-explanatory. Of particular note, however, are these two variables:

```
var HOME_NET any
var EXTERNAL_NET any
```

HOME_NET specifies which IP address spaces should be considered local. The default is set so that any IP address is included as part of the home network. Networks can be specified using CIDR notation (i.e., *xxx.xxx.xxx.xxx/yy*). You can also specify multiple subnets and IP addresses by enclosing them in brackets and separating them with commas:

```
var HOME_NET [10.1.1.0/24,192.168.1.0/24]
```

HOME_NET can also be automatically set to the network address of a particular interface by setting the variable to $eth0_ADDRESS. In this particular case, $eth0_ADDRESS sets it to the network address of eth0.

The EXTERNAL_NET variable allows you to explicitly specify IP addresses and networks that are not a part of HOME_NET. Unless a subset of HOME_NET is considered hostile, you can just keep the default value, which is any.

The rest of the variables that deal with IP addresses or network ranges—DNS_SERVERS, SMTP_SERVERS, HTTP_SERVERS, SQL_SERVERS, and TELNET_SERVERS—are set to $HOME_NET by default. These variables are used within the ruleset that comes with the Snort distribution and can be used to fine-tune a rules behavior. For instance, rules that deal with SMTP-related attack signatures use the SMTP_SERVERS variable to filter out traffic that isn't actually related to the rule. Fine-tuning these variables not only leads to more relevant alerts and less false positives, but also to higher performance.

Another important variable is RULE_PATH, which is used later in the configuration file to include rulesets. The sample configuration file sets it to `../rules` but, to be compatible with the previous examples, this should be set to `./rules` since *snort.conf* and the *rules* directory are both in */usr/local/etc/snort*.

The next section in the configuration file allows you to configure Snort's built-in preprocessors. These do anything from reassembling fragmented packets to decoding HTTP traffic to detecting portscans. For most situations, the default configuration is sufficient. However, if you need to tweak any of these settings, the configuration file is fully documented with each preprocessor's options.

If you've compiled in database support, you'll probably want to enable the database output plug-in, which will cause Snort to store any alerts that it generates in your database. Enable this plug-in by putting lines similar to these in your configuration file:

```
output database: log, mysql, user=snort password=snortpass dbname=SNORT \
host=dbserver
output database: alert mysql, user=snort password=snortpass dbname=SNORT \
host=dbserver
```

The first line configures Snort to send any information generated by rules that specify the log action to the database. Likewise, the second line tells Snort to send any information generated by rules that specify the alert action to the database. For more information on the difference between the log and alert actions, see "Write Your Own Snort Rules" [Hack #86].

If you're going to use a database with Snort, you'll need to create a new database, and possibly a new database user account. The Snort source code's *contrib* directory includes scripts to create databases of the supported types: *create_mssql*, *create_mysql*, *create_oracle.sql*, and *create_postgresql*.

If you are using MySQL, you can create a database and then create the proper tables by running a command like this:

```
# mysql SNORT -p < ./contrib/create_mysql
```

The rest of the configuration file deals mostly with the rule signatures Snort will use when monitoring network traffic for intrusions. These rules are categorized and stored in separate files, and are activated by using the include directive. For testing purposes (or on networks with light traffic) the default configuration is sufficient, but you should look over the rules and decide which rule categories you really need and which ones you don't.

Now that all of the hard configuration and setup work is out of the way, you should test your *snort.conf* file. You can do this by running something similar to the following command:

```
# snort -T -c /usr/local/etc/snort/snort.conf
```

Snort will report any errors that it finds and then exit. If there aren't any errors, run Snort with a command similar to this:

```
# snort -Dd -z est -c /usr/local/etc/snort/snort.conf
```

Two of these flags, -d and -c, were used previously (to tell Snort to decode packet data and to use the specified configuration file, respectively). The other two are new. The -D flag tells Snort to print out some startup messages and then fork into the background. The -z est argument tells Snort's streams preprocessor plug-in to ignore TCP packets that aren't part of established sessions, which makes your Snort system much less susceptible to spoofing attacks and certain DoS attacks. Some other useful options are -u and -g, which let Snort drop its privileges and run under the user and group that you specify. These are especially useful with the -t option, which will chroot( ) Snort to the directory that you specify. Now you should start to see logs appearing in */var/log/snort*.

See Also

- Chapter 11, "Simple Intrusion Detection Techniques," in *Building Secure Servers with Linux*, by Michael D. Bauer (O'Reilly)

HACK #83 Keep Track of Alerts
Use ACID to make sense of your IDS logs.

Once you have set up Snort to log information to your database [Hack #82]), you may find it hard to cope with all the data that it generates. Very busy and high-profile sites can generate a huge number of Snort warnings that eventually need to be tracked down. One way to alleviate the problem is to install *ACID* (*http://acidlab.sourceforge.net*).

ACID, otherwise known as the Analysis Console for Intrusion Databases, is a web-based frontend to databases that contain alerts from intrusion detection systems. It features the ability to search for alerts based on a variety of criteria, such as alert signature, time of detection, source and destination address and ports, as well as payload or flag values. *ACID* can display the packets that triggered the alerts, as well as decode their layer-3 and layer-4 information. *ACID* also contains alert management features that allow you to group alerts based on incident, delete acknowledged or false positive alerts, email alerts, or archive them to another database. *ACID* also provides many different statistics on the alerts in your database based on time, the sensor they were generated by, signature, and packet-related statistics such as protocol, address, or port.

To install *ACID*, you'll first need a web server and a working installation of PHP (e.g., Apache and mod_php), as well as a Snort installation that has been configured to log to a database (e.g., MySQL). You will also need a couple of PHP code libraries: ADODB (*http://php.weblogs.com/adodb*) for database abstraction and either PHPlot (*http://www.phplot.com*) or JPGraph (*http://www.aditus.nu/jpgraph*) for graphics rendering.

After you have downloaded these packages, unpack them into a directory that can be used to execute PHP content on the web server. Next, change to the directory that was created by unpacking the *ACID* distribution (i.e., *./acid*) and edit the *acid_conf.php* file. Here you will need to tell *ACID* where to find ADODB and JPGraph, as well as how to connect to your Snort database.

You can do this by changing these variables to similar values that fit your situation:

```
$Dblib_path = "../adodb";
$Dbtype = "mysql";
$alert_dbname = "SNORT";
$alert_host = "localhost";
$alert_port = "";
$alert_user="snort";
$alert_password = "snortpass";
```

This will tell *ACID* to look for the ADODB code in the *adodb* directory at the same directory level as the *acid* directory. In addition, it will tell *ACID* to connect to a MySQL database called SNORT that is running on the local machine, using the user snort with the password snortpass. Since it is connecting to a MySQL server on the local machine, there is no need to specify a port number. If you want to connect to a database running on another system, you should specify 3389, which is the default port used by MySQL.

Additionally, you can configure an archive database for *ACID* using variables that are similar to the ones used to configure the alert database. The following variables will need to be set to use *ACID*'s archiving features:

```
$archive_dbname
$archive_host
$archive_port
$archive_user
$archive_password
```

To tell *ACID* where to find the graphing library that you want to use, you will need to set the $ChartLib_path variable. If you are using JPGraph 1.13 and have unpacked it from the same directory you unpacked the *ACID* distribution, you would enter something like this:

```
$ChartLib_path = "../jpgraph-1.13/src";
```

Congratulations! You're finished mucking about in configuration files for the time being. Now open a web browser and go to the URL that corresponds to the directory where you unpacked *ACID*. You should then be greeted with a database setup page as shown in Figure 7-1.

Before you can use *ACID*, it must create some database tables for its own use. To do this, click the Create ACID AG button. After this, you should see a screen confirming that the tables were created. In addition, you can have *ACID* create indexes for your events table if this was not done prior to setting up *ACID*. Indexes will greatly speed up queries as your events table grows, at the expense of using a little more disk space. Once you are done with the setup screen, you can click the Home link to go to the main *ACID* page, as seen in Figure 7-2.

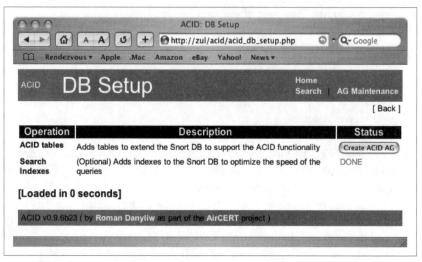

Figure 7-1. The ACID database setup page

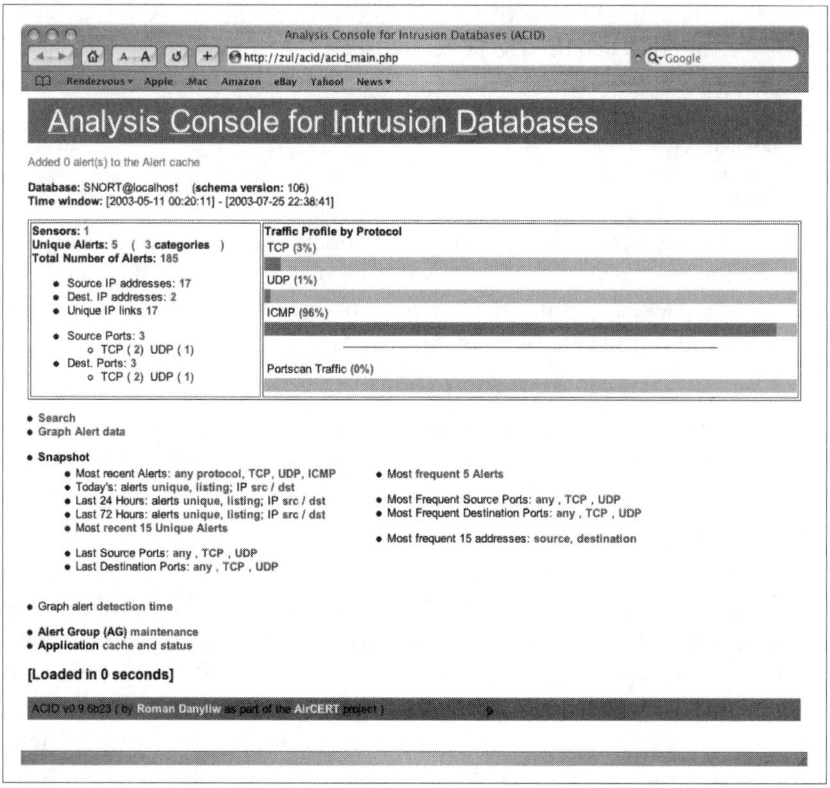

Figure 7-2. ACID's main page

ACID has a fairly intuitive user interface. The main table provides plenty of links to see many useful views of the database at a glance, such as the list of source or destination IP addresses associated with the alerts in your database, as well as the source and destination ports.

HACK #84 Real-Time Monitoring

Use Sguil's advanced GUI to monitor and analyze IDS events in a timely manner.

One thing that's crucial when analyzing your IDS events is to be able to correlate all your audit data from various sources, to determine the exact trigger for the alert and what actions should be taken. This could involve anything from simply querying a database for similar alerts to viewing TCP stream conversations. One tool to help facilitate this is *Sguil* (*http://sguil. sourceforge.net*), the Snort GUI for Lamerz. In case you're wondering, *Sguil* is pronounced "sgweel" (to rhyme with "squeal").

Sguil is a graphical analysis console written in Tcl/Tk that brings together the power of such tools as Ethereal (*http://www.ethereal.com*), TcpFlow (*http://www.circlemud.org/~jelson/software/tcpflow/*), and Snort's portscan and TCP stream decoding processors into a single unified application, where it correlates all the data from each of these sources. *Sguil* uses a client/server model and is made up of three parts: a plug-in for *Barnyard* (*op_guil*), a server (*sguild*), and a client (*sguil.tk*). Agents installed on each of your NIDS sensors are used to report back information to the *Sguil* server. The server takes care of collecting and correlating all the data from the sensor agents, and handles information and authentication requests from the GUI clients.

Before you begin, you'll need to download the *Sguil* distribution from the project's web site and unpack it somewhere. This will create a directory that reflects the package and its version number (e.g., *sguil-0.3.0*).

The first step in setting up *Sguil* is creating a MySQL database for storing its information. You should also create a user that *Sguil* can use to access the database:

```
$ mysql -u root -p
Enter password:
Welcome to the MySQL monitor.  Commands end with ; or \g.
Your MySQL connection id is 546 to server version: 3.23.55

Type 'help;' or '\h' for help. Type '\c' to clear the buffer.

mysql> CREATE DATABASE SGUIL;
Query OK, 1 row affected (0.00 sec)
```

```
mysql> GRANT SELECT,INSERT,UPDATE,DELETE ON SGUIL.* \
 TO sguil IDENTIFIED BY 'sguilpass';
Query OK, 0 rows affected (0.06 sec)

mysql> FLUSH PRIVILEGES;
Query OK, 0 rows affected (0.06 sec)

mysql>
```

Now you'll need to create *Sguil*'s database tables. To do this, locate the *create_sguildb.sql* file. It should be in the *server/sql_scripts* subdirectory of the directory that was created when you unpacked the *Sguil* distribution. You'll need to feed this as input to the mysql command like this:

```
$ mysql -u root -p SGUIL < create_sguildb.sql
```

sguild requires several Tcl packages in order to run. The first is Tclx (*http://tclx.sourceforge.net*), which is an extensions library for Tcl. The second is mysqltcl (*http://www.xdobry.de/mysqltcl/*). Both of these can be installed with the standard ./configure && make install routine.

You can verify that they were installed correctly by running the following commands:

```
$ tcl
tcl>package require Tclx
8.3
tcl>package require mysqltcl
2.40
tcl>
```

If you want to use SSL to encrypt the traffic between the GUI and the server, you will also need to install tcltls (*http://sourceforge.net/projects/tls/*). After installing it, you can verify that it was installed correctly by running this command:

```
$ tcl
tcl>package require tls
1.41
tcl>
```

Now you'll need to go about configuring *sguild*. First, you'll need to create a directory suitable for holding its configuration files (i.e., */etc/sguild*). Then copy *sguild.users*, *sguild.conf*, *sguild.queries*, and *autocat.conf* to the directory that you created.

For example:

```
# mkdir /etc/sguild
# cd server
# cp autocat.conf sguild.conf sguild.queries \
  sguild.users /etc/sguild
```

This assumes that you're in the directory that was created when you unpacked the *Sguil* distribution. You'll also want to copy the *sguild* script to somewhere more permanent, such as */usr/local/sbin* or something similar.

Now edit *sguild.conf* and tell it how to access the database you created. If you used the database commands shown previously to create the database and user for *Sguil*, you would set these variables to the following values:

```
set DBNAME SGUIL
set DBPASS sguilpass
set DBHOST localhost
set DBPORT 3389
set DBUSER sguil
```

In addition, *sguild* requires access to the Snort rules used on each sensor in order for it to correlate the different pieces. You can tell *sguild* where to look for these by setting the RULESDIR variable.

For instance, the following line will tell *sguild* to look for rules in */etc/snort/ rules*:

```
set RULESDIR /etc/snort/rules
```

However, *sguild* needs to find rules for each sensor that it monitors here, so this is really just the base directory for the rules. When looking up rules for a specific host it will look for them in a directory corresponding to the hostname within the directory that you specified (e.g., zul's rules would be in */etc/snort/rules/zul*).

Optionally, if you want to use SSL to encrypt *sguild*'s traffic (which you should), you'll need to create an SSL certificate and key pair [Hack #45]. After you've done that, move them to */etc/sguild/certs* and make sure they're named *sguild.key* and *sguild.pem*.

Next, you'll need to add users for accessing *sguild* from the *Sguil* GUI. To do this, use a command similar to this:

```
# sguild -adduser andrew
Please enter a passwd for andrew:
Retype passwd:
User 'andrew' added successfully
```

You can test out the server at this point by connecting to it with the GUI client. All you need to do is edit the *sguil.conf* file and change the SERVERHOST variable to point to the machine on which *sguild* is installed. In addition, if you want to use SSL, you'll need to change the following variables to values similar to these:

```
set OPENSSL 1
set TLS_PATH /usr/lib/tls1.4/libtls1.4.so
```

Now test out the client and server by running *sguil.tk*. After a moment you should see a login window like Figure 7-3.

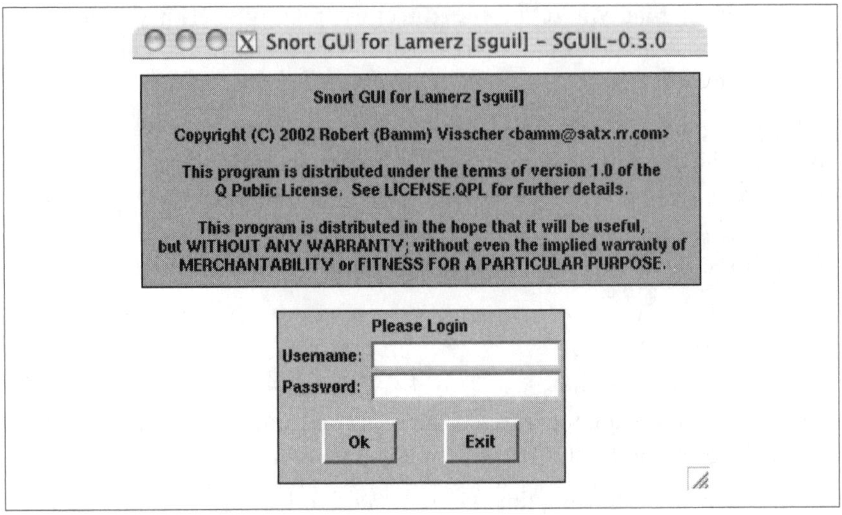

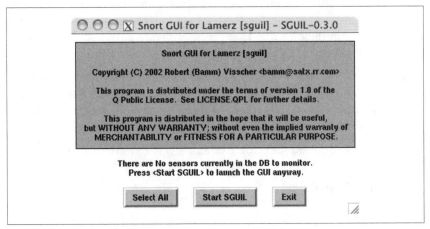

Figure 7-3. The Sguil login dialog

Enter in the information that you used when you created the user and click OK. After you've done that, you should see a dialog like Figure 7-4.

Figure 7-4. Sguil's no available sensors dialog

Since you won't have any sensors to monitor yet, click Exit.

To set up a *Sguil* sensor, you'll need to patch your Snort source code. You can find the patches that you'll need in the *sensor/snort_mods/2_0/* subdirectory of the *Sguil* source distribution. Now change to the directory that contains the Snort source code, go to the *src/preprocessors* subdirectory, and patch *spp_portscan.c* and *spp_stream4.c*.

For example:

```
$ cd ~/snort-2.0.5/src/preprocessors
$ patch spp_portscan.c < \
 ~/sguil0.3.0/sensor/snort_mods/2_0/spp_portscan_sguil.patch
patching file spp_portscan.c
$ patch spp_stream4.c < \
 ~/sguil-0.3.0/sensor/snort_mods/2_0/spp_stream4_sguil.patch
patching file spp_stream4.c
Hunk #9 succeeded at 988 (offset -5 lines).
Hunk #11 succeeded at 3324 (offset -5 lines).
Hunk #13 succeeded at 3674 (offset -5 lines).
```

Then compile Snort just as you normally would [Hack #82]. After you've done that, edit your *snort.conf* and enable the portscan and stream4 preprocessors:

```
preprocessor portscan: $HOME_NET 4 3 /var/log/snort/portscans gw-ext0
preprocessor stream4: detect_scans, disable_evasion_alerts, keepstats db \
/var/log/snort/ssn_logs
```

The first line enables the portscan preprocessor and tells it to trigger a portscan alert if connections to four different ports within a three-second interval have been received from the same host. In addition, the portscan preprocessor will keep its logs in */var/log/snort/portscans*. The last field on the line is the name of the sensor. The second line enables the stream4 preprocessor, directs it to detect stealth portscans, and to not alert on overlapping TCP datagrams. It also tells the stream4 preprocessor to keep its logs in */var/log/snort/ssn_logs*.

You'll also need to set up Snort to use its unified output format, so that you can use *Barnyard* to handle logging Snort's alert and log events:

```
output alert_unified: filename snort.alert, limit 128
output log_unified: filnemae snort.log, limit 128
```

Next, create a crontab entry for the *log_packets.sh* script that comes with *Sguil*. This script starts an instance of Snort solely to log packets. This crontab line will have the script restart the Snort logging instance every hour:

```
00 0-23/1 * * * /usr/local/bin/log_packets.sh restart
```

You should also edit the variables at the beginning of the script and change them to suit your needs. These variables tell the script where to find the Snort binary (SNORT_PATH), where to have Snort log packets to (LOG_DIR), what interface to sniff on (INTERFACE), and what command-line options to use (OPTIONS). Pay special attention to the OPTIONS variable. Here is where you can tell snort what user and group to run as; the default won't work unless you've created a sguil user and group. In addition, you can specify what traffic to not log by setting the FILTER variable to a BPF (i.e., tcpdump-style) filter.

Next, you'll need to compile and install *Barnyard* [Hack #92], but only run the configure step for now. After that, patch in the *op_sguil* output plug-in provided by *Sguil*. To do this, copy *sensor/barnyard_mods/op_sguil.** to the *output-plugins* directory in the *Barnyard* source tree.

For instance:

```
$ cd ~/barnyard-0.1.0/src/output-plugins
$ cp ~/sguil-0.3.0/sensor/barnyard_mods/op_sguil.* .
```

Now edit the Makefile in that directory to add *op_sguil.c* and *op_sguil.h* to the libop_a_SOURCES variable, and add *op_sguil.o* to the libop_a_OBJECTS variable.

After you've done that, edit *op_plugbase.c* and look for a line that says:

```
#include "op_acid_db.h"
```

Add another line below it so that it becomes:

```
#include "op_acid_db.h"
#include "op_sguil.h"
```

Now look for another line like this:

```
AcidDbOpInit( );
```

and add another line below it so that it looks like this:

```
AcidDbOpInit( );
SguilOpInit( );
```

Now run make from the current directory; when that completes, change to the top-level directory of the source distribution and run make install. To configure *Barnyard* to use the *Sguil* output plug-in, add a line similar to this one to your *barnyard.conf*:

```
output sguil: mysql, sensor_id 0, database SGUIL, server localhost, user
sguil, sguilpass, sguild_host localhost, sguild_port 7736
```

Now you can start *Barnyard* as you would normally. After you do that, you'll need to set up *Sguil*'s sensor agent script, *sensor_agent.tcl*, which can be found in the *sensor* directory of the source distribution. Before running the script, you'll need to edit several variables to fit your situation:

```
set SERVER_HOST localhost
set SERVER_PORT 7736
set HOSTNAME gw-ext0
set PORTSCAN_DIR /var/log/snort/portscans
set SSN_DIR /var/log/snort/ssn_logs
set WATCH_DIR /var/log/snort
```

The PORTSCAN_DIR and SSN_DIR variables should be set to where the Snort portscan and stream4 preprocessors log to.

Now all you need to do is set up *xscriptd* on the same system that you installed *sguild* on. This script is responsible for collecting the packet dumps from each sensor, pulling out the requested information, and then sending it back to the GUI client. Before running it, you'll need to edit some variables in this script too:

```
set LOCALSENSOR 1
set LOCAL_LOG_DIR /var/log/snort/archive
set REMOTE_LOG_DIR /var/log/snort/dailylogs
```

If you're running *xscriptd* on the same host as the sensor, set LOCALSENSOR to 1. Otherwise, set it to 0. The LOCAL_LOG_DIR variable sets where *xscriptd* will archive the data it receives when it queries the sensor, and REMOTE_LOG_DIR sets where *xscriptd* will look on the remote host for the packet dumps. If you're installing *xscriptd* on a host other than the sensor agent, you'll need to set up SSH client keys [Hack #73] in order for it to retrieve data from the sensors. You'll also need to install tcpflow (*http://www.circlemud.org/~jelson/software/tcpflow/*) and p0f (*http://www.stearns.org/p0f/*) on the host that you install *xscriptd* on.

Now that everything's set up, you can start *sguild* and *xscriptd* with commands similar to these:

```
# sguild -O /usr/lib/tls1.4/libtls1.4.so
# xscriptd -O /usr/lib/tls1.4/libtls1.4.so
```

If you're not using SSL, you should omit the -O /usr/lib/tls1.4/libtls1.4.so portions of the commands. Otherwise, you should make sure that the argument to -O points to the location of libtls on your system.

Getting *Sguil* running isn't trivial, but it is well worth the effort. Once everything is running, you will have a very good overview of precisely what is happening on your network. *Sguil* presents data from a bunch of sources simultaneously, giving you a good view of the big picture that is sometimes impossible to see when simply looking at your NIDS logs.

HACK #85 Manage a Sensor Network

Use SnortCenter's easy-to-use web interface to manage your NIDS sensors.

Managing an IDS sensor and keeping track of the alerts it generates can be a daunting task, and even more so when you're dealing with multiple sensors. One way to unify all your IDS management tasks into a single application is to use *SnortCenter* (*http://users.pandora.be/larc/*), a management system for Snort.

SnortCenter is comprised of a web-based console and sensor agents that are run on each machine in your NIDS infrastructure. It lets you unify all of your management and monitoring duties into one program, which can help you get your work done quickly. *SnortCenter* has its own user authentication scheme, and supports encrypted communication between the web-based management console and the individual sensor agents. This enables you to update multiple sensors with new Snort rules or create new rules of your own and push them to your sensors securely. *SnortCenter* also allows you to start and stop your sensors remotely through its management interface. To monitor the alerts from your sensors, *SnortCenter* can integrate with *ACID* [Hack #83].

To set up *SnortCenter*, you'll first need to install the management console on a web server that has both PHP support and access to a MySQL database server where *SnortCenter* can store its configuration database. To install the management console, download the distribution from the download page (*http://users.pandora.be/larc/download/*) and unpack it. This will create a directory called *www* (so be sure not to unpack it where there's already a *www* directory) containing SnortCenter's PHP scripts, graphics, and SQL schemas. Then, copy the contents of the *www* directory to a suitable location within your web server's document root.

For example:

```
# tar xfz snortcenter-v1.0-RC1.tar.gz
# cp -R www /var/www/htdocs/snortcenter
```

In order for *SnortCenter* to communicate with your database, you'll need to install ADODB (*http://php.weblogs.com/adodb*) as well. This is a PHP package that provides database abstraction functionality. After you've downloaded the ADODB code, unpack it into your document root (e.g., */var/www/htdocs*).

You'll also need to install curl (*http://curl.haxx.se*). Download the source distribution, unpack it, and run ./configure && make install. Alternatively, it might be available with your operating system (Red Hat has a curl RPM, and *BSD includes it in the ports tree).

After that's out of the way, you'll need to edit *SnortCenter*'s *config.php* (e.g., */var/www/htdocs/snortcenter/config.php*) and change these variables to similar values that fit your situation:

```
$DBlib_path = "../adodb/";
$DBtype = "mysql";
$DB_dbname   = "SNORTCENTER";
$DB_host     = "localhost";
$DB_port     = "";
$DB_user     = "snortcenter";
$DB_password = "snortcenterpass";
$hidden_key_num =1823701983719312;
```

This configuration will tell *SnortCenter* to look for the ADODB code in the *adodb* directory located at the same directory level as the one containing *SnortCenter*. In addition, it will tell *SnortCenter* to connect to a MySQL database called SNORTCENTER that is running on the local machine as the user snortcenter with the password snortcenterpass. Since it is connecting to a MySQL server on the local machine, there is no need to specify a port. If you want to connect to a database running on another system, you should specify 3389 for the port, which is the default used by MySQL. Set $hidden_key_num to a random number.

After you're done editing *config.php*, you'll need to create the database and user you specified and set the proper password for it:

```
$ mysql -u root -p mysql
Enter password:
Reading table information for completion of table and column names
You can turn off this feature to get a quicker startup with -A

Welcome to the MySQL monitor.  Commands end with ; or \g.
Your MySQL connection id is 27 to server version: 3.23.55

Type 'help;' or '\h' for help. Type '\c' to clear the buffer.

mysql> create database SNORTCENTER;
Query OK, 1 row affected (0.01 sec)

mysql> GRANT SELECT,INSERT,UPDATE,DELETE ON SNORTCENTER.* TO \
snortcenter@localhost IDENTIFIED BY 'snortcenterpass';
Query OK, 0 rows affected (0.00 sec)

mysql> FLUSH PRIVILEGES;
Query OK, 0 rows affected (0.02 sec)

mysql> Bye
```

Now create the database tables:

```
$ mysql -u root -p SNORTCENTER < snortcenter_db.mysql
```

Congratulations, it's time to try out *SnortCenter*! To do this, go to the URL that corresponds to where you installed it within your document root (e.g., *http://example.com/snortcenter/*). You should see something like Figure 7-5.

Enter in the default login/password admin/change, and then click the Login button. After you do that, you should see a page similar to Figure 7-6.

Now that you know that the management console has been installed successfully, you can move on to installing the agent. But before doing that, you should change the password for the admin account. To do this, click on the Admin button, then click on the User Administration menu item that appears. After that, click on View Users. You should then see a page like Figure 7-7.

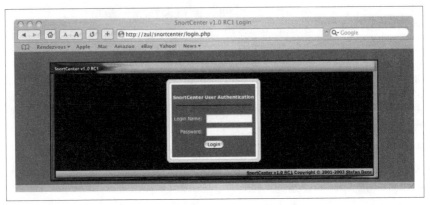

Figure 7-5. The SnortCenter login page

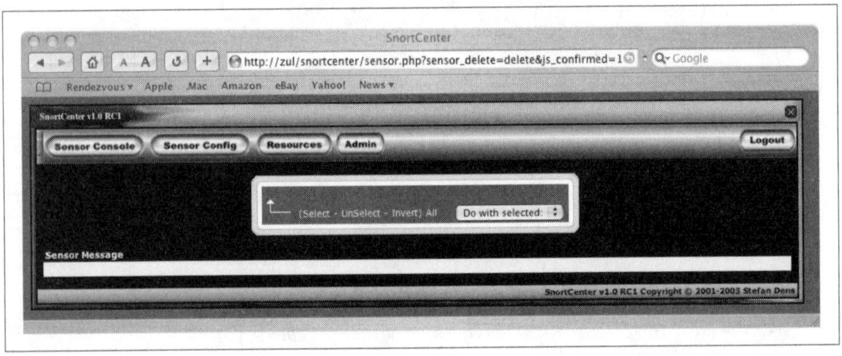

Figure 7-6. The initial SnortCenter main page

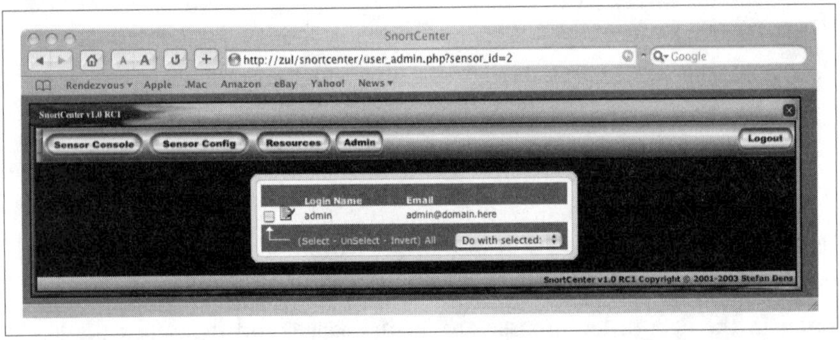

Figure 7-7. SnortCenter's user listing page

Clicking on the icon to the left of the username should bring you to a page similar to Figure 7-8; here you can edit the admin account's information, including the password.

Now you can go on to set up your sensor agents (really, I'm serious this time).

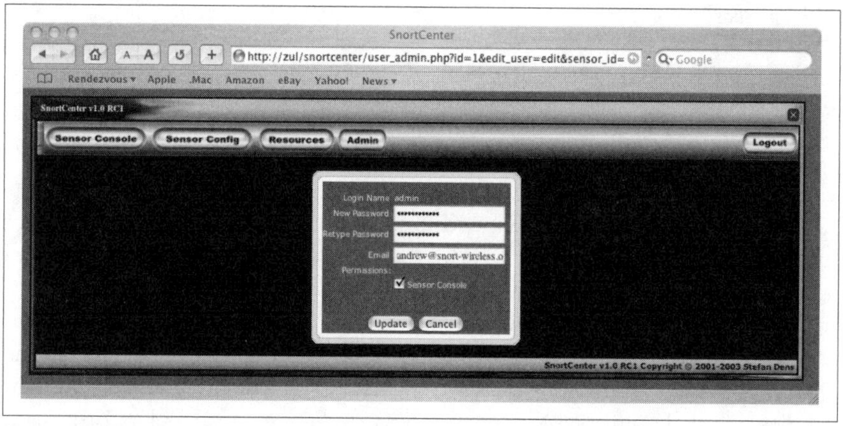

Figure 7-8. Changing the admin account's password and email address

SnortCenter's sensor agents are written in Perl and require the Net::SSLeay module to communicate with the management console through a secure channel. If you have Perl's CPAN module installed, you can install Net::SSLeay easily by running the following command:

```
# perl -MCPAN -e "install Net::SSLeay"
```

To install the sensor code, you'll first need to unpack it. This will create a directory called *sensor* containing all of the sensor agent code. Then copy that directory to a suitable permanent location.

For example:

```
# tar xfz /tmp/snortcenter-agent-v1.0-RC1.tar.gz
# cp -R sensor /usr/local/snortcenter
```

Next you'll need to create an SSL certificate for the sensor. You can do this by running the following command:

```
# cd /usr/local/snortcenter
# mkdir conf
# openssl req -new -x509 -days 3650 -nodes \
 -out conf/sensor.pem -keyout conf/sensor.pem
```

Alternatively, you can create a signed certificate [Hack #45] and use that.

After you've done that, run the sensor agent's setup script:

```
# sh setup.sh
****************************************************************************
*  Welcome to the SnortCenter Sensor Agent setup script, version 1.0 RC1  *
****************************************************************************


Installing Sensor in /usr/local/snortcenter ...


****************************************************************************
```

The Sensor Agent uses separate directories for configuration files and log
files.
Unless you want to place them in a other directory, you can just accept the
defaults.

```
Config file directory [/usr/local/snortcenter/conf]:
```

This script will prompt you for several pieces of information, such as the
sensor agent's configuration file and log directories, the full path to the perl
binary (e.g., /usr/bin/perl), as well as the location of your snort binary and
rules. In addition, it will ask you questions about your operating system,
what port and IP address you want the sensor agent to listen on (the default
is TCP port 2525), and what IP addresses are allowed to connect to the
agent. In particular, it will ask you to set a login and password that the management console will use for logging into the agent. After it has prompted
you for all the information it needs, it will start the sensor agent on the port
and IP address specified in the configuration file. You can now test out the
sensor agent by accessing it with your web browser (be sure to use *https*
instead of *http*). You should see a page similar to Figure 7-9 after entering
the login information contained in the setup script.

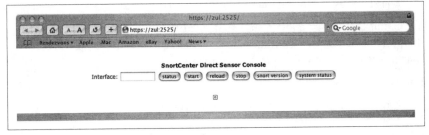

Figure 7-9. The sensor agent direct console page

Now you can go back to the main management console and add the sensor
to it. To do this, log back into the management console and select Add Sensor from the Sensor Console menu. After doing this, you should see something similar to Figure 7-10.

Fill in the information that you used when running the setup script and click
the Save button. When the next page loads, the sensor that you just added
should appear in the sensor list. You can push a basic configuration to the
sensor by opening the Admin menu, then selecting the Import/Update Rules
item, and then Update from Internet. After you've done that, go back to the
sensor list by clicking View Sensors in the Sensor Consoles menu, and then
click the Push hyperlink for the sensor. To start Snort on that particular sensor, click the Start link. After you've done that, you should see a page similar to Figure 7-11.

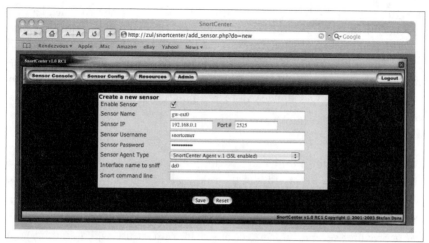

Figure 7-10. Adding a sensor agent

Figure 7-11. SnortCenter's sensor list after starting a sensor

You can now configure your sensor by using the Sensor Config and Resources menus. Once you've created a configuration you're satisfied with, you can push it to your sensor(s) by going back to the sensor list and selecting Push.

HACK #86 Write Your Own Snort Rules

Customize Snort for your own needs quickly and easily by leveraging its flexible rule engine and language.

One of the best features of Snort is its rule engine and language. Snort's rule engine provides an extensive language that enables you to write your own rules, allowing you to extend it to meet the needs of your own network.

A Snort rule can be broken down into two basic parts, the rule header and options for the rule. The rule header contains the action to perform, the protocol that the rule applies to, and the source and destination addresses and ports. The rule options allow you to create a descriptive message to associate with the rule, as well as check a variety of other packet attributes by making use of Snort's extensive library of plug-ins.

Here's the general form of a Snort rule:

```
action proto src_ip src_port direction dst_ip dst_port (options)
```

When a packet comes in, its source and destination IP addresses and ports are then compared to the rules in the ruleset. If any of them are applicable to the packet, then the options are compared to the packet. If all of these comparisons return a match, then the specified action is taken.

Snort provides several built-in actions that you can use when crafting your rules. To simply log the packet that matches a rule, use the log action. The alert action generates an alert using the method specified in your configuration file or on the command line, in addition to logging the packet. One nice feature is that you can have very general rules and then create exceptions by writing a rule that uses the pass action. This works especially well when you are using the rules distributed with Snort, but are frequently getting false positives for some of them. If this happens and it's not a security risk to ignore them, you can simply write a pass rule for it.

The last two built-in rule actions are used together to dynamically modify Snort's ruleset at runtime. These are the activate and dynamic actions. Rules that use the dynamic action are just like a log rule, except they will be considered only after they have been enabled by an activate rule. To accomplish this, Snort enforces the use of the activates and activated_by rule options in order to know what dynamic rules to enable once an activate rule has been triggered. In addition, dynamic rules are required to specify a count option in order for Snort to limit how many packets the rule will record.

For instance, if you wanted to start recording packets once an exploit of a SSH daemon on 192.168.1.21 was noticed, you could use a couple of rules similar to these:

```
activate tcp any any -> 192.168.1.21 22 (content:"/bin/sh"; activates:1; \
msg:"Possible SSH buffer overflow"; )
dynamic tcp any any -> 192.168.1.21 22 (activated_by:1; count:100;)
```

These two rules aren't completely foolproof, but if someone were to run an exploit with shell code against an SSH daemon, it would most likely send the string */bin/sh* in the clear in order to spawn a shell on the system being attacked. In addition, since SSH is encrypted, strings like that wouldn't be sent to the daemon under normal circumstances. Once the first rule is triggered, it will activate the second one, which will record 100 packets and then stop. This is useful, since you might be able to catch the intruder downloading or installing a root kit within those first few packets and be able to analyze the compromised system much more quickly.

You can also define custom rule actions, in addition to those that Snort has built-in. This is done with the ruletype keyword:

```
ruletype redalert
{
    type alert
    output alert_syslog: LOG_AUTH LOG_ALERT
    output database: log, mysql, user=snort dbname=snort host=localhost
}
```

This custom rule action tells Snort that it behaves like the alert rule action, but specifies that the alerts should be sent to the syslog daemon, while the packet will be logged to a database. When defining a custom action, you can use any of Snort's output plug-ins, just as you would if you were configuring them as your primary output method.

Snort's detection engine supports several protocols. The proto field is used to specify what protocol your rule applies to. Valid values for this field are ip, icmp, tcp, and udp.

The next fields in a Snort rule are used to specify the source and destination IP addresses and ports of the packet, as well as the direction the packet is traveling. Snort can accept a single IP or a list of addresses. When specifying a list of IP address, you should separate each one with a comma and then enclose the list within square brackets, like this:

```
[192.168.1.1,192.168.1.45,10.1.1.24]
```

When doing this, be careful not to use any whitespace. You can also specify ranges of IP addresses using CIDR notation, or even include CIDR ranges within lists. Snort also allows you to apply the logical NOT operator (!) to an IP address or CIDR range to specify that the rule should match all but that address or range of addresses.

As with IP addresses, Snort can accept single ports as well as ranges. To specify a range, use a colon character to separate the lower bound from the upper bound. For example, if you wanted to specify all ports from 1 to 1024, you would do it like this:

```
1:1024
```

You can also apply the NOT operator to a port, and you can specify a range of ports without an upper or lower bound.

For instance, if you only wanted to examine ports greater than 1024, you would do it this way:

```
1024:
```

Similarly, you could specify ports less than 1024 by doing this:

```
:1024
```

If you do not care about the IP address or port, you can simply specify any.

Moving on, the direction field is used to tell Snort which IP address and port is the source and which pair is the destination. In earlier versions of Snort you could use either -> or <- to specify the direction. However, the <- operator was removed since you can make either one equivalent to the other by just switching the IP addresses and port numbers. Snort does have another direction operator in addition to ->, though. Specifying <> as the direction tells Snort that you want the rule to apply bidirectionally. This is especially useful when using log rules or dynamic rules, since you can log both sides of the TCP stream rather than just one direction.

The next part of the rule includes the options. This part lets you specify many other attributes to check against. Each option is implemented through a Snort plug-in. When a rule that specifies an option is triggered, Snort will run through the option's corresponding plug-in to perform the check against the packet. Snort has over 40 plug-ins—too many to cover in detail in this hack. Here are some of the more useful ones.

The single most useful option is msg. This option allows you to specify a custom message that will be logged in the alert when a packet matching the rule is detected. Without it, most alerts wouldn't make much sense at first glance. This option takes a string enclosed in quotes as its argument.

For example, this specifies a logical message whenever Snort notices any traffic that is sent from 192.168.1.35:

```
alert tcp 192.168.1.35 any -> any any (msg:"Traffic from 192.168.1.35";)
```

Be sure not to include any escaped quotes within the string. Snort's parser is a simple one and does not support escaping characters.

Another useful option is content, which allows you to search a packet for a sequence of characters or hexadecimal values. If you are searching for a string, you can just put it in quotes. In addition, if you want it to do a case-insensitive search, you can add nocase; to the end of all your options. However, if you are looking for a sequence of hexadecimal digits, you must enclose them in | characters.

This rule will trigger when it sees the digit 0x90:

```
alert tcp any any -> any any (msg:"Possible  exploit"; content:"|90|";)
```

This digit is the hexadecimal equivalent of the NOP instruction on the x86 architecture and is often seen in exploit code since it can be used to make buffer overflow exploits easier to write.

The offset and depth options can be used in conjunction with the content option to limit the searched portion of the data payload to a specific range of bytes.

If you wanted to limit content matches for NOP instructions to between bytes 40 and 75 of the data portion of a packet, you could modify the previously shown rule to look like this:

```
alert tcp any any -> any any (msg:"Possible  exploit"; content:"|90|";  \
offset:40; depth:75;)
```

You can also match against packets that do not contain the specified sequence by prefixing it with a !. In addition, many shell code payloads can be very large compared to the normal amount of data carried in a packet sent to a particular service. You can check the size of a packet's data payload by using the dsize option. This option takes a number as an argument. In addition, you can specify an upper bound by using the < operator, or you can choose a lower bound by using the > operator. Upper and lower bounds can be expressed with <>.

For example:

```
alert tcp any any -> any any (msg:"Possible  exploit"; content:"|90|";  \
offset:40; depth:75; dsize: >6000;)
```

This modifies the previous rule to match only if the data payload's size is greater than 6000 bytes, in addition to the other options criteria.

To check the TCP flags of a packet, Snort provides the flags option. This option is especially useful for detecting portscans that employ various invalid flag combinations.

For example, this rule will detect when the SYN and FIN flags are set at the same time:

```
alert any any -> any any (flags: SF,12; msg: "Possible SYN FIN scan";)
```

Valid flags are S for SYN, F for FIN, R for RST, P for PSH, A for ACK, and U for URG. In addition, Snort lets you check the values of the two reserved flag bits. You can specify these by using either 1 or 2. You can also match packets that have no flags set by using 0. There are also several operators that the flags option will accept. You can prepend either a +, *, or ! to the flags, to match on all the flags plus any others, any of the flags, or only if none of the flags are set, respectively.

One of the best features of Snort is that it provides many plug-ins that can be used in the options field of a rule. The options discussed here should get you off to a good start. However, if you want to write more complex rules, consult Snort's excellent rule documentation, which contains full descriptions and examples for each of Snort's rule options. The Snort User's Manual is available at *http://www.snort.org/docs/writing_rules/*.

HACK #87 Prevent and Contain Intrusions with Snort_inline

Install Snort_inline on your firewall to contain intrusions, or to stop them as they're happening.

Wouldn't it be nice if your NIDS could not only detect intrusions, but also do something about them? It would be nice if it could actually stop the intrusion occurring on the host that was being attacked, but the next best thing would be to block the network traffic that's propagating the attack. One tool that can do this for you is *Snort_inline (http://snort-inline.sf.net)*.

Snort_inline is a patch to Snort that modifies it to read data from the Linux kernel's Netfilter queue, which allows Snort to effectively integrate itself with the firewall. This allows it to not only detect intrusions, but to decide whether to drop packets or to forward them to another host (using Libnet). This of course requires that your kernel be compiled with IP queue support, either statically or as a module.

You can see if you have the module by running a command like this:

```
$ locate ip_queue.o
/usr/src/linux-2.4.20-8/net/ipv4/netfilter/ip_queue.o
/usr/src/linux-2.4.20-8/net/ipv4/netfilter/.ip_queue.o.flags
/lib/modules/2.4.20-8/kernel/net/ipv4/netfilter/ip_queue.o
```

In this case, you can see that the module is available by looking at the last line of the output. If that doesn't exist, you can check to see whether the file */proc/net/ip_queue* exists. If you can't find the module, but that file exists, then it means IP queue support is compiled into your kernel statically. If neither file exists, you'll need to enable it in your kernel and recompile.

In addition to requiring IP queue support, *Snort_inline* also needs libipq. This is a library that comes with Netfilter and is used by applications to communicate with Netfilter's queue. You can check to see if it's installed on your system by running this command:

```
$ locate libipq
/usr/include/libipq.h
/lib/libipq.a
```

If you don't see output similar to this, chances are that you don't have libipq installed. You can install it by downloading the iptables source from the Netfilter distribution site (*http://www.netfilter.org*). For instructions on compiling it, refer to "Fool Remote Operating System Detection Software" [Hack #41]. After compilation is finished, run make install-dev, since libipq is not installed by default.

In addition to those libraries, you'll also need the Libnet packet injection library (*http://www.packetfactory.net/projects/libnet/*). To install Libnet, simply download the source distribution, unpack it, and then run ./configure && make install as root.

Now that all the prerequisites are out of the way, you can compile *Snort_inline*. First download and unpack the source distribution, and then change to the directory that it creates. Then run this command:

```
$ ./configure --enable-inline && make
```

You can also use any configure options that you'd normally use with Snort, since at it's heart *Snort_inline* is still Snort.

Don't be alarmed if your compile aborts with the following error:

```
gcc -DHAVE_CONFIG_H -I. -I. -I../.. -I../.. -I../../src -I../../src/sfutil -
I/usr/include/pcap -I../../src/output-plugins -I../../src/detection-plugins
-I../../src/preprocessors -I../../src/preprocessors/flow -I../../src/
preprocessors/portscan -I../../src/preprocessors/flow/int-snort  -I../../
src/preprocessors/HttpInspect/include  -I/usr/include/pcre -I/usr/local/
include  -g -O2 -Wall -DGIDS -D_BSD_SOURCE -D__BSD_SOURCE -D__FAVOR_BSD -
DHAVE_NET_ETHERNET_H -DLIBNET_LIL_ENDIAN -c `test -f 'spo_alert_fast.c' ||
echo './'`spo_alert_fast.c
In file included from /usr/include/linux/netfilter_ipv4/ip_queue.h:10,
                 from /usr/include/libipq.h:37,
                 from ../../src/inline.h:8,
                 from ../../src/snort.h:38,
                 from spo_alert_fast.c:51:
/usr/include/linux/if.h:59: redefinition of `struct ifmap'
/usr/include/linux/if.h:77: redefinition of `struct ifreq'
/usr/include/linux/if.h:126: redefinition of `struct ifconf'
make[3]: *** [spo_alert_fast.o] Error 1
make[3]: Leaving directory `/home/andrew/snort_inline-2.1.0/src/output-
plugins'
make[2]: *** [all-recursive] Error 1
make[2]: Leaving directory `/home/andrew/snort_inline-2.1.0/src'
make[1]: *** [all-recursive] Error 1
make[1]: Leaving directory `/home/andrew/snort_inline-2.1.0'
make: *** [all] Error 2
```

This is caused by */usr/include/linux/netfilter_ipv4/ip_queue.h* including */usr/include/linux/if.h* instead of */usr/include/net/if.h* (a problem that the author encountered while writing this). You can fix this by simply editing *ip_queue.h* and changing this line near the top of the file:

```
#include <linux/if.h>
```

to this:

```
#include <net/if.h>
```

You can then restart the compilation from where it left off by simply typing make, or, if you're paranoid, you can use this command to completely start over:

```
$ make clean && make
```

After compilation has finished, become root and type make install.

You can now configure *Snort_inline* just as you would configure Snort regularly. However, it's recommended that you run a separate instance of Snort if you want alerting and use *Snort_inline* solely for setting firewall rules.

In addition to modifying Snort to capture packets from Netfilter rather than libpcap, the *Snort_inline* patch also adds three new rule types, as well as a new rule option. The new rule types are drop, sdrop, and reject. The drop rule type will drop the packet that triggered the rule without notifying the sending host, much like the iptables DROP target, and will log that it has done so. The sdrop rule type is similar, except that packets are silently dropped with no log entry to tell you that it occurred. Using the reject rule type will block the offending packet, but will notify the sending host with either a TCP RST or an ICMP port unreachable message, depending on whether the packet that triggered the rule used the TCP or UDP protocols, respectively. The new rule option added by *Snort_inline* allows you to replace arbitrary content within a packet with whatever you choose. The only restriction is that the replacement byte stream must be the same length as the original. This is implemented with the replace rule option and is used in conjunction with the content rule option to select what is to be replaced.

To run *Snort_inline*, start it just as you would start Snort. *Snort_inline* does add a new command-line switch, though: -Q tells it to use IP queues rather than libpcap to gather packets. So, you'll need to use this option if you want to use it in inline mode.

The only thing left to do before actually running it in inline mode is to configure the kernel to send the packets to the IP queues. This is done with the iptables command:

```
# iptables -F
# iptables -A INPUT -j QUEUE
# iptables -A OUTPUT -j QUEUE
# iptables -A FORWARD -j QUEUE
```

This will push all traffic going in, out, and through the machine into an IP queue from which *Snort_inline* will read its packets. You can then start snort_inline as you would Snort (just don't forget to use the -Q option):

```
# snort_inline -Qvc /etc/snort/snort_inline.conf
```

If you're administering the machine remotely, you'll probably want to start snort_inline before enabling the QUEUE targets, since it's snort_inline that will actually pass the packets back and forth. Otherwise, your remote logins will be dropped as soon as you put the iptables rules in place. If you're particularly paranoid, have your QUEUE target rules ignore packets coming from a certain IP address or range of addresses.

HACK #88 Automated Dynamic Firewalling with SnortSam

Use SnortSam to prevent intrusions by putting dynamic firewall rules in place to stop in-progress attacks.

An alternative to running Snort on your firewall and having it activate filtering rules on the machine it's running on [Hack #87] is to have Snort communicate which filtering rules should be put in place when the an intrusion is detected on an external firewall. To do this, you can use *SnortSam* (*http://www.snortsam.net*).

SnortSam uses Snort's plug-in architecture and extends Snort with the ability to notify a remote firewall, which then dynamically applies filtering rules to stop attacks that are in progress. Unlike *Snort_inline*, which is highly dependent on Linux, *SnortSam* supports a wide variety of firewalls, such as Checkpoint, Cisco, Netscreen, Firebox, OpenBSD's pf, and even Linux's ipchains and iptables interfaces to Netfilter. *SnortSam* is made up of two components, a Snort plug-in and a daemon.

To set up *SnortSam*, first download the source distribution and then unpack it. After you've done that, go into the directory it created and run this command:

```
$ sh makesnortsam.sh
```

This will build the snortsam binary, which you can then copy to a suitable place in your path (e.g., */usr/bin* or */usr/local/bin*).

Now download the patch for Snort, which you can get from the same site as *SnortSam*. After you've done that, unpack it:

```
$ tar xvfz snortsam-patch.tar.gz
NOTE
patchsnort.sh
patchsnort.sh.asc
```

```
snortpatch8
snortpatch8.asc
snortpatch9
snortpatch9.asc
snortpatchb
snortpatchb.asc
```

Next, run patchsnort.sh and specify the directory where you're keeping Snort's source:

```
$ sh patchsnort.sh snort-2.0.5
Patching Snort version 2.0...
patching file spo_alert_fwsam.c
patching file spo_alert_fwsam.h
patching file twofish.c
patching file twofish.h
patching file plugbase.c
Hunk #1 succeeded at 29 with fuzz 2 (offset -73 lines).
Hunk #2 succeeded at 639 with fuzz 2 (offset 77 lines).
Patching Makefiles...
Done
```

Now compile Snort as you would normally [Hack #82].

Before running *SnortSam*, you must create a configuration file for it. *SnortSam*'s configuration syntax is pretty easy to use, but there are quite a few options, so only a subset of the available ones will be discussed here.

One useful option is accept, which lets you tell *SnortSam* what Snort sensors are allowed to connect to it. This option can take a CIDR-format address range, a hostname, or a single IP address. You can optionally specify a password as well. If you don't specify a password, the one specified by the defaultkey option is used.

For example, if you wanted to allow all hosts from the network 192.168.1.0/24 with the password qwijybo, you could put a line like this in your configuration file:

```
accept 192.168.1.0/24, qwijybo
```

To specify multiple hosts on network address ranges, you can use multiple accept entries.

Another useful option is dontblock. This enables you to construct a whitelist of hosts and networks that *SnortSam* will not block under any circumstances. This option takes hostnames, single IP addresses, and CIDR addresses; you can also use multiple dontblock entries, just as you can with accept.

To improve *SnortSam*'s performance, you may want to use the skipinterval option. This option lets you tell *SnortSam* how long to skip identical blocking requests before it will resume applying rules for that request. This ensures that *SnortSam* isn't constantly requesting the firewall to block the same IP address and port over and over again. The skipinterval option takes a single number as its argument, which specifies how many seconds to wait.

You'll probably want to keep tabs on what *SnortSam*'s doing, since you're allowing it to modify your firewall's rules. One way is to use the logfile option, which will cause *SnortSam* to log events such as program start, blocking and unblocking requests, and any errors that were encountered. This option takes a single argument, which is the filename that the logs will be written to. The log file that you specify will be created in */var/log*.

A couple of other useful options are daemon and bindip. The daemon option simply tells *SnortSam* to fork into the background and run as a daemon; it does not take any arguments. The bindip option, on the other hand, allows you to specify which IP address to listen on, which is useful when the machine that *SnortSam* is running on has multiple addresses available.

For instance, if you wanted *SnortSam* to listen only on 192.168.1.15, you would use a line like this:

```
bindip 192.168.1.15
```

In addition, the default port that *SnortSam* listens on is 898, but you can change this with the port option.

After you're done with *SnortSam*'s options, you'll need to tell it what kind of firewall to communicate with and how to do it. To use *SnortSam* with a Checkpoint Ffwexec or fwsamW-1 firewall, you can specify either the fwexec or fwsam keywords. Use fwexec when you when you want to run *SnortSam* on the host that the firewall is install fwexec or fwsamed on, and use fwsam when you want to communicate with a remote firewall.

The fwexec keyword takes the full pathname to the fw executable as its only argument, whereas the fwsam keyword uses the hostname or IP of the fire-wall. In addition, you'll need to modify the *fwopsec.conf* file on your firewall to include the following line:

```
sam_server port 1813
```

To use *SnortSam* with a PIX firewall, you'll need to use the pix keyword and specify the IP address of the firewall as well as the Telnet and enable mode passwords.

For example:

```
pix 192.16.1.2 telnetpw enablepw
```

Or, if your firewall is set up to do user authentication, you can use user/ password in place of the Telnet password.

If you want to use *SnortSam* with OpenBSD's PF or Linux's iptables, you'll need to use the pf or iptables keywords. For basic usage, all you need to do is specify the interface on which to block packets.

To configure the Snort side of things, you'll need to add the alert_fwsam output plug-in to the output plug-ins that you're already using. This plug-in takes a hostname and an optional port to connect to, along with a password. If *SnortSam* is using the default port, you don't need to specify the port here.

For example:

```
output alert_fwsam: firewall/mypassword firewall2:1025/mypassword
```

Notice that you can list multiple instances of *SnortSam* to send block requests to by separating them with whitespace.

Any rules that you want to trigger a firewall rule should be modified to use the fwsam rule option. This option takes as its arguments what to block and for how long the block should be in effect. To block the source of the packet that caused the alert, use src; to block the destination, use dst. If you want to block both, use either. For the duration you can use a number along with a modifier specifying what unit it's in (i.e., seconds, minutes, hours, days, weeks, months, or years), or you can use 0 to specify an indefinite period of time.

For instance, to block the source address of the packet that triggered a rule for five minutes, you could add this to your rule options:

```
fwsam: src, 5 minutes;
```

Now that everything is configured, start *SnortSam* by running a command similar to this:

```
# snortsam /usr/local/etc/snortsam.conf
```

Of course, you'll need to substitute the full path to your configuration file if it's not */usr/local/etc/snortsam.conf*. As for Snort, just start it as you normally would.

For more information on using *SnortSam* with other types of firewalls, be sure to check out the *README* files included with the source distribution.

HACK #89 Detect Anomalous Behavior

Detect attacks and intrusions by monitoring your network for abnormal traffic, regardless of the actual content.

Most NIDS monitor the network for specific signatures of attacks and trigger alerts when one is spotted on the network. Another means of detecting intrusions is to generate a statistical baseline of the traffic on the network and flag any traffic that doesn't fit the statistical norms. One intrusion detection system of this type is *Spade* (*http://www.silicondefense.com/software/spice/*).

Spade, or the Statistical Anomaly Detection Engine, is actually a modified version of Snort that extends its functionality into the realm of anomaly-based intrusion detection. The *Spade* preprocessor uses Snort to monitor the network and then constructs probability tables based on the traffic that it sees. It then uses this table to generate an anomaly between 0 and 1 for each packet (i.e., 0 is a definite normal, and 1 is a definite anomaly).

Installing *Spade* is easy. Just download the source distribution, unpack it, and change into the directory that it created. Then type a command similar to this, which will patch your Snort source code:

```
$ make SNORTBASE=../snort-2.0.5
```

Of course, if your Snort source tree isn't at *../snort-2.0.5*, you'll need to specify a different path.

Now change to the directory containing the Snort source code, and compile and install Snort as you normally would [Hack #82]. Once you've done that, you'll need to configure Snort to use *Spade*. You have two choices here: setting it up to use only *Spade* functionality or using normal Snort functionality along with *Spade*. For the former, you can use the *spade.conf* located in the *Spade* source distribution as a starting point.

Most of the defaults are fine. However, you will need to set the SPADEDIR variable to a place where Snort has read and write access. *Spade* will keep various logs and check-pointing information here so that it does not lose its probability table whenever Snort is restarted.

For example:

```
var SPADEDIR /var/log/snort/spade
```

It is also important that you tell *Spade* what network is your "home" network. You can do this by using a line similar to this one in your configuration file:

```
peprocessor spade-homenet: 192.168.1.0/24
```

You can specify multiple networks by separating them with commas and enclosing the list in square brackets.

If you want to run Snort with *Spade* and traditional Snort functionality, you can just include your *spade.conf* in your *snort.conf* with a line like this:

```
include spade.conf
```

Run Snort just as you did before. *Spade* will now send its output to any of the output plug-ins that you have configured when it detects anomalous behavior. This is triggered when a given packet's anomaly score is in the range of .8 to .9 (it depends on the type of packet). Any alerts generated by *Spade* will be prefixed with `Spade:` and will include a description of the packet's deviant behavior and its anomaly score.

Automatically Update Snort's Rules
Keep your Snort rules up-to-date with Oinkmaster.

If you have only a handful of IDS sensors, keeping your Snort rules up-to-date is a fairly quick and easy process. However, as the number of sensors grows it can become more difficult. Luckily, you automatically update your Snort rules with *Oinkmaster* (*http://oinkmaster.sourceforge.net/news.shtml*).

Oinkmaster is a Perl script that does much more than just download new Snort rules. It will also modify the newly downloaded rules according to rules that you specify or selectively disable them, which is useful when you've modified the standard Snort rules to fit your environment more closely or have disabled a rule that was reporting too many false positives.

To install *Oinkmaster*, simply download the source distribution and unpack it. Then copy the *oinkmaster.pl* file from the directory that it creates to some suitable place on your system. In addition, you'll need to copy the *oinkmaster.conf* file to either */etc* or */usr/local/etc*. The *oinkmaster.conf* that comes with the source distribution is full of comments explaining all the minute options that you can configure. *Oinkmaster* is most useful for when you want to update your rules but have a set of rules that you don't want enabled and that are already commented out in your current Snort rules. To have *Oinkmaster* automatically disable these rules, use the `disablesid` directive with the Snort rule ID that you want disabled when your rules are updated.

For instance, you may get a lot of ICMP unreachable datagrams on your network and have determined that you don't want to receive alerts when Snort detects this type of traffic. So, you decided to comment out the rule in your *icmp.rules* file:

```
# alert icmp any any -> any any (msg:"ICMP Destination Unreachable
(Communication Administratively Prohibited)"; itype: 3; icode: 13; sid:485;
classtype:misc-activity; rev:2;)
```

This is only one rule, so it's easy to remember to go back and comment it out again after updating your rules, but this can become quite a chore when you've done the same thing with several dozen other rules. If you use *Oinkmaster*, putting the following line in your *oinkmaster.conf* file will disable the preceding rule after *Oinkmaster* has updated your rules with the newest ones available from *snort.org*:

```
disablesid 485
```

Then, when you want to update your rules, run *oinkmaster.pl* and tell it where you'd like the updated rules to be placed:

```
# oinkmaster.pl -o /etc/snort/rules
```

Now you won't have to remember which rules to disable ever again.

Create a Distributed Stealth Sensor Network

H A C K
#91

Keep your IDS sensors safe from attack, while still giving yourself access to their data.

Your IDS sensors are the early warning system that can both alert you to an attack and provide needed evidence for investigating a break-in after one has occurred. You should take extra care to protect them and the data that they collect. One way to do this is to run your IDS sensors in *stealth mode*.

To do this, simply don't configure an IP address for the interface that your IDS software will be collecting data from. Putting the interface up, but without specifying an IP address, can do this.

For example:

```
# tcpdump -i eth1
tcpdump: bind: Network is down
# ifconfig eth1 up promisc
# ifconfig eth1
eth1      Link encap:Ethernet  HWaddr 00:DE:AD:BE:EF:00
          UP BROADCAST PROMISC MULTICAST  MTU:1500  Metric:1
          RX packets:0 errors:0 dropped:0 overruns:0 frame:0
          TX packets:0 errors:0 dropped:0 overruns:0 carrier:0
          collisions:0 txqueuelen:100
          RX bytes:0 (0.0 b)  TX bytes:0 (0.0 b)
          Interrupt:11 Base address:0x1c80

# /usr/sbin/tcpdump -i eth1
tcpdump: WARNING: eth1: no IPv4 address assigned
tcpdump: listening on eth1
```

After you've put the interface up, just start your IDS [Hack #82]. Your IDS will run as normal, but since there is no way to directly access the machine, it is very difficult to attack it.

However, just like potential attackers, you will be unable to access the machine remotely. Therefore, if you want to manage the sensor remotely, you'll need to put in a second network interface. Of course, if you did this and hooked it up to the same network that the IDS sensor is monitoring, it would totally defeat the purpose of running the other interface without an IP address. To keep the traffic isolated, you should create a separate network for managing the IDS sensors. You can of course attach this network to one that is remotely accessible and then firewall it heavily.

Another approach is to access the box using an alternate channel, such as a serial port connected to another machine that does have a network connection. Just run a console on the serial port, and take care to heavily secure the second machine. You could also connect a modem (remember those?) to an unlisted phone number or, better yet, an unlisted extension on your office's PBX. Depending on your situation, simply using the console for access may be the simplest and most secure method.

Whichever method you decide to use for remote access is a choice you'll have to make by weighing the value of increased security against the inconvenience of jumping through hoops to access the machine. Security nearly always involves a trade-off between convenience and confidence.

HACK #92   Use Snort in High-Performance Environments with Barnyard

Decouple Snort's output stage so it can keep pace with the packets.

Snort by itself is fine for monitoring small networks or networks with low amounts of traffic, but it does not scale very well without some additional help. The problem is not with Snort's detection engine itself, but stems from the fact that Snort is a single-threaded application. Because of this, whenever an alert or log event is triggered, Snort must first send the alert or log entry to its final destination before it can go back to looking at the incoming data stream. This isn't such a big deal if you're just having Snort write to a file, but it can become a problem if you are logging to a database, which can cause Snort to wait a relatively long time for the database insert to complete. This of course is exacerbated when you're having Snort log to a remote database server.

To solve this, another application called *Barnyard* (*http://www.snort.org/dl/barnyard/*) was written. Functionally, *Barnyard* is the equivalent of Snort's output plug-ins all rolled into one program, with a frontend for reading in files that Snort generates and then sending them to the same database or other destination that you would normally have Snort log to. The only drawback to *Barnyard* is its limited database support: *Barnyard* supports only MySQL, whereas Snort supports MySQL, PostgreSQL, Oracle, and ODBC outputs (*Barnyard* claims to support PostgreSQL, but unfortunately its current support is shaky at best).

After downloading *Barnyard* and unpacking it, change to the directory it created and run its configure script:

```
$ ./configure --enable-mysql
```

This will enable MySQL support when *Barnyard* is compiled. If you've installed your MySQL libraries and include files in a nonstandard place (i.e., underneath the */usr* or */usr/local* hierarchies), you'll probably need to add the `--with-mysql-includes` and `--with-mysql-libraries` command-line options.

After you're done with the configure script, you can compile *Barnyard* by running make. When it finishes compiling, install it by becoming root and running make install.

Before you use *Barnyard*, you'll need to configure Snort to use its unified output format. This is a binary format that includes both the alert information and the data for the packet that triggered the alert, and it is the only type of input that *Barnyard* will understand.

To configure Snort to use the unified output format for both alert and log events, add lines similar to these to your Snort configuration (e.g., */etc/snort/snort.conf* or */usr/local/etc/snort/snort.conf*):

```
output alert_unified: filename snort.alert, limit 128
output log_unified: filnemae snort.log, limit 128
```

The filenames specified here are the basenames for the files that Snort will write its alert and log event information to. When it writes a file, it will append the current Unix timestamp to the end of the basename. In addition, the size of these files will be limited to 128MB.

Now you'll need to create a configuration file for use with *Barnyard*. To run *Barnyard* in daemon mode and have it automatically fork itself into the background, add this line to your configuration file:

```
config daemon
```

If you're going to be logging to a database for use with *ACID* [Hack #83], you'll also want to add two lines similar to these:

```
config hostname: colossus
config interface: eth0
```

These two lines should be set to the name of the machine that you're running *Barnyard* on and the interface that Snort is reading packets from. Next, you'll need to actually tell *Barnyard* to read your unified log files.

You can do this for alert events by using this line:

```
processor dp_alert
```

Or, if you want to process log events, use this line:

```
processor dp_log
```

Note that *Barnyard* can process only one type of unified log at a time. So, if you want it to process both alert and log events, you'll need to run an instance of *Barnyard* for each type.

Now all that's left to configure is where *Barnyard* will send the data. If you want to use Snort's fast alert mode to generate single-line abbreviated alerts, you can use the `alert_fast` output plug-in:

```
output alert_fast: fast_alerts.log
```

Or, if you want *Barnyard* to generate ASCII packet dumps of the data contained in the unified logs, you can use a line similar to this:

```
output log_dump: ascii_dump.log
```

To have *Barnyard* output to your syslog daemon, you can use the `alert_syslog` plug-in just like you would in your *snort.conf*. For instance, if you wanted to send data to the local *syslogd* and use the auth facility and the alert log level, you could use a line like this:

```
output alert_syslog: LOG_AUTH LOG_ALERT
```

Or, if you want to send to a remote syslog daemon, you can use a line similar to this:

```
output alert_syslog: hostname=loghost, LOG_AUTH LOG_ALERT
```

You can also have *Barnyard* create Pcap-formatted files from the data in the unified logs. This is useful for analyzing the data later in tools such as Ethereal. To do this, use the `log_pcap` plug-in:

```
output log_pcap: alerts.pcap
```

Finally, you can also have *Barnyard* output to a database by using the `alert_acid_db` plug-in for logging alert events and the `log_acid_db` for capturing log events.

For instance, this line would send alerts to the SNORT MySQL database running on dbserver using the username snort:

```
output alert_acid_db: mysql, sensor_id 0, database SNORT, server dbserver,
user snort
```

The `sensor_id` is the one assigned by *ACID* to the particular instance of Snort that is gathering the data. You can find what sensor ID to use by clicking on the Sensors link on *ACID*'s front page [Hack #83], which will show you a list of the sensors that are currently logging to *ACID*.

The `log_acid_db` plug-in is similar, except it does not use the `sensor_id` option:

```
output log_acid_db: mysql, database SNORT, server dbserver, user snort,
detail full
```

You can start *Barnyard* by simply using a command similar to the following if Snort's configuration files are stored in */etc/snort* and Snort is set to keep its logs in */var/log/snort*:

```
# barnyard -f snort.alert
```

Of course, this assumes that you used snort.alert when configuring Snort's alert_unified plug-in. If your Snort configuration files aren't stored in */etc/snort*, you can specify the locations of all the files that *Barnyard* needs to access by running a command similar to this one:

```
# barnyard -c /usr/local/etc/snort/barnyard.conf \
-g /usr/local/etc/snort/gen-msg.map \
-s /usr/local/etc/snort/sid-msg.map -f snort.alert
```

This would tell *Barnyard* where to find all the files it needs if they are in */usr/local/etc/snort* (and are too stubborn to create a symlink to */etc/snort*). If you're using a directory other than */var/log/snort* to store Snort's logs, you can specify it with the -d option.

Congratulations. With *Barnyard* running, you should be able to handle much larger volumes of traffic without dropping log entries or missing a single packet.

HACK #93 Detect and Prevent Web Application Intrusions

Protect your web server and dynamic content from intrusions.

Detecting intrusions that utilize common protocols and services is a job that a network intrusion detection system is well suited for. However, due to the complexity of web applications and the variety of attacks they can be vulnerable to, it is more difficult to detect and prevent intrusions without generating many false positives. This is especially true for web applications that use SSL, since this requires you to jump through hoops to enable the NIDS to actually get access to the unencrypted traffic coming to and from the web server. One way to get around these issues is to integrate the intrusion detection system into the web server itself. This is just what *mod_security* (*http://www.modsecurity.org*) does for the popular Apache (*http://www.apache.org*) web server.

mod_security, as the name suggests, is a module for the Apache web server that is meant to increase the security of a web server by providing facilities for filtering requests and performing arbitrary actions based on user-specified rules. In addition, *mod_security* will also perform various sanity checks that normalize the requests that the web server receives. With the proper filtering rules, *mod_security* can be effective at defeating directory traversal, cross-site scripting, SQL injection, and buffer overflow attacks.

To install *mod_security*, download and unpack the source distribution. If you wish to install it as a DSO (i.e., a module), you can do so easily with the *apxs* utility. First change to the directory appropriate for the version of Apache that you are using—*apache1* or *apache2*. Then run a command like this:

```
# apxs -cia mod_security.c
```

This will compile *mod_security* and configure Apache to load it at startup. If you would like to statically compile *mod_security*, you will have to rebuild Apache. If you are using Apache 1.x, you can compile it statically by copying *mod_security.c* to the *src/modules/extra* directory in the Apache source tree. Then, when you run Apache's configure script, use these command-line switches:

```
--activate-module=src/modules/extra/mod_security
--enable-module=security
```

Now that *mod_security* has been installed, you'll need to enable it. You can do this by putting the following lines in your *httpd.conf* file:

```
<IfModule mod_security.c>
    SecFilterEngine On
</IfModule>
```

This will enable the request normalization features of *mod_security* for all requests made to the web server. Alternatively, you can enable it only for dynamic content by setting the SecFilterEngine variable to DynamicOnly. When *mod_security* is enabled, it will intercept all requests coming into the web server and perform several checks on it before passing it through any user-defined filters and finally either servicing or denying the requests. During these sanity checks, *mod_security* will convert several different types of evasive character sequences to their more commonly used equivalent forms. Thus the character sequences // and /./ will be transformed to /, and on Windows the \ character will be converted to /. In addition, any URL-encoded characters will be decoded. In addition to these checks, *mod_security* can also be configured to scan the payload of POST method requests and validate URL encoding and Unicode encoding contained within requests.

To enable these features, add these lines to your *httpd.conf*:

```
SecFilterScanPOST On
SecFilterCheckURLEncoding On
SecFilterCheckUnicodeEncoding On
```

URL encoding allows someone making a request to encode characters by using hexadecimal values, which use the numbers 0 through 9 and the letters A through F prefixed by the % character. When URL-encoding validation is enabled, *mod_security* simply ensures that any URL-encoded characters don't violate the hexadecimal numbering system. When performing Unicode validation, *mod_security* basically does the same type of thing—ensure that the string seen by the web server in fulfilling the request is a valid Unicode string. Unicode validation is useful if your web server is running on an operating system that supports Unicode or your web application makes use of it.

To avoid buffer overflow exploits, you can also limit the range of bytes that are allowed in request strings. For instance, to allow only printable characters (and not ones that might show up in exploit shell code), add a line like this to your *httpd.conf*:

```
SecFilterForceByteRange 32 126
```

User-defined filters are created with either the `SecFilter` or the `SecFilterSelective` keyword. You can use `SecFilter` to search just the query string, or you can use `SecFilterSelective` if you would like to filter requests based on the value of an internal web server variable. Both of these filtering keywords can accept regular expressions.

The following are filtering rules that can help prevent some common attacks.

The following rule will filter out requests that contain the character sequence `../`:

```
SecFilter "\.\./"
```

Even though the web server will interpret the `../` correctly and disallow access if it ends up resolving to something outside of its document root, that may not be the case for scripts or applications that are on your server. This rule prevents such requests from being processed.

Cross-site scripting (XSS) attacks are invoked by inserting HTML or Java-Script into an existing page so that other users will execute it. Such attacks can be used to read a user's session cookie and gain full control of that user's information. You can prevent these attacks by having *mod_security* filter out requests that contain JavaScript.

To disallow JavaScript in requests, use a rule like this:

```
SecFilter "<[[:space:]]*script"
```

In addition, you can disallow HTML by using this rule:

```
SecFilter "<(.|\n)+>"
```

SQL-injection attacks are similar to XSS attacks, except in this case attackers modify a variable that is used for an SQL query in such a way that they can execute arbitrary SQL commands.

To protect against this class of attacks, you can employ rules similar to these:

```
SecFilter "delete[[:space:]]+from"
SecFilter "insert[[:space:]]+into"
SecFilter "select.+from"
```

This rule prevents SQL injection in a cookie called sessionid:

```
SecFilterSelective COOKIE_sessionid "!^(|[0-9]{1,9})$"
```

If a sessiondid cookie is present, the request can proceed only if the cookie contains one to nine digits.

This rule requires HTTP_USER_AGENT and HTTP_HOST headers in every request:

```
SecFilterSelective "HTTP_USER_AGENT|HTTP_HOST" "^$"
```

You can search on multiple variables by separating each variable in the list with a | character. Attackers often investigate using simple tools (even Telnet) and don't send all headers as browsers do. Such requests can be rejected, logged, and monitored.

This rule rejects file uploads:

```
SecFilterSelective "HTTP_CONTENT_TYPE" multipart/form-data
```

This is a simple but effective protection, rejecting requests based on the content type used for file upload.

This rule logs requests without an Accept header, so you can examine them later:

```
SecFilterSelective "HTTP_ACCEPT" "^$" log,pass
```

Again, manual requests frequently do not include all HTTP headers. The Keep-Alive header is another good candidate. Notice that in addition to the variable and search string this rule contains the keywords log and pass, which specify the actions to take if a request matches the rule. In this case, any requests that match will be logged to Apache's error log, and then the request will go on for further processing by the web server. If you do not specify an action for a filter rule, the default action will be used.

You can specify the default action like this:

```
SecFilterDefaultAction "deny,log,status:500"
```

If you set this as the default action, the web server will deny all requests that match filter rules and that do not specify a custom action. In addition, they will be logged and then redirected to an HTTP 500 status page, which will inform the client that an internal server error occurred. Other possible actions are allow, which is similar to pass, but stops other filters from being tried; redirect, which redirects the client to an arbitrary URL; exec, which executes an external binary or script; and chain, which allows you to effectively AND rules together.

In addition to filtering, *mod_security* provides extensive auditing features, allowing you to keep logs of the full request sent to the server. To turn on audit logging, add lines similar to these to your *httpd.conf*:

```
SecAuditEngine On
SecAuditLog logs/audit_log
```

However, this will log all requests sent to the web server. Obviously, this can generate quite a lot of data very quickly. To only log requests that triggered a filter rule, set the SecAuditEngine variable to RelevantOnly. Alternatively, you can set this variable to DynamicOrRelevant, which will log requests to dynamic content or requests that triggered a filter rule.

As with most other Apache configuration directives, you can enclose *mod_security* configuration directives within a <Location> tag to specify individual configurations for specific scripts or directory hierarchies.

mod_security is a very powerful tool for protecting your web applications, but it should not take the place of actually validating input in your application or other secure coding practices. If at all possible, it is best to employ such methods in addition to using a tool such as *mod_security*.

See Also

- "Introducing mod_security": *http://www.onlamp.com/pub/a/apache/2003/11/26/mod_security.html*
- Mod_security Reference Manual v1.7.4: *http://www.modsecurity.org/documentation/modsecurity-manual-1.7.4.pdf*

Simulate a Network of Vulnerable Hosts
HACK #94   Use honeyd to fool would-be attackers into chasing ghosts.

As the saying goes, you will attract more flies with honey than with vinegar. (I've never understood that saying; who wants to attract flies, anyway?) A honeypot is used to attract the "flies" of the Internet: script kiddies and hacker wannabes that have nothing better to do with their time than scan for vulnerable hosts and try to attack them. A honeypot does this by pretending to be a server running vulnerable services, but is in fact collecting information about the attackers who think themselves so clever.

Whether you want to simulate one or one thousand vulnerable network hosts, *honeyd* (*http://www.honeyd.org*) makes the job as simple as editing a configuration file and running a daemon. The *honeyd* daemon can simulate thousands of hosts simultaneously and will let you configure what operating system each host will appear as when scanned with operating system detection tools like Nmap [Hack #42]. Each system that *honeyd* simulates will appear to be a fully functioning node on the network. Besides simply creating hosts that respond to pings and traceroutes, *honeyd* also lets you configure what services each host appears to be running. You can either use simple scripts to emulate a given service or have *honeyd* act as a proxy and forward requests to another host for servicing.

honeyd has several prerequisites that you'll need to install before building the daemon itself. These are libevent (*http://www.monkey.org/~provos/libevent/*), libdnet (*http://libdnet.sourceforge.net*), and libpcap (*http://www.tcpdump.org*). These can be easily installed by downloading and unpacking them and then using the standard ./configure && make install procedure. After the libraries are installed, you can install *honeyd* the same way. Then copy the service emulation scripts from the source distribution to somewhere more permanent (e.g., */usr/local/share/honeyd/scripts*). There are only a few scripts that come with *honeyd* itself, but there are additional service emulation scripts available on *honeyd*'s contributions page (*http://www.citi.umich.edu/u/provos/honeyd/contrib.html*).

Once *honeyd* has been installed, you'll need to create a configuration file that defines the types of operating systems and services *honeyd* will emulate, and the IP addresses *honeyd* will respond to. First, create some operating system templates:

```
### Windows computers
create windows-web
set windows-web personality "MS Windows2000 Professional RC1/W2K Advance
Server Beta3"
set windows-web  default tcp action reset
set windows-web default udp action reset
add windows-web tcp port 80 "perl scripts/win2k/iisemulator-0.95
/iisemul8.pl"
add windows-web tcp port 139 open
add windows-web tcp port 137 open
add windows-web tcp port 5900 "sh scripts/win2k/vnc.sh"
add windows-web udp port 137 open
add windows-web udp port 135 open

create windows-xchng
set windows-xchng personality "MS Windows2000 Professional RC1/W2K Advance
Server Beta3"
set windows-xchng default tcp action reset
set windows-xchng default udp action reset
add windows-xchng tcp port 25 "sh scripts/win2k/exchange-smtp.sh"
add windows-xchng tcp port 110 "sh scripts/win2k/exchange-pop3.sh"
add windows-xchng tcp port 119 "sh scripts/win2k/exchange-nntp.sh"
```

```
add windows-xchng tcp port 143 "sh scripts/win2k/exchange-imap.sh"
add windows-xchng tcp port 5900 "sh scripts/win2k/vnc.sh"
add windows-xchng tcp port 139 open
add windows-xchng tcp port 137 open
add windows-xchng udp port 137 open
add windows-xchng udp port 135 open


### Linux 2.4.x computer
create linux
set linux personality "Linux 2.4.7 (X86)"
set linux default tcp action reset
set linux default udp action reset
add linux tcp port 110 "sh scripts/pop3.sh"
add linux tcp port 25 "sh scripts/smtp.sh"
add linux tcp port 21 "sh scripts/ftp.sh"
```

And then bind them to the IP addresses that you want to use:

```
bind 192.168.0.10 windows-web
bind 192.168.0.11 windows-xchng
bind 192.168.0.12 linux
```

Save this configuration file in a good place (e.g., */usr/local/share/honeyd/ honeyd.conf*). Then start *honeyd* and arpd like this:

```
# arpd 192.168.0.10-192.168.0.12
# cd /usr/local/share/honeyd
# honeyd -p nmap.prints -x xprobe2.conf -a nmap.assoc \
 -0 pf.os -f honeyd.conf
honeyd[5861]: started with -p nmap.prints -x xprobe2.conf -a nmap.assoc -0
pf.os -f honeyd.conf
honeyd[5861]: listening on eth0: (arp or ip proto 47 or (ip )) and not ether
src 00:0c:29:e2:2b:c1
Honeyd starting as background process
```

Now try running Nmap on the IP addresses that *honeyd* is handling:

```
# nmap -sS -sU -O 192.168.0.10-12

Starting nmap V. 3.00 ( www.insecure.org/nmap/ )
Interesting ports on  (192.168.0.10):
(The 3063 ports scanned but not shown below are in state: closed)
Port       State     Service
80/tcp     open      http
135/udp    open      loc-srv
137/tcp    open      netbios-ns
137/udp    open      netbios-ns
139/tcp    open      netbios-ssn
5900/tcp   open      vnc
Remote operating system guess: MS Windows2000 Professional RC1/W2K Advance
Server Beta3
Uptime 2.698 days (since Sun Jan 11 03:52:35 2004)
```

```
Interesting ports on  (192.168.0.11):
(The 3060 ports scanned but not shown below are in state: closed)
Port      State        Service
25/tcp    open         smtp
110/tcp   open         pop-3
119/tcp   open         nntp
135/udp   open         loc-srv
137/tcp   open         netbios-ns
137/udp   open         netbios-ns
139/tcp   open         netbios-ssn
143/tcp   open         imap2
5900/tcp  open         vnc
Remote operating system guess: MS Windows2000 Professional RC1/W2K Advance
Server Beta3
Uptime 2.172 days (since Sun Jan 11 16:29:38 2004)

Interesting ports on  (192.168.0.12):
(The 1598 ports scanned but not shown below are in state: closed)
Port      State        Service
21/tcp    open         ftp
25/tcp    open         smtp
110/tcp   open         pop-3
Remote operating system guess: Linux 2.4.7 (X86)
```

You can certainly see that *honeyd* fools Nmap. But what happens when you
try to access one of the services that are purportedly running? Try connecting to the port 25 of the fake Windows mail server:

```
$ telnet 192.168.0.11 25
Trying 192.168.0.11...
Connected to 192.168.0.11.
Escape character is '^]'.
220 bps-pc9.local.mynet Microsoft ESMTP MAIL Service, Version: 5.0.2195.5329
ready at  Mon Jan 12 12:55:04 MST 2004
EHLO kryten
250-bps-pc9.local.mynet Hello [kryten]
250-TURN
250-ATRN
250-SIZE
250-ETRN
250-PIPELINING
250-DSN
250-ENHANCEDSTATUSCODES
250-8bitmime
250-BINARYMIME
250-CHUNKING
250-VRFY
250-X-EXPS GSSAPI NTLM LOGIN
250-X-EXPS=LOGIN
250-AUTH GSSAPI NTLM LOGIN
250-AUTH=LOGIN
250-X-LINK2STATE
```

```
250-XEXCH50}
250 OK
```

Pretty effective at first glance isn't it? If you'd like to specify some real services for attackers to play with, you can use the proxy keyword to forward any port to a host on another machine. For example, this will forward SSH requests from our imaginary Linux host to the machine at 192.168.1.100:

```
add linux tcp port 22 proxy 192.168.0.100:22
```

In addition to running the service emulation scripts, *honeyd* can limit inbound or outbound bandwidth, or even slow down access to a particular service. This can be used to tie up spammer's resources, by holding open an apparently open mail relay. The possibilities provided by *honeyd* are limited only by your imagination and the time you're willing to spend building your virtual fly-catching network.

HACK #95 Record Honeypot Activity

Keep track of everything that happens on your honeypot.

Once an attacker has fallen prey to your honeypot and gained access to it, it is critical that you monitor all activity on that machine. By monitoring every tiny bit of activity on your honeypot, you can not only learn the intentions of your uninvited guest, but can often learn about new techniques for compromising a system as the intruder tries to gain further access. Besides, if you're not interested in what attackers are trying to do, why run a honeypot at all?

One of the most effective methods for tracking every packet and keystroke is to use a kernel-based monitoring tool. This way nearly everything that the attacker does on your honeypot can be monitored, even if the attackers use encryption to protect their data or network connection. One powerful package for monitoring a honeypot at the kernel level is *Sebek* (*http://www. honeynet.org/tools/sebek/*).

Sebek is a loadable kernel module for Linux and Solaris that intercepts key system calls in the kernel and monitors them for interesting information. It then transmits the data to a listening server and hides the presence of the transmissions from the local system. *Sebek* is actually made up of two kernel modules. The first, *sebek.o*, actually does the monitoring. The other module is *cleaner.o*, which protects *sebek.o* from being discovered.

To build the kernel modules on Linux, first make sure that */usr/src/linux-2.4* points to the source code of the kernel that you want to compile the modules for. Either unpack the kernel source under this directory or symlink it to an existing kernel source tree. You can then download the source distribution, unpack it, and build it with the usual commands:

```
$ ./configure
$ make
```

This will generate a tar archive containing the kernel modules and an installer script. Copy this archive to your honeypot to complete the installation.

Here's what's inside:

```
$ tar tf sebek-linux-2.1.4-bin.tar
sebek-linux-2.1.4-bin/
sebek-linux-2.1.4-bin/sebek.o
sebek-linux-2.1.4-bin/cleaner.o
sebek-linux-2.1.4-bin/sbk_install.sh
```

Before installing the modules on your honeypot, you'll need to edit the *sbk_ install.sh* script and modify several variables that tell *sebek.o* where to send the information that it collects. These variables are DESTINATION_MAC, DESTINATION_IP, SOURCE_PORT, and DESTINATION_PORT. These should all be set to point to the *Sebek* server that you will build in a moment. Make sure to use the same DESTINATION_PORT for all honeypots that you'll be operating. In addition, you'll need to set the MAGIC_VAL variable to the same value on all your honeypots. This variable, in conjunction with DESTINATION_PORT, is used to hide traffic from other honeypots that you are operating. If you want *Sebek* to only collect keystrokes from your honeypot, you can set the KEYSTROKE_ONLY variable to 1.

Now run the install script on your honeypot:

```
# sh sbk_install.sh
Installing Sebek:
   sebek.o installed successfully
   cleaner.o installed successfully
   cleaner.o removed successfully
```

Once *Sebek* is installed, be sure to remove the archive and installation files. The presence of these files on a system is a pretty clear indication that it is a honeypot, and it could tip off intruders.

There are two ways to receive the data from *Sebek*. The simplest is to run the *Sebek* server, which will sniff for the information and automatically extract it for you. If you prefer to collect the data manually, you can use a sniffer on the host that you configured in the *sbk_install.sh* script and later use *Sebek*'s data extraction utility to pull the information out of your packet dumps.

To install the server, download the source distribution, unpack it, and go into the directory that it created. Then run this command:

```
$ ./configure && make
```

After compilation has finished, become root and run make install. This will install *sbk_extract*, *sbk_ks_log.pl*, and *sbk_upload.pl*. To extract information sent from a honeypot, use *sbk_extract*. You can run it in sniffer mode by using the -i and -p options to specify which interface to listen on and which destination port to look for, respectively. If you want to process packets that have already been captured using a packet capture tool, use the -f option to specify the location of the packet dump file. Once you've extracted the data, you can use *sbk_ks_log.pl* to display the attacker's keystrokes.

Sebek also has an optional web interface that uses PHP and MySQL to allow more complex queries of the collected data. In addition to logged keystrokes, the web interface can extract files that have been uploaded to the honeypot. The *sbk_upload.pl* script uploads the logs to the web interface. Installation of the web interface is a bit more involved, since it requires an Apache server, PHP, and a MySQL 4 database. For more details, consult *Sebek*'s homepage at *http://www.honeynet.org/tools/sebek/*.

Recovery and Response
Hacks 96–100

Incident recovery and response is a very broad topic, and there are many opinions on the proper methods to use and actions to take once an intrusion has been discovered. Just as the debate rages on regarding vi versus emacs, Linux versus Windows, and BSD versus everything else, there is much debate in the computer forensics crowd on the "clean shutdown" versus "pull the plug" argument. A whole book could be written on recovering from and responding to an incident since there are many things to consider when doing so, and the procedure you should use is far from well defined.

With this in mind, this chapter is not meant to be a guide on what to do when you first discover an incident, but it does show you how to perform tasks that you might decide to undertake in the event of a successful intrusion. In reading this chapter, you will learn how to properly create a filesystem image to use for forensic investigation of an incident, methods for verifying that files on your system haven't been tampered with, and some ideas on how to quickly track down the owner of an IP address.

HACK #96 Image Mounted Filesystems
Make a bit-for-bit copy of your system's disk for forensic analysis.

Before you format and reinstall the operating system on a recently compromised machine, you should take the time to make duplicates of all the data stored on the system. Having an exact copy of the contents of the system is not only invaluable for investigating a break-in, but may be necessary for pursuing any future legal actions. Before you begin, you should make sure that your md5sum, dd, and fdisk binaries are not compromised (you *are* running *Tripwire* [Hack #97] or otherwise have installed your packages using RPM [Hack #98], right?).

But hang on a second. Once you start wondering about the integrity of your system, where do you stop? Hidden processes could be running, waiting for the root user to log in on the console and ready to remove all evidence of the break-in. Likewise, there could be scripts installed to run at shutdown to clean up log entries and delete any incriminating files. Once you've determined that it is likely that a machine has been compromised, you may want to simply power down the machine (yes, just switch it off!) and boot from an alternate media. Use a boot CD or another hard drive that has a known good copy of the operating system. That way you can know without a doubt that you are starting the system from a known state, eliminating the possibility of hidden processes that could taint your data before you can copy it. The downside to this procedure is that it will obviously destroy any evidence of running programs or data stored on a RAM disk. However, chances are very good that the intruder has installed other backdoors that will survive a reboot, and these changes will most certainly be saved to the disk.

To make a bit-for-bit copy of our disks, we'll use the dd command. But before we do this we'll generate a checksum for the disk so that we can check our copy against the disk contents, to ensure that it is indeed an exact copy.

To generate a checksum for the partition we wish to image, run this command:

```
# md5sum /dev/hda2 > /tmp/hda2.md5
```

In this case we're using the second partition of the first IDE disk on a Linux system. Now that that's out of the way, it's time to make an image of the disk:

```
# dd if=/dev/hda of=/tmp/hda.img
```

Note that you will need enough space in /tmp to hold a copy of the entire /dev/hda hard drive. This means that /tmp shouldn't be a RAM disk and should not be stored on /dev/hda. Write it to another hard disk altogether.

Why do you want to image the whole disk? If you image just a partition, it is not an exact copy of what is on the disk. An attacker could store information outside of the partition, and this wouldn't be copied if you just imaged the partition itself. In any case, we can always reconstruct a partition image as long as we have an image of the entire disk.

In order to create separate partition images, we will need some more information. Run fdisk to get the offsets and sizes for each partition in sectors. To get the sectors offsets for the partition, run this:

```
# fdisk -l -u /dev/hda
Disk /dev/hda: 4294 MB, 4294967296 bytes
```

```
255 heads, 63 sectors/track, 522 cylinders, total 8388608 sectors
Units = sectors of 1 * 512 = 512 bytes

   Device Boot    Start      End    Blocks   Id  System
/dev/hda1    *       63    208844   104391   83  Linux
/dev/hda2        208845   7341704  3566430   83  Linux
/dev/hda3       7341705   8385929  522112+   82  Linux swap
```

Be sure to save this information for future reference, just in case you want to create the separate image files at a later date.

Now create an image file for the second partition:

```
# dd if=hda.img of=hda2.img bs=512 skip=208845 count=$[7341704-208845]
7132859+0 records in
7132859+0 records out
```

Note that the count parameter does some shell math for us: the size of the partition is the location of the last block (7341704) minus the location of the first block (208845). Be sure that the bs parameter matches the block size reported by fdisk (usually 512, but it's best to check it when you run fdisk). Finally, we'll generate a checksum of the image file and then compare it against the original one we created:

```
# md5sum hda2.img > /tmp/hda2.img.md5 && diff /tmp/hda2.md5 /tmp/hda2.img.md5
```

The checksum for the image matches that of the actual partition exactly, so we know we have a good copy. Now you can rebuild the original machine and look through the contents of the copy at your leisure.

HACK #97 Verify File Integrity and Find Compromised Files

Use Tripwire to alert you to compromised files or verify file integrity in the event of a compromise.

One tool that can help you detect intrusions on a host and also ascertain what happened after the fact is *Tripwire* (*http://sourceforge.net/projects/tripwire*). *Tripwire* is part of a class of tools known as *file integrity checkers*, which can detect the presence of important changed files on your systems. This is desirable because intruders who have gained access to a system will often install what's known as a *root kit*, in an attempt to both cover their tracks and maintain access to the system. A root kit usually accomplishes this by modifying key operating system utilities such as *ps*, *ls*, and other programs that could give away the presence of a backdoor program. This usually means that these programs will be patched to not report that a certain process is active or that certain files exist on the system. Attackers could also modify the system's MD5 checksum program (e.g., *md5* or *md5sum*) to report correct checksums for all the binaries that they have replaced. Since using MD5 checksums is usually one of the primary ways to verify whether a file has been modified, it should be clear that something else is sorely needed.

This is where *Tripwire* comes in handy. It stores a snapshot of your files in a known state, so you can periodically compare the files against the snapshot to discover discrepancies. With this snapshot, *Tripwire* can track changes in a file's size, inode number, permissions, or other attributes, such as the file's contents. To top all of this off, *Tripwire* encrypts and signs its own files, to detect if it has been compromised itself.

Tripwire is driven by two main components: a policy and a database. The policy lists all files and directories that *Tripwire* should snapshot, along with rules for identifying violations (i.e., unexpected changes). For example, a simple policy might treat any changes in */root*, */sbin*, */bin*, and */lib* as violations. The *Tripwire* database contains the snapshot itself, created by evaluating the policy against your filesystems. Once setup is complete, you can compare filesystems against the snapshot at any time, and *Tripwire* will report any discrepancies.

Along with the policy and database, *Tripwire* also has configuration settings, stored in a file that controls global aspects of its behavior. For example, the configuration specifies the locations of the database, policy file, and tripwire executable.

Tripwire uses two cryptographic keys to protect its files. The site key protects the policy file and the configuration file, and the local key protects the database and generated reports. Multiple machines with the same policy and configuration may share a site key, but each machine must have its own local key for its database and reports.

One caveat with *Tripwire* is that its batch-oriented method of integrity checking gives intruders a window of opportunity to modify a file after it has been legitimately modified and before the next integrity check has been run. The modified file will be flagged, but it will be expected (because you know that the file is modified) and probably dismissed as a legitimate change to the file. For this reason, it is best to update your *Tripwire* snapshot as often as possible. Failing that, you should note the exact time that you modified a file, so you can compare it with the modification time that *Tripwire* reports.

Tripwire is available with the latest versions of Red Hat and as a port on FreeBSD. However, if you're not running either of those, you'll need to compile it from source. To compile *Tripwire*, download the source package and unpack it. Next, check whether you have a symbolic link from */usr/bin/gmake* to */usr/bin/make*. (Operating systems outside the world of Linux don't always come with GNU make, so *Tripwire* explicitly looks for gmake, but this is simply called make on most Linux systems.) If you don't have such a link, create one.

Another thing to check for is a full set of subdirectories in */usr/share/man*. *Tripwire* will need to place manpages in *man4*, *man5*, and *man8*. On systems where these are missing, the installer will create files named after those directories, rather than creating directories and placing the files within the appropriate ones. For instance, a file called */usr/man/man4* would be created instead of a directory of the same name containing the appropriate manual pages.

Now change your working directory to *Tripwire* source's root directory (e.g., *./tripwire-2.3.1-2*) and read the *README* and *INSTALL* files. Both are brief but important.

Finally, change to the source tree's *src* directory (e.g., *./tripwire-2.3.1-2/src*) and make any necessary changes to the variable definitions in *src/Makefile*. Be sure to verify that the appropriate SYSPRE definition is uncommented (SYSPRE = i686-pc-linux or SYSPRE = sparc-linux, etc.).

Now you're ready to compile. While still in *Tripwire*'s *src* directory, enter this command:

```
$ make release
```

Then, after compilation has finished, run these commands:

```
$ cd ..
$ cp ./install/install.cfg .
$ cp ./intall/install.sh
```

Now open *install.cfg* with your favorite text editor to fine-tune the configuration variables. While the default paths are probably fine, you should at the very least examine the Mail Options section, which is where we initially tell *Tripwire* how to route its logs. Note that these settings can be changed later.

If you set TWMAILMETHOD=SENDMAIL and specify a value for TWMAILPROGRAM, *Tripwire* will use the specified local mailer (sendmail by default) to deliver its reports to a local user or group. If instead you set TWMAILMETHOD=SMTP and specify values for TWSMTPHOST and TWSMTPPORT, *Tripwire* will mail its reports to an external email address via the specified SMTP server and port.

Once you are done editing *install.cfg*, it's time to install *Tripwire*. While still in the root directory of the *Tripwire* source distribution, enter the following:

```
# sh ./install.sh
```

You will be prompted for site and local passwords: the site password protects *Tripwire*'s configuration and policy files, whereas the local password protects *Tripwire*'s databases and reports. This allows the use of a single policy across multiple hosts, to centralize control of *Tripwire* policies but distribute responsibility for database management and report generation.

If you do not plan to use *Tripwire* across multiple hosts with shared policies, there's nothing wrong with setting the site and local *Tripwire* passwords on a given system to the same string. In either case, choose a strong passphrase that contains some combination of upper- and lowercase letters, punctuation (which can include whitespace), and numerals.

When you install *Tripwire* (whether via binary package or source build), a default configuration file is created, */etc/tripwire/tw.cfg*. You can't edit this file, because it's an encrypted binary, but for your convenience, a clear-text version of it, *twcfg.txt*, should also reside in */etc/tripwire*. If it does not, you can create the text version with this command:

```
# twadmin --print-cfgfile > /etc/tripwire/twcfg.txt
```

By editing this file, you can make changes to the settings you used when installing *Tripwire*, and you can change the location where *Tripwire* will look for its database. This can be done by setting the DBFILE variable. One interesting use of this is to set the variable to a directory within the */mnt* directory hierarchy. Then, after the database has been created you can copy it to a CD-ROM and remount it there whenever you need to perform integrity checks.

After you are done editing the configuration file, you can re-encrypt it by running this command:

```
# twadmin --create-cfgfile --site-keyfile ./site.key twcfg.txt
```

You should also remove the *twcfg.txt* file.

You can then initialize *Tripwire*'s database by running this command:

```
# tripwire --init
```

Since this uses the default policy file that *Tripwire* installed, you will probably see errors related to files and directories not being found. These errors are nonfatal, and the database will finish initializing. If you want to get rid of these errors, you can edit the policy and remove the files that were reported as missing.

First you'll need to decrypt the policy file into an editable plain text format. You can do this by running the following command:

```
# twadmin --print-polfile > twpol.txt
```

Then comment out any files that were reported as missing. You will probably want to look through the file and determine whether any files that you would like to catalog aren't already in there. For instance, you will probably want to monitor all SUID files on your system [Hack #2]. *Tripwire*'s policy-file language can allow for far more complex constructs than simply listing one file per line; read the twpolicy(4) manpage for more information if you'd like to use some of these features.

After you've updated your policy, you'll also need to update *Tripwire*'s database. You can do this by running the following command:

```
# tripwire --update-policy twpol.txt
```

To perform checks against your database, run this command:

```
# tripwire --check
```

This will print a report to the screen and leave a copy of it in */var/lib/tripwire/report*. If you want *Tripwire* to automatically email the report to the configured recipients, you can add --email-report to the end of the command. You can view the reports by running twprint.

For example:

```
# twprint --print-report --twrfile \
/var/lib/tripwire/report/colossus-20040102-205528.twr
```

Finally, to reconcile changes that *Tripwire* reports with its database, you can run a command similar to this one:

```
# tripwire --update --twrfile \
/var/lib/tripwire/report/colossus-20040102-205528.twr
```

You can and should schedule *Tripwire* to run its checks as regularly as possible. In addition to keeping your database in a safe place, such as on a CD-ROM, you'll also want to make backup copies of your configuration, policy, and keys. Otherwise you will not perform an integrity check in the event that someone (malicious or not) deletes them.

See Also

- twpolicy (4)
- The section "Using Tripwire" in *Building Secure Servers with Linux*, by Michael D. Bauer (O'Reilly)

Find Compromised Packages with RPM
HACK #98   Verify operating system installed files in an RPM-based distribution.

So you've had a compromise and need to figure out which files (if any) were modified by the intruder, but you didn't install *Tripwire*? Well, all is not lost if your distribution uses RPM for its package management system. While not as powerful as *Tripwire*, RPM can be useful for finding to what degree a system has been compromised. RPM keeps MD5 signatures for all the files it has ever installed. We can use this functionality to check the packages on a system against its signature database. In addition to MD5 checksums, you can also check a file's size, user, group, mode, and modification time against that which is stored in the system's RPM database.

To verify a single package, run this:

```
rpm -V package
```

If the intruder modified any binaries, it's very likely that the ps command was one of them. Let's check its signature:

```
# which ps
/bin/ps
# rpm -V `rpm -qf /bin/ps`
S.5....T   /bin/ps
```

Here we see from the S, 5, and T that the file's size, checksum, and modification time has changed from when it was installed—not good at all. Note that only files that do not match the information contained in the package database will result in output.

If we want to verify all packages on the system, we can use the usual rpm option that specifies all packages, -a:

```
# rpm -Va
S.5....T   /bin/ps
S.5....T c /etc/pam.d/system-auth
S.5....T c /etc/security/access.conf
S.5....T c /etc/pam.d/login
S.5....T c /etc/rc.d/rc.local
S.5....T c /etc/sysconfig/pcmcia
.......T c /etc/libuser.conf
S.5....T c /etc/ldap.conf
.......T c /etc/mail/sendmail.cf
S.5....T c /etc/sysconfig/rhn/up2date-uuid
.......T c /etc/yp.conf
S.5....T   /usr/bin/md5sum
.......T c /etc/krb5.conf
```

There are other options that can be used to limit what gets checked on each file. Some of the more useful ones are -nouser, -nogroup, -nomtime, and -nomode. These can be used to eliminate a lot of the output that results from configuration files that you've modified.

Note that you'll probably want to redirect the output to a file, unless you narrow down what gets checked by using the command-line options. Running rpm -Va without any options can result in quite a lot of output resulting from modified configuration files and such.

This is all well and good, but ignores the possibility that someone has compromised key system binaries and that they may have compromised the RPM database as well. If this is the case, we can still use RPM, but we'll need to obtain the file the package was installed from in order to verify the installed files against it.

The worst-case scenario is that the rpm binary itself has been compromised. It can be difficult to be certain of this unless you boot from an alternate media, as mentioned earlier. If this is the case, you should locate a safe rpm binary to use for verifying the packages.

First find the name of the package that owns the file. You can do this by running:

```
rpm -qf filename
```

Then you can locate that package from your distribution media, or download it from the Internet. After doing so, you can verify the installed files against what's in the package using this command:

```
rpm -Vp package file
```

RPM can be used for quite a number of useful things, including verifying the integrity of system binaries. However, it should not be relied on for this purpose. If at all possible, something like *Tripwire* [Hack #97] or AIDE (*http:// sourceforge.net/projects/aide*) should be used instead.

HACK #99 Scan for Root Kits

Use chkrootkit to determine the extent of a compromise.

If you suspect that you have a compromised system, it is a good idea to check for root kits that the intruder may have installed. In short, a root kit is a collection of programs that intruders often install after they have compromised the root account of a system. These programs will help the intruders clean up their tracks, as well as provide access back into the system. Because of this, root kits will sometimes leave processes running so that the intruder can come back easily and without the system administrator's knowledge. This means that some of the system's binaries (like ps, ls, and netstat) will need to be modified by the root kit in order to not give away the backdoor processes that the intruder has put in place. Unfortunately, there are so many different root kits that it would be far too time-consuming to learn the intricacies of each one and look for them manually. Scripts like *chkrootkit* (*http://www.chkrootkit.org*) will do the job for you automatically.

In addition to detecting over 50 different root kits, *chkrootkit* will also detect network interfaces that are in promiscuous mode, altered *lastlog* files, and altered *wtmp* files. These files contain times and dates of when users have logged on and off the system, so if they have been altered, this is evidence of an intruder. In addition, *chkrootkit* will perform tests in order to detect kernel module–based root kits. C programs that are called by the main *chkrootkit* script perform all of these tests.

It isn't a good idea to install *chkrootkit* on your system and simply run it periodically, since an attacker may simply find the installation and change it so that it doesn't detect his presence. A better idea may be to compile it and put it on removable or read-only media. To compile *chrootkit*, download the source package and extract it. Then go into the directory that it created and type make sense.

Running *chkrootkit* is as simple as just typing ./chkrootkit from the directory it was built in. When you do this, it will print each test that it performs and the result of the test:

```
# ./chrootkit
ROOTDIR is `/'
Checking `amd'... not found
Checking `basename'... not infected
Checking `biff'... not found
Checking `chfn'... not infected
Checking `chsh'... not infected
Checking `cron'... not infected
Checking `date'... not infected
Checking `du'... not infected
Checking `dirname'... not infected
Checking `echo'... not infected
Checking `egrep'... not infected
Checking `env'... not infected
Checking `find'... not infected
Checking `fingerd'... not found
Checking `gpm'... not infected
Checking `grep'... not infected
Checking `hdparm'... not infected
Checking `su'... not infected
```

That's not very interesting, since the machine hasn't been infected (yet). *chrootkit* can also be run on disks mounted in another machine; just specify the mount point for the partition with the -r option, like this:

```
# ./chrootkit -r /mnt/hda2_image
```

Also, since *chrootkit* depends on several system binaries, you may want to verify them before running the script (using the Tripwire [Hack #97] or RPM [Hack #98] methods). These binaries are awk, cut, egrep, find, head, id, ls, netstat, ps, strings, sed, and uname. However, if you have known good backup copies of these, you can specify the path to them by using the -p option. For instance, if you copied them to a CD-ROM and then mounted it under */mnt/cdrom*, you would use a command like this:

```
# ./chrootkit -p /mnt/cdrom
```

You can also add multiple paths by separating each one with a :. Instead of maintaining a separate copy of each of these binaries, you could simply keep a statically compiled copy of BusyBox handy (*http://www.busybox.net*). Intended for embedded systems, BusyBox can perform the functions of over 200 common binaries, and does so using a very tiny binary with symlinks. A floppy, CD, or USB keychain (with the read-only switch enabled) with *chkrootkit* and a static BusyBox installed can be a quick and handy tool for checking the integrity of your system.

HACK #100   Find the Owner of a Network
Track down network contacts using WHOIS databases.

Looking through your IDS logs, you've seen some strange traffic coming from another network across the Internet. When you look up the IP address in DNS, it resolves as something like *dhcp-103.badguydomain.com*. Who do you contact to help track down the person who sent this traffic? You're probably already aware that you can use the whois command to find out contact information for owners of Internet domain names. If you haven't used whois, it's as simple as typing, well, "whois":

```
$ whois badguydomain.com
Registrant:
    Dewey Cheatum

    Registered through: GoDaddy.com
    Domain Name: BADGUYDOMAIN.COM

    Domain servers in listed order:
        PARK13.SECURESERVER.NET
        PARK14.SECURESERVER.NET
    For complete domain details go to:
    http://whois.godaddy.com
```

Unfortunately, this whois entry isn't as helpful as it might be. Normally, administrative and technical contacts are listed, complete with a phone number and email and snail mail addresses. Evidently, *godaddy.com* has a policy of releasing this information only through their web interface, apparently to cut down on spam harvesters. But if the registrant's name is listed as "Dewey Cheatum," how accurate do you think the rest of this domain record is likely to be? Although domain registrants are "required" to give legitimate information when setting up a domain, I can tell you from experience that using whois in this way is a great tool for tracking down honest people.

Since this approach doesn't get you anywhere, what other options do you have? You can use the whois command again, this time using it to query the number registry for the IP address block of the offending address.

Number registries are entities that owners of large blocks of IP addresses must register with, and are split up according to geographic region. The main difficulty is picking the correct registry to query, but the WHOIS server for ARIN (American Registry for Internet Numbers) is generally the best bet—it will tell you the correct registry to query if the IP address is not found in its own database.

With that in mind, let's try out a query using the offending IP address:

```
# whois -h whois.arin.net 208.201.239.103
[Querying whois.arin.net]
[whois.arin.net]
Final results obtained from whois.arin.net.
Results:
UUNET Technologies, Inc. UUNET1996B (NET-208-192-0-0-1)
                               208.192.0.0 - 208.255.255.255
SONIC.NET, INC. UU-208-201-224 (NET-208-201-224-0-1)
                               208.201.224.0 - 208.201.255.255

# ARIN WHOIS database, last updated 2004-01-18 19:15
# Enter ? for additional hints on searching ARIN's WHOIS database.
```

Our query returned multiple results, which will happen sometimes when an owner of a larger IP block has delegated a subblock to another party. In this case, UUNET has delegated a subblock to Sonic.net.

Now we'll run a query with Sonic.net's handle:

```
# whois -h whois.arin.net NET-208-201-224-0-1
Checking server [whois.arin.net]
Results:

OrgName:    SONIC.NET, INC.
OrgID:      SNIC
Address:    2260 Apollo Way
City:       Santa Rosa
StateProv:  CA
PostalCode: 95407
Country:    US

ReferralServer: rwhois://whois.sonic.net:43

NetRange:   208.201.224.0 - 208.201.255.255
CIDR:       208.201.224.0/19
NetName:    UU-208-201-224
NetHandle:  NET-208-201-224-0-1
Parent:     NET-208-192-0-0-1
```

```
NetType:       Reallocated
Comment:
RegDate:       1996-09-12
Updated:       2002-08-23

OrgTechHandle: NETWO144-ARIN
OrgTechName:   Network Operations
OrgTechPhone:  +1-707-522-1000
OrgTechEmail:  noc@sonic.net

# ARIN WHOIS database, last updated 2004-01-18 19:15
# Enter ? for additional hints on searching ARIN's WHOIS database.
```

From the output, you can see that we have a contact listed with a phone number and email. This is most likely the ISP who serves the miscreant who is causing the trouble. Now you have a solid contact who should know exactly who is behind *badguydomain.com*. You can let them know about the suspicious traffic you're seeing, and get the situation resolved.

Incidentally, you may have trouble using whois if you are querying some of the new TLDs (such as *.us*, *.biz*, *.info*, etc.). One great shortcut for automatically finding the proper whois server is to use the whois proxy at *geektools.com*. It automatically forwards your request to the proper whois server, based on the TLD you are requesting. I specify an alias such as this in my *.profile* to always use the geektools proxy:

```
alias whois='whois -h whois.geektools.com'
```

Now when I run whois from the command line, I don't need to remember the address of a single whois server. The folks at geektools have a bunch of other nifty tools to make sysadmin tasks easier. Check them out at *http://geektools.com*.

—*Rob Flickenger*

Index

Symbols

| character
 enclosing hexadecimal vales in Snort rules, 242
 searching on multiple variables, 260
../ character sequence in requests, 259
: (colon), in port ranges for Snort rules, 241
-> (direction operator), in Snort rules, 242
! (logical NOT) operator
 matching IP addresses and ports for Snort rules, 241
 TCP flag matching, Snort rules, 243
* operator, TCP flag matching in Snort rules, 243
+ operator, TCP flag matching in Snort rules, 243
<> (direction operator), in Snort rules, 242

A

ac command (process accounting), 154
Accept header, logging requests without, 260
accept option, SnortSam, 248
access.conf file (pam_access module), 39
ACID (Analysis Console for Intrusion Databases), 224–227
 archiving database, configuring, 225

Barnyard logging of Snort events, 255
 database tables, creating for, 225
 graphing, configuring, 225
 libraries used with, 224
 sensor ID, 256
ACLs (access control lists), 5–8
 application availability, restricting for users, 63
 grsecurity, 26, 30
 Windows event logs, securing, 56
activate and dynamic actions, Snort rules, 240
Address Resolution Protocol (see ARP)
address space layouts, randomization with grsecurity, 28
address spoofing
 detecting ARP spoofing, 67–69
 preventing for internal addresses with FilterPacket, 79
ADODB (PHP code library), 224, 234
AIDE, 276
alerts
 configuring Snort for, 223
 generated by Spade, 252
 IDS sensor, tracking, 233–239
 Snort NIDS
  analyzing with Sguil, 227–233
  handling with Barnyard, 255
  tracking with ACID, 224–227
  unified output format, 255
Analysis Console for Intrusion Databases (see ACID)

We'd like to hear your suggestions for improving our indexes. Send email to *index@oreilly.com*.

anomalous network behavior, detecting
    with Spade, 250–252
Apache web server
    configuring to listen on specific
        interface, 16
    installing with SSL and
        suEXEC, 121–125
    mod_security, 257–261
append-only (file attribute), 8
    preventing removal of, 9
applications
    restricting availability to users, 63
    restricting with grsecurity, 30–32
AppSec program (Windows), 64
Argus (Audit Record Generation and
        Utilization System), 169
    ra command, querying
        with, 169–171
    XML output, 170
ARIN (American Registry for Internet
        Numbers), 279
ARP (Address Resolution Protocol)
    arpd, starting with honeyd, 263
    cache poisioning, 67
    creating static ARP table, 69–71
    detecting ARP spoofing, 67–69
    proxy arp, 216
    sniffdet tool, ARP test, 120
arp command, 69
    finding system MAC address, 91
Arpwatch, 68, 118
attacks
    filtering rules that help to
        prevent, 259
    (see also entries under individual
        attack names)
auditing
    enabling on Windows systems, 55
    mod_security features for, 261
authenticated gateway, creating, 80–82
authentication
    MySQL source, using with
        proftpd, 21–23
    PAM, controlling login
        access, 38–42
authpf shell (OpenBSD), 80–82
AutoRPM (system update package), 45
Avaya Labs, LibSafe technology, 24

B

backdoors
    checking for, 3
    installed during root kit attacks, 276
    listening services that check
        for, 14–16
bandwidth usage
    graphing, 164–166
    tracking for machine with firewall
        rules, 171
Barnyard, 231
    compiling and installing for
        Sguil, 232
    using with Snort, 254–257
        configuring Barnyard, 255
        limited database support, 254
        logging, 255
bash shell
    restricted, 42
    setting up in chroot( )
        environment, 19
binaries, disallowing execution of, 2
    on Linux, 3
    setuid, cautions with sudo utility, 11
    SUID or SGID bit, 4
BIND, securing, 125–127
    restricting zone transfers, 127
bindip option, SnortSam, 249
bit-for-bit copy of system disks, 269
block-policy option (PacketFilter), 76
    modifying for specific rules, 78
booting compromised machine from an
        alternate media, 269
browsers
    acceptable formats for CA certs, 112
    Internet Explorer, listing files opened
        by, 53
    Mozilla, testing squid proxy, 194
    securing and accelerating with squid
        proxy over SSH, 193–195
BSDs
    IPsec connections under
        FreeBSD, 179–181
    IPsec connections under
        OpenBSD, 182
    netstat program, listing listening
        ports, 15
    OpenBSD and PacketFilter, 75–80

crytography (*continued*)
    public keys, security concerns
        with, 193
    SFS (Self-certifying File
        System), 131–133
    SSL encryption, 198–200
    TLS encryption, setting up for
        SMTP, 115–117
curses-based GUI, configuring kernel to
    enable grsecurity, 26

D

daemon option, SnortSam, 249
data size for packets (Snort, dsize
    option), 243
databases
    Barnyard output to, 256
    Barnyard support for, 254
    MySQL (see MySQL)
    NIDS, tracking alerts with
        ACID, 224–227
    round-robin database (RRD), 164
    Snort, configuring to use, 223
    Tripwire database, 271, 274
dd command, 269
debugging, logging information for, 137
default shares (Windows networks), 51
defaultkey option, SnortSam, 248
deny policy (PacketFilter), 78
depth and offset options, Snort
    rules, 243
DESX encryption algorithm, 62
device nodes
    in chroot( ) environment, 3
    creating from programs in chroot( )
        environment, 19
    for daemons in sandbox
        environment, 21
    preventing creation of with
        grsecurity, 28
/dev/mem and /dev/kmem, preventing
    access to, 9
directories
    dividing into read-only and
        read-write, 2
    loose permissions, scanning for, 5
dmesg utility, preceventing nonroot
    users from using, 28

DNS
    HTTP proxy difficulties with, 195
    SOCKS 4 problems with, 197
    testing by sniffdet tool, 121
    TXT records, using in encrypted
        connections, 188
domain name, scanning remote
    Windows systems by, 52
domain registrants, finding, 278
dontblock option, SnortSam, 248
drop option (PacketFilter), 76
drop, sdrop, and reject rules, Snort_
    inline, 246
dsize option, Snort rules, 243
Dsniff, 68
dynamic and activate actions, Snort
    rules, 240

E

echo action, swatch, 147
effective UID (EUID), changing to 0 in
    chroot( ) environment, 18
egress filtering of network traffic, 86
Ethereal protocol analyzer, 172
    device name for monitoring,
        obtaining, 174
    remote capture device, using
        with, 175
    Sguil, use with, 227
Ethernet addresses, translation of IP
    addresses to, 67
Ethernet sniffers, detecting
    remotely, 117–121
Ettercap, 68
event logs (Windows), 138
    securing, 56
exec action, swatch, 148
execution of binaries, disallowing, 2
    on Linux, 3

F

facilities and priorities, filtering log
    messages on, 136
fdisk command, 269
Ffwexec or fwsamW-1 firewall, using
    with SnortSam, 249
FIFO restrictions (grsecurity), 28
file attributes, protecting logs
    with, 8–10

M

P

packages (compromised), finding with RPM, 274–276

packet sniffers
  examining SSH connection tunneled through HTTP, 201
  rpcapd remote capture device, using with, 172–175
  WinDump, 174

PacketFilter (PF), 75–80
  authenticated gateway, creating, 80–82
  blocking packets used for operating-system probes, 93
  pf.conf file, editing
    defining table of IP addresses, 75
    macros, 75
    options, 76
    packet-filtering rules, 78
    traffic normalization rules, 77
  SnortSam, using with, 250

paging file (Windows), clearing at shutdown, 62

PAM (pluggable authentication modules), 38–42
  pam_access module, 38
  pam_limits module, 44
  pam_stack module, 38
  pam_time module, 38

partitions (disk), imaging, 269

passwd program, SUID or SGID bit, 3

passwords
  command execution without password, 11
  (see also authentication)

patch utility, applying grsecurity patch to kernel, 26

patching system security holes, automation of, 45

PaX (grsecurity), 29

Pcap-formatted files, creating with Barnyard, 256

Perl modules, necessary for swatch tool, 147

Perl scripts, running through CGI interface, 125

Perl, sensor agents for SnortCenter, 237

permissions
  creating flexible hierarchies with POSIX ACLs, 5–8
  world- and group-writable, 5

PF (see PacketFilter)

pfctl command, 75

PHP
  libraries for SnortCenter, 234
  programs, running through CGI interface, 125
  Sebek package, use by, 267
  using with ACID, 224

PHPlot, 224

PIDs (process IDs)
  listing for listening services, 14–16
  stunnel PID file, 199

ping program
  finding system MAC address, 91
  monitoring statistics from web server, 164

pipe action, swatch, 148

PIX firewall, using with SnortSam, 249

pluggable authentication modules (see PAM)

pluto, 177

Point-to-Point Tunneling Protocol (see PPTP tunneling)

poisioning the ARP cache, 67

policies, systrace, 33–35
  automated generation of, 35–37

POP, encrypting with SSL, 113–114

POP3 traffic, encrypting and forwarding with SSH, 190

PoPToP (PPTP server), 184
  connecting to with Windows machine, 185

port forwarding
  honeyd, using with, 265
  httptunnel, using, 201
  SSH, using as SOCKS proxy, 195–198
  SSH, using for, 189–191
  stunnel, using, 199

port security (Ethernet switches), 119

ports
  monitor port, 68
  open, listing for Windows systems, 54
  scanning for listening services, 14–16
  SnortSam port option, 249
  specifying for packets in Snort rules, 241

portscan and stream4 preprocessors, Snort, 231, 232

S

T

Colophon

Our look is the result of reader comments, our own experimentation, and feedback from distribution channels. Distinctive covers complement our distinctive approach to technical topics, breathing personality and life into potentially dry subjects.

The image on the cover of *Network Security Hacks* is barbed wire. The type of barbed wire pictured in the cover image was patented by Joseph Glidden in 1874. Glidden improved on earlier attempts at manufacturing wire fencing by fashioning sharp barbs, spacing them along a smooth wire, and then twisting another wire around the first to hold the barbs in place. Advertised as "Cheaper than dirt and stronger than steel," barbed wire was immediately adopted by farmers in the American west as a way to control their herds. The days of free-roaming cattle and cowboys were soon numbered, but battles over barbs were fought both in court and on the ranch. Opponents called barbed wire "the Devil's rope," and the Cole Porter song "Don't Fence Me In" mourned this change in the western landscape. Barbed wire was here to stay, though—in addition to agricultural use, it has become a ubiquitous component of warfare and is a common feature of high-security areas such as prisons.

Genevieve d'Entremont was the production editor and copyeditor for *Network Security Hacks*. Brian Sawyer proofread the book. Philip Dangler and Claire Cloutier provided quality control. Jamie Peppard provided production support. Ellen Troutman-Zaig wrote the index. Rob Flickenger wrote the Preface.

Hanna Dyer designed the cover of this book, based on a series design by Edie Freedman. The cover image is a photograph from *gettyimages.com*. Emma Colby produced the cover layout with QuarkXPress 4.1 using Adobe's Helvetica Neue and ITC Garamond fonts.

Melanie Wang designed the interior layout, based on a series design by David Futato. This book was converted by Andrew Savikas to FrameMaker 5.5.6 with a format conversion tool created by Erik Ray, Jason McIntosh, Neil Walls, and Mike Sierra that uses Perl and XML technologies. The text font is Linotype Birka; the heading font is Adobe Helvetica Neue Condensed; and the code font is LucasFont's TheSans Mono Condensed. The illustrations that appear in the book were produced by Robert Romano and Jessamyn Read using Macromedia FreeHand 9 and Adobe Photoshop 6. This colophon was written by Philip Dangler.

Need in-depth answers fast?

Access over 2,000 of the newest and best technology books online

Safari Bookshelf is the premier electronic reference library for IT professionals and programmers—a must-have when you need to pinpoint exact answers in an instant.

Access over 2,000 of the top technical reference books by twelve leading publishers including O'Reilly, Addison-Wesley, Peachpit Press, Prentice Hall, and Microsoft Press. Safari provides the technical references and code samples you need to develop quality, timely solutions.

Try it today with a FREE TRIAL
Visit *www.oreilly.com/safari/max/*

For groups of five or more, set up a free, 30-day corporate trial
Contact: *corporate@oreilly.com*

What Safari Subscribers Say:

"The online books make quick research a snap. I usually keep Safari up all day and refer to it whenever I need it."
—Joe Bennett, Sr. Internet Developer

"I love how Safari allows me to access new books each month depending on my needs. The search facility is excellent and the presentation is top notch. It is one heck of an online technical library."
—Eric Winslow, Economist-System,
Administrator-Web Master-Programmer

Related Titles Available from O'Reilly

Hacks

Amazon Hacks

BSD Hacks

Digital Photography Hacks

eBay Hacks

Excel hacks

Google Hacks

Harware Hacking Projects for Geeks

Linux Desktop Hacks

Linux Server Hacks

Mac OS X Hacks

Mac OS X Panther Hacks

Spidering Hacks

TiVo Hacks

Windows Server Hacks

Windows XP Hacks

Wireless Hacks

Keep in touch with O'Reilly

1. Download examples from our books

To find example files for a book, go to:

www.oreilly.com/catalog

select the book, and follow the "Examples" link.

2. Register your O'Reilly books

Register your book at *register.oreilly.com*

Why register your books? Once you've registered your O'Reilly books you can:

- Win O'Reilly books, T-shirts or discount coupons in our monthly drawing.
- Get special offers available only to registered O'Reilly customers.
- Get catalogs announcing new books (US and UK only).
- Get email notification of new editions of the O'Reilly books you own.

3. Join our email lists

Sign up to get topic-specific email announcements of new books and conferences, special offers, and O'Reilly Network technology newsletters at:

elists.oreilly.com

It's easy to customize your free elists subscription so you'll get exactly the O'Reilly news you want.

4. Get the latest news, tips, and tools

http://www.oreilly.com

- "Top 100 Sites on the Web"—PC Magazine
- CIO Magazine's Web Business 50 Awards

Our web site contains a library of comprehensive product information (including book excerpts and tables of contents), downloadable software, background articles, interviews with technology leaders, links to relevant sites, book cover art, and more.

5. Work for O'Reilly

Check out our web site for current employment opportunities:

jobs.oreilly.com

6. Contact us

O'Reilly & Associates
1005 Gravenstein Hwy North
Sebastopol, CA 95472 USA

TEL: 707-827-7000 or 800-998-9938
         (6am to 5pm PST)

FAX: 707-829-0104

order@oreilly.com
For answers to problems regarding your order or our products.
To place a book order online, visit:

www.oreilly.com/order_new

catalog@oreilly.com
To request a copy of our latest catalog.

booktech@oreilly.com
For book content technical questions or corrections.

corporate@oreilly.com
For educational, library, government, and corporate sales.

proposals@oreilly.com
To submit new book proposals to our editors and product managers.

international@oreilly.com
For information about our international distributors or translation queries. For a list of our distributors outside of North America check out:

international.oreilly.com/distributors.html

adoption@oreilly.com
For information about academic use of O'Reilly books, visit:

academic.oreilly.com

O'REILLY®

Our books are available at most retail and online bookstores.
To order direct: 1-800-998-9938 • *order@oreilly.com* • *www.oreilly.com*
Online editions of most O'Reilly titles are available by subscription at *safari.oreilly.com*